IP Multicast, Volume II
Advanced Multicast Concepts and Large-Scale Multicast Design

Josh Loveless, CCIE No. 16638

Ray Blair, CCIE No. 7050

Arvind Durai, CCIE No. 7016

T0313680

Cisco Press

800 East 96th Street

Indianapolis, Indiana 46240 USA

IP Multicast, Volume II

Advanced Multicast Concepts and Large-Scale Multicast Design

Josh Loveless, Ray Blair, and Arvind Durai

Copyright© 2018 Cisco Systems, Inc.

Published by:
Cisco Press
800 East 96th Street
Indianapolis, IN 46240 USA

Printed in the United States of America

1   18

Library of Congress Control Number: 2017962613

ISBN-13: 978-1-58714-493-6

ISBN-10: 1-58714-493-X

Warning and Disclaimer

Trademark Acknowledgments

All terms mentioned in this book that are known to be trademarks or service marks have been appropriately capitalized. Cisco Press or Cisco Systems, Inc., cannot attest to the accuracy of this information. Use of a term in this book should not be regarded as affecting the validity of any trademark or service mark.

Special Sales

For information about buying this title in bulk quantities, or for special sales opportunities (which may include electronic versions; custom cover designs; and content particular to your business, training goals, marketing focus, or branding interests), please contact our corporate sales department at corpsales@pearsoned.com or (800) 382-3419.

For government sales inquiries, please contact governmentsales@pearsoned.com.

For questions about sales outside the U.S., please contact intlcs@pearson.com.

Feedback Information

At Cisco Press, our goal is to create in-depth technical books of the highest quality and value. Each book is crafted with care and precision, undergoing rigorous development that involves the unique expertise of members from the professional technical community.

Readers' feedback is a natural continuation of this process. If you have any comments regarding how we could improve the quality of this book, or otherwise alter it to better suit your needs, you can contact us through email at feedback@ciscopress.com. Please make sure to include the book title and ISBN in your message.

We greatly appreciate your assistance.

Editor-in-Chief: Mark Taub

Alliances Manager, Cisco Press: Arezou Gol

Product Line Manager: Brett Bartow

Managing Editor: Sandra Schroeder

Development Editor: Marianne Bartow

Project Editor: Mandie Frank

Copy Editor: Kitty Wilson

Technical Editors: Nick Garner; Yogi Raghunathan

Editorial Assistant: Vanessa Evans

Designer: Chuti Prasertsith

Composition: codemantra

Indexer: Erika Millen

Proofreader: Abby Manheim

Americas Headquarters
Cisco Systems, Inc.
San Jose, CA

Asia Pacific Headquarters
Cisco Systems (USA) Pte. Ltd.
Singapore

Europe Headquarters
Cisco Systems International BV Amsterdam,
The Netherlands

Cisco has more than 200 offices worldwide. Addresses, phone numbers, and fax numbers are listed on the Cisco Website at www.cisco.com/go/offices.

Cisco and the Cisco logo are trademarks or registered trademarks of Cisco and/or its affiliates in the U.S. and other countries. To view a list of Cisco trademarks, go to this URL: www.cisco.com/go/trademarks. Third party trademarks mentioned are the property of their respective owners. The use of the word partner does not imply a partnership relationship between Cisco and any other company. (1110R)

About the Authors

Josh Loveless, CCIE No. 16638, is a systems engineering manager for Cisco Systems. He has been with Cisco since 2012, providing architecture and support services for tier 1 service providers as well as for many of Cisco's largest enterprise customers, specializing in large-scale routing and switching designs. Prior to joining Cisco, he spent 15 years working for large service providers and enterprises as both an engineer and an architect, as well as providing training and architecture services to some of Cisco's trusted partners. Josh maintains two CCIE certifications, Routing and Switching and Service Provider.

Ray Blair, CCIE No. 7050, is a distinguished systems engineer and has been with Cisco Systems since 1999. He uses his years of experience to align technology solutions with business needs to ensure customer success. Ray started his career in 1988, designing industrial monitoring and communication systems. Since that time, he has been involved with server/database administration and the design, implementation, and management of networks that included networking technologies from ATM to ZMODEM. He maintains three CCIE certifications in Routing and Switching, Security, and Service Provider (No. 7050), and he is also a Certified Information Systems Security Professional (CISSP), and a Certified Business Architect (No. 00298). Ray is coauthor of three Cisco Press books, *Cisco Secure Firewall Services Module, Tcl Scripting for Cisco IOS,* and *IP Multicast, Volume 1.* He speaks at many industry events and is a Cisco Live distinguished speaker.

Arvind Durai, CCIE No. 7016, is a director of solution integration for Cisco Advanced Services. Arvind is a chief architect for advanced services for the West Enterprise Region, an organization of around 100 consultants focused on customer success for approximately 150 enterprise accounts. Over the past 18 years, Arvind has been responsible for supporting major Cisco customers in the enterprise sector, including financial, retail, manufacturing, e-commerce, state government, utility, and health care sectors. Some of his focuses have been on security, multicast, network virtualization, data center enterprise cloud adoption, automation, and software-defined infrastructure, and he has authored several white papers on various technologies. He has been involved in multicast designs for several enterprise customers in different verticals. He is also one of the contributors to the framework for the Advanced Services Multicast Audit tool, which helps customers assess their operational multicast network to industry best practices. Arvind maintains two CCIE certifications, Routing and Switching and Security, and also is a Certified Business Architect. He holds a bachelor of science degree in electronics and communication, a master's degree in electrical engineering, and a master's degree in business administration. He has coauthored four Cisco Press books: *Cisco Secure Firewall Services Module, Virtual Routing in the Cloud, Tcl Scripting for Cisco IOS,* and *IP Multicast:, Volume 1.* He has also coauthored IEEE WAN smart grid architecture and presented in many industry forums, such as IEEE and Cisco Live.

About the Technical Reviewers

Nick Garner, CCIE No. 17871, is a solutions integration architect for Cisco Systems. He has been in Cisco Advanced Services, supporting customers in both transactional and subscription engagements, for 8 years. In his primary role, he has deployed and supported large-scale data center designs for prominent clients in the San Francisco Bay Area. His primary technical focus, outside of data center routing and switching designs, has been security and multicast. Prior to joining Cisco, Nick worked for a large national financial institution as a network security engineer. Nick maintains two CCIE certifications, Routing and Switching and Security.

Yogeshwaran Raghunathan, CCIE No. 6583, is a senior solutions integration architect on the Advanced Services team at Cisco Systems. Yogi holds an MBA and an engineering degree in electronics and communication from CIT (Coimbatore, India). He has 22 years of experience working in the networking industry, 17 of them with Cisco Systems, supporting various service providers in North America. Yogi's hands-on experience in building and supporting large service provider networks has exposed him to complex MPLS architectures, thus enabling different perspectives on the new world of SDN and MPLS deployment. Yogi has in recent years been involved in design, implementation, and planning for large web provider networks. He can be reached at yraghuna@cisco.com.

Dedications

This book is dedicated to my wonderful family and to all my friends who have supported my career throughout many difficult years.—Josh Loveless

This book is dedicated to my wife, Sonya, and my children, Sam, Riley, Sophie, and Regan. You guys mean the world to me!—Ray Blair

This book is dedicated to my parents and family for their support and blessings.—Arvind Durai

Acknowledgments

Josh Loveless: A special thank you goes to my coauthors, Ray Blair and Arvind Durai, for the great work they have done completing this two-volume set on IP Multicast. I would also like to thank the technical reviewers, Yogi and Nick, and all the editors at Pearson for all the tireless work they put into making this book pop!

Ray Blair: As with everything else in my life, I thank my Lord and Savior for his faithful leading that has brought me to this place. Thank you, Josh and Arvind, for partnering in this endeavor, Nick and Yogi for your excellent reviews, and Pearson for your support.

Arvind Durai: Thank you, Monica and Akhhill, for your continuous support and patience that helped me complete my fifth book.

Thank you, Ray and Josh, for making this journey of writing *IP Multicast, Volume 1* and *Volume 2* a joyful ride.

A special thanks to Brett Bartow, Yogi Raghunathan, and Nick Garner for your valuable contributions.

As always, thank you, God, for giving me guidance, opportunity, and support in all my endeavors!

Contents at a Glance

Contents

Command Syntax Conventions

The conventions used to present command syntax in this book are the same conventions used in the IOS Command Reference. The Command Reference describes these conventions as follows:

■ **Boldface** indicates commands and keywords that are entered literally as shown. In actual configuration examples and output (not general command syntax), boldface indicates commands that are manually input by the user (such as a **show** command).

■ *Italic* indicates arguments for which you supply actual values.

■ Vertical bars (|) separate alternative, mutually exclusive elements.

■ Square brackets ([ ]) indicate an optional element.

■ Braces ({ }) indicate a required choice.

■ Braces within brackets ([{ }]) indicate a required choice within an optional element.

Note This book covers multiple operating systems, and icons and router names indicate the appropriate OS that is being referenced. IOS and IOS-XE use router names like R1 and R2 and are referenced by the IOS router icon. IOS-XR routers use router names like XR1 and XR2 and are referenced by the IOS-XR router icon.

Reader Services

Register your copy at www.ciscopress.com/title/ISBN for convenient access to downloads, updates, and corrections as they become available. To start the registration process, go to www.ciscopress.com/register and log in or create an account*. Enter the product ISBN 9781587144936 and click Submit. When the process is complete, you will find any available bonus content under Registered Products.

*Be sure to check the box that you would like to hear from us to receive exclusive discounts on future editions of this product.

Introduction

IP Multicast, Volume 2 covers advanced IP Multicast designs and protocols specific to Cisco Systems routers and switches. It includes pragmatic discussion of common features, deployment models, and field practices for advanced IP Multicast networks. The discussion culminates with commands and methodologies for implementing and troubleshooting advanced Cisco IP Multicast networks.

Who Should Read This Book?

IP Multicast, Volume 2 is intended for any professional supporting IP Multicast networks. This book primarily targets the following groups, but network managers and administrators will also find value from the included case studies and feature explanations:

- IP network engineers and architects

- Network operations technicians

- Network consultants

- Security professionals

- Collaboration specialists and architects

How This Book Is Organized

This book is organized into six chapters that cover the following topics:

- **Chapter 1, "Interdomain Routing and Internet Multicast":** This chapter explains the fundamental requirements for interdomain multicast and the three pillars of interdomain design: control plane for source identification, control plane for receiver identification, and downstream control plane.

- **Chapter 2, "Multicast Scalability and Transport Diversification":** Transportation of multicast messages requires consideration of several factors, especially when cloud service providers do not support native multicast. This chapter introduces the key concepts of cloud services and explains the elements required to support multicast services.

- **Chapter 3, "Multicast MPLS VPNs":** Multicast VPNs provide the ability to logically separate traffic on the same physical infrastructure. Most service providers and many enterprise customers implement Multiprotocol Label Switching (MPLS) so they can separate or isolate traffic into logical domains or groups, generally referred to as virtual private networks (VPNs). This chapter discusses the options for implementing multicast VPNs.

- **Chapter 4, "Multicast in Data Center Environments":** This chapter explains the use of multicast in the data center. Understanding the nuances of how multicast functions in myriad solutions is critical to the success of your organization. The goal of this chapter is to provide insight into the operation of multicast, using the most popular methods for data center implementation, including virtual port channel (VPC), Virtual Extensible LAN (VXLAN), and Application Centric Infrastructure (ACI).

- **Chapter 5, "Multicast Design Solutions":** This chapter examines several archetypical network design models. One of the models represents a specific network strategy that meets a specific commercial purpose—a trade floor. Another model is a general design for a specific industry, focusing on the deployment of multicast in a hospital environment. The intent of this chapter is to provide a baseline for each type of design as well as examples of best practices for multicast deployments.

- **Chapter 6, "Advanced Multicast Troubleshooting":** This chapter explains the basic methodology for troubleshooting IP Multicast networks.

Chapter 1

Interdomain Routing and Internet Multicast

This chapter explains the fundamental requirements for interdomain multicast and the three pillars of interdomain design: the control plane for source identification, the control plane for receiver identification, and the downstream control plane.

Introduction to Interdomain Multicast

Applications may require support for multicasting over large and diverse networks, such as the Internet. It is possible that a sender may exist on one side of a diverse network, far away from potential receivers. Multicast receivers could exist on any network, including networks that are altogether foreign to the sender's network, being under completely different administrative control with different policies governing multicast forwarding.

In such scenarios, there is no reasonable expectation that all Layer 3 devices in the forwarding path will share similar configurations or policies. This is certainly the reality of multicast applications that use the Internet. Therefore, additional protocols and configuration outside basic multicast transport are required to provide internetwork multicast service. Why is this the case? Aren't large internetworks, such as the Internet, using the same Internet Protocol (IP) for multicasting? If each network is administered using different rules, how does anything on the Internet work? As discussed in the book *IP Multicast, Volume 1*, the de facto standard forwarding protocol for IP Multicast is Protocol Independent Multicast (PIM). If PIM is universal, why are different policies required? A brief introduction to Internet principles will answer these questions and help you understand why additional consideration is needed when designing multicast applications across internetworks.

Internet Protocol was created as a "best effort" service. Even when IP was expanded to enable the World Wide Web (WWW) and multinetwork connectivity, best effort was a universal maxim. This maxim still exists; it dictates the forwarding behavior of today's Internet and also, therefore, that of any other large multidomain network. Best effort in this context means that as IP traffic passes from one network to the next, it is assumed that each transit network is properly configured for optimal forwarding to any appropriate destinations. There are no guarantees of optimal forwarding—or even that packets will make it to the final destination at all.

Note   The concept of best-effort forwarding is universal and applies to all IP traffic: unicast, multicast, and broadcast. This introduction briefly explores this concept, which further exposes the need for additional forwarding mechanisms for multicast traffic across diverse networks. While basic in nature, this review establishes the foundation for multicast forwarding across internetworks. An advanced understanding of unicast Internet forwarding, including the use of Border Gateway Protocol (BGP), is assumed throughout this chapter.

If you examine the Internet from a macro perspective, you see that it is essentially a mesh of connections between many disparate networks. Typically, Internet service providers (ISPs) connect to each other for transit and/or peering to provide interconnection to other service providers or customers.

End customers include all manner of connections, including homes, cellular networks, small and medium-sized businesses, research institutions, hospitals, governments, enterprise businesses, and others. Figure 1-1 shows a small, isolated example of how this interconnectivity works, using a fictional company called Mcast Enterprises.

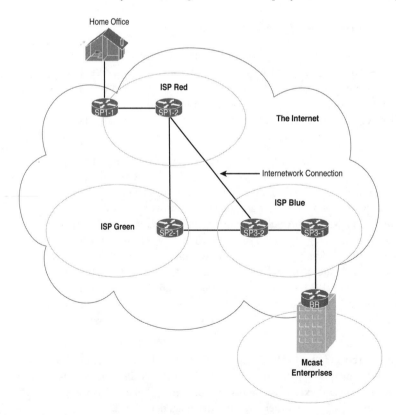

Figure 1-1   *Mcast Enterprises Interconnectivity*

Each of the network entities (surrounded by an oval) shown in Figure 1-1 is known as an *autonomous system (AS)*—that is, a network that has administrative and operational boundaries, with clear demarcations between itself and any other network AS. Like IP addresses, autonomous systems are numbered, and the assignment of numbers is controlled by the Internet Assigned Numbers Authority (IANA). Figure 1-2 shows the previous Internet example network represented as simple AS bubbles using private autonomous system numbers (ASNs).

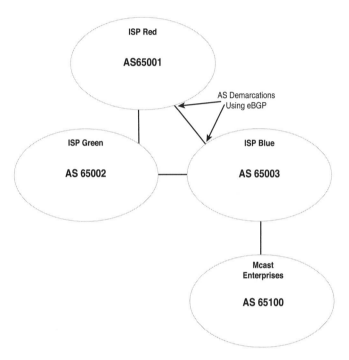

Figure 1-2   *The Mcast Enterprises Network as a System of Connected Autonomous Systems*

Note   ASNs, as defined by the IETF, are public, just like IP addresses. However, as with IP addresses, there is a private number range that is reserved for use in non-public networks. The standard 16-bit private ASN range is 64512–65535, which is defined by RFC 6996 (a 2013 update to RFC 1930). Even though Internet functions may be discussed, all numbers used in this text (for IP addressing, ASNs, and multicast group numbers) are private to prevent confusion with existing Internet services and to protect public interest.

Some routing information is shared between the interconnected ASs to provide a complete internetwork picture. Best-effort forwarding implies that as routers look up destination information and traffic transits between ASs, each AS has its own forwarding rules. To illustrate this concept, imagine that a home user is connected to ISP Red (AS 65001) and sends an IP web request to a server within Mcast Enterprises (AS 65100). The enterprise does not have a direct connection to ISP Red. Therefore, ISP Red must forward the

packets to ISP Blue, and ISP Blue can then forward the traffic to the enterprise AS with
the server. ISP Red knows that ISP Blue can reach the enterprise web server at address
10.10.1.100 because ISP Blue shared that routing information with all the ASs it is
connected to. ISP Red does not control the network policy or functions of ISP Blue and
must trust that the traffic can be successfully passed to the server. In this situation, ISP
Blue acts as a transit network. Figure 1-3 illustrates this request.

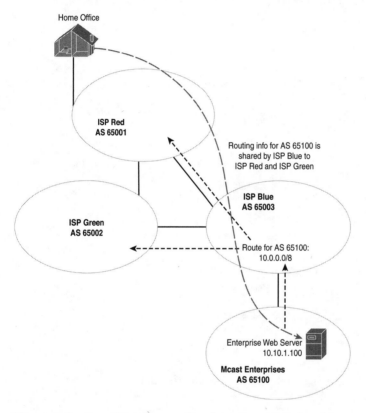

Figure 1-3   *Best-Effort Forwarding from One AS to Another*

Some protocols are designed to make best-effort forwarding between ASs more precise.
This set of protocols is maintained by the IETF, an international organization that gov-
erns all protocols related to IP forwarding, including PIM and BGP. The IETF—like the
Internet—is an open society in which standards are formed collaboratively. This means
there is no inherent administrative mandate placed on network operating system vendors
or networks connecting to the Internet to follow protocol rules precisely or even in the
same way.

This open concept is one of the more miraculous and special characteristics of the
modern Internet. Networks and devices that wish to communicate across network
boundaries should use IETF-compliant software and configurations. Internet routers
that follow IETF protocol specifications should be able to forward IP packets to

any destination on any permitted IP network in the world. This assumes that every Internet-connected router shares some protocols with its neighbors, and those protocols are properly implemented (as discussed further later in this chapter); each router updates neighbor ASs with at least a summary of the routes it knows about. This does not assume that every network is configured or administered in the same way.

For example, an AS is created using routing protocols and policies as borders and demarcation points. In fact, routing protocols are specifically built for these two purposes. Internal routing is handled by an Interior Gateway Protocol (IGP). Examples of IGPs include Open Shortest Path First (OSPF) and Intermediate System-to-Intermediate System (IS-IS). Routers use a chosen IGP on all the routed links within the AS. When routing protocols need to share information with another AS, an External Gateway Protocol (EGP) is used to provide demarcation. This allows you to use completely separate routing policies and security between ASs that might be obstructive or unnecessary for internal links.

Border Gateway Protocol version 4 (BGPv4) is the EGP that connects all Internet autonomous systems together. Figure 1-4 shows an expanded view of the Mcast Enterprises connectivity from Figure 1-3, with internal IGP connections and an EGP link with ISP Blue. Mcast Enterprises shares a single summary route for all internal links to ISP Blue via BGP.

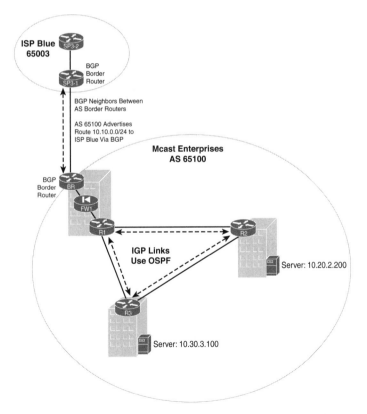

Figure 1-4   *AS Demarcation: IGP Links Using OSPF and EGP Links Using BGP*

The separation between internal (IGP) and external (EGP) routes provides several important benefits. The first is protection of critical internal infrastructure from outside influence, securing the internal routing domain. Both security and routing policies can be applied to the EGP neighborship with outside networks. Another clear benefit is the ability to better engineer traffic. Best-effort forwarding may be acceptable for Internet connections and internetwork routing. However, you definitely need more finite control over internal routes. In addition, if there are multiple external links that share similar routing information, you may want to control external path selection or influence incoming path selection—without compromising internal routing fidelity. Finally, you may choose to import only specific routes from external neighbors or share only specific internal routes with outside neighbors. Selective route sharing provides administrators control over how traffic will or will not pass through each AS.

Why is all this relevant to multicast? PIM is the IETF standard for Any-Source Multicast (ASM) and Source-Specific Multicast (SSM) in IP networks. Many people refer to PIM as a multicast routing protocol. However, PIM is unlike any IGP or EGP. It is less concerned with complex route sharing policy than with building loop-free forwarding topologies or trees. PIM uses the information learned from IP unicast routing protocols to build these trees. PIM networking and neighborships have neither an internal nor an external characteristic. PIM neighborships on a single router can exist between both IGP neighbors and EGP neighbors. If multicast internetworking is required between two ASs, PIM is a requirement. Without this relationship, a tree cannot be completed.

Crossing the administrative demarcation point from one AS to another means crossing into a network operating under a completely different set of rules and with potentially limited shared unicast routing information. Even when all the routers in two different networks are using PIM for forward multicasting, forming a forwarding tree across these networks using PIM alone is virtually impossible because Reverse Path Forwarding (RPF) information will be incomplete. In addition, it is still necessary to secure and create a prescriptive control plane for IP Multicast forwarding as you enter and exit each AS. The following sections explore these concepts further and discuss how to best forward multicast application traffic across internetworks and the Internet.

What Is a Multicast Domain? A Refresher

Before we really discuss interdomain multicast forwarding, let's clearly define the characteristics of a multicast domain. Just like the unicast routing protocols OSPF, IS-IS, and EIGRP, PIM routers have the capability to dynamically share information about multicast trees. Most networks use only one IGP routing protocol for internal route sharing and routing table building, and there are some similarities between multicast domains and unicast domains.

When an IGP network is properly designed, routers in the network have the same routes in their individual routing information base (RIB). The routes may be summarized into larger entries on some routers—even as far as having only one summary (default) route on stub routers. Often times this process is controlled by the use of configured route sharing policy. Link-state routing protocols, such as IS-IS or OSPF, can use regions or areas to achieve summarization and route selection. The routing protocol dynamically provides the necessary routing information to all the segmented routers that need the information, allowing network architects to create boundaries between various portions of a network.

The deployed IGP also has a natural physical boundary. When the interface of an IGP router is not configured to send/receive IGP information, that interface bounds the IGP. This serves the purpose of preventing internal routing information from leaking to routers that should not or do not need internal information.

As discussed earlier in this chapter, routes between two autonomous systems are shared through the use of an EGP, and BGP is the EGP of the Internet. Most administrators configure BGP to share only essential IGP-learned routes with external routers so that only internal networks meant for public access are reachable by external devices. The routing process of the IGP is kept separate and secure from external influence. For most networks, the natural boundary of the internal routing domain lies between the IGP and the EGP of the network.

Multicast networks must also have boundaries. These boundaries may be drastically different from those of the underlying unicast network. Why? It is important to remember that IP Multicast networks are overlays on the IGP network, and most network routers can have only one PIM process. PIM uses the information found in the RIB from router to router to build both a local multicast forwarding tree and a networkwide forwarding tree. Let's quickly review how this works.

As you know, when a router forwards unicast IP traffic, it is concerned only with the destination of the packet. The router receives a packet from an upstream device, reads the IP destination from the packet header, and then makes a path selection, forwarding the packet toward the intended destination. The RIB contains the destination information for the router to make the best forwarding decision. As explained in *IP Multicast, Volume 1*, multicast forwarding uses this same table but completely different logic to get packets from the source to multiple receivers on multiple paths. Receivers express interest in a multicast stream (a flow of IP packets) by subscribing to a particular group address. PIM tracks these active groups and subscribed receivers. Because receivers can request the stream from nearly any location in the network, there are many possible destination paths.

The multicast router needs to build a forwarding tree that includes a root at the source of the stream and branches down any paths toward joined receivers. The branches of the tree cannot loop back to the source, or the forwarding paradigm of efficiency will be entirely broken. PIM uses the RIB to calculate the source of packets rather than the destination. Forwarding of this nature, away from a source and toward receivers, with source route verification, is called Reverse Path Forwarding (RPF).

When a multicast packet arrives at a router, the first thing the router does is perform an RPF check. The IP source of the packet header and the interface on which it was received are compared to the RIB. If the RIB contains a proper best route to the source on the same interface on which the packet was received, the RPF check is successful. PIM then forwards that packet, as long as it has a proper tree constructed (or can construct a new tree) for the destination group.

If the required entries are not in the unicast RIB and the RPF table, the router drops any multicast packets to prevent a loop. The router doesn't just make these RPF checks independently for every packet. RPF checks are performed by the PIM process on the router, and they are also used for building the multicast forwarding tree. If a packet fails the RPF check, the interface on which the packet is received is not added to any trees for the destination group. In fact, PIM uses RPF in almost all tree-building activities.

In addition, PIM as a protocol is independent of any unicast routing protocols or unicast forwarding. Proper and efficient multicast packet forwarding is PIM's main purpose; in other words, PIM is designed for tree building and loop prevention. As of this writing, most PIM domains run PIM Sparse-Mode (PIM–SM). A quick review of PIM–SM mechanics provides additional aid in the exploration of multicast domains.

There are two types of forwarding trees in PIM–SM: the shortest-path tree (also known as a source tree) and the shared tree. The source tree is a tree that flows from the source (the root of the tree) to the receivers (the leaves) via the shortest (most efficient) network path. You can also think of the source as a server and the receivers as clients of that server. As mentioned earlier, clients must be connected to the Layer 3 network to be included in the tree. This allows the router to see the best path between the source and the receivers.

The subscribed clients become a "group," and, in fact, clients use a multicast group address to perform the subscription. Internet Group Management Protocol (IGMP) is the protocol that manages the client subscription process. IGMP shares the IP group subscriptions with PIM. PIM then uses those groups to build the source tree and shares the tree information with other PIM neighbors.

Note   This review is only meant to be high level as it is germane to understanding why additional protocols are required for interdomain routing. If any of these topics are more than a simple review for you, you can find a deeper study of IGMP, PIM mechanics, and tree building in additional texts, such as *IP Multicast, Volume 1*.

Keep in mind that there may be many locations in a network that have a receiver. Any time a router has receivers that are reached by multiple interfaces, the tree must branch, and PIM must RPF check any received sources before adding forwarding entries to the router's Multicast Forwarding Information Base (MFIB). A source tree in a multicast forwarding table is represented by an (S, G) entry (for source, group). The (S, G) entry contains RPF information such as the interface closest to the source and the interfaces in the path of any downstream receivers.

The branches in the entry are displayed as a list of outgoing interfaces, called an outgoing interface list (OIL). This is essentially how PIM builds the source tree within the forwarding table. Neighboring PIM routers share this information with each other so that routers will independently build proper trees, both locally and across the network. Example 1-1 shows what a completed tree with incoming interfaces and OILs look like on an IOS-XE router by using the **show ip mroute** command.

Example 1-1 *Completed Trees*

```
R1# show ip mroute
IP Multicast Routing Table
Flags: D - Dense, S - Sparse, B - Bidir Group, s - SSM Group, C - Connected,
       L - Local, P - Pruned, R - RP-bit set, F - Register flag,
       T - SPT-bit set, J - Join SPT, M - MSDP created entry, E - Extranet,
       X - Proxy Join Timer Running, A - Candidate for MSDP Advertisement,
       U - URD, I - Received Source Specific Host Report,
       Z - Multicast Tunnel, z - MDT-data group sender,
       Y - Joined MDT-data group, y - Sending to MDT-data group,
       G - Received BGP C-Mroute, g - Sent BGP C-Mroute,
       N - Received BGP Shared-Tree Prune, n - BGP C-Mroute suppressed,
       Q - Received BGP S-A Route, q - Sent BGP S-A Route,
       V - RD & Vector, v - Vector, p - PIM Joins on route,
       x - VxLAN group
Outgoing interface flags: H - Hardware switched, A - Assert winner, p - PIM Join
 Timers: Uptime/Expires
 Interface state: Interface, Next-Hop or VCD, State/Mode

(*, 239.1.1.1), 2d01h/00:03:22, RP 192.168.100.100, flags: SJC
  Incoming interface: Ethernet2/0, RPF nbr 10.1.5.1
  Outgoing interface list:
    Ethernet0/0, Forward/Sparse, 2d01h/00:03:22

(10.1.1.1, 239.1.1.1), 00:04:53/00:02:31, flags: T
  Incoming interface: Ethernet1/0, RPF nbr 10.1.3.1
  Outgoing interface list:
    Ethernet0/0, Forward/Sparse, 00:04:53/00:03:22
```

It would be very difficult for every router to manage this process completely indepen-dently in a very large network, or if there were a great number of sources (which is a benefit of opting for a source tree multicast design that provides an optimal path for fast convergence). In addition, distribution of the PIM tree information could become very cumbersome to routers that are in the path of multiple source, receivers, or groups. This is especially true if sources only send packets between long intervals, consequently causing repeated table time-outs and then subsequent tree rebuilding and processing. The shared tree is the answer to this problem in the PIM–SM network, giving routers a measure of protocol efficiency.

The main function of the shared tree is to shift the initial tree-building process to a single router. The shared tree flows from this single router toward the receivers. An addi-tional benefit of the shared tree occurs when clients are subscribed to a group but there is not yet any active source for the group. The shared tree allows each router in the path to maintain state for the receivers only so that reprocessing of the tree branches does not need to occur again when a source comes online. The central processing location of the shared tree is known as the rendezvous point (RP).

When a receiver subscribes to a group through IGMP, the PIM process on the local router records the join, and then RPF checks the receivers against the location of the RP. If the RP is not located in the same direction as the receiver, PIM creates a local tree with the RP as the root and the receiver-bound interfaces in the OIL as the leaves or branches. The shared tree is represented in the Multicast Routing Information Base (MRIB) and MFIB as a (*, G) entry. PIM shares this information with its neighbors in the direction of the RP.

When the source begins sending packets to a group, the source-connected router regis-ters the source with the RP and forwards the packets to the RP via unicast tunneling. The RP acts as a temporary conduit to the receivers, with packets flowing down the shared tree toward the receivers from the RP. Meanwhile, the RP signals the source-connected router to begin building a source tree. PIM on the source-connected router builds the tree and then shares the (S, G) information with its neighbors. (For more on this concept, see *IP Multicast, Volume 1*.)

If a PIM neighbor is in the path of the multicast flow, the router joins the source tree while also sharing the information via PIM to its neighbors. Only the routers in the path must build the source tree, which improves processing efficiency. The RP is removed from any forwarding for the (S, G) once the source tree is complete, unless of course the RP happens to be in the path of the flow. (This process is very quick, taking only milliseconds on geographically small domains.) All routers in the path must use the same RP for each group in order for this to work. Each router maintains a table of group-to-RP mappings to keep RP information current. If any router in the path has a group mapping that is incongruent with that of its neighbor, the shared-tree construction fails. RP-to-group mappings are managed through either static RP configurations or through dynamic RP protocols, such as Cisco's Auto-RP or the open standard protocol Bootstrap Router (BSR).

Figure 1-5 illustrates the differences between a source tree and the shared tree in a basic network.

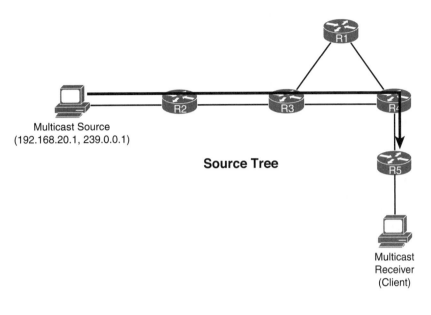

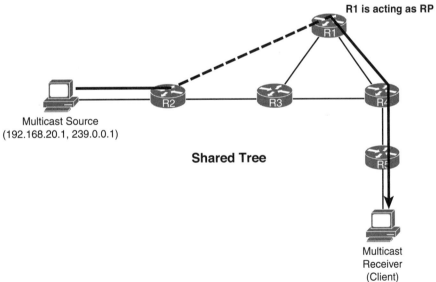

Figure 1-5   *Basic Source Tree versus Shared Tree*

With this reminder and understanding of RPF and PIM mechanics, let's establish that a PIM router must have three critical components to build a complete multicast forwarding tree. These three components must be present in every multicast domain and are the primary pillars of interdomain forwarding. Let's call them the three pillars of interdomain design:

- **The multicast control plane for source identification:** The router must know a proper path to any multicast source, either from the unicast RIB or learned (either statically or dynamically) through a specific RPF exception.

- **The multicast control plane for receiver identification:** The router must know about any legitimate receivers that have joined the group and where they are located in the network.

- **The downstream multicast control plane and MRIB:** The router must know when a source is actively sending packets for a given group. PIM–SM domains must also be able to build a shared tree from the local domain's RP, even when the source has registered to a remote RP in a different domain.

So far, this chapter has covered a lot of basics—multicast 101, you might say. These basics are inherently fundamental to understanding the critical components of interdomain multicast forwarding. In order to route multicast packets using PIM, the following must occur: *(1) Routers must be able to build proper forwarding trees (2) independent of any remote unicast routing processes and (3) regardless of the location of the source or (4) the receivers for a given multicast group.* This includes instances where sources and receivers are potentially separated by many administrative domains.

Inside an AS, especially one with only a single multicast domain, network administrators could use many methods for fulfilling these four criteria. All of the network is under singular control, so there is no concern about what happens outside the AS. For example, a network administrator could deploy multiple routing processes to satisfy the first requirement. He or she could even use multiple protocols through the use of protocol redistribution. The sophisticated link-state protocols OSPF and IS-IS provide built-in mechanisms for very tightly controlling route information sharing. PIM routers, on the other hand, can share-tree state information with any PIM neighbors and have no similar structures, needing only to satisfy the four criteria. A PIM domain forms more organically through both PIM configuration and protocol interaction. This means there are many ways to define a multicast domain. In its simplest terms, a multicast domain could be the administrative reach of the PIM process. Such a domain would include any router that is configured for PIM and has a PIM neighbor(s), IGMP subscribed receivers, or connected sources. A multicast domain could mirror exactly the administrative domain or autonomous system of the local network.

To understand this concept, let's look more closely at Mcast Enterprises, the fictional example from earlier in this chapter. Figure 1-6 shows Mcast Enterprises using a single AS, with one IGP and one companywide multicast domain that includes all IP Multicast groups (224.0.0.0/10). If there is no PIM neighborship with the border ISP (Router SP3-1 from Figure 1-1), the PIM domain ends naturally at that border.

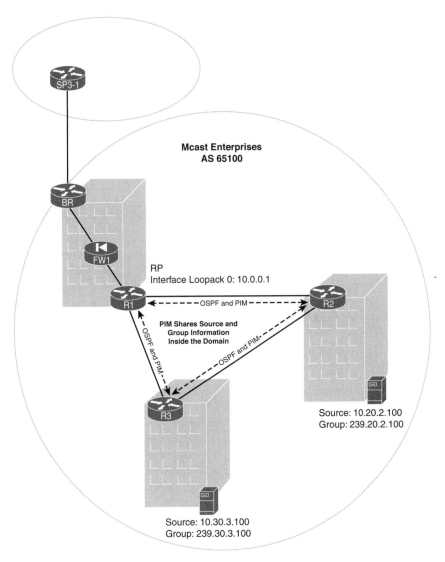

Figure 1-6 *A Single AS with a Single Multicast Domain*

In this case, the domain exists wherever PIM is configured, but what if PIM were configured between the AS border router (BR) of Mcast Enterprises and ISP Blue (SP3-1)?
Wouldn't the domain then encompass both autonomous systems?

Such a broad definition of a domain may not be very useful. If a domain encompasses
any PIM-connected routers, a single multicast domain could extend across the global
Internet! While that might be convenient for the purposes of multicast forwarding, it
would not be secure or desirable.

A domain can also be defined by the potential reach of a multicast packet, encompassing
all the paths between sources and receivers. However, to have all multicast sources and

groups available to all routers within a given domain, even inside a single AS may not be the best design. It may also not be very efficient, depending on the locations of sources, receivers, and RPs.

Clearly, PIM networks can use very flexible definitions for domains. The scope and borders of a multicast domain are essentially wherever an administrator designs them to be. This means that multicast domains also need much tighter and more distinctly configured boundaries than their unicast counterparts. For example, organizations that source or receive multicast flows over the global Internet need a secure boundary between internal and external multicast resources, just like they have for unicast routing resources. After all, an Internet multicast application could potentially use RPF information or send/receive packets from nearly anywhere.

PIM Domain Design Types

Because the definitions of multicast domains are fluid, it is important to define those types of domains that make logical sense and those most commonly deployed. You also need to establish some guidelines and best practices around how best to deploy them. In almost all cases, the best design is the one that matches the particular needs of the applications running on the network. Using an application-centered approach means that administrators are free to define domains according to need rather than a set prescriptive methodology.

The primary focus of defining a domain is drawing borders or boundaries around the desired reach of multicast applications. To accomplish this, network architects use router configurations, IP Multicast groups and scoping, RP placement strategies, and other policy to define and create domain boundaries. If the multicast overlay is very simple, then the domain may also be very simple, even encompassing the entire AS (refer to Figure 1-6). This type of domain would likely span an entire IGP network, with universal PIM neighbor relationships between all IGP routers. A single RP could be used for all group mappings. In this type of domain, all multicast groups and sources would be available to all systems within the domain.

These types of domains with AS-wide scope are becoming more and more rare in practice. Application and security requirements often require tighter borders around specific flows for specific applications. An administrator could use scoping in a much more effective way.

Domains by Group, or Group Scope

In many cases, the best way to scope a domain is by application. It is best practice for individual applications to use different multicast groups across an AS. That means that you can isolate an application by group number and scope the domain by group number. This is perhaps the most common method of bounding a domain in most enterprise networks.

It is also very common to have numerous applications with similar policy requirements within a network. They may need the same security zoning, or the same quality of service (QoS), or perhaps similar traffic engineering. In these cases, you can use group scopes to accomplish the proper grouping of applications for policy purposes. For example, a local-only set of applications with a singular policy requirement could be summarized by a summary address. Two applications using groups 239.20.2.100 and 239.20.2.200 could be localized by using summary address 239.20.0.0/16. To keep these applications local to a specific geography, the domain should use a single RP or an Anycast RP pair for that specific domain.

Figure 1-7 shows just such a model—a domain scoping in the Mcast Enterprises network using a combination of geography and application type, as defined by a group scope. Assuming that this network is using PIM–SM, each domain *must* have at least one active RP mapped to the groups in the scope that is tied to the local region-specific application or enterprise-specific groups. (Operational simplicity would require separate nodes representing RPs for different scope.) In this case, R1, R2, and R3 are RPs/border routers for their respective domains.

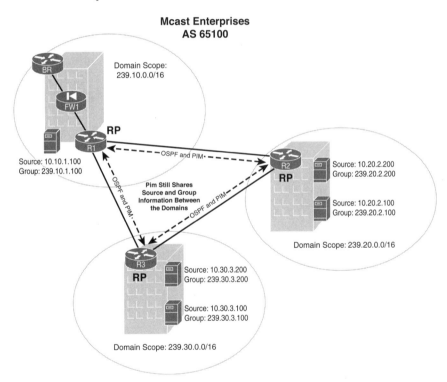

Figure 1-7   *Domain Scope Using Application and Geography Type*

Chapter 5, "IP Multicast Design Considerations and Implementation," in *IP Multicast, Volume 1* explains domain scoping at length and provides additional examples of how to scope a domain based on application, geography, or other properties. Most IP Multicast problems that occur in networks happen because the networks haven't been properly segmented. (This is actually often true of unicast networks as well.) A well-defined scope that is based on applications can be very helpful in achieving proper segmentation.

Domains by RP Scope

In some larger networks, the location and policy of the applications are of less concern than the resiliency of network resources. If there are many applications and the multicast network is very busy, RP resources could simply be overloaded. It may be necessary to scope on RP location rather than on application type or group.

Scoping by RP allows the network architect to spread multicast pathing resources across the network. It is not uncommon to use Anycast RP groupings to manage such large deployments. For example, with the network shown in Figure 1-7, instead of using each router as a single RP, all three routers could be grouped together for Anycast RP in a single large domain. Figure 1-8 shows an updated design for Mcast Enterprises for just such a scenario.

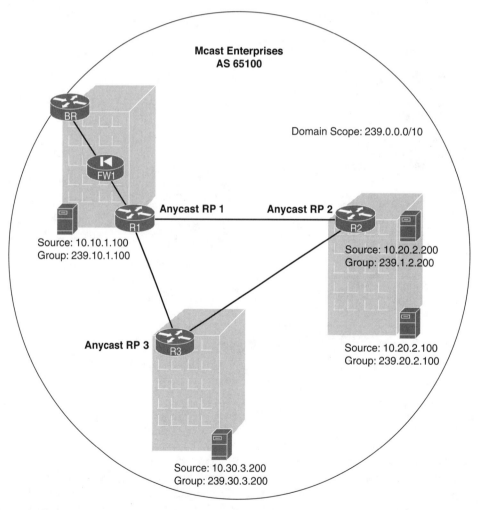

Figure 1-8   *A Single Domain Scoped with Anycast RP*

The advantage of this design is that no one RP can become a single point of failure, and there is geographic resistance to overutilization of RP resources. This design is common among enterprises with many applications, senders, and receivers spread out across large geographies. There is no limitation to the way in which scoping can occur, and multiple domains can overlap each other to achieve the best of both the RP domain scope and the group scope design methodologies.

Overlapping Domains and Subdomains

If the network design requires multiple types of domains and accompanying policies, it is likely that a hybrid design model is required. This type of design might include many multicast domains that overlap each other in certain places. There could also be sub-domains of a much larger domain.

Let's look one more time at the Mcast Enterprises network, this time using a hybrid design (see Figure 1-9). In this case, an application is sourced at R2 with group 239.20.2.100. That application is meant to be a geographically local resource and should not be shared with the larger network. In addition, R2 is also connected to a source for group 239.1.2.200, which has an AS-wide scope.

Remember that each domain needs a domain-specific RP or RP pair. In this case, R2 is used as the local domain RP and R1 as the RP for an AS-wide scoped domain. Because the 239.20/16 domain is essentially a subset of the private multicast group space desig-nated by 239.0.0.0/8, the 239.20/16 domain is a subdomain of the much larger domain that uses R1 as the RP. This design also uses two additional subdomains, with R1 as local RP and R3 as local RP.

For further domain resiliency, it would not be unreasonable to use R1 as a backup or Anycast RP for any of the other groups as well. In these cases, you would use very spe-cific source network filters at the domain boundaries. Otherwise, you may want to look more closely at how to accomplish forwarding between these domains. Table 1-1 breaks down the scope and RP assignments for each domain and subdomain.

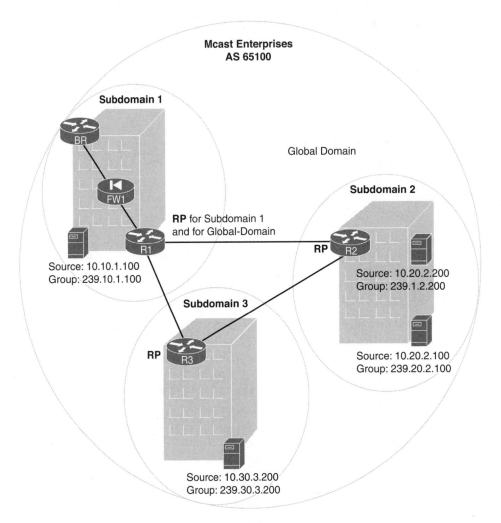

Figure 1-9   *Overlapping Domains and Subdomains*

Table 1-1   *Overlapping Domain Scopes for Figure 1-9*

Domain	RP Assignment	Group Mapping/Scope
Global domain	R1	239.0.0.0/8
Subdomain 1	R1	239.10.0.0/16
Subdomain 2	R2	239.20.0.0/16
Subdomain 3	R3	239.30.0.0/16

In a hybrid design scenario, such as the example shown in Figure 1-9, it may be necessary to forward multicast traffic down a path that is not congruent with the unicast path; this is known as *traffic engineering*. In addition, Mcast Enterprises may have some multicast applications that require forwarding to the Internet, as previously discussed, or forwarding between the domains outlined in Figure 1-9, which is even more common. Additional protocols are required to make this type of interdomain forwarding happen.

Forwarding Between Domains

Now that you understand the three pillars of interdomain design and the types of domains typically deployed, you also need to meet these pillar requirements in order to forward traffic from one domain to another domain. If any of these elements are missing from the network design, forwarding between domains simply cannot occur. But how does a network build an MRIB for remote groups or identify sources and receivers that are not connected to the local domain?

Each domain in the path needs to be supplemented with information from all the domains in between the source and the receivers. There are essentially two ways to accomplish this: statically or dynamically. A static solution involves a network administrator manually entering information into the edge of the network in order to complete tree building that connects the remote root to the local branches. Consider, for example, two PIM–SM domains: one that contains the source of a flow and one that contains the receivers.

The first static tree-building method requires the source network to statically nail the multicast flow to the external interface, using an IGMP static-group join. Once this is accomplished, if it is a PIM–SM domain, the receiver network can use the edge router as either a physical RP or a virtual RP to which routers in the network can map groups and complete shared and source trees. This is shown in Figure 1-10, using the Mcast Enterprises network as the receiver network and ISP Blue as the source network. Both networks are using PIM–SM for forwarding.

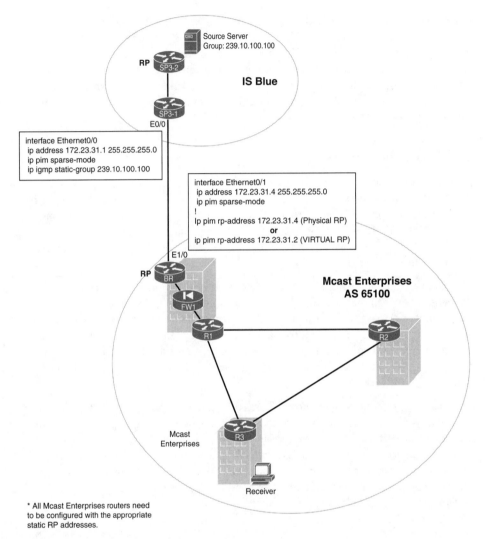

Figure 1-10 *Static Interdomain Solution*

When the edge router is used for RP services, it can pick up the join from the remote network and automatically form the shared and source trees as packets come in from the source network. If Mcast Enterprises does not wish to use the edge router as an RP but instead uses a centralized enterprise RP like R1, tree building will fail as the edge router will not have the shared-tree information necessary for forwarding. The second interdomain static tree-building method solves this problem by using a PIM dense-mode proxy (see Figure 1-11), which normally provides a proxy for connecting a dense-mode domain to a sparse-mode domain.

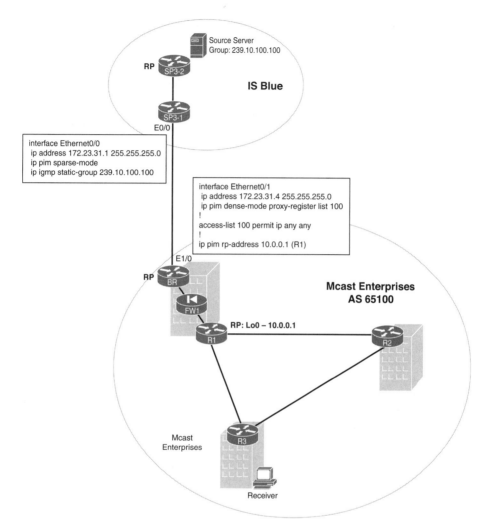

Figure 1-11 *Static Interdomain Forwarding Using a PIM Dense-Mode Proxy*

Static methods are fine for certain network situations. For example, a services company that has an extranet connection and unidirectional flows could create a simple interdomain solution like the ones shown previously. Not only is such a solution simple, it provides a clear demarcation between two domains, leaving each domain free to use any domain design type desired.

Every static configuration in networking also has weaknesses. If any scale to the solution is required, it is likely that these static methods simply will not work. For example, scaling statically across three or more domains requires that each flow be nailed up statically at each edge. With a large number of flows, this can become an administrative nightmare that grows exponentially with the number of connections and domains. In addition, the source domain will have almost no control over subscriptions and bandwidth usage of flows as they pass outside the source domain.

If scale and sophisticated flow management are required, dynamic information sharing for the three pillars is also required. Dynamic methods use existing IGP/EGP protocols in conjunction with three additional multicast-specific protocols that an architect can implement between domains to share information: Multicast BGP (MBGP), PIM, and Multicast Source Discovery Protocol (MSDP). The remainder of this chapter deals with the configuration and operation of these three protocols in a multidomain environment.

Autonomous System Borders and Multicast BGP

As discussed earlier, each Internet-connected organization has unique needs and requirements that drive the implementation of IETF protocol policies and configurations. A unique Internet-connected network, with singular administrative control, is commonly referred to as an *autonomous system* (*AS*). The Internet is essentially a collection of networks, with ASs connected together in a massive, global nexus. A connection between any two ASs is an administrative demarcation (border) point. As IP packets cross each AS border, a best-effort trust is implied; that is, the packet is forwarded to the final destination with reasonable service.

Each border-connecting router needs to share routing information through a common protocol with its neighbors in any other AS. This does not mean that the two border routers use the same protocols, configuration, or policy to communicate with other routers inside the AS. It is a near certain guarantee that an ISP will have a completely different set of protocols and configurations than would an enterprise network to which it provides service.

The AS border represents a policy- and protocol-based plane of separation between routing information that an organization wishes to make public and routing information that it intends to keep private. Routing protocols used within the AS are generally meant to be private.

The modern Internet today uses Border Gateway Protocol (BGP)—specifically version 4, or BGPv4—as the EGP protocol for sharing forwarding information between AS border routers. Any IP routing protocol could be used internally to share routes among intra-AS IP routers. Internal route sharing may or may not include routes learned by border routers via BGP. Any acceptable IP-based IGP can be used within the AS.

Figure 1-12 expands on the AS view and more clearly illustrates the demarcation between internal and external routing protocols. In this example, not only is there an AS demarcation between Mcast Enterprises and ISP Blue but Mcast Enterprises has also implemented a BGP confederation internally. Both AS border routers share an eBGP neighborship. All Mcast Enterprises routes are advertised by the BR to the Internet via SP3-1, the border router of ISP Blue. Because Mcast Enterprises is using a confederation, all routes are advertised from a single BGP AS, AS 65100. In this scenario, BR advertises a single summary prefix of 10.0.0.0/8 to the Internet via ISP Blue.

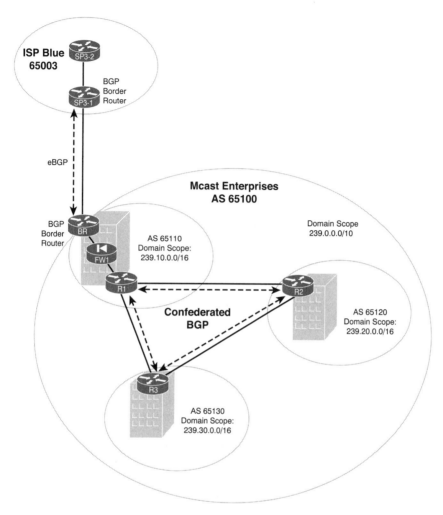

Figure 1-12 *Inter-AS Routing Through BGP*

Note BGP confederations are not required in this design. The authors added confederations in order to more fully illustrate multicast BGP relationships.

As mentioned earlier, the practice of best-effort networking also applies to internetworks that are not a part of the Internet. Large internetworks may wish to segregate network geographies for specific policy or traffic engineering requirements. Many enterprises use BGP with private AS numbers to accomplish this task. In some ways, this mirrors the best-effort service of the Internet but on a much smaller scale. However, what happens when multicast is added to tiered networks or interconnected networks such as these? Can multicast packets naturally cross AS boundaries without additional considerations?

Remember the three pillars of interdomain design. Autonomous system borders naturally create a problem for the first of these requirements: the multicast control plane for source identification. Remember that the router must know a proper path to any multicast source, either from the unicast RIB or learned (either statically or dynamically) through a specific RPF exception.

There is no RPF information from the IGP at a domain boundary. Therefore, if PIM needs to build a forwarding tree across a domain boundary, there are no valid paths on which to build an OIL. If any part of the multicast tree lies beyond the boundary, you need to add a static or dynamic RPF entry to complete the tree at the border router.

As discussed in *IP Multicast, Volume 1*, static entries are configured by using the **ip mroute** command in IOS-XE and NX-OS. For IOS-XR, you add a static entry by using the **static-rpf** command. However, adding static RPF entries for large enterprises or ISPs is simply not practical. You need a way to transport this information across multiple ASs, in the same way you transport routing information for unicast networks. Autonomous system border routers typically use BGP to engineer traffic between ASs. The IETF added specific, multiprotocol extensions to BGPv4 for this very purpose.

RFC 2283 created multiprotocol BGPv4 extensions (the most current RFC is RFC 4760, with updates in RFC 7606). This is often referred to as Multiprotocol Border Gateway Protocol (MBGP). MBGP uses the same underlying IP unicast routing mechanics inherent in BGPv4 to forward routing and IP prefix information about many other types of protocols. Whereas BGPv4 in its original form was meant to carry routing information and updates exclusively for IPv4 unicast, MBGP supports IPv6, multicast, and label-switched virtual private networks (VPNs) (using MPLS VPN technology, as discussed in Chapter 3, "Multicast MPLS VPNs"), and other types of networking protocols as well. In the case of multicast, MBGP carries multicast-specific route prefix information against which routers can RPF check source and destination multicast traffic. The best part of this protocol arrangement is that MBGP can use all the same tuning and control parameters for multicast prefix information sharing that apply to regular IPv4 unicast routing in BGP.

The MBGP RFC accomplishes extends BGP reachability information by adding two additional path attributes, MP_REACH_NLRI and MP_UNREACH_NLRI. NLRI, or Network Learning Reachability Information, is essentially a descriptive name for the prefix, path, and attribute information shared between BGP speakers. These two additional attributes create a simple way to learn and advertise multiple sets of routing information, individualized by an address family. MBGP address families include IPv4 unicast, IPv6 unicast, Multiprotocol Label Switching labels, and, of course, IPv4 and IPv6 multicast.

The main advantage of MBGP is that it allows AS-border and internal routers to support noncongruent (traffic engineered) multicast topologies. This is discussed at length in Chapter 5 in *IP Multicast, Volume 1*. This concept is particularly relevant to Internet multicast and interdomain multicast. Multicast NLRI reachability information can now be shared with all the great filtering and route preferencing of standard BGP for unicast, allowing Internet providers to create a specific feed for multicast traffic.

Configuring and Verifying MBGP for Multicast

Configuring and operating MBGP is extraordinarily easy to do, especially if you already have a basic understanding of BGP configurations for IPv4 unicast. The routing information and configuration is essentially identical standard BGPv4 for unicast prefixes. The differences between a unicast BGP table and multicast BGP table occur because of specific filtering or sharing policies implemented per address family, leading to potentially noncongruent tables.

MBGP configuration begins by separating BGP neighbor activations by address family. A non-MBGP configuration typically consists of a series of neighbor statements with filter and routing parameters. Example 1-2 is a non-MBGP-enabled configuration on the BR between the other routers in Mcast Enterprises and ISP Blue from Figure 1-12.

Example 1-2 *Standard BGP Configuration*

```
BR(config)# router bgp 65100
BR(config-router)# neighbor 10.0.0.1 remote-as 65100
BR(config-router)# neighbor 10.0.0.1 update-source Loopback0
BR(config-router)# neighbor 10.0.0.2 remote-as 65100
BR(config-router)# neighbor 10.0.0.2 update-source Loopback0
BR(config-router)# neighbor 10.0.0.3 remote-as 65100
BR(config-router)# neighbor 10.0.0.3 update-source Loopback0

BR(config-router)# neighbor 172.23.31.1 remote-as 65003
BR(config-router)# network 10.0.0.0
```

MBGP commands can be separated into two configuration types: BGP neighborship commands and BGP policy commands. In IOS-XE and NX-OS, all neighbors and neighbor-related parameters (for example, remote-as, MD5 authentication, update-source, AS pathing info, timers, and so on) must be configured and established under the global BGP routing process subconfiguration mode. BGP policy commands (such as route-map filters, network statements, and redistribution), are no longer configured globally but by address family.

Let's look more closely at an example of an MBGP configuration. Figure 1-13 shows a snapshot of just the external, unicast, BGP connection between the BR and the border route in ISP Blue, SP3-1.

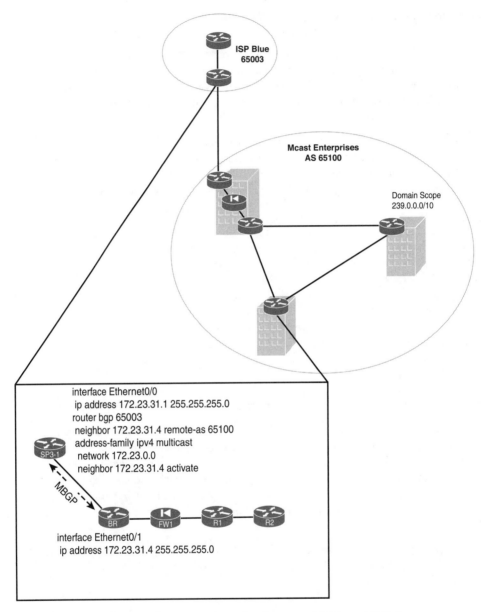

Figure 1-13 *MBGP Configuration Snapshot Between the BR and SP3-1*

Example 1-3 shows the same router configuration on the BR from above but this time using address families for IPv4 unicast and IPv4 multicast, with the additional multicast configuration. In this example, BR is using IOS-XE.

Example 1-3 *MBGP Address-Family Configuration on the BR*

```
BR(config)# router bgp 65100
BR(config-router)# neighbor 10.0.0.1 remote-as 65100
BR(config-router)# neighbor 10.0.0.1 update-source Loopback0
BR(config-router)# neighbor 172.23.31.1 remote-as 65003
BR(config-router-af)# address-family ipv4
BR(config-router-af)# network 10.0.0.0
BR(config-router-af)# neighbor 10.0.0.1 activate
BR(config-router-af)# neighbor 172.23.31.1 activate
BR(config-router-af)# exit-address-family
BR(config-router)# address-family ipv4 multicast
BR(config-router-af)# network 10.0.0.0
BR(config-router-af)# neighbor 10.0.0.1 activate
BR(config-router-af)# neighbor 172.23.31.1 activate
BR(config-router-af)# exit-address-family
```

The **activate** command option under each configured address family is critical and is required for any peer to activate information sharing for a specific NLRI—in this case IPv4 unicast and multicast. It is important to note that a neighbor does not have to have consistent address-family activation. For example, a neighbor may be activated for multicast NLRI sharing, but not for unicast. Once the neighbor is activated, all policy commands must be entered under an address family.

> **Note** BGP neighbor commands must be consistent across peers, regardless of address-family activation. This means that a peer must be established with a neighbor router in compliance with all the explicit RFC neighborship requirements for BGP. For example, you must use consistent AS numbers between global peers. You cannot have two peerings with the same node in multiple ASs. The standard rules of BGP still apply, regardless of the policy configuration.

In IOS-XR (a service provider–oriented operating system), multiprotocol usage is essentially assumed in the configuration. Address families are required for almost all protocol configurations, and policy commands are entered per neighbor and per address family. Example 1-4 shows the same configuration as before, for the BR at Mcast Enterprises using IOS-XR.

Example 1-4   *BGP Address-Family Configuration for IOS-XR on the BR*

```
RP/0/0/CPU0:BR(config)# router bgp 65100
RP/0/0/CPU0:BR(config-bgp)# address-family ipv4 unicast
RP/0/0/CPU0:BR(config-bgp-af)# network 10.0.0.0
RP/0/0/CPU0:BR(config-bgp-af)# exit
RP/0/0/CPU0:BR(config-bgp)# address-family ipv4 multicast
RP/0/0/CPU0:BR(config-bgp-af)# network 10.0.0.0
RP/0/0/CPU0:BR(config-bgp-af)# exit
RP/0/0/CPU0:BR(config-bgp)# neighbor 10.0.0.1
RP/0/0/CPU0:BR(config-bgp-nbr)# remote-as 65100
RP/0/0/CPU0:BR(config-bgp-nbr)# address-family ipv4 unicast
RP/0/0/CPU0:BR(config-bgp-nbr-af)# exit
RP/0/0/CPU0:BR(config-bgp-nbr)# address-family ipv4 multicast
RP/0/0/CPU0:BR(config-bgp)# neighbor 172.23.31.1
RP/0/0/CPU0:BR(config-bgp-nbr)# remote-as 65003
RP/0/0/CPU0:BR(config-bgp-nbr)# address-family ipv4 unicast
RP/0/0/CPU0:BR(config-bgp-nbr-af)# exit
RP/0/0/CPU0:BR(config-bgp-nbr)# address-family ipv4 multicast
RP/0/0/CPU0:BR(config-bgp-nbr-af)# commit
RP/0/0/CPU0:BR(config-bgp-nbr-af)# end
```

This method of policy configuration provides unique and potentially incongruent tables between NLRI address families in BGP. Activation and policy do not need to be consistent between NLRI (address family) instances. It also naturally stands to reason that checking the multicast BGP table requires different commands from checking the unicast table. To learn more about this type of BGP configuration, check out the many Cisco Press books written about BGP and BGP design. *Internet Routing Architectures* by Sam Halabi would be a good place to start.

Any BGP commands that are used to check on neighborship status and establishment parameters are universal. Commands like **show ip bgp neighbors** in IOS-XE do not change. In fact, this is still the best command to use to check on the neighborship status of an MBGP peer. However, additional information about new NLRI address families is also included. The BR output in Example 1-5 shows this in action.

Example 1-5   show ip bgp neighbors *(Truncated) on the BR*

```
BR# sh ip bgp neighbors
BGP neighbor is 10.0.0.1,  remote AS 65100, internal link
  BGP version 4, remote router ID 10.0.0.1
  BGP state = Established, up for 00:31:41
  Last read 00:00:14, last write 00:00:48, hold time is 180, keepalive interval is
    60 seconds
  Neighbor sessions:
    1 active, is not multisession capable (disabled)
  Neighbor capabilities:
    Route refresh: advertised and received(new)
    Four-octets ASN Capability: advertised and received
    Address family IPv4 Unicast: advertised and received
    Address family IPv4 Multicast: advertised
    Enhanced Refresh Capability: advertised and received
    Multisession Capability:
    Stateful switchover support enabled: NO for session 1
  Message statistics:
    InQ depth is 0
    OutQ depth is 0

                      Sent       Rcvd
    Opens:              1          1
    Notifications:      0          0
    Updates:            9          1
    Keepalives:        35         36
    Route Refresh:      0          0
    Total:             45         38
  Default minimum time between advertisement runs is 0 seconds

For address family: IPv4 Unicast
  Session: 10.0.0.1
  BGP table version 18, neighbor version 18/0
  Output queue size : 0
  Index 4, Advertise bit 1
  4 update-group member
  Slow-peer detection is disabled
    Slow-peer split-update-group dynamic is disabled
```

```
                                    Sent        Rcvd
    Prefix activity:                ----        ----
       Prefixes Current:             4           0
       Prefixes Total:               7           0
       Implicit Withdraw:            0           0
       Explicit Withdraw:            3           0
       Used as bestpath:            n/a          0
       Used as multipath:           n/a          0


                                  Outbound    Inbound
    Local Policy Denied Prefixes:  --------    -------
       Total:                         0           0
    Number of NLRIs in the update sent: max 2, min 0
    Last detected as dynamic slow peer: never
    Dynamic slow peer recovered: never
    Refresh Epoch: 1
    Last Sent Refresh Start-of-rib: never
    Last Sent Refresh End-of-rib: never
    Last Received Refresh Start-of-rib: never
    Last Received Refresh End-of-rib: never
                                    Sent        Rcvd
       Refresh activity:            ----        ----
          Refresh Start-of-RIB       0           0
          Refresh End-of-RIB         0           0


For address family: IPv4 Multicast
  BGP table version 2, neighbor version 1/2
  Output queue size : 0
  Index 0, Advertise bit 0
  Uses NEXT_HOP attribute for MBGP NLRIs
  Slow-peer detection is disabled
  Slow-peer split-update-group dynamic is disabled
                                    Sent        Rcvd
    Prefix activity:                ----        ----
       Prefixes Current:             0           0
       Prefixes Total:               0           0
       Implicit Withdraw:            0           0
       Explicit Withdraw:            0           0
       Used as bestpath:            n/a          0
       Used as multipath:           n/a          0


                                  Outbound    Inbound
    Local Policy Denied Prefixes:  --------    -------
       Total:                         0           0
    Number of NLRIs in the update sent: max 0, min 0
    Last detected as dynamic slow peer: never
```

```
Dynamic slow peer recovered: never
Refresh Epoch: 1
Last Sent Refresh Start-of-rib: never
Last Sent Refresh End-of-rib: never
Last Received Refresh Start-of-rib: never
Last Received Refresh End-of-rib: never
                                  Sent      Rcvd
        Refresh activity:         ----      ----
      Refresh Start-of-RIB          0         0
      Refresh End-of-RIB            0         0
```

Additional verification commands for the IPv4 multicast address family are generally found using the **ipv4 multicast** keyword in many standard BGP commands. For example, the command for showing the standard IPv4 unicast BGP prefix table is **show ip bgp**. Notice in Example 1-6 what happens to the BGP multicast prefix table when **ipv4 multicast** is added. In this instance, the two tables are not congruent, as indicated by the highlighted multicast table output.

Example 1-6   show ip bgp *versus* show ip bgp ipv4 multicast

```
BR# show ip bgp
BGP table version is 18, local router ID is 10.0.0.4
Status codes: s suppressed, d damped, h history, * valid, > best, i - internal,
              r RIB-failure, S Stale, m multipath, b backup-path, f RT-Filter,
              x best-external, a additional-path, c RIB-compressed,
Origin codes: i - IGP, e - EGP, ? - incomplete
RPKI validation codes: V valid, I invalid, N Not found

     Network          Next Hop          Metric LocPrf Weight Path
 *>  10.0.0.0         0.0.0.0                0          32768 i
 *>  172.21.0.0       172.23.31.1                          0 65003 65001 i
 *>  172.22.0.0       172.23.31.1                          0 65003 65002 i
 *>  172.23.0.0       172.23.31.1            0             0 65003 i


BR# show ip bgp ipv4 multicast
BGP table version is 2, local router ID is 10.0.0.4
Status codes: s suppressed, d damped, h history, * valid, > best, i - internal,
              r RIB-failure, S Stale, m multipath, b backup-path, f RT-Filter,
              x best-external, a additional-path, c RIB-compressed,
Origin codes: i - IGP, e - EGP, ? - incomplete
RPKI validation codes: V valid, I invalid, N Not found

     Network          Next Hop          Metric LocPrf Weight Path
 *>  10.0.0.0         0.0.0.0                0          32768 i
 *   172.23.0.0       172.23.31.1            0             0 65003 i
```

Note   This is only a basic introduction to MBGP configuration. It is beyond the scope of this text to delve deeply into the interworking of the BGP protocol stack. If you are planning to configure interdomain multicast, it is recommend that you spend time getting acquainted with BGP. It will also help you in better understanding the material presented in Chapter 3.

Domain Borders and Configured Multicast Boundaries

As mentioned earlier, most autonomous systems use IGPs and EGPs to establish clear demarcation points and borders. The easiest way to create a clear border around a PIM domain is to simply configure the router to *not* apply PIM–SM to border interfaces. Without PIM–SM configuration for those interfaces, no neighborships form between the border router inside the AS and the border router of the neighboring AS.

What does this mean for the PIM–SM domain border in an interdomain forwarding model? If PIM is not sharing join/leave information between the neighboring border routers, the second critical element in the three pillars of interdomain design—the multicast control plane for receiver identification—becomes a problem. Remember that—the router must know about any legitimate receivers that have joined the group and where they are located in the network.

Here then, is the big question: Is a PIM–SM relationship required between ASs in order to perform multicast interdomain forwarding? The short answer is yes! There are certainly ways to work around this requirement (such as by using protocol rules), but the best recommendation is to configure PIM on any interdomain multicast interfaces in order to maintain PIM neighborships with external PIM routers.

Why is this necessary? The biggest reason is that the local domain needs the join/prune PIM–SM messages for any receivers that may not be part of the local domain. Remember that without the (*, G) information, the local RP cannot help the network build a shared tree linking the source and receivers through the RP. Let's examine this relationship in action in an example.

Let's limit the scope to just the PIM relationship between the BR in Mcast Enterprises and SP3-1. In this particular instance, there is a receiver for an Internet multicast group, 239.120.1.1, connected to R2, as shown in Figure 1-14, with additional PIM configuration on the interface on BR. SP3-1 does not have PIM configured on the interface facing the BR, interface Ethernet0/0.

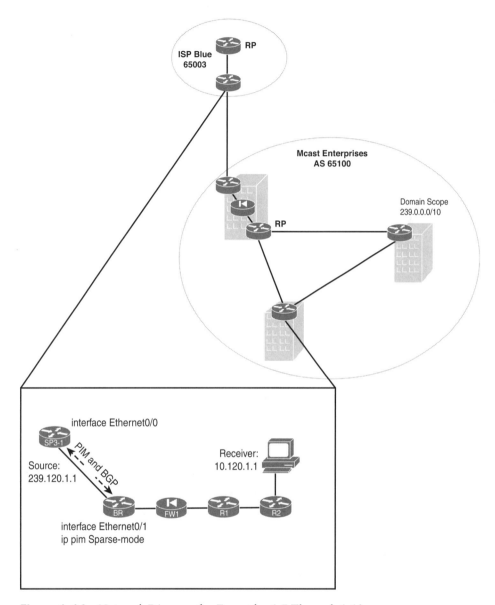

Figure 1-14   *Network Diagram for Examples 1-7 Through 1-10*

As you can see from the **show ip mroute 239.120.1.1** command output in Example 1-7, router SP3-1 has no entries for 239.120.1.1. It does not have a PIM relationship to the BR in Mcast Enterprises, so there is no way for the BR to share that information.

Example 1-7   *No* ip mroute *Entries*

```
SP3-1# show ip mroute 239.120.1.1
Group 239.120.1.1 not found
```

If PIM–SM is configured on SP3-1, a neighborship forms between the BR and SP3-1. Once this is up, SP3-1 learns the (*, G) entry from the BR. This can be seen by debugging PIM with the command **debug ip pim**. Example 1-8 shows output for this command on SP3-1.

Example 1-8   *debug ip pim on SP3-1*

```
SP3-1(config-if)# int e0/0
SP3-1(config-if)# do debug ip pim
SP3-1(config-if)# ip pim sparse-mode
SP3-1(config-if)#
*Feb 19 22:34:49.481: %PIM-5-NBRCHG: neighbor 172.23.31.4 UP on interface
  Ethernet0/0
*Feb 19 22:34:49.489: PIM(0): Changing DR for Ethernet0/0, from 0.0.0.0 to
  172.23.31.4
SP3-1(config-if)#
*Feb 19 22:34:49.489: %PIM-5-DRCHG: DR change from neighbor 0.0.0.0 to 172.23.31.4
  on interface Ethernet0/0
SP3-1(config-if)#
*Feb 19 22:34:50.622: PIM(0): Check DR after interface: Ethernet0/0 came up!
SP3-1(config-if)#
*Feb 19 22:34:56.239: PIM(0): Building Triggered (*,G) Join / (S,G,RP-bit) Prune
  message for 239.120.1.1
*Feb 19 22:34:56.239: PIM(0): Check RP 172.23.0.2 into the (*, 239.120.1.1) entry
```

As you can see, once the neighbor is up, router BR sends a PIM join/prune message to SP3-1, indicating that a receiver for group 239.120.1.1 is registered to the Mcast Enterprises multicast domain. SP3-1 now uses this message to build a state entry for the (*, 239.120.1.1) tree. Without this message, there is no way for SP3-1 or any other upstream routers to know that a receiver is located down the E0/0 path toward the BR of Mcast Enterprises.

There's also another problem here. Have you already identified it? SP3-1 is looking for an RP on which to build a shared tree for the (*, G) join that it just received. However, as you can see from the last message in the **debug** output, the RP for this domain is 172.23.0.2, which is located through a different interface, interface E0/1. This means the RPF check for the (*, G) is going to fail, and the outgoing interface list for (*, G) will have an outgoing interface list (OIL) of NULL. Until that issue is resolved, all the packets from the domain are dropped in the bit bucket.

You can verify all this with the **show ip mroute 239.120.1.1** command on SP3-1 and by pinging the group from the ISP-Blue domain. Pinging 239.120.1.1 from SP3-1 should make SP3-1 E0/0 a source for that group, and the ping should fail because it is unable to cross the domain. Example 1-9 shows this behavior in action.

Example 1-9 *Multicast Reachability Failure for 239.120.1.1*

```
SP3-1# sh ip mroute 239.120.1.1
IP Multicast Routing Table
Flags: D - Dense, S - Sparse, B - Bidir Group, s - SSM Group, C - Connected,
       L - Local, P - Pruned, R - RP-bit set, F - Register flag,
       T - SPT-bit set, J - Join SPT, M - MSDP created entry, E - Extranet,
       X - Proxy Join Timer Running, A - Candidate for MSDP Advertisement,
       U - URD, I - Received Source Specific Host Report,
       Z - Multicast Tunnel, z - MDT-data group sender,
       Y - Joined MDT-data group, y - Sending to MDT-data group,
       G - Received BGP C-Mroute, g - Sent BGP C-Mroute,
       N - Received BGP Shared-Tree Prune, n - BGP C-Mroute suppressed,
       Q - Received BGP S-A Route, q - Sent BGP S-A Route,
       V - RD & Vector, v - Vector, p - PIM Joins on route
Outgoing interface flags: H - Hardware switched, A - Assert winner, p - PIM Join
 Timers: Uptime/Expires
 Interface state: Interface, Next-Hop or VCD, State/Mode

(*, 239.120.1.1), 00:00:20/stopped, RP 172.23.0.2, flags: SP
  Incoming interface: Ethernet0/1, RPF nbr 172.23.1.2
  Outgoing interface list: Null

(172.23.31.1, 239.120.1.1), 00:00:20/00:02:39, flags: PT
  Incoming interface: Ethernet0/0, RPF nbr 0.0.0.0
  Outgoing interface list: Null

SP3-1# ping 239.120.1.1
Type escape sequence to abort.
Sending 1, 100-byte ICMP Echos to 239.120.1.1, timeout is 2 seconds:
...
```

You can see in Example 1-9 that the ping does fail, as expected. It is important to remember that BGP is included in this network configuration—in particular, MBGP for the IPv4 multicast NLRI address family. The issue is not that the RPF check for the source has failed but rather that the RPF check against the RP has failed because the RP is in a different direction and has no knowledge of the (*, G) to marry with the source. Something else is needed to complete the tree. This is addressed this in the next section.

Note   There is also an interesting relationship between using PIM interfaces at domain borders and MBGP. If an external multicast MBGP peer is configured on a router on an interface that has no PIM configuration, you get some very odd behavior in BGP.

One of the many rules of BGP states that for a route to be valid, the route and interface to the next hop must also be valid and learned via the routing table and not recursively through BGP. In the case of multicast MBGP, BGP refers to the PIM topology table in the router to determine if the next-hop interface is valid. If the interface on which the external MBGP (E-MBGP) route was learned is not enabled in the PIM topology, the route fails the best-path selection algorithm and shows in the BGP table as "inaccessible." If you are using MBGP to carry multicast NLRI data across domains, make sure the cross-domain interfaces on which BGP is configured are also configured for an interdomain PIM neighborship. This is shown in Example 1-10, using the IOS-XE command **show ip bgp ipv4 multicast**. Example 1-10 reveals that the prefix is received from the peer but is not installed in the RPF table.

Example 1-10   *BGP IPv4 Multicast Prefix Acceptance With and Without Active PIM on the External Peer Interface*

```
BR# show ip bgp ipv4 multicast
BGP table version is 2, local router ID is 10.0.0.4
Status codes: s suppressed, d damped, h history, * valid, > best, i - internal,
              r RIB-failure, S Stale, m multipath, b backup-path, f RT-Filter,
              x best-external, a additional-path, c RIB-compressed,
Origin codes: i - IGP, e - EGP, ? - incomplete
RPKI validation codes: V valid, I invalid, N Not found
     Network          Next Hop          Metric LocPrf Weight Path
 *>  10.0.0.0         0.0.0.0                0         32768 i
 *   172.23.0.0       172.23.31.1            0             0 65003 i


BR# show ip bgp ipv4 multicast 172.23.0.0
BGP routing table entry for 172.23.0.0/16, version 0
Paths: (1 available, no best path)
Flag: 0x820
  Not advertised to any peer
  Refresh Epoch 2
  65003, (received & used)
```

Next, you need to add PIM to the MBGP peering interface, as shown in Example 1-11.

Example 1-11   *Adding PIM to Complete the RPF Check for BGP*

```
BR(config)# interface ethernet0/1
BR(config-if)# ip pim sparse-mode
*Feb 19 20:46:06.252: %PIM-5-NBRCHG: neighbor 172.23.31.1 UP on interface
  Ethernet0/1
*Feb 19 20:46:07.640: %PIM-5-DRCHG: DR change from neighbor 0.0.0.0 to 172.23.31.4
  on interface Ethernet0/1


BR# show ip bgp ipv4 multicast
BGP table version is 2, local router ID is 10.0.0.4
```

```
Status codes: s suppressed, d damped, h history, * valid, > best, i - internal,
              r RIB-failure, S Stale, m multipath, b backup-path, f RT-Filter,
              x best-external, a additional-path, c RIB-compressed,
Origin codes: i - IGP, e - EGP, ? - incomplete
RPKI validation codes: V valid, I invalid, N Not found

     Network          Next Hop          Metric LocPrf Weight Path
 *>  10.0.0.0         0.0.0.0                0         32768 i
 *   172.23.0.0       172.23.31.1            0             0 65003 i
```

Clearing the BGP neighbors, using the command **clear ip bgp** *, immediately clears the prefix table, as shown in Example 1-12.

Example 1-12   *Clearing the BGP Table*

```
BR# clear ip bgp *
*Feb 19 20:46:29.014: %BGP-5-ADJCHANGE: neighbor 10.0.0.1 Down User reset
*Feb 19 20:46:29.014: %BGP_SESSION-5-ADJCHANGE: neighbor 10.0.0.1 IPv4 Multicast
  topology base removed from session  User reset
*Feb 19 20:46:29.014: %BGP_SESSION-5-ADJCHANGE: neighbor 10.0.0.1 IPv4 Unicast
  topology base removed from session  User reset
*Feb 19 20:46:29.014: %BGP-5-ADJCHANGE: neighbor 172.23.31.1 Down User reset
*Feb 19 20:46:29.014: %BGP_SESSION-5-ADJCHANGE: neighbor 172.23.31.1 IPv4 Multicast
  topology base removed from session  User reset
*Feb 19 20:46:29.014: %BGP_SESSION-5-ADJCHANGE: neighbor 172.23.31.1 IPv4 Unicast
  topology base removed from session  User reset
BR#
*Feb 19 20:46:29.929: %BGP-5-ADJCHANGE: neighbor 10.0.0.1 Up
*Feb 19 20:46:29.942: %BGP-5-ADJCHANGE: neighbor 172.23.31.1 Up
```

Once the neighbor is up, the prefix is received again and is chosen as a BGP best path, as shown in Example 1-13, again using the **show ip bgp ipv4 multicast** command.

Example 1-13   *RPF and BGP Alignment*

```
BR# show ip bgp ipv4 multicast
BGP table version is 2, local router ID is 10.0.0.4
Status codes: s suppressed, d damped, h history, * valid, > best, i - internal,
              r RIB-failure, S Stale, m multipath, b backup-path, f RT-Filter,
              x best-external, a additional-path, c RIB-compressed,
Origin codes: i - IGP, e - EGP, ? - incomplete
RPKI validation codes: V valid, I invalid, N Not found
     Network          Next Hop          Metric LocPrf Weight Path
 *>  10.0.0.0         0.0.0.0                0         32768 i
 *>  172.23.0.0       172.23.31.1            0             0 65003 i
```

Multicast Source Discovery Protocol

The first and second pillars of interdomain design are addressed extensively in the previous section. Let's look more closely at the third pillar: the downstream multicast control plane and MRIB. Remember that the router must know when a source is actively sending packets for a given group. PIM–SM domains must also be able to build a shared tree from the local domain's RP, even when the source has registered to a remote RP in a different domain.

For multidomain or interdomain forwarding, you need ways to deal specifically with these requirements. If a source is in a remote SM domain and actively sending packets, it is registered to an RP that is also not in the domain. That domain will have built the appropriate tree(s) to distribute the packets via PIM. Without the RP in the local domain knowing about the source, no shared tree can be built by the local RP. In addition, how can you RPF check the source tree if you don't know about that source?

The IETF created Multicast Source Discovery Protocol (MSDP) to address this specific issue. The IETF defined MSDP in RFC 3618 as a stop-gap measure for bridging PIM–SM domains until IETF members could establish other PIM extensions to accomplish the same thing. MSDP soon became more than a stop-gap; it is now an industry standard and requirement for PIM–SM interdomain forwarding. As discussed in *IP Multicast, Volume 1*, the usefulness of MSDP was even extended to allow for RP redundancy via Anycast RP, as initially defined in RFC 3446. MSDP's main purpose is to allow a local RP to notify RPs in other domains about the active sources about which it knows.

MSDP accomplishes this by allowing an RP to peer with other RPs via a Transport Control Protocol (TCP) connection to share active multicast source information. This is very similar to the way BGP routers use TCP connections to create neighborships for sharing prefix and path information across autonomous systems. In fact, MSDP, like BGP, uses ASNs in its calculations for building active source tables.

Configuring a basic MSDP peer is quite simple. For the most part, the configuration steps are similar to those for configuring basic BGP, though with some exceptions. Tables 1-2 through 1-4 show the configuration commands needed to enable peering between RPs in IOS-XE, NX-OS, and IOS-XR.

Table 1-2   *IOS-XE MSDP Peering Commands*

Router(Config)#**ip msdp** [**vrf** *vrf-name*] **peer** { *peer-name* | *peer-address* } [**connect-source** *interface-type interface-number*] [**remote-as** *as-number*]

Router(config)#**no ip msdp** [**vrf** *vrf-name*] **peer** { *peer-name* | *peer-address* }

Syntax Options	Purpose
vrf	(Optional) Supports the multicast VPN routing and forwarding (VRF) instance.
vrf-name	(Optional) Specifies the name assigned to the VRF.
peer-name peer-address	Specifies the Domain Name System (DNS) name or IP address of the router that is to be the MSDP peer.

Syntax Options	Purpose
connect-source *interface-type interface-number*	(Optional) Specifies the interface type and number whose primary address becomes the source IP address for the TCP connection. This interface is on the router being configured.
remote-as *as-number*	(Optional) Specifies the autonomous system number of the MSDP peer. This keyword and argument are used for display purposes only.

Table 1-3   *NX-OS MSDP Peering Commands*

Nexus(config)#**ip msdp peer** *peer-address* **connect-source** *if-type if-number* [**remote-as** *asn*]

Nexus(config)#**no ip msdp peer** *peer-address* [**connect-source** *if-type if-number*] [**remote-as** *asn*]

Syntax Options	Purpose
connect-source	Configures a local IP address for a TCP connection.
if-type	Specifies the interface type. For more information, use the question mark (?) online help function.
if-number	Specifies the interface or subinterface number. For more information about the numbering syntax for the networking device, use the question mark (?) online help function.
remote-as *asn*	(Optional) Configures a remote autonomous system number.
connect-source	Configures a local IP address for a TCP connection.

Table 1-4   *IOS-XR MSDP Peering Commands*

RP/0/RP0/CPU0:router(config)#**router msdp**

RP/0/RP0/CPU0:router(config-msdp)#(no)**originator-id** *type interface-path-id*

RP/0/RP0/CPU0:router(config-msdp)#(no) **peer** *peer-address*

Syntax Options	Purpose
type	Specifies the interface type. For more information, use the question mark (?) online help function.
interface-path-id	Specifies the physical interface or virtual interface.
peer-address	Specifies the IP address or DNS name of the router that is to be the MSDP peer.

Example 1-14 shows a sample MSDP peering configuration on router SP3-2 to peer with the RP and border router, SP2-1 (172.22.0.1), in ISP Green, as depicted in the mock-Internet example.

Example 1-14   *Basic MSDP Configuration, SP3-1 to SP2-1*

```
SP3-2>en
SP3-2# config t
Enter configuration commands, one per line.  End with CNTL/Z.
SP3-2(config)# ip msdp peer 172.22.0.1 connect-source lo0
```

Figure 1-15 shows the mock-Internet map expanded. (The configuration snippet in Example 1-14 is from a router using IOS-XE.)

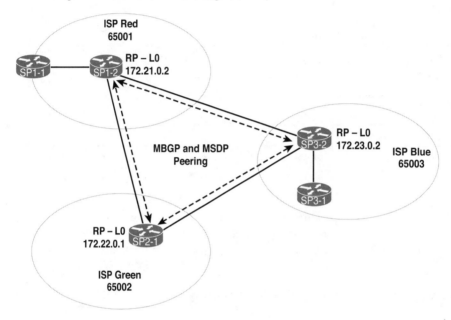

Figure 1-15   *Mock-Internet Map*

As you know, when a source-connected router sees new packets coming from a source, it registers that source with its local RP. If the local RP is enabled for MSDP, it completes the shared tree and, if validated, it creates a special state entry called a source active (SA). The local RP then shares that SA information with any MSDP peer RPs in other domains.

A remote RP that receives this SA advertisement validates the source against its own RPF table. Once validated, the remote RP uses the source and location information to calculate an interdomain forwarding tree, if it has subscribed receivers for that source's group in its local PIM–SM domain. It also forwards the SA entry to any other peers to which it is connected, except for the peer from which it received the SA advertisement. This processing allows a remote RP to learn about remote active sources, while facilitating the shared-tree and source-tree building process for the local domain, completing multicast forwarding trees across multiple domains. This means that in Example 1-14, the RP in

ISP Blue (SP3-1) receives SA advertisements from the configured MSDP peer and RP in ISP Green (SP2-1, 172.22.0.1).

Aside from being necessary to interdomain multicast forwarding, MSDP has some inherent advantages. For one, because a single RP for the entire Internet is not required, no one entity is responsible for the quality of local domain forwarding. Each AS can implement its own RP strategy and connect to other domains in a best-effort manner, just as with unicast routing. Administrators can also use policy to control MSDP sharing behavior, which means autonomous systems can use a single domain strategy for both internal and external forwarding. Shared multicast trees always stay local to the domain, even when join messages are shared with neighboring domains. When receivers are downstream from the remote domain, a (*, G) entry is created only for that domain, with branches at the border edge interface. Because RP resources are only required within the local domain, there are no global resource exhaustion problems or global reliability issues.

MSDP uses TCP port 639 for peering sessions. Also like BGP, MSDP has a specific state machine that allows it to listen for peers, establish TCP connections, and maintain those connections while checking for accuracy and authorization. Figure 1-16 illustrates the MSDP state machine described in RFC 3618.

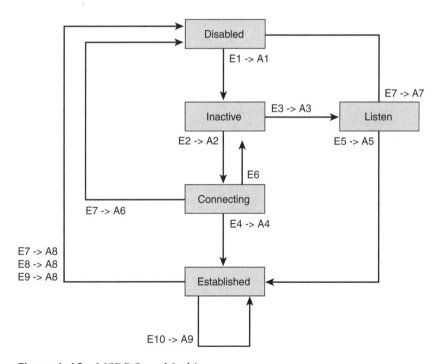

Figure 1-16 *MSDP State Machine*

Table 1-5 explains the Events (EX) and Actions (AX) of the state machine shown in Figure 1-16.

Table 1-5 *MSDP State Machine Events and Actions*

Event/Action	Description
E1	MSDP peering is configured and enabled.
E2	The peer IP address is less than the MSDP source address.
E3	The peer IP address is greater than the MSDP source address.
E4	TCP peering is established (active/master side of the connection).
E5	TCP peering is established (active/master side of the connection).
E6	The connect retry timer has expired.
E7	MSDP peering is disabled.
E8	The hold timer has expired.
E9	A TLV format error has been detected in the MSDP packet.
E10	Any other error is detected.
A1	The peering process begins, with resources allocated and peer IP addresses compared.
A2	TCP is set to Active OPEN and the connect retry timer is set to [ConnectRetry-Period].
A3	TCP is set to Passive OPEN (listen).
A4	The connect retry timer is deleted, and the keepalive TLV is sent, while the keepalive and hold timer are set to configured periods.
A5	The keepalive TLV is sent, while the keepalive and hold timer are set to configured periods.
A6	The TCP Active OPEN attempt is aborted, and MSDP resources for the peer are released.
A7	The TCP Passive OPEN attempt is aborted, and MSDP resources for the peer are released.
A8	The TCP connection is closed, and MSDP resources for the peer are released.
A9	The packet is dropped.

Figure 1-17, which includes configuration commands, shows how to enable basic MSDP peering between the RP router in Mcast Enterprises (R1) and the RP for ISP Blue (SP3-2).

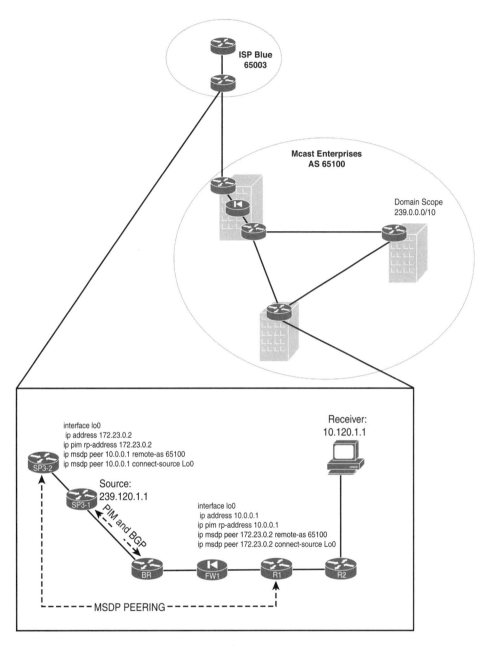

Figure 1-17   *Basic MSDP Peering Configuration, R1 to SP3-2*

You can watch the state machine in action by using the **debug ip msdp peer** command. Example 1-15 shows the state machine debug on R1 using IOS-XE.

Example 1-15   *MSDP State Machine:* **debug ip msdp peer**

```
*Feb 20 21:33:40.390: MSDP(0): 172.23.0.2: Sending TCP connect
*Feb 20 21:33:40.392: %MSDP-5-PEER_UPDOWN: Session to peer 172.23.0.2 going up
*Feb 20 21:33:40.392: MSDP(0): 172.23.0.2: TCP connection established
*Feb 20 21:33:41.004: MSDP(0): Received 3-byte TCP segment from 172.23.0.2
*Feb 20 21:33:41.004: MSDP(0): Append 3 bytes to 0-byte msg 116 from 172.23.0.2, qs 1
*Feb 20 21:33:41.004: MSDP(0): 172.23.0.2: Received 3-byte msg 116 from peer
*Feb 20 21:33:41.004: MSDP(0): 172.23.0.2: Keepalive TLV
*Feb 20 21:33:41.218: MSDP(0): 172.23.0.2: Sending Keepalive message to peer
*Feb 20 21:33:42.224: MSDP(0): 172.23.0.2: Originating SA message
*Feb 20 21:33:42.224: MSDP(0): start_index = 0, mroute_cache_index = 0, Qlen = 0
*Feb 20 21:33:42.225: MSDP(0): 172.23.0.2: Building SA message from SA cache
*Feb 20 21:33:42.225: MSDP(0): start_index = 0, sa_cache_index = 0, Qlen = 0
*Feb 20 21:33:42.225: MSDP(0): Sent entire sa-cache, sa_cache_index = 0, Qlen = 0
```

As you can see from the highlighted portions of the debugging output in Example 1-15, MSDP exchanges TLV (Type-Length-Value) between these TCP peers to maintain multicast source states. All MSDP routers send TLV messages using the same basic packet format (see Figure 1-18).

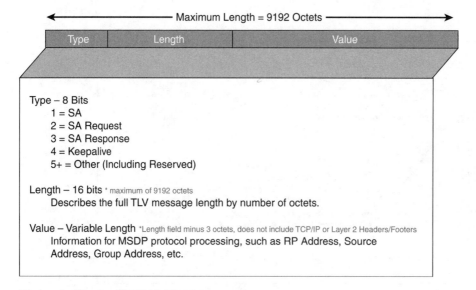

Figure 1-18   *Basic MSDP TLV Message Format*

Depending on the type of communication, the VALUE field in the TLV message may vary dramatically. As shown in Figure 1-18, there are four basic, commonly used TLV messages types. MSDP uses these TLVs to exchange information and maintain peer connections. The message type is indicated in the TYPE field of the packet. These are the four basic message types:

■ **SA message:** Basic advertisement of SA information to a peer, including the RP address on which it was learned, the source IP, and the group IP.

■ **SA Request message:** A request for any known SAs for a given group (usually this occurs because of configuration, in an attempt to reduce state creation latency).

■ **SA Response message:** A response with SA information to an SA Request message.

■ **Keepalive:** Sent between peers when there are no current SA messages to maintain the TCP connection.

Each of these message types populates the VALUE field with different information necessary for MSDP processing. Figure 1-19 shows an expanded view of the VALUE field parameters for an SA message, and Figure 1-20 illustrates the VALUE field parameters for a Keepalive message.

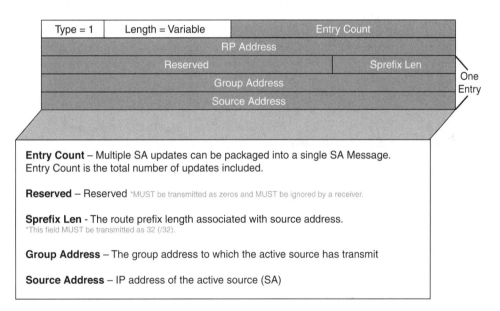

Figure 1-19   *VALUE Field Parameters for an MSDP TLV Message*

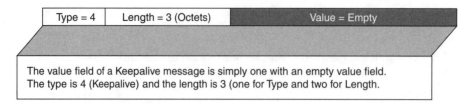

Figure 1-20 *VALUE Field Parameters for an MSDP Keepalive Message*

It is important to note that the TCP connections used between RP routers are dependent on the underlying IP unicast network. This means there must be IP reachability between the peers, just as there would be for BGP. However, unlike with BGP, there is no measuring of the hop count of external systems and no requirement that the RPs be directly connected. Any MSDP peer must be a proper RPF peer, meaning that an RPF check is applied to received SA advertisements to ensure loop-free forwarding across domains. There are three MSDP rules that require BGP ASN checking for loop prevention. The rules that apply to RPF checks for SA messages are dependent on the BGP peerings between the MSDP peers:

- **Rule 1: When the sending MSDP peer is also an internal MBGP peer, MSDP checks the BGP MRIB for the best path to the RP that originated the SA message.** If the MRIB contains a best path, the MSDP peer uses that information to RPF check the originating RP of the SA. If there is no best path in the MRIB, the unicast RIB is checked for a proper RPF path. If no path is found in either table, the RPF check fails. The IP address of the sending MSDP peer must be same as the BGP neighbor address (not the next hop) in order to pass the RPF check.

- **Rule 2: When the sending MSDP peer is also an external MBGP peer, MSDP checks the BGP MRIB for the best path to the RP that originated the SA message.** If the MRIB contains a best path, the MSDP peer uses that information to RPF check the originating RP of the SA. If there is no best path in the MRIB, the unicast RIB is checked for a proper RPF path. A best path must be found in either of the tables, or the RPF check fails. After the best path is found, MSDP checks the first autonomous system in the path to the RP. The check succeeds and the SA is accepted if the first AS in the path to the RP is the same as the AS of the BGP peer (which is also the sending MSDP peer). Otherwise, the SA is rejected.

- **Rule 3: When the sending MSDP peer is not an MBGP peer at all, MSDP checks the BGP MRIB for the best path to the RP that originated the SA message.** If the MRIB contains a best path, the MSDP peer uses that information to RPF check the originating RP of the SA. If there is no best path in the MRIB, the unicast RIB is checked for a proper RPF path. If no path is found in either table, the RPF check fails. When the previous check succeeds, MSDP then looks for a best path to the MSDP peer that sent the SA message. If a path is not found in the MRIB, the peer searches the unicast RIB. If a path is not found, the RPF check fails.

RPF checks are not performed in the following cases:

- When the advertising MSDP peer is the only MSDP peer (which is the case if only a single MSDP peer or a default MSDP peer is configured).

- With mesh group peers.

- When the advertising MSDP peer address is the originating RP address contained in the SA message.

The advertisement must pass one of the three rules; otherwise, MSDP fails the update and tosses out any received SA information. MSDP should have a properly populated MBGP table for that interaction to work. Therefore, you can say that it is a requirement for both MBGP and MSDP to be configured on each RP maintaining interdomain operations.

MSDP makes exceptions for IGP checking, as previously mentioned, but they are not commonly used, except for Anycast RP. MSDP uses several additional underlying RPF checks to ensure a loop-free forwarding topology. Some of the most important checks are discussed in subsequent sections of this chapter. RFC 3618 section 10.1.3 lists the primary SA acceptance and forwarding rules for loop prevention. For a full understanding of MSDP loop prevention mechanisms, refer to the RFCs that define MSDP, such as 3618. In addition, loop prevention is one of the primary purposes of PIM–SM, and all standard PIM–SM loop-prevention checks are also deployed.

Understanding Source Actives (SA) and MSDP Mechanics

Source actives (SAs) are the key to MSDP operations. Recall that in PIM–SM mechanics, when the first-hop router (FHR) receives a multicast packet from a source, its first order of business is to register the source's IP address with the RP, while encapsulating the first few packets in generic routing encapsulation (GRE) and sending those to the RP as well. The RP then takes that source information and builds a shared tree, with the RP as the root, branching toward any known receivers. It stands to reason, then, that the RP(s) in a given domain can essentially function as an authority on any active sources sending within the domain.

That's where MSDP comes in to play. If the RP is also running MSDP, the router takes that source state information and builds a special table, a record of all the active sources in the network. This table is called the SA cache, and an entry in the table is known as a source active, hence the name SA. MSDP was created to not only create the SA cache but share it with other peers, as outlined earlier in this chapter.

This is why MSDP is so functional and was the original standard for the Anycast RP mechanism. Two or more RPs with the same address collectively have the complete picture of all SAs in the network. If they share that SA information among themselves, they all have a complete cache, which enables them to act in concert when necessary.

However, Anycast RP mechanics was not the original, functional intent of MSDP. Rather, it was a "discovery" of sorts, made after its creation. MSDP was specifically designed to bridge IP Multicast domains over the public Internet. This means that each ISP could independently control multicast update information without relying on another ISP as the authority or relying on a single Internet-wide RP—which would have been an administrative and security nightmare.

It is important to note that MSDP in and of itself *does not* share multicast state information or create forwarding trees between domains. That is still the job of PIM–SM, and PIM–SM is still an absolute requirement within a domain for those functions. MSDP's only role is to actively discover and share sources on the network. Let's review MSDP mechanics, including the process of updating the SA cache and sharing SA information with other MSDP peers.

The first step in the process of sharing SA information is for the FHR to register an active source with the RP. The RP, running MSDP, creates an SA entry in the cache and immediately shares that entry with any of its known peers. Let's take a look at this in practice in the example network from Figure 1-15, where the router SP3-2 is the RP and MSDP source for ISP Blue. You can use the border router in ISP Green, SP2-1, as the source by sending a ping sourced from its loopback address, 172.22.0.1. Using the **debug ip msdp details** and **debug ip pim rp 239.120.1.1** commands on SP3-2, you can watch the active source being learned, populated into the SA cache, updating the PIM MRIB, and then being sent to the MSDP peer R1. Example 1-16 displays the output of these commands.

Example 1-16   **debug ip pim 239.120.1.1** *and* **debug ip msdp details** *on RP SP3-2*

```
*Feb 23 04:36:12.640: MSDP(0): Received 20-byte TCP segment from 172.22.0.1
*Feb 23 04:36:12.640: MSDP(0): Append 20 bytes to 0-byte msg 3432 from 172.22.0.1,
  qs 1
*Feb 23 04:36:12.640: MSDP(0): WAVL Insert SA Source 172.22.0.1 Group 239.120.1.1 RP
  172.22.0.1 Successful
*Feb 23 04:36:12.643: PIM(0): Join-list: (172.22.0.1/32, 239.120.1.1), S-bit set
*Feb 23 04:36:12.643: PIM(0): Check RP 172.23.0.2 into the (*, 239.120.1.1) entry
*Feb 23 04:36:12.643: PIM(0): Adding register decap tunnel (Tunnel1) as accepting
  interface of (*, 239.120.1.1).
*Feb 23 04:36:12.643: PIM(0): Adding register decap tunnel (Tunnel1) as accepting
  interface of (172.22.0.1, 239.120.1.1).
*Feb 23 04:36:12.643: PIM(0): Add Ethernet0/0/172.23.1.1 to (172.22.0.1,
  239.120.1.1), Forward state, by PIM SG Join
*Feb 23 04:36:12.643: PIM(0): Insert (172.22.0.1,239.120.1.1) join in nbr
  172.23.2.1's queue
*Feb 23 04:36:12.643: PIM(0): Building Join/Prune packet for nbr 172.23.2.1
*Feb 23 04:36:12.643: PIM(0):  Adding v2 (172.22.0.1/32, 239.120.1.1), S-bit Join
*Feb 23 04:36:12.643: PIM(0): Send v2 join/prune to 172.23.2.1 (Ethernet0/1)
*Feb 23 04:36:12.658: PIM(0): Received v2 Join/Prune on Ethernet0/0 from 172.23.1.1,
  to us
*Feb 23 04:37:22.773: MSDP(0): start_index = 0, mroute_cache_index = 0, Qlen = 0
*Feb 23 04:37:22.773: MSDP(0): Sent entire mroute table, mroute_cache_index = 0,
  Qlen = 0
```

As you can see from the debugging output in Example 1-16, SP3-2 first learns of the MSDP SA from RP SP2-1, of ISP Green, which also happens to be the source. SP3-2's PIM process then adds the (*, G) entry and then the (S, G) entry, (*, 239.120.1.1) and (172.22.0.1, 239.120.1.1), respectively. Then, when the RP is finished creating the state, MSDP immediately forwards the SA entry to all peers. There is no split-horizon type loop prevention in this process. You can see the MSDP SA cache entry for source 172.22.0.1, or any entries for that matter, by issuing the command **show ip msdp sa-cache [*x.x.x.x*]** (where the optional [*x.x.x.x*] is the IP address of either the group or the source you wish to examine). Example 1-17 shows the output from this command on SP3-2, running IOS-XE.

Example 1-17   show ip msdp sa-cache *on SP3-2*

```
SP3-2# show ip msdp sa-cache
MSDP Source-Active Cache - 1 entries
(172.22.0.1, 239.120.1.1), RP 172.22.0.1, MBGP/AS 65002, 00:04:47/00:04:02, Peer
  172.22.0.1
Learned from peer 172.22.0.1, RPF peer 172.22.0.1,
SAs received: 5, Encapsulated data received: 1
```

Note from this output that the SA cache entry includes the (S, G) state of the multicast flow, as well as the peer from which it was learned and the MBGP AS in which that peer resides. This MBGP peer information in the entry comes from a combination of the configured MSDP peer remote-as parameter and cross-checking that configuration against the actual MBGP table. That is a loop-prevention mechanism built into MSDP because there is no split-horizon update control mechanism. In fact, it goes a little deeper than what you see here on the surface.

Just like PIM, MSDP uses RPF checking to ensure that the MSDP peer and the SA entry are in the appropriate place in the path. At the end of the SA cache entries is an RPF peer statement which indicates that the peer has been checked. You know how a router RPF checks the (S, G) against the unicast RIB. But how exactly does a router RPF check an MSDP peer? It consults the BGP table, looking for the MBGP next hop of the originating address; that is the RP that originated the SA. The next-hop address becomes the RPF peer of the MSDP SA originator. In this example, that is router SP2-1, with address 172.22.0.1. Any MSDP messages that are received on an interface—not the RPF peer for that originator—are automatically dropped. This functionality is called *peer-RPF flooding*. If MBGP is not configured, the unicast IPv4 BGP table is used instead. However, because of the peer-RPF flooding mechanism built into MSDP, MBGP or BGP is required for proper cross-domain multicast forwarding. Without this information, you would essentially black hole all foreign domain traffic, regardless of the PIM and MSDP relationships between domain edge peers.

> **Note**   For MSDP peers within a single domain, such as those used for Anycast RP, there is no requirement for MBGP or BGP prefixes. In this case, the peer-RPF flooding mechanism is automatically disabled by the router. There is also no requirement for BGP or MBGP within an MSDP mesh group, as discussed later in this section.

In addition to these checks, there are two other checks that the MSDP-enabled RP performs before installing an SA entry in the cache and enabling PIM to complete the (S, G) tree toward the source. The first check is to make sure that there is a valid (*, G) entry in the MRIB table and that the entry has valid interfaces included in the OIL. If there are group members, the RP sends the (S, G) joins toward the remote source. Once this occurs, the router at the AS boundary encapsulates the multicast packets from the joined stream and tunnels them to the RP for initial shared tree forwarding. When the downstream last-hop router (LHR) receives the packets, standard PIM mechanics apply, and eventually a source tree is formed between the FHR (in this case, the domain border router closest to the source) and the LHR.

The LHR could be a router directly connected to receivers subscribed to the group via IGMP. However, the LHR could also simply be the downstream edge of the domain where the domain is only acting as transit for the multicast traffic, bridging the (*, G) and (S, G) trees between two unconnected domains. This is exactly what ISP Blue is doing in the Mcast Enterprises network, where SP3-1 is the LHR of ISP Green's multicast domain and AS. In these cases, there may be no local (*, G) entry at the local RP until the remote, downstream domain registers receivers and joins the (*, G). Until then, the SA entry is invalid, and the RP does not initiate PIM processing. When a host in the remote downstream domain subscribes to the group, the LHR in that domain sends a (*, G) to its local RP. Because that RP and the transit domain RP have an existing valid SA entry, both domains can then join, as needed, the (S, G) all the way back to the remote domain.

The originating RP keeps track of the source. As long as the source continues sending packets, the RP sends SA messages every 60 seconds. These SA messages maintain the SA state of downstream peers. The MSDP SA cache has an expiration timer for SA entries. The timer is variable, but for most operating systems, it is 150 seconds. (Some operating systems, such as IOS-XR, offer a configuration option to change this timer setting.) If a valid, peer-RPF checked SA message is not received before the entry timer expires, the SA entry is removed from the cache and is subsequently removed from any further SA messages sent to peers.

Configuring and Verifying MSDP

The configuration tasks involved with MSDP are fairly simple and straightforward. You start by configuring the MSDP peering between two RP routers. The configuration commands are shown earlier in this chapter for peer configuration on IOS-XE. Table 1-6 details the configuration commands and options for basic peering on IOS-XE, IOS-XR, and NX-OS. For IOS XR, it is important to note that all MSDP configuration commands are entered globally under the **router msdp** configuration mode. At each peer configuration, you enter the **msdp-peer** configuration mode, as indicated by the * in the IOS-XR section of the table.

Table 1-6   *MSDP Peer Commands*

Operating System	Command
IOS/XE	`ip msdp peer`{peer-name / peer-address} [`connect-source` type number] [`remote-as` as-number]
IOS XR	`peer` peer-address *(config-msdp-peer)# **remote-as** as-number; `connect-source` type [interface-path-id]
NX-OS	`ip msdp peer` peer-ip-address `connect-source` interface [`remote-as` as-number]

Note   It is very unlikely that NX-OS on any platform will be found at the AS edge of a domain. It is more common to see NX-OS cross-domain forwarding at the data center edge. For this reason, many of the more sophisticated MSDP features are not available in NX-OS. In addition, you must first enable the MSDP feature on a Nexus platform before it is configurable. You use the **feature msdp** global configuration mode command to enable MSDP.

Note   MSDP configuration on IOS-XR requires, first, the installation and activation of the multicast package installation envelope (PIE). After this is done, all PIM, multicast routing, and MSDP configuration commands are available for execution. Remember that, compared to classic Cisco operating systems, IOS-XR commands are more structured, and most parameters are entered one at a time rather than on a single line, as shown in Table 1-6.

Like their BGP counterparts, MSDP peers can have configured descriptions for easier identification, and they can use password authentication with MD5 encryption to secure the TCP peering mechanism. Table 1-7 shows the commands needed to implement peer descriptions.

Table 1-7   *MSDP Peer Descriptions*

Operating System	Command
IOS/XE	`ip msdp` [`vrf` vrf-name] `description` { peer-name | peer-address } text
IOS XR	`peer` peer-address (config-msdp-peer)# **description** peer-address text
NX-OS	`ip msdp description` peer-address text

Table 1-8 shows the commands needed to configure peer security through password authentication.

Table 1-8   *MSDP Peer Password Authentication and Encryption*

Operating System	Command
IOS/XE	`ip msdp` [`vrf` *vrf-name*] `password peer` { *peer-name* | *peer-address* } [*encryption-type*] *string*
IOS XR	`peer` *peer-address* (*config-msdp-peer*)`#` `password` { `clear` | `encrypted` } *password*
NX-OS	`ip msdp password` *peer-address password*

Note   When a password is configured on a peer, encryption of TCP data packets is not implied. Only the password exchange is encrypted using MD5 hashing. Each of the commands has an option for entering an unencrypted password. That unencrypted password option (**clear** in IOS-XR and **encryption-type** 0 in IOS-XE) only enables the configuration entry of a password in plaintext. Otherwise, the MD5 hash value of the password, which shows up after configuration, is required. For first-time configuration of passwords, it is recommended that you use plaintext. In addition, it is important to understand that changing a password after peer establishment does not immediately bring down an MSDP peering session. Instead, the router continues to maintain the peering until the peer expiration timer has expired. Once this happens, the password is used for authentication. If the peering RP has not been configured for authentication with the appropriate password, then the local peer fails the TCP handshake process, and peering is not established.

Speaking of timers, it is possible to change the default TCP peer timers in MSDP, just as it is with BGP peers. The most important timer is the MSDP peer keepalive timer. Recall from the discussion of the MSDP state machine that if there are no SA messages to send to a peer, the TCP must still be maintained. This is done through the use of peer keepalives. If no keepalive is received within the configured peering hold timer, the session is torn down. Each Cisco operating system has a different set of defaults for these timers. Table 1-9 shows how to adjust the keepalive timer and the peer hold timer for each operating system, along with default timer values. These commands are entered per peer.

Table 1-9   *MSDP Peer Timer Commands*

Operating System	Command	Default
IOS/XE	`ip msdp` [`vrf` *vrf-name*] `keepalive` { *peer-address* | *peer-name* } *keepalive-interval hold-time-interval*	60-second *keepalive-interval*, 75-second *hold-time-interval*
IOS XR	No equivalent command.	N/A
NX-OS	`ip msdp keepalive` *peer-address interval timeout*	60-second *interval*, 90-second *timeout*

In addition, by default, an MSDP peer waits a given number of seconds after an MSDP peer session is reset before attempting to reestablish the MSDP connection. Table 1-10 shows the commands needed for each operating system to change the default timer.

Table 1-10   *Adjusting MSDP Peer Reset Timers*

Operating System	Command	Default
IOS/XE	`ip msdp` [`vrf` *vrf-name*] `timer` `connection-retry-interval`	30 seconds
IOS XR	`No equivalent command.`	N/A
NX-OS	`ip msdp reconnect-interval` *interval*	10 seconds

Note   With any peer timer, if a timer change is required for a given peering session, it is highly recommended that both MSDP peers be configured with the same timer.

The commands introduced so far are used to configure and establish peering between two RPs acting as MSDP peers. The commands affect how the peer TCP session will behave. Now let's explore additional commands that affect how an MSDP-configured RP behaves once a peer is established. These additional commands, tuning options for MSDP, and many of the options are similar to the options available for BGP peers, such as entry timers, origination IDs, and entry filtering.

Perhaps the most important MSDP tuning knob allows you to create a mesh group of MSDP peers. In networking, a mesh exists when there is a link between each pair of peers, such that every peer has a direct path to every other peer, without taking unnecessary hops. In some multicast interdomain networks, such as intra-AS interdomain deployments, it is common have MSDP peers connected together in a mesh. Such a design could significantly reduce the number of MSDP messages that are needed between peers. Remember that any time an MSDP peer receives and validates an SA entry, it forwards that entry to all its peers by default. If the peers are connected in a mesh, it is completely unnecessary for all the mesh peers to duplicate messages that are already sent between peers on the network. The MSDP mesh group commands configure RP routers to circumvent this behavior. An SA received from one member of the mesh group is not replicated and sent to any other peers in the same mesh group, thus eliminating potentially redundant SA messages.

A mesh group has another potential advantage for interdomain operations. Because each RP has direct knowledge of the other SAs in the mesh group, no MBGP is required for MSDP RPF checking. Thus, you can have MSDP without the added complication of MBGP within an internal network scenario, such as Anycast RP. Table 1-11 shows the commands required to configure a mesh group for MSDP.

Table 1-11 *MSDP Mesh Group Commands*

Operating System	Command
IOS/XE	ip msdp [vrf *vrf-name*] mesh-group *mesh-name* { *peer-address* | *peer-name* }
IOS XR	peer *peer-address* (config-msdp-peer)# mesh-group *name*
NX-OS	ip msdp mesh-group *peer-address name*

Note It is unlikely that you will find MSDP mesh groups outside an AS. Most Internet peering requires MBGP for Internet multicast. Using mesh groups may be the most efficient way of bridging internal PIM domains using Anycast RP.

When an MSDP router creates a new SA entry, it includes the interface-configured IP address of the RP in the update as the originator ID. The router uses the originator ID to perform the MSDP RPF check against the MSDP speaker. Usually, the same interface is used as both the RP and the MSDP peering source. However, there are times when a logical RP is required, and you need to change the MSDP originator ID to prevent an MSDP RPF failure. The **originator-id** command allows an administrator to change the originator ID in advertised SA entries. By default, the originator ID should be the address of the RP configured on the router. If there are multiple RPs configured on the same router, you need to set the originator ID manually. If no originator ID is defined, routers use the highest IP configured as RP or, if there is no configured RP, the highest loopback interface IP as the originator ID. Table 1-12 shows the originator ID commands. In order to mitigate confusion, it is best practice to define the originator ID manually in all cases to ensure that the originator ID and the MBGP source IP are the same.

Table 1-12 *MSDP Originator ID Commands*

Operating System	Command
IOS/XE	ip msdp [vrf *vrf-name*] originator-id *interface-type interface-number*
IOS XR	router msdp (config-msdp)# originator-id *type interface-path-id*
NX-OS	ip msdp originator-id *if-type if-number*

If you have ever configured BGP, you know there needs to be a way to shut down a peer without removing it from configuration. The **shutdown** command accomplishes this. A similar command exists for MSDP, allowing someone to shut down the MSDP peering, closing the TCP session with the remote MSDP peer, without removing the peer from configuration. This simplifies basic MSDP operations. Table 1-13 shows the MSDP **shutdown** command for each OS. The **shutdown** command is issued within the appropriate configuration mode for the peer.

Table 1-13 *MSDP Shutdown Commands*

Operating System	Command
IOS/XE	`ip msdp [ vrf` *vrf-name* `] shutdown {` *peer-address* `|` *peer-name* `}`
IOS XR	`peer` *peer-address* `(config-msdp-peer)# shutdown`
NX-OS	`ip msdp shutdown` *peer-address*

It may also be necessary at times to clear an MSDP peering session or other MSDP information. You do so by using the **clear** command. Like its BGP counterpart, this is not a configuration command but is instead performed from the EXEC mode of the router. The **clear ip msdp peer** command simply resets the MSDP TCP session for a specific peer, allowing the router to immediately flush entries for the cleared peer. The **clear ip msdp sa-cache** command only flushes the SA cache table without clearing peering sessions, allowing the router to rebuild the table as it receives ongoing updates.

MSDP peering security through authentication, discussed earlier in this chapter, should be a requirement for any external peering sessions. MSDP also has built-in capabilities for blocking specific incoming and outgoing SA advertisements. This is accomplished using SA filters. An SA filter is configured and works very similarly to a BGP filter. The difference is that an SA filter can specify sources, groups, or RPs to permit or deny. Tables 1-14 and 1-15 show the commands to filter inbound and outbound by MSDP peer.

Table 1-14 *SA Filter In Commands*

Operating System	Command
IOS/XE	`ip msdp [ vrf` *vrf-name* `] sa-filter in {` *peer-address* `|` *peer-name* `} [ list` *access-list-name* `] [ route-map` *map-name* `] [ rp-list {` *access-list-range* `|` *access-list-name* `} ] [ rp-route-map` route-mappreference `]`
IOS XR	`peer` *peer-address* `(config-msdp-peer)# sa-filter in { list` *access-list-name* `| rp-list` *access-list-name* `}`
NX-OS	`ip msdp sa-policy` *peer-address* *policy-name* `in`

Table 1-15 *SA Filter Out Commands*

Operating System	Command
IOS/XE	`ip msdp` [**vrf** *vrf-name*] **sa-filter out** { *peer-address* | *peer-name* } [**list** *access-list-name*] [**route-map** *map-name*] [**rp-list** { *access-list-range* | *access-list-name* }] [**rp-route-map** *route-map reference*]
IOS XR	**peer** *peer-address* `(config-msdp-peer)#` **sa-filter out** { **list** *access-list-name* | **rp-list** *access-list-name* }
NX-OS	`ip msdp` **sa-policy** *peer-address policy-name* **out**

It is also possible to protect router resources on an MSDP speaker by limiting the total number of SA advertisements that can be accepted from a specific peer. The **sa-limit** command is used for this purpose. The command is peer specific and is detailed for each OS in Table 1-16.

Table 1-16 *MSDP SA Limit*

Operating System	Command
IOS/XE	`ip msdp` [**vrf** *vrf-name*] **sa-limit** { *peer-address* | *peer-name* } [*sa-limit*]
IOS XR	No equivalent command. Use the **filter** commands to control SA cache resource usage.
NX-OS	`ip msdp` **sa-limit** *peer-address limit*

Note The mechanics of an SA limit are very straightforward. The router keeps a tally of SA messages received from the configured peer. Once the limit is reached, additional SA advertisements from a peer are simply ignored. It is highly recommended that you use this command. The appropriate limit should depend on the usage. A transit Internet MSDP peer needs a very high limit, whereas an Internet-connected enterprise AS is likely to use a very small limit that protects the enterprise MSDP speaker from Internet multicast SA leakage.

Many other MSDP commands are useful but are beyond the scope of this discussion. For more information about MSDP configuration and operations, refer to the multicast command reference for the router and operating system in use. These command references are available at www.cisco.com.

Basic MSDP Deployment Use Case

Let's look at a very basic network scenario using MSDP and selective MSDP filters across an enterprise multicast domain. In this use case, the network designer can achieve single-RP deployment for the enterprise and create filters local to the enterprise multicast boundary by localizing the filters to the local domain.

The only consideration for this design is scalability of total number of MSDP peers. If the enterprise has hundreds of local domains, scalability of mesh group to 100+ peers needs to be reviewed with a single RP. The diagram in Figure 1-21 illustrates the configuration example for this use case.

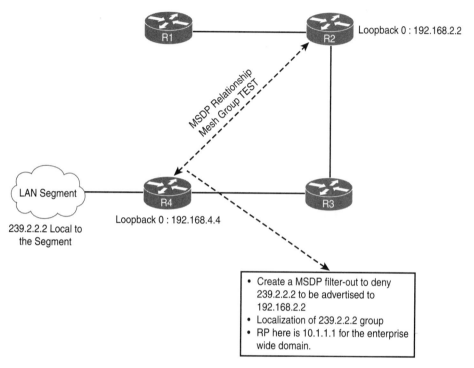

Figure 1-21   *Topology MSDP Use Case Example*

Note the following important points about this design:

■ R4 and R2 are part of the MSDP mesh group TEST. More routers than are shown in the topology can be added to the mesh group. The number of routers in a mesh group should be considered a design constraint and evaluated on a per-platform basis.

■ 239.2.2.2 is a local group localized to R4 only.

■ The RP, 10.1.1.1, is located at every mesh group router and advertised via BSR; this RP is enterprisewide. The localization of the group is aligned to MSDP SA messages (Anycast RP), and the local router (which is also a mesh group member) determines whether the source active message needs to be forwarded to the global PIM domain.

■ The control point to localize is based on a selected MSDP mesh group router, which also plays a role as a border router.

■ The use of an MSDP filter to deny 239.2.2.2 being sent to other MSDP peers allows R4 to localize the group and participate in global 239.1.1.1, which is enterprisewide.

These elements are illustrated in Example 1-18.

Example 1-18   *Snapshot of R4 Configuration*

```
hostname r4
!
ip multicast-routing
ip cef
!
interface Loopback0
 ip address 192.168.4.4 255.255.255.255
 ip pim sparse-mode
 ip igmp join-group 239.2.2.2
 ip igmp join-group 239.1.1.1
!
interface Loopback100
 ip address 1.1.1.1 255.255.255.255
 ip pim sparse-mode
!
router eigrp 1
 network 0.0.0.0
 eigrp router-id 192.168.4.4
!
ip forward-protocol nd
!
!
ip pim bsr-candidate Loopback100 0
ip pim rp-candidate Loopback100 interval 10
ip msdp peer 192.168.2.2 connect-source Loopback0
ip msdp sa-filter out 192.168.2.2 list 100
ip msdp cache-sa-state
ip msdp originator-id Loopback0
ip msdp mesh-group TEST 192.168.2.2
!
!
!
access-list 100 deny   ip host 192.168.4.4 host 239.2.2.2
access-list 100 deny   ip host 192.168.41.4 host 239.2.2.2
access-list 100 permit ip any any
```

In Example 1-18, R4 represents a local domain and takes part in the enterprisewide mesh group. A single RP for the enterprise, represented as 1.1.1.1, is a part of every mesh group router (as shown in loopback 100) and is advertised to all downstream routers enterprisewide using BSR. The BSR candidate is the same 1.1.1.1 IP address enterprisewide. The source active state is exchanged based on MSDP (RFC 3446). Controlling the MSDP SA message is the key to controlling distribution of the local group information. This is done by using the **msdp filter-out** command at R4 to contain the localized group. **ACL 100 deny R4 to send 239.2.2.2 to enterprise mesh-group** and **ip any any** allow it to receive other enterprise groups.

The host from the LAN segment connected to R4 transmits 239.2.2.2. The state at R4 is shown in Example 1-19, using the **show ip mroute** command on R4.

Example 1-19 *R4 Multicast State for Group 239.2.2.2*

```
r4# show ip mroute 239.2.2.2


(*, 239.2.2.2), 00:22:12/stopped, RP 1.1.1.1, flags: SJCL
  Incoming interface: Null, RPF nbr 0.0.0.0
  Outgoing interface list:
    Loopback0, Forward/Sparse, 00:22:12/00:02:06

(192.168.41.4, 239.2.2.2), 00:00:13/00:02:46, flags: LM
  Incoming interface: Ethernet0/0, RPF nbr 10.1.3.1
  Outgoing interface list:
    Loopback0, Forward/Sparse, 00:00:13/00:02:46
```

Example 1-20 displays the RP information at R4, using the **show ip pim rp mapping** command.

Example 1-20 *RP Mapping Info on R4*

```
r4# sh ip pim rp mapping
PIM Group-to-RP Mappings
This system is a candidate RP (v2)
This system is the Bootstrap Router (v2)

Group(s) 224.0.0.0/4
  RP 1.1.1.1 (?), v2
    Info source: 1.1.1.1 (?), via bootstrap, priority 0, holdtime 25
        Uptime: 05:24:36, expires: 00:00:17
r4#
```

The MSDP peer group at R2, even though it has a local join for 239.2.2.2, does not receive the flow. R2 is part of the global RP domain 1.1.1.1. This is illustrated in Example 1-21, using the commands **show ip mroute** and **show ip msdp sa-cache**; no SA message is received.

Example 1-21   *R2 MSDP Has No SA-Cache Entry for 239.2.2.2*

```
r2# sh ip mroute 239.2.2.2
IP Multicast Routing Table
Flags: D - Dense, S - Sparse, B - Bidir Group, s - SSM Group, C - Connected,
       L - Local, P - Pruned, R - RP-bit set, F - Register flag,
       T - SPT-bit set, J - Join SPT, M - MSDP created entry, E - Extranet,
       X - Proxy Join Timer Running, A - Candidate for MSDP Advertisement,
       U - URD, I - Received Source Specific Host Report,
       Z - Multicast Tunnel, z - MDT-data group sender,
       Y - Joined MDT-data group, y - Sending to MDT-data group,
       G - Received BGP C-Mroute, g - Sent BGP C-Mroute,
       N - Received BGP Shared-Tree Prune, n - BGP C-Mroute suppressed,
       Q - Received BGP S-A Route, q - Sent BGP S-A Route,
       V - RD & Vector, v - Vector, p - PIM Joins on route,
       x - VxLAN group
Outgoing interface flags: H - Hardware switched, A - Assert winner, p - PIM Join
 Timers: Uptime/Expires
 Interface state: Interface, Next-Hop or VCD, State/Mode

(*, 239.2.2.2), 00:24:07/00:03:01, RP 1.1.1.1, flags: S
  Incoming interface: Null, RPF nbr 0.0.0.0
  Outgoing interface list:
    Ethernet0/0, Forward/Sparse, 00:24:07/00:03:01

r2# sh ip msdp sa
r2# sh ip msdp sa-cache
MSDP Source-Active Cache - 0 entries
r2#
```

Next, the host connected to R1 sends packets to group 239.1.1.1, which functions like a global multicast group with receivers at R2 and R4. Since there are no filters for 239.1.1.1, it functions as a global enterprise group.

The **show ip mroute** command output at R2 shows the flow for 239.1.1.1, as displayed in Example 1-22.

Example 1-22   *Flow for Group 239.1.1.1*

```
r2# sh ip mroute

 Interface state: Interface, Next-Hop or VCD, State/Mode

(*, 239.1.1.1), 00:29:03/stopped, RP 1.1.1.1, flags: SJCL
  Incoming interface: Null, RPF nbr 0.0.0.0
  Outgoing interface list:
    Loopback0, Forward/Sparse, 00:29:03/00:02:58

(192.168.1.1, 239.1.1.1), 00:00:05/00:02:54, flags: LA
  Incoming interface: Ethernet0/0, RPF nbr 10.1.1.1
  Outgoing interface list:
    Ethernet1/0, Forward/Sparse, 00:00:05/00:03:24
    Loopback0, Forward/Sparse, 00:00:05/00:02:58
```

At R4, the MSDP SA cache information now shows that the router has learned the SA entry from R2 for group 239.1.1.1. This is proven using the **show ip msdp sa-cache** and **show ip mroute** commands again at R4. Example 1-23 illustrates this output.

Example 1-23   *MSDP SA-Cache on R4 with an Entry for Group 239.1.1.1*

```
r4# show ip msdp sa-cache
MSDP Source-Active Cache - 1 entries
(192.168.1.1, 239.1.1.1), RP 192.168.2.2, AS ?,00:08:49/00:05:52, Peer 192.168.2.2

r4# show ip mroute
IP Multicast Routing Table

(*, 239.1.1.1), 00:30:39/stopped, RP 1.1.1.1, flags: SJCL
 Incoming interface: Null, RPF nbr 0.0.0.0
  Outgoing interface list:
    Loopback0, Forward/Sparse, 00:30:39/00:02:31

(192.168.1.1, 239.1.1.1), 00:01:29/00:01:29, flags: LM
  Incoming interface: Ethernet0/0, RPF nbr 10.1.3.1
  Outgoing interface list:
    Loopback0, Forward/Sparse, 00:01:29/00:02:31
```

Intradomain versus Interdomain Design Models

As you can see from what has been discussed in this chapter, there are some major protocol differences between forwarding IP multicast traffic inside a domain and between domains. However, the principles of designing and securing the domains are relatively ubiquitous. The major differences come when you cross AS boundaries and how they are treated.

Let's examine the differences between the two design models. The following sections use the Mcast Enterprises network to configure both intra-AS multidomain forwarding and inter-AS interdomain forwarding. This network and ISPs from the running example can serve both purposes. You can use the **show** command in these scenarios to examine how forwarding works in an interdomain scenario.

Intra-AS Multidomain Design

Intra-AS multidomain forwarding is accomplished in multiple ways. Some of the options for structuring domains within an AS are discussed earlier in this chapter (in the section "What Is a Multicast Domain? A Refresher"). This section shows the most likely configuration for Mcast Enterprises and examines the configuration of such a network more closely.

For this example, assume that there is one large enterprisewide domain that encompasses all Mcast Enterprises groups, represented by the multicast supernet 239.0.0.0/10. In addition, Mcast Enterprises has individual domain scopes for each of its three locations, using 239.10.0.0/16, 239.20.0.0/16, and 230.30.0.0/16, respectively. BGP is configured in a confederation with the global ASN 65100.

Each of the three routers, R1, R2, and R3, is acting as the local RP for its respective domain. The loopback 0 interface of R1 is also acting as the RP for the enterprisewide domain. There is external MBGP peering between the BR and SP3-1, as well as MSDP peering between the loopbacks of R1 and SP3-2. Internally, BGP and MBGP connections are part of a BGP confederation. There is no global RP; instead, each domain has a single RP for all multicast groups. To bridge the gaps between domains, MSDP is configured between each peer in a mesh group called ENTERPRISE. This network design is represented by the network diagram in Figure 1-22.

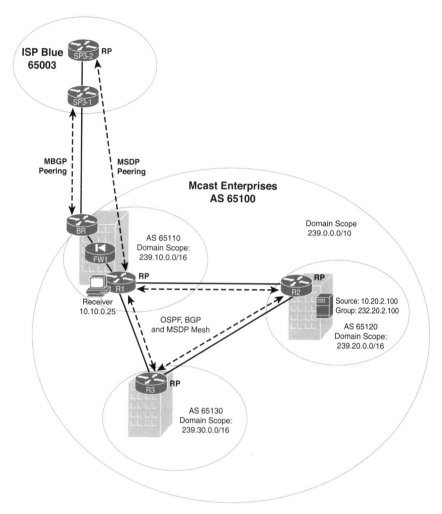

Figure 1-22 *Network Diagram for the Mcast Enterprises Final Solution*

Note   The design shown in Figure 1-22 depicts the intra-AS network as well as the previously configured external connections for clarity.

Now that you have the design, you can configure the network. Figure 1-23 shows the physical topology of the network with the connecting interfaces of each router.

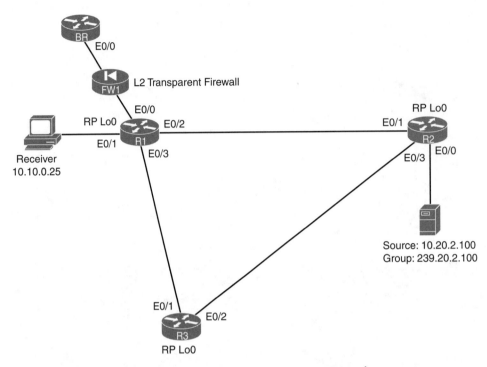

Figure 1-23 *Physical Topology of the Mcast Enterprises Network*

Example 1-24 details the final configurations for each of these routers within the domain, using IOS-XE.

Example 1-24 *Final Configurations for Mcast Enterprises*

```
R1
ip multicast-routing
ip cef
!
interface Loopback0
 ip address 10.0.0.1 255.255.255.255
 ip pim sparse-mode
!
interface Ethernet0/0
 ip address 10.1.4.1 255.255.255.0
 ip pim sparse-mode
!
interface Ethernet0/1
 ip address 10.10.0.1 255.255.255.0
 ip pim sparse-mode
interface Ethernet0/2
```

```
 ip address 10.1.2.1 255.255.255.0
 ip pim sparse-mode
!
interface Ethernet0/3
 ip address 10.1.3.1 255.255.255.0
 ip pim sparse-mode
!
router ospf 10
 network 10.0.0.0 0.255.255.255 area 0
 router-id 10.0.0.1
!
router bgp 65101
 bgp router-id 10.0.0.1
 bgp log-neighbor-changes
 bgp confederation identifier 65100
 bgp confederation peers 65120 65130
 neighbor 10.0.0.2 remote-as 65120
 neighbor 10.0.0.2 ebgp-multihop 2
 neighbor 10.0.0.2 update-source Loopback0
 neighbor 10.0.0.3 remote-as 65103
 neighbor 10.0.0.3 ebgp-multihop 2
 neighbor 10.0.0.3 update-source Loopback0
 neighbor 10.0.0.4 remote-as 65110
 neighbor 10.0.0.4 update-source Loopback0
 !
 address-family ipv4
  neighbor 10.0.0.2 activate
  neighbor 10.0.0.3 activate
  neighbor 10.0.0.4 activate
 exit-address-family
 !
 address-family ipv4 multicast
  neighbor 10.0.0.2 activate
  neighbor 10.0.0.3 activate
  neighbor 10.0.0.4 activate
 exit-address-family
!
ip bgp-community new-format
!
ip pim rp-address 10.0.0.1 10 override
ip pim send-rp-announce Loopback0 scope 32 group-list 1
ip pim send-rp-discovery Loopback0 scope 32
ip msdp peer 172.23.0.2 connect-source Loopback0 remote-as 65003
```

```
ip msdp peer 10.0.0.2 connect-source Loopback0
ip msdp peer 10.0.0.3 connect-source Loopback0
ip msdp cache-sa-state
ip msdp mesh-group ENTERPRISE 10.0.0.2
ip msdp mesh-group ENTERPRISE 10.0.0.3
!
access-list 1 permit 239.0.0.0 0.63.255.255
access-list 10 permit 239.10.0.0 0.0.255.255
R2
ip multicast-routing
ip cef
!
interface Loopback0
 ip address 10.0.0.2 255.255.255.255
 ip pim sparse-mode
!
interface Ethernet0/0
 ip address 10.20.2.1 255.255.255.0
 ip pim sparse-mode
!
interface Ethernet0/1
 ip address 10.1.2.2 255.255.255.0
 ip pim sparse-mode
!
interface Ethernet0/3
 ip address 10.2.3.2 255.255.255.0
 ip pim sparse-mode
!
router ospf 10
 network 10.0.0.0 0.255.255.255 area 0
 router-id 10.0.0.2
!
router bgp 65102
 bgp router-id 10.0.0.2
 bgp log-neighbor-changes
 bgp confederation identifier 65100
 bgp confederation peers 65110 65130
 neighbor 10.0.0.1 remote-as 65110
 neighbor 10.0.0.1 ebgp-multihop 2
 neighbor 10.0.0.1 update-source Loopback0
 neighbor 10.0.0.3 remote-as 65130
 neighbor 10.0.0.3 ebgp-multihop 2
```

```
 neighbor 10.0.0.3 update-source Loopback0
 !
 address-family ipv4
  neighbor 10.0.0.1 activate
  neighbor 10.0.0.3 activate
 exit-address-family
 !
 address-family ipv4 multicast
  neighbor 10.0.0.1 activate
  neighbor 10.0.0.3 activate
 exit-address-family
!
ip bgp-community new-format
!
ip pim rp-address 10.0.0.2 20 override
ip msdp peer 10.0.0.3 connect-source Loopback0
ip msdp peer 10.0.0.1 connect-source Loopback0
ip msdp cache-sa-state
ip msdp mesh-group ENTERPRISE 10.0.0.3
ip msdp mesh-group ENTERPRISE 10.0.0.1
!
access-list 20 permit 239.20.0.0 0.0.255.255

R3
ip multicast-routing
ip cef
!
interface Loopback0
 ip address 10.0.0.3 255.255.255.255
 ip pim sparse-mode
!
interface Ethernet0/0
 no ip address
 ip pim sparse-mode
!
interface Ethernet0/1
 ip address 10.1.3.3 255.255.255.0
 ip pim sparse-mode
!
interface Ethernet0/2
 ip address 10.2.3.3 255.255.255.0
```

```
 ip pim sparse-mode
!
router ospf 10
 network 10.0.0.0 0.255.255.255 area 0
 router-id 10.0.0.3
!
router bgp 65103
 bgp router-id 10.0.0.3
 bgp log-neighbor-changes
 bgp confederation identifier 65100
 bgp confederation peers 65110 65120
 neighbor 10.0.0.1 remote-as 65110
 neighbor 10.0.0.1 ebgp-multihop 2
 neighbor 10.0.0.1 update-source Loopback0
 neighbor 10.0.0.2 remote-as 65120
 neighbor 10.0.0.2 ebgp-multihop 2
 neighbor 10.0.0.2 update-source Loopback0
 !
 address-family ipv4
  neighbor 10.0.0.1 activate
  neighbor 10.0.0.2 activate
 exit-address-family
 !
 address-family ipv4 multicast
  neighbor 10.0.0.1 activate
  neighbor 10.0.0.2 activate
 exit-address-family
!
ip bgp-community new-format
!
ip pim rp-address 10.0.0.3 30 override
ip msdp peer 10.0.0.1 connect-source Loopback0
ip msdp peer 10.0.0.2 connect-source Loopback0
ip msdp cache-sa-state
ip msdp mesh-group ENTERPRISE 10.0.0.1
ip msdp mesh-group ENTERPRISE 10.0.0.2
!
access-list 30 permit 239.30.0.0 0.0.255.255

BR
ip multicast-routing
ip cef
!
```

```
interface Loopback0
 ip address 10.0.0.4 255.255.255.255
 ip pim sparse-mode
!
interface Ethernet0/0
 ip address 10.1.4.4 255.255.255.0
 ip pim sparse-mode
!
interface Ethernet0/1
 ip address 172.23.31.4 255.255.255.0
 ip pim sparse-mode
!
router ospf 10
 passive-interface Ethernet0/1
 network 10.0.0.0 0.255.255.255 area 0
 network 172.23.31.0 0.0.0.255 area 0
!
router bgp 65101
 bgp router-id 10.0.0.4
 bgp log-neighbor-changes
 bgp confederation identifier 65100
 bgp confederation peers 65110 65120 65130
 neighbor 10.0.0.1 remote-as 65110
 neighbor 10.0.0.1 update-source Loopback0
 neighbor 172.23.31.1 remote-as 65003
 !
 address-family ipv4
  network 10.0.0.0
  neighbor 10.0.0.1 activate
  neighbor 172.23.31.1 activate
  neighbor 172.23.31.1 soft-reconfiguration inbound
 exit-address-family
 !
 address-family ipv4 multicast
  network 10.0.0.0
  neighbor 10.0.0.1 activate
  neighbor 172.23.31.1 activate
  neighbor 172.23.31.1 soft-reconfiguration inbound
 exit-address-family
!
ip bgp-community new-format
!
ip route 10.0.0.0 255.0.0.0 Null0
```

Note   Example 1-24 shows only the configuration commands that are relevant to the network diagram shown in Figure 1-22. Additional configurations for connecting Mcast Enterprises to ISP Blue are covered earlier in this chapter.

In this configuration, each domain has its own RP. This RP structure does not isolate local domain groups, but it does isolate domain resources. MBGP shares all necessary multicast RPF entries for the global domain. Because there is a full OSPF and MBGP mesh, there is no requirement to add the remote-as command option to MSDP peering configuration statements. The mesh group takes care of that while also reducing extra traffic on the internal network.

Note   The global domain 239.0.0.0/10 was chosen to keep configurations simple. In this configuration, there are no control ACLs built in for the domains corresponding to AS numbers 65101 through 65103. This is why individual domain groups are no longer isolated by the configuration. In practice, it is more appropriate to lock down the domains according to a specific policy. This type of security policy is discussed later in this chapter.

You can verify that you have in fact achieved successful division of domains by using the **show ip pim** command in conjunction with specific groups that are controlled by the different RPs. You can also use the **show ip mroute** command to verify that the trees have been successfully built to the correct RPs. Look at R2, for example, and see if local group 239.20.2.100 is local to the RP on R2 and if global group 239.1.2.200 is using the RP on R1. Example 1-25 provides this output.

Example 1-25   *Verify Proper Interdomain Segregation*

```
R2# show ip pim rp 239.20.2.100
Group: 239.20.2.100, RP: 10.0.0.2, next RP-reachable in 00:00:19
R2#
R2#
R2#show ip mroute
IP Multicast Routing Table
Flags: D - Dense, S - Sparse, B - Bidir Group, s - SSM Group, C - Connected,
       L - Local, P - Pruned, R - RP-bit set, F - Register flag,
       T - SPT-bit set, J - Join SPT, M - MSDP created entry, E - Extranet,
       X - Proxy Join Timer Running, A - Candidate for MSDP Advertisement,
       U - URD, I - Received Source Specific Host Report,
       Z - Multicast Tunnel, z - MDT-data group sender,
       Y - Joined MDT-data group, y - Sending to MDT-data group,
       G - Received BGP C-Mroute, g - Sent BGP C-Mroute,
       N - Received BGP Shared-Tree Prune, n - BGP C-Mroute suppressed,
       Q - Received BGP S-A Route, q - Sent BGP S-A Route,
       V - RD & Vector, v - Vector, p - PIM Joins on route
```

```
Outgoing interface flags: H - Hardware switched, A - Assert winner, p - PIM Join
 Timers: Uptime/Expires
 Interface state: Interface, Next-Hop or VCD, State/Mode

(*, 239.20.2.100), 01:58:11/stopped, RP 10.0.0.2, flags: SJCL
  Incoming interface: Null, RPF nbr 0.0.0.0
  Outgoing interface list:
    Ethernet0/2, Forward/Sparse, 01:58:11/00:02:33

(10.20.2.100, 239.20.2.100), 00:01:31/00:01:28, flags: LTA
  Incoming interface: Ethernet0/0, RPF nbr 0.0.0.0
  Outgoing interface list:
    Ethernet0/1, Forward/Sparse, 00:01:31/00:02:56
    Ethernet0/2, Forward/Sparse, 00:01:31/00:02:33
```

In addition, you can use the **show ip msdp sa-cache** command, as shown in Example 1-26, to see that the MSDP process on R1 has registered the (S, G) state for the group.

Example 1-26   *Verifying the MSDP SA Cache Entry for 239.20.2.100*

```
R1# show ip msdp sa-cache
MSDP Source-Active Cache - 1 entries
(10.20.2.100, 239.20.2.100), RP 10.0.0.2, MBGP/AS 65101, 00:03:04/00:05:10, Peer
  10.0.0.2
```

Finally, you can verify that interdomain forwarding is working if a client connected to R1 can receive a multicast stream from a server on R3. Connect client 10.10.0.25 as shown in Figure 1-24.

Begin a ping to group 239.20.2.100 from a server with IP address 10.20.2.100 connected to R2, as shown in Example 1-27

Example 1-27   *Verifying Cross-Domain Packet Forwarding*

```
Server2# ping 239.20.2.100
Type escape sequence to abort.
Sending 1, 100-byte ICMP Echos to 239.20.2.100, timeout is 2 seconds:

Reply to request 0 from 10.10.0.25, 7 ms
```

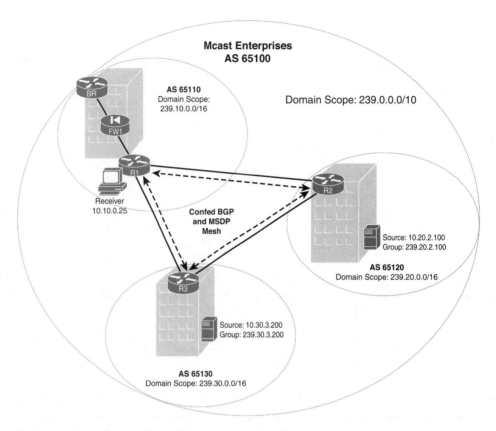

Figure 1-24   *Client 10.10.0.25 in Domain AS65110*

Inter-AS and Internet Design

Inter-AS interdomain multicast is very similar to intra-AS. The key difference is, of course, the requirement that MSDP, MBGP, and PIM be fully operational in each connected domain. The edge of the AS is the control point for cross-domain traffic.

We have already examined configurations for the Mcast Enterprises network. You can complete the solution by configuring each of the ISP routers in the complete network. Figure 1-25 shows the interface details for the ISP routers.

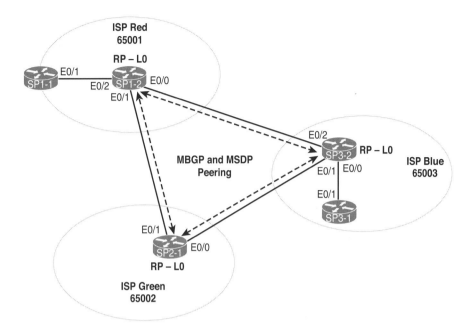

Figure 1-25   *Internet Multicast Network*

Example 1-28 details the configuration of each of the SPX-X routers, making them capable of carrying multicast traffic from the Mcast Enterprises network to ISP-connected customers.

> **Note**   Example 1-28 shows only the configuration commands relevant to the network diagram shown in Figure 1-25. Additional configurations for connecting Mcast Enterprises to ISP Blue are covered earlier in this chapter.

Example 1-28   *Final ISP Multicast Configurations*

```
SP3-1:
ip multicast-routing
ip cef
!
!
interface Loopback0
 ip address 172.23.0.1 255.255.255.255
!
interface Ethernet0/0
 ip address 172.23.31.1 255.255.255.0
```

```
 ip pim sparse-mode
!
interface Ethernet0/1
 ip address 172.23.1.1 255.255.255.0
 ip pim sparse-mode
!
router ospf 1
 passive-interface Ethernet0/0
 network 172.23.0.0 0.0.255.255 area 0
!
router bgp 65003
 bgp log-neighbor-changes
 neighbor 172.23.0.2 remote-as 65003
 neighbor 172.23.0.2 update-source Loopback0
 neighbor 172.23.31.4 remote-as 65100
 !
 address-family ipv4
  network 172.23.0.0
  neighbor 172.23.0.2 activate
  neighbor 172.23.31.4 activate
  neighbor 172.23.31.4 soft-reconfiguration inbound
 exit-address-family
 !
 address-family ipv4 multicast
  network 172.23.0.0
  neighbor 172.23.0.2 activate
  neighbor 172.23.31.4 activate
 exit-address-family
!
ip pim rp-address 172.23.0.2
ip route 172.23.0.0 255.255.0.0 Null0


SP3-2:
ip multicast-routing
ip cef
!
interface Loopback0
 ip address 172.23.0.2 255.255.255.255
!
interface Ethernet0/0
 ip address 172.23.1.2 255.255.255.0
 ip pim sparse-mode
!
```

```
interface Ethernet0/1
 ip address 172.23.2.2 255.255.255.0
 ip pim sparse-mode
!
interface Ethernet0/2
 ip address 172.21.13.2 255.255.255.0
 ip pim sparse-mode
!
router ospf 1
 passive-interface Ethernet0/1
 passive-interface Ethernet0/2
 network 172.21.0.0 0.0.255.255 area 0
 network 172.23.0.0 0.0.255.255 area 0
!
router bgp 65003
 bgp log-neighbor-changes
 neighbor 172.21.13.1 remote-as 65001
 neighbor 172.23.0.1 remote-as 65003
 neighbor 172.23.0.1 update-source Loopback0
 neighbor 172.23.2.1 remote-as 65002
 !
 address-family ipv4
  network 172.23.0.0
  neighbor 172.21.13.1 activate
  neighbor 172.23.0.1 activate
  neighbor 172.23.2.1 activate
 exit-address-family
 !
 address-family ipv4 multicast
  network 172.23.0.0
  neighbor 172.21.13.1 activate
  neighbor 172.23.0.1 activate
  neighbor 172.23.2.1 activate
 exit-address-family
!
ip bgp-community new-format
!
ip pim rp-address 172.23.0.2
ip msdp peer 10.0.0.1 connect-source Loopback0 remote-as 65100
ip msdp peer 172.22.0.1 connect-source Loopback0 remote-as 65002
ip msdp peer 172.21.0.2 connect-source Loopback0 remote-as 65001
ip msdp cache-sa-state
ip route 172.23.0.0 255.255.0.0 Null0
```

```
SP2-1:
ip multicast-routing
ip cef
!
interface Loopback0
 ip address 172.22.0.1 255.255.255.255
 ip pim sparse-mode
!
interface Ethernet0/0
 ip address 172.23.2.1 255.255.255.0
 ip pim sparse-mode
!
interface Ethernet0/1
 ip address 172.21.12.1 255.255.255.0
 ip pim sparse-mode
!
router bgp 65002
 bgp log-neighbor-changes
 neighbor 172.21.12.2 remote-as 65001
 neighbor 172.23.2.2 remote-as 65003
 !
 address-family ipv4
  network 172.22.0.0
  neighbor 172.21.12.2 activate
  neighbor 172.21.12.2 soft-reconfiguration inbound
  neighbor 172.23.2.2 activate
  neighbor 172.23.2.2 soft-reconfiguration inbound
 exit-address-family
 !
 address-family ipv4 multicast
  network 172.22.0.0
  neighbor 172.21.12.2 activate
  neighbor 172.21.12.2 soft-reconfiguration inbound
  neighbor 172.23.2.2 activate
  neighbor 172.23.2.2 soft-reconfiguration inbound
 exit-address-family
!
ip bgp-community new-format
!
ip msdp peer 172.23.0.2 connect-source Loopback0 remote-as 65003
ip msdp peer 172.21.0.2 connect-source Loopback0 remote-as 65001
ip msdp cache-sa-state
ip route 172.22.0.0 255.255.0.0 Null0

SP1-1:
ip multicast-routing
```

```
ip cef
!
interface Loopback0
 ip address 172.21.0.1 255.255.255.255
 ip pim sparse-mode
!
interface Ethernet0/0
 ip address 172.21.100.1 255.255.255.0
 ip pim sparse-mode
!
interface Ethernet0/1
 ip address 172.21.1.1 255.255.255.0
 ip pim sparse-mode
!
router ospf 1
 network 172.21.0.0 0.0.255.255 area 0
!
router bgp 65001
 bgp log-neighbor-changes
 neighbor 172.21.0.2 remote-as 65001
 neighbor 172.21.0.2 update-source Loopback0
 !
 address-family ipv4
  network 172.21.0.0
  neighbor 172.21.0.2 activate
 exit-address-family
 !
 address-family ipv4 multicast
  network 172.21.0.0
  neighbor 172.21.0.2 activate
 exit-address-family
!
ip bgp-community new-format
!
ip pim rp-address 172.21.0.2
ip route 172.21.0.0 255.255.0.0 Null0

SP1-2:
ip multicast-routing
ip cef
no ipv6 cef
!
interface Loopback0
 ip address 172.21.0.2 255.255.255.255
 ip pim sparse-mode
!
```

```
interface Ethernet0/0
 ip address 172.21.13.1 255.255.255.0
 ip pim sparse-mode
!
interface Ethernet0/1
 ip address 172.21.12.2 255.255.255.0
 ip pim sparse-mode
!
interface Ethernet0/2
 ip address 172.21.1.2 255.255.255.0
 ip pim sparse-mode
!
router ospf 1
 passive-interface Ethernet0/0
 passive-interface Ethernet0/1
 passive-interface Ethernet1/0
 network 172.21.0.0 0.0.255.255 area 0
!
router bgp 65001
 bgp log-neighbor-changes
 neighbor 172.21.0.1 remote-as 65001
 neighbor 172.21.0.1 update-source Loopback0
 neighbor 172.21.12.1 remote-as 65002
 neighbor 172.21.13.2 remote-as 65003
 !
 address-family ipv4
  network 172.21.0.0
  neighbor 172.21.0.1 activate
  neighbor 172.21.12.1 activate
  neighbor 172.21.13.2 activate
 exit-address-family
 !
 address-family ipv4 multicast
  network 172.21.0.0
  neighbor 172.21.0.1 activate
  neighbor 172.21.12.1 activate
  neighbor 172.21.13.2 activate
 exit-address-family
!
ip bgp-community new-format
!
ip pim rp-address 172.21.0.2
ip msdp peer 172.22.0.1 connect-source Loopback0 remote-as 65002
ip msdp peer 172.23.0.2 connect-source Loopback0 remote-as 65003
ip msdp cache-sa-state
ip route 172.21.0.0 255.255.0.0 Null0
```

Now that the ISP networks are configured to carry multicast across the mock Internet, you should be able to connect a client to any of the ISPs and receive multicast from a server in the Mcast Enterprises network. Use Figure 1-26 as the end-to-end visual for this exercise.

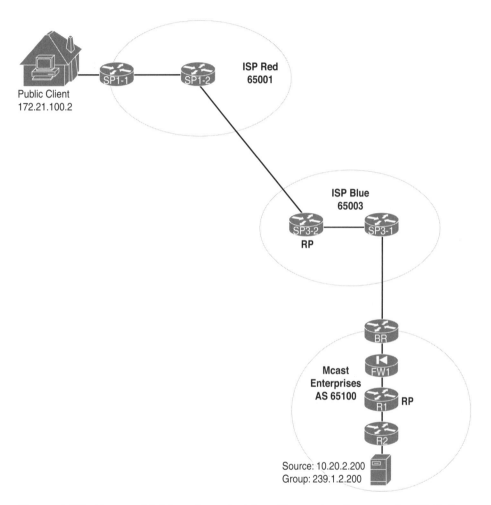

Figure 1-26 *Internet Multicast from the Mcast Enterprises Server to the ISP-Red Connected Client*

Make Server 2 with IP address 10.20.2.200 a source for group 239.1.2.200 (which resides in the global Mcast Enterprise domain) by simply using the **ping** command from the server's terminal. Notice the ping replies from the client connected to ISP-1 with IP address 172.21.100.2. If successful, there should be a complete shared tree and a complete source tree at each RP in the path (R1, SP3-2, and SP1-2), which you can see by using the **show ip mroute** command on each router. Example 1-29 shows the execution of the **ping** on Server 2 and the command output from the RPs.

Example 1-29 *Completed Multicast Tree from the Mcast Enterprise Server to the ISP-1 Connected Client*

```
Server 2
Server2# ping 239.1.2.200
Type escape sequence to abort.
Sending 1, 100-byte ICMP Echos to 239.1.2.200, timeout is 2 seconds:


Reply to request 0 from 172.21.100.2, 4 ms


R1
R1# show ip mroute 239.1.2.200
IP Multicast Routing Table
Flags: D - Dense, S - Sparse, B - Bidir Group, s - SSM Group, C - Connected,
       L - Local, P - Pruned, R - RP-bit set, F - Register flag,
       T - SPT-bit set, J - Join SPT, M - MSDP created entry, E - Extranet,
       X - Proxy Join Timer Running, A - Candidate for MSDP Advertisement,
       U - URD, I - Received Source Specific Host Report,
       Z - Multicast Tunnel, z - MDT-data group sender,
       Y - Joined MDT-data group, y - Sending to MDT-data group,
       G - Received BGP C-Mroute, g - Sent BGP C-Mroute,
       N - Received BGP Shared-Tree Prune, n - BGP C-Mroute suppressed,
       Q - Received BGP S-A Route, q - Sent BGP S-A Route,
       V - RD & Vector, v - Vector, p - PIM Joins on route
Outgoing interface flags: H - Hardware switched, A - Assert winner, p - PIM Join
 Timers: Uptime/Expires
 Interface state: Interface, Next-Hop or VCD, State/Mode

(*, 239.1.2.200), 00:17:07/stopped, RP 10.0.0.1, flags: SP
  Incoming interface: Null, RPF nbr 0.0.0.0
  Outgoing interface list: Null

(10.20.2.200, 239.1.2.200), 00:17:07/00:01:43, flags: TA
  Incoming interface: Ethernet0/2, RPF nbr 10.1.2.2
  Outgoing interface list:
    Ethernet0/0, Forward/Sparse, 00:07:34/00:02:48


SP3-2:
SP3-2# show ip mroute 239.1.2.200
IP Multicast Routing Table
Flags: D - Dense, S - Sparse, B - Bidir Group, s - SSM Group, C - Connected,
       L - Local, P - Pruned, R - RP-bit set, F - Register flag,
```

```
           T - SPT-bit set, J - Join SPT, M - MSDP created entry, E - Extranet,
           X - Proxy Join Timer Running, A - Candidate for MSDP Advertisement,
           U - URD, I - Received Source Specific Host Report,
           Z - Multicast Tunnel, z - MDT-data group sender,
           Y - Joined MDT-data group, y - Sending to MDT-data group,
           G - Received BGP C-Mroute, g - Sent BGP C-Mroute,
           N - Received BGP Shared-Tree Prune, n - BGP C-Mroute suppressed,
           Q - Received BGP S-A Route, q - Sent BGP S-A Route,
           V - RD & Vector, v - Vector, p - PIM Joins on route
Outgoing interface flags: H - Hardware switched, A - Assert winner, p - PIM Join
 Timers: Uptime/Expires
 Interface state: Interface, Next-Hop or VCD, State/Mode


(*, 239.1.2.200), 00:08:37/stopped, RP 172.23.0.2, flags: SP
   Incoming interface: Null, RPF nbr 0.0.0.0
   Outgoing interface list: Null


(10.20.2.200, 239.1.2.200), 00:08:37/00:02:48, flags: T
   Incoming interface: Ethernet0/0, RPF nbr 172.23.1.1, Mbgp
   Outgoing interface list:
     Ethernet0/2, Forward/Sparse, 00:08:37/00:02:45


SP1-2
SP1-2# show ip mroute 239.1.2.200
IP Multicast Routing Table
Flags: D - Dense, S - Sparse, B - Bidir Group, s - SSM Group, C - Connected,
           L - Local, P - Pruned, R - RP-bit set, F - Register flag,
           T - SPT-bit set, J - Join SPT, M - MSDP created entry, E - Extranet,
           X - Proxy Join Timer Running, A - Candidate for MSDP Advertisement,
           U - URD, I - Received Source Specific Host Report,
           Z - Multicast Tunnel, z - MDT-data group sender,
           Y - Joined MDT-data group, y - Sending to MDT-data group,
           G - Received BGP C-Mroute, g - Sent BGP C-Mroute,
           N - Received BGP Shared-Tree Prune, n - BGP C-Mroute suppressed,
           Q - Received BGP S-A Route, q - Sent BGP S-A Route,
           V - RD & Vector, v - Vector, p - PIM Joins on route
Outgoing interface flags: H - Hardware switched, A - Assert winner, p - PIM Join
 Timers: Uptime/Expires
 Interface state: Interface, Next-Hop or VCD, State/Mode


(*, 239.1.2.200), 00:11:51/00:03:23, RP 172.21.0.2, flags: S
   Incoming interface: Null, RPF nbr 0.0.0.0
   Outgoing interface list:
     Ethernet0/2, Forward/Sparse, 00:11:51/00:03:23
```

```
(10.20.2.200, 239.1.2.200), 00:09:12/00:02:06, flags: MT
  Incoming interface: Ethernet0/0, RPF nbr 172.21.13.2, Mbgp
  Outgoing interface list:
    Ethernet0/2, Forward/Sparse, 00:09:12/00:03:23
```

Success! As you can see, inter-AS interdomain multicast is fairly simple to understand and implement. These basic principles can be applied across the global Internet or across any multidomain network in which AS boundaries exist.

Protecting Domain Borders and Interdomain Resources

No Internet-connected organization provides Internet users unfettered access to internal resources. This maxim is not just true for common unicast IP traffic but is also true, sometimes especially so, for multicast traffic. Remember that multicast traffic is still, at its core, IP traffic, and so it is vulnerable to nearly any standard IP attack vector. IP multicast may even be more vulnerable to exploit than unicast. This increased vulnerability occurs because of the nature of multicast traffic, its reliance on an underlying unicast network, and the additional service protocols enabled/required by multicast.

Multicast packets are very different from unicast packets. Intended receivers could be nearly anywhere geographically. In a unicast framework, generally the sender has a very specific receiver—one that can be authorized for communications through a two-way TCP exchange. No such mechanism exists for multicast. Senders rarely know who is subscribed to a feed or where they may be located. This is known as a *push data model*, and there is rarely an exchange of data between senders and receivers. It is very difficult to authenticate, encrypt, or control distribution in a push data model. Remember that the main purpose of multicast is increased efficiency, and you must make sacrifices in certain other network aspects—such as control, centralized resources, and security—to achieve it.

Furthermore, if the underlying IP unicast network is not secure, the multicast overlay is equally vulnerable to exploit or error. Any time a multicast domain is implemented, every effort should be taken to secure the underlying unicast infrastructure, and additional measures should be taken for reliability and resilience. An unsecured unicast network makes for an unsecured multicast network.

Chapter 5 in *IP Multicast, Volume 1* discusses at length how to internally secure a multicast domain, as well as how to protect the domain border. However, most of those protections prevent leakage of multicast messages inside or outside the domain or protect domain resources, such as RP memory, from overuse. Such protections are even more important in a multidomain scenario, especially if internal domains are exposed to Internet resources. It is strongly suggested that you review the material from *IP Multicast, Volume 1* to ensure that internal domain resources are protected as well as possible.

In addition to these measures, further considerations for the domain border should be accounted for. One such consideration is the use of firewalls in the multicast domain. Firewalls can simultaneously protect both the unicast and multicast infrastructures inside a zone, domain, or autonomous system. You may have noticed that there is a transparent firewall (FW1) in all the network designs for Mcast Enterprises. It is best practice to always have a firewall separating secure zones, such as the public Internet from internal network resources. Also consider additional services that are required for or enabled by multicast. This is especially true at the domain border. Clearly, if you are going to connect multicast domains to other domains outside your immediate control, you must be very serious about securing that domain and the domain border. The following sections examine some of these items more closely.

Firewalling IP Multicast

There are two ways to implement traffic handling in a network firewall: in L2 transparent mode or in L3 routed mode. Each has different implications on multicast traffic handling. For example, routed mode on a Cisco ASA, by default, does not allow multicast traffic to pass between interfaces, even when explicitly allowed by an ACL. Additional multicast configuration is required.

> **Note** An in-depth discussion of the ASA and Firepower firewall is beyond the scope of this text. For more information about multicast support on these devices, please look to Cisco's published command references, design guides, and configuration guides. They provide specific, in-depth sections dedicated to IP multicast and firewall configuration.

In transparent mode, firewalling multicast is much easier. L2 transparent mode can natively pass IP multicast traffic without additional configuration. There are two major considerations when using transparent mode to secure a multicast domain:

- **Multicast usage on any management interfaces of the firewall:** Many network configuration and control tools can use multicast for more efficient communications across the management plane of the network. If this is a requirement for your transparent firewall, you need to explicitly permit multicast traffic on the management interface. Typically, the management interface is a fully functional IP routed interface that is walled off from the other interfaces on the firewall, and consequently it needs this additional configuration for multicast operation.

- **The passing of multicast packets between firewall zones:** In an L2 configuration, this should be very simple to accomplish. Each firewall manufacturer has different configuration parameters for permitting multicast traffic across the zone boundaries. An architect or engineer needs to understand the role and capabilities of each firewall and what is required for multicast to work both through the firewall and to the firewall.

As a rule, firewalling multicast between critical security zones is recommended, just as for any other traffic. Multicast is still IP, which carries with it many of the same vulnerabilities as regular unicast traffic. Additional multicast-specific vulnerabilities may also apply. These should be mitigated to the extent possible to secure vital infrastructure traffic. For configuring multicast on Cisco firewalls (ASA and Firepower), look for multicast security toolkits and product-specific design guides at www.cisco.com.

Controlling Domain Access through Filtering

Perhaps the most important way to protect a multicast domain with external sources or receivers is to filter out certain prefixes from participation. Remember that MSDP speakers are also RPs, which play a critical role in the network. You need to protect MSDP routers from resource exhaustion and attack vectors such as denial of service (DoS). Proper filtering of MSDP messages can also limit this type of exposure to vulnerability.

IP Multicast, Volume 1 discusses methods of closing a domain completely to outside multicast or PIM traffic. That, of course, does not work the same in an interdomain scenario. Properly filtering traffic is, therefore, a must. There are many ways to implement interdomain filtering, and the best security strategy incorporates all of them. You should focus on three essential types of filters that should be deployed in every domain that allows cross-domain communications:

- Domain boundary filters

- MSDP filters

- MBGP filters

The first and most obvious type of filter is applied at the domain border router, specifically on PIM border interfaces. PIM uses boundary lists to block unwanted sources and groups. Table 1-17 shows the commands for configuring boundary lists.

Table 1-17 *Multicast Boundary Commands*

Operating System	Command
IOS/XE	`ip multicast boundary` *access-list* [`filter-autorp` `|` `block source` `|` `in` `|` `out`]
IOS XR	`(config-mcast-default-ipv4-if)#` `boundary` *access-list*
NX-OS	`ip pim jp-policy` *policy-name* [`in` `|` `out`]

Note The **boundary** command acts differently on each OS, and the NX-OS equivalent is to set up a PIM join/prune policy. The **in** and **out** keywords specify the direction in which the filter applies on an interface. For NX-OS and IOS-XE, when the direction is not specified, both directions are assumed by default. For more information about this command in each OS, please refer to the most recent published command reference.

These commands allow PIM to permit or deny tree building for specific (S, G) pairs at a specified interface. When an (S, G) is denied, PIM does not allow that interface to become a part of the source tree. Additional consideration for IOS-XE can be taken for shared trees, (*, G), by using an all-0s host ID in the access control list (ACL). However, this is only part of a good boundary filter policy. In addition to implementing the **boundary** command, border interface ACLs should also include basic filtering for packets destined to group addresses inside a domain. This is especially relevant on Internet- or extranet-facing interfaces. Be sure your border ACLs block incoming multicast for any unauthorized group access. Firewalls can also help in this regard.

Even with this protection at the edge, your network could still be vulnerable to other types of multicast-based attacks. For example, if the network edge is ever misconfigured and MBGP is not properly filtered, the domain could quickly become transit for traffic in which it should not be a forwarding participant. Resource exhaustion is another common attack vector to which an administrator should pay special attention. You should consider standard BGP protections and protecting RP resources on MSDP speakers that peer externally.

Standard MBGP filters can prevent learning unwanted source prefixes from specific networks. Remember that MBGP prefix entries are simply RPF entries for a router to check against. Network engineers should configure filters that prevent improper RPF checks. This type of filtering functions and is configured in exactly the same manner as any other BGP filtering. You can simply deny incoming or outgoing advertisements of unwanted source prefixes. For more information on BGP prefix filtering, refer to current published documentation at www.cisco.com.

Let's look at this type of filtering in practice on the Mcast Enterprise network, with the added elements shown in Figure 1-26 (in the previous section). In this scenario, the sole purpose of Mcast Enterprise's participation in Internet interdomain multicast is to make a multicast service available to the public Internet. The server connected to R2 with IP address 10.20.2.200 is the source of this traffic, and receivers can be located on the public Internet. The public stream from this server is using group 239.1.2.200.

There is no reason for any outside, public, multicast stream to reach receivers within the Mcast Enterprises AS. Therefore, Mcast Enterprises should implement the following filters to protect the domain and other internal infrastructure:

- Place an inbound ACL blocking all incoming multicast traffic from the Internet on BR interface E0/0. (Be sure to allow all PIM routers on 224.0.0.13.)

- Place an ACL that allows multicast traffic only for group 239.1.2.200 and all PIM routers on the same BR interface in an outbound direction.

- Place an inbound route filter on the BR's MBGP peer with SP3-2 that prevents any external source prefixes from being learned.

- Place an MBGP advertisement filter on the same peering on the BR, allowing advertisement of only the source prefix required for group 239.1.2.200 (in this case, a summary route for 10.2.0.0/16).

- Place an inbound MSDP SA filter on router R1 to prevent any inbound SA learning.

- Place an outbound MSDP SA filter on R1 to allow the sharing of the SA cache entry for (10.20.2.200, 239.1.2.200) only.

Example 1-30 shows these additional configuration elements for routers BR and R1, using simple access list and route maps for simplicity.

Example 1-30   *Filtering Configuration for Public Internet Services*

```
BR
interface Ethernet0/1
 ip address 172.23.31.4 255.255.255.0
 ip access-group MCAST_IN in
 ip access-group MCAST_OUT out
 ip pim sparse-mode
!
router bgp 65101
!
 address-family ipv4 multicast
  neighbor 172.23.31.1 route-map MBGP_IN in
  neighbor 172.23.31.1 route-map MBGP_OUT out
!
ip access-list MCAST_IN
 permit ip host 224.0.0.13 any
 deny   ip 224.0.0.0 15.255.255.255 any
 permit ip any any
ip access-list standard MCAST-OUT
 permit 239.1.2.200
 permit 224.0.0.13
 deny   224.0.0.0 15.255.255.255
 permit any
ip access-list standard PUBLIC_SOURCE
 permit 10.2.0.0 0.0.255.255
!
!
route-map MBGP_OUT permit 10
 match ip address PUBLIC_SOURCE
!
route-map MBGP_OUT deny 20
!
route-map MBGP_IN deny 10


R1
ip msdp peer 172.23.0.2 connect-source Loopback0 remote-as 65003
ip msdp sa-filter in 172.23.0.2 route-map MSDP_IN
ip msdp sa-filter out 172.23.0.2 list MSDP_OUT
!
ip access-list extended MSDP_OUT
 permit ip any host 239.1.2.200
!
!
route-map MSDP_IN deny 10
```

Note The transparent firewall discussed earlier can act as a secondary safeguard against unwanted inbound multicast traffic if the filtering on the BR fails. In addition, the firewall can be implemented to help prevent internal multicast leakage to the BR and beyond, protecting sensitive internal communications. An optional ACL could also be added at R1 to prevent the other internal domains of Mcast Enterprises from leaking to the firewall, thus easing the processing burden on the firewall ASICs. In addition, the router ACLs given in this example are rudimentary in nature. In practice, these elements would be added to much more effective and extensive ACLs that include standard AS border security elements.

As you can see, there are many places and ways to enable domain filtering. Each one serves a specific purpose and should be considered part of a holistic protection strategy. Do not assume, for example, that protecting the domain border is enough. Domain resources such as RP memory on MSDP speakers must also be protected.

Another element of filtering that will become obvious as it is implemented is the need to have concise and useful domain scoping. Because the network in the example is properly scoped, writing policy to protect applications is relatively straightforward. Poor scoping can make filtering extremely difficult—maybe even impossible—in a very large multidomain implementation. Therefore, scoping should not only be considered an essential element of good domain and application design but also an essential element of multicast security policy.

Service Filtering at the Edge

The final step in securing the multidomain multicast solution is to lock down any services at the edge. This keeps the domain secure from resource overutilization and unauthorized service access attempts. You should consider killing IGMP packets from external networks, limiting unwanted unicast TCP ACKs to a source, and using Time-to-Live (TTL) scoping for multicast packets.

Locking down IGMP and eliminating TCP Acknowledgements (ACKs) is very straight-forward. These should be added to any inbound border ACLs at the edge of the AS or domain. TTL scoping is discussed at length in Chapter 5 in *IP Multicast, Volume 1*.

The only other thing to consider for service filtering at the edge is the use of Session Advertisement Protocol (SAP). SAP is a legacy protocol that harkens back to the days of MBONE. SAP and its sister protocol Session Description Protocol (SDP) were used to provide directory information about a service that was offered via IP multicast. The idea was to advertise these services, making it easier for clients to subscribe to. However, through the course of time, the Internet community found it was simply easier and safer to hard-code addresses.

In more recent years, SAP and SDP have become an attack vector for multicast specific DDoS assaults. There is no reason to have SAP running in your network. Many Cisco operating systems shut it down by default. However, the authors feel it is better to be certain and deconfigure SAP services on multicast-enabled interfaces in the network, regardless of default settings. This should be considered a crucial and important step for *any* multicast design, regardless of domain scope. The IOS-XE command for disabling SAP is **no ip sap listen**, and it is entered at the interface configuration mode prompt. For the corresponding command in other operating systems, please see the command references at www.cisco.com.

Interdomain Multicast Without Active Source Learning

As mentioned earlier in this chapter, most multicast networks are built using Any-Source Multicast (ASM), with PIM Sparse-Mode (PIM–SM) acting as the multicast tree-builder. It is obvious that PIM–SM with MBGP and MSDP is the de facto standard for Internet-based interdomain multicast. Is there a way, though, to achieve similar results without all the additional source learning and active source sharing among domain RPs?

The answer is a resounding yes! Interdomain multicast can also be achieved by using the Source-Specific Multicast (SSM) model without all the headaches of MBGP and MSDP. In addition, IPv6 includes ways to implement an ASM PIM–SM model that does not require MSDP or MBGP. Let's very quickly examine the differences in how to implement interdomain multicast much more simply using these models.

SSM

Remember the three pillars of interdomain design? Here they are, listed again for your convenience:

- **The multicast control plane for source identification:** The router must know a proper path to any multicast source, either from the unicast RIB or learned (either statically or dynamically) through a specific RPF exception.

- **The multicast control plane for receiver identification:** The router must know about any legitimate receivers that have joined the group and where they are located in the network.

- **The downstream multicast control plane and MRIB:** The router must know when a source is actively sending packets for a given group. PIM–SM domains must also be able to build a shared tree from the local domain's RP, even when the source has registered to a remote RP in a different domain.

In an SSM-enabled domain, the third pillar is addressed inherently by the nature of the SSM PIM implementation. When a receiver wants to join an SSM group, it must not only specify the group address but also specify the specific source it wishes to hear from. This means that every time a receiver subscribes to a group, the last-hop router (LHR; the router connected to the receiver) already knows where the source is located. It will only ever build a source tree directly to the source of the stream. This means there is no RP required! It also means that SA caching is not needed for this type of communication, and no shared trees are required either.

If the source is in another domain, PIM routers simply share the (S, G) join directly toward the source, regardless of its location. If the domains are completely within an AS, it is also very unlikely that MBGP is necessary to carry RPF information for sources as the source is generally part of a prefix entry in the IGP-based RIB of each internal router. Multicast domains can still be segregated by scoping and border ACLs (which should be a requirement of any domain border, regardless of PIM type), ensuring that you have security in place for multicast traffic.

Note   BGP or MBGP is still required, of course, if you are crossing IGP boundaries. Using MBGP may, in fact, still be the best way of controlling source RPF checks between domains, but its use should be dictated by the overall design.

The SSM interdomain model is therefore substantially easier to implement. Consider what would happen to the intra-AS design at Mcast Enterprises. Figure 1-27 redraws the final solution Mcast Enterprises network shown in Figure 1-22 but using SSM. As you can see, this is a much simpler design, with no MBGP, no MSDP, and no RPs.

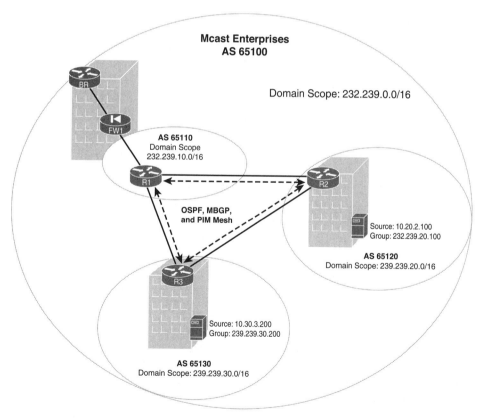

Figure 1-27   *Mcast Enterprises Final Design, Using SSM*

> **Note**   The IP Multicast group address has been updated to reflect private SSM addresses per RFC 5771.

Wait a minute! If SSM is really so much easier to implement for interdomain multicast, why isn't the entire Internet using it instead of PIM–SM? This is a good question. There are three answers. First, as a feature, SSM is a relatively recent addition to many networks; it is specified in RFC 4607, published in 2006. Legacy infrastructure support is an important element in any network, including the Internet. Changing the standards is a time-consuming and sometimes expensive process.

The second reason SSM is not the Internet standard for interdomain multicast is control. The PIM–SM model gives autonomous systems far more control over the flow of multicast between domains. While you can still have good interdomain security with SSM, there are far fewer control points. It would be much more difficult to isolate internal domain traffic from external traffic, and mistaken configurations could have far-reaching consequences. The PIM–SM model with MSDP follows the same command and control principles as BGP for this very reason. In fact, achieving similar segmentation with SSM would likely require that many companies use very specific host IPs advertised exclusively by MBGP and that MBGP filtering become the primary method of multicast resource protection—which it was not necessarily designed to do. Thus, an improperly configured SSM domain could cause far-reaching havoc, maybe even globally.

That being said, at the time of this writing at least, SSM interdomain multicast is perfectly suited to intra-AS interdomain multicast. An understanding of basic traffic filtering and basic SSM operations is all that is needed to get started. For more information on SSM operations, refer to *IP Multicast, Volume 1*.

The third and most relevant reason is that ISP support for multicast is simply not ubiquitous. While it is possible to get multicast across the global Internet, as described in the latter half of this chapter, it is certainly not pervasive as of this writing. It may very well be that in the future, with additional improvements to SSM forwarding, you will see pervasive Internet multicast. However, for the time being, the complexities and lack of uniform support for PIM–SM standards make Internet-based multicast a less attractive service than unicast replication.

IPv6 with Embedded RP

Using IPv6 for interdomain multicast is very simple. For the most part, the configuration of the networks previously shown is identical, only using IPv6 addressing and IPv6 address families to complete the configurations. IPv6-based intra-AS interdomain multicast does have a big advantage over its IPv4 counterpart. IPv6 can simplify the deployment of RPs and eliminate the need for MSDP by using embedded RP.

The embedded RP function of IPv6 allows the address of the RP to be embedded in an IPv6 multicast message. When a downstream router or routers see the group address, the RP information is extracted, and a shared tree is immediately built. In this way, a single centrally controlled RP can provide RP services for multiple domains. This solution works for both interdomain and intra-domain multicast.

The format of the embedded RP address is shown in Figure 1-28 and includes the following:

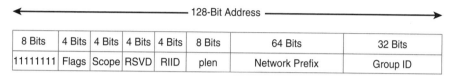

8 Bits	4 Bits	4 Bits	4 Bits	4 Bits	8 Bits	64 Bits	32 Bits
11111111	Flags	Scope	RSVD	RIID	plen	Network Prefix	Group ID

Figure 1-28 *IPv6 with Embedded RP Addressing*

- **11111111:** All group addresses must begin with this bit pattern.

- **Flags:** The 4 bits are defined as 0, R, P, and T, where the most significant bit is 0, R when set to 1 indicates an embedded RP address, and P and T must both equal 1. (For additional information, please refer to RFC 3306/7371.)

- **Scope:**
  - 0000–0: Reserved
  - 0001–1: Node-local scope
  - 0010–2: Link-local scope
  - 0011–3: Unassigned
  - 0100–4: Unassigned
  - 0101–5: Site-local scope
  - 0110–6: Unassigned
  - 0111–7: Unassigned
  - 1000–8: Organization-local scope
  - 1001–9: Unassigned
  - 1010–A: Unassigned
  - 1011–B: Unassigned
  - 1100–C: Unassigned
  - 1101–D: Unassigned
  - 1110–E: Global scope
  - 1111–F: Reserved

- **RIID (RP Interface ID):** Anything except 0.

- **Plen (prefix length):** Indicates the number of bits in the network prefix field and must not be equal to 0 or greater than 64.

To embed the RP address in the message, the prefix must begin with FF70::/12, as shown in Figure 1-29.

8 Bits	4 Bits	4 Bits
11111111	Flags	Scope

Binary:	11111111	0111	xxxx
Hex:	FF	7	x

Figure 1-29 *Embedded RP Address Prefix*

You need to copy the number of bits from the network prefix as defined by the value of plen. Finally, the RIID value is appended to the last four least significant bits, as shown in Figure 1-30.

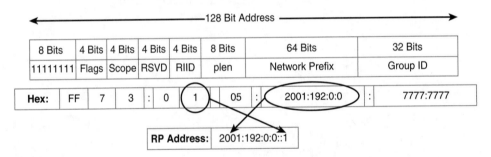

Figure 1-30 *Determining the Embedded RP Address*

Figure 1-31 provides an example of embedding an RP address.

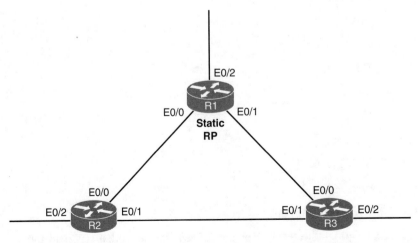

Figure 1-31 *Embedded RP Configuration Example Network*

Example 1-31 provides the configurations for the routers shown in Figure 1-31.

Example 1-31   *Configurations for IPv6 Embedded RP*

```
hostname R1
ipv6 unicast-routing
ipv6 multicast-routing
!
interface Loopback0
 ip address 192.168.0.1 255.255.255.255
 ipv6 address 2001:192::1/128
 ipv6 enable
 ipv6 ospf 65000 area 0
!
interface Ethernet0/0
 no ip address
 ipv6 address 2001:192:168:21::1/64
 ipv6 enable
 ipv6 ospf 65000 area 0
!
interface Ethernet0/1
 no ip address
 ipv6 address 2001:192:168:31::1/64
 ipv6 enable
 ipv6 ospf 65000 area 0
!
interface Ethernet0/2
 no ip address
 load-interval 30
 ipv6 address 2001:192:168:41::1/64
 ipv6 enable
 ipv6 ospf 65000 area 0
!
ipv6 pim rp-address 2001:192::1

!
ipv6 router ospf 65000
 router-id 192.168.0.1


hostname R2
ipv6 unicast-routing
ipv6 multicast-routing
!
interface Loopback0
ip address 192.168.0.2 255.255.255.255
```

```
 ipv6 address 2001:192:168::2/128
 ipv6 enable
 ipv6 ospf 65000 area 0
!
interface Ethernet0/0
 no ip address
 ipv6 address 2001:192:168:21::2/64
 ipv6 enable
 ipv6 ospf 65000 area 0
!
interface Ethernet0/1
 no ip address
 ipv6 address 2001:192:168:32::2/64
 ipv6 enable
 ipv6 ospf 65000 area 0
!
interface Ethernet0/2
 no ip address
 ipv6 address 2001:192:168:52::2/64
 ipv6 enable
 ipv6 ospf 65000 area 0
!
ipv6 router ospf 65000
 router-id 192.168.0.2


hostname R3
ipv6 unicast-routing
ipv6 multicast-routing
!
interface Loopback0
 ip address 192.168.0.3 255.255.255.255
 ipv6 address 2001:192:168::3/128
 ipv6 enable
 ipv6 ospf 65000 area 0
!
interface Ethernet0/0
 no ip address
 load-interval 30
 ipv6 address 2001:192:168:31::3/64
 ipv6 enable
 ipv6 ospf 65000 area 0
!
interface Ethernet0/1
 no ip address
```

```
  ipv6 address 2001:192:168:32::3/64
  ipv6 enable
  ipv6 ospf 65000 area 0
 !
 interface Ethernet0/2
  no ip address
  ipv6 address 2001:192:168:63::3/64
  ipv6 enable
  ipv6 mld join-group FF73:105:2001:192::1
  ipv6 ospf 65000 area 0
 !
 ipv6 router ospf 65000
  router-id 192.168.0.3
```

As you can see from the configurations in Example 1-31, there isn't anything too fancy. The highlighted commands on R1 defines R1 as the RP using the loopback 0 interface, with the **ipv6 pim rp-address 2001:192::1** command, and the second is on R3, which statically defines a join group by using the **ipv6 mld join-group FF73:105:2001:192::1** command.

Note The **ipv6 mld join-group** command should be used only temporarily, for trouble-shooting purposes only.

You may have noticed that the only router with an RP mapping is R1. Because you are embedding the RP information in the multicast message, it is not necessary to define an RP on every router.

From R2, you can watch the behavior in action by using a simple **ping** command. As shown in Example 1-32, you can ping the FF73:105:2001:192::1 address configured as a join group on R3.

Example 1-32 *Embedded RP Example*

```
R2# ping FF73:105:2001:192::1
Output Interface: ethernet0/1
Type escape sequence to abort.
Sending 5, 100-byte ICMP Echos to FF73:105:2001:192::1, timeout is 2 seconds:
Packet sent with a source address of 2001:192:168:32::2

Reply to request 0 received from 2001:192:168:63::3, 8 ms
Reply to request 1 received from 2001:192:168:63::3, 1 ms
Reply to request 2 received from 2001:192:168:63::3, 1 ms
Reply to request 3 received from 2001:192:168:63::3, 1 ms
Reply to request 4 received from 2001:192:168:63::3, 1 ms
Success rate is 100 percent (5/5), round-trip min/avg/max = 1/2/8 ms
5 multicast replies and 0 errors.
```

You can see that all the ping packets received replies from R3 (2001:192:168:63::3).

On R3, you can verify the existence of both the (*, G) and (S, G) entries with the command shown in Example 1-33.

Example 1-33   *Verifying the PIM Entry with RP Mapping*

```
R3# show ipv6 mroute FF73:105:2001:192::1
Multicast Routing Table
Flags: D - Dense, S - Sparse, B - Bidir Group, s - SSM Group,
       C - Connected, L - Local, I - Received Source Specific Host Report,
       P - Pruned, R - RP-bit set, F - Register flag, T - SPT-bit set,
       J - Join SPT, Y - Joined MDT-data group,
       y - Sending to MDT-data group,
       g - BGP signal originated, G - BGP Signal received,
       N - BGP Shared-Tree Prune received, n - BGP C-Mroute suppressed,
       q - BGP Src-Active originated, Q - BGP Src-Active received
       E - Extranet
Timers: Uptime/Expires
Interface state: Interface, State

(*, FF73:105:2001:192::1), 00:13:34/00:02:55, RP 2000::1, flags: SCL
  Incoming interface: Null
  RPF nbr: ::
  Immediate Outgoing interface list:
    Ethernet0/2, Forward, 00:13:34/00:02:55

(2001:192:168:32::2, FF73:105:2001:192::1), 00:03:02/00:00:27, flags: SFT
  Incoming interface: Ethernet0/1
  RPF nbr: FE80::A8BB:CCFF:FE00:210, Registering
  Immediate Outgoing interface list:
    Tunnel0, Forward, 00:03:02/never
    Ethernet0/2, Forward, 00:03:02/00:02:35
```

Notice that multicast messages are received from interface Ethernet0/1 and sent to the destination interface, Ethernet0/2.

Even though this example is an intra-domain configuration, using IPv6 with embedded RP is a great solution for intra-AS interdomain multicasting. A single RP can be used for all domains, with the mapping function being performed by embedded RP. No additional protocols or interdomain configuration are required as the embedded RP for each group mapping propagates throughout the IPV6 network. However, this is not a very good solution for inter-AS interdomain multicast. The largest difficulty of such a design is the use of a single RP to service multiple ASs. For additional details, refer to RFC 3956.

Summary

This chapter reviews the fundamental requirements for interdomain forwarding of IP multicast flows. An understanding of PIM domains and how they are built on the three pillars of interdomain design is critical for architecting this type of forwarding. Remember that these are the three pillars:

- **The multicast control plane for source identification:** The router must know a proper path to any multicast source, either from the unicast RIB or learned (either statically or dynamically) through a specific RPF exception.

- **The multicast control plane for receiver identification:** The router must know about any legitimate receivers that have joined the group and where they are located in the network.

- **The downstream multicast control plane and MRIB:** The router must know when a source is actively sending packets for a given group. PIM–SM domains must also be able to build a shared tree from the local domain's RP, even when the source has registered to a remote RP in a different domain.

Multicast BGP, PIM, and MSDP satisfy the requirements of the three pillars. With these protocols, you should be able to configure any multidomain or interdomain network, including designs that are both internal and cross the public Internet. This chapter also reviews ways to eliminate the use of MSDP by using SSM or IPv6 embedded RP within the network.

References

RFC 3306

RFC 7371

RFC 5771

RFC 3956

RFC 4607

RFC 3446

RFC 3618

RFC 7606

RFC 4760

RFC 2283

RFC 1930

RFC 6996

Chapter 2

Multicast Scalability and Transport Diversification

Public cloud services are very commonly used in enterprise networks, and it is therefore important to understand how multicast messages are carried to and from a cloud service provider. Transportation of multicast messages requires consideration of several factors, especially when the cloud service providers do not support native multicast. This chapter introduces the key concepts of cloud services and explains the elements required to support multicast services.

Why Is Multicast Not Enabled Natively in a Public Cloud Environment?

Currently, public cloud environments do not have multicast enabled. This is the case because sending a packet to every host in the customer-owned cloud segment would have implications on the data plane and control plane traffic in terms of scalability of the cloud fabric. As enterprise customers add to the cloud more resources with a need for multicast, the cloud platform needs increased capacity and must meet other considerations for dynamic multicast demand. Such changes can be expensive, and speculative calculation can impact the user experience for the cloud consumers.

The calculation of changes needed becomes more complex and difficult to estimate when multitenancy is added to the equation. Allowing multicast protocol in the cloud fabric can have an impact on the performance of the cloud fabric. However, for enterprise customers that require multicast communication for business-relevant applications, it is difficult to adopt cloud services.

Enterprise Adoption of Cloud Services

Enterprise customers tend to adopt cloud services for a number of reasons, including agile provisioning, lower cost of investment, reduced operational and capital expense, closeness to geocentric user population, and speed of developing a product. Figure 2-1 illustrates the most common types of cloud models.

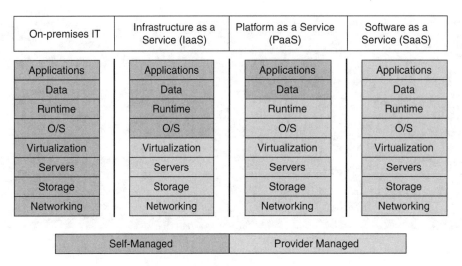

Figure 2-1   *Data Center and Cloud Types*

Many cloud offerings allow consumers to utilize storage, network, and compute resources. The consumer can manage these three components to deploy and run specific applications. This is known as infrastructure as a service (IaaS). Organizations that consume resources from the cloud can outsource the support operation for maintaining the IT infrastructure and the hardware cost and can move toward a "pay-as-you-use" model. Platform as a service (PaaS) abstracts many of the standard application stack–level functions and offers those functions as a service. Developers can leverage the tool sets that are readily available in the cloud and can focus on the application logic rather than worrying about the underlying infrastructure. Software as a service (SaaS) gives consumers the ability to use a hosted software licensing and delivery model, delivering an application as a service for an organization.

IaaS is commonly used to host application resources in the cloud, and it can accommodate multicast requirements. Many enterprise customers are moving toward a hybrid approach of application deployment in the cloud. One example of a hybrid deployment is having the web tier hosted in the cloud, while the application and database tiers are hosted in the customer's on-premises data center. Having the web tier hosted in the cloud provides a cost-effective solution to offer a global service offering, as web applications can be positioned closer to the geographic regions. Cloud applications have ties to the application stack and internal data and require enterprise features such as security, preferred routing, and multicast. Therefore, it is essential to have a thorough understanding of how all these elements interact with one another during the planning, implementation, and migration stages. Many cloud service providers (CSP) do not provide support for multicast. The use of multicast may not be needed for all the enterprise applications, but it is critical for a few that need the support for multicast to function appropriately.

The following sections are dedicated to explaining how multicast is supported in a cloud environment.

Cloud Connectivity to an Enterprise

Connectivity for an enterprise to a cloud service provider can be achieved in three different ways:

- Internet-based connectivity

- Direct connectivity to the cloud provider

- Cloud broker–based connectivity to the cloud provider

With Internet-based connectivity, the enterprise is connected to the cloud service provider via an Internet connection, as shown in Figure 2-2. The enterprise normally uses an encrypted virtual private network (VPN) service to the virtual data center located at the cloud provider. The enterprise customer may leverage the VPN-based service managed by the cloud service provider or a self-managed service.

Figure 2-2 *Internet-Based Connectivity: Hybrid Model*

Direct connectivity to the cloud provider requires the service provider to terminate the virtual circuit (VC) from the enterprise to the service provider (that is, the network service provider [NSP]). The NSP provides network connectivity to access the cloud asset. There is a one-to-one mapping of circuits from each enterprise to the service provider. The direct connectivity concept is illustrated in Figure 2-3.

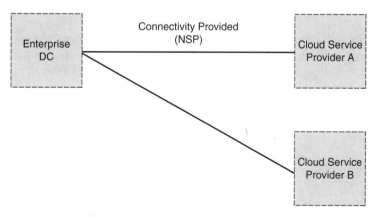

Figure 2-3 *Direct Connectivity to the Cloud Provider*

A new variant of direct connectivity for network service providers is to merge the cloud service provider access with an SP-managed Layer 3 VPN solution that connects branch offices and enterprise data centers. This implementation strategy allows the service provider to tie a VC to a specific customer connection to multiple cloud providers; it is known as cloud broker. Many cloud brokers also provide colocation services to enterprise and cloud service providers. Figure 2-4 illustrates the direct connectivity concept using a cloud broker.

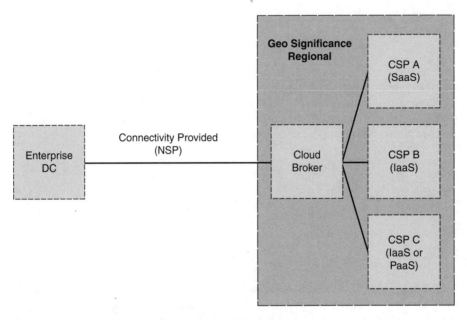

Figure 2-4 *Cloud Broker–Based Connectivity to a CSP*

The cloud broker type of access provides the flexibility of being able to access multiple CSPs from the same connection from the enterprise. The connectivity from the enterprise to the cloud broker is provided by the NSP. Most cloud brokers also provide a carrier-neutral facility (such as colocation services) space and Internet exchange points. Using a cloud broker allows an enterprise to consolidate its pipe to the cloud service provider and also provides access to multiple cloud service providers. Figure 2-5 illustrates a functional description of a cloud broker.

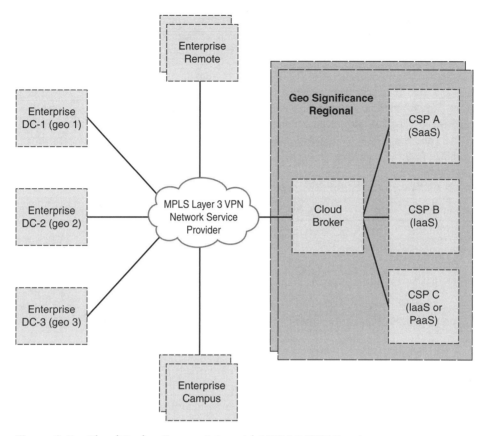

Figure 2-5   *Cloud Broker Connectivity with NSP L3 VPN Service*

Network service providers also offer Layer 3 VPN services to access the cloud broker (for example, AT&T NetBond, Verizon Secure Cloud Interconnect). Without the Layer 3 VPN service, each enterprise data center requires a point-to-point connection with the NSP to the regional cloud broker or must use the IPsec VPN over Internet connectivity model. The Layer 3 VPN service allows an enterprise campus or remote sites to have access to the cloud service provider directly, without transiting the enterprise data center. Localization of enterprise security services for cloud usage is accomplished in the cloud broker's colocation facility.

Virtual Services in a Cloud

Many enterprise architects prefer having control of the services in their tenant space within the cloud infrastructure. The concept of network functions virtualization (NFV) becomes a feasible solution especially when using IaaS cloud service.

NFV involves implementing in software network service elements such as routing, load balancing, VPN services, WAN optimization, and firewalls. Each of these services is referred to as a virtual network function (VNF). The NFV framework stitches together VNFs by using service chaining. In this way, provisioning of the network services can be aligned with service elements. The NFV elements can be automated using the same workflow related to the application services, thus making them easier to manage. These cloud services can then provide a solution for enterprise features to be available in an IaaS infrastructure.

Using a CSR 1000v device as a VNF element provides a customer with a rich set of features in the cloud. The CSR 1000v is an IOS-XE software router based on the ASR 1001. The CSR 1000v runs within a virtual machine, which can be deployed on x86 server hardware. There are a lot of commonalities between the system architecture for the CSR 1000v and the ASR 1000. As shown in Table 2-1, a CSR 1000v provides an enterprise feature footprint in the cloud.

Table 2-1 *Enterprise Feature Footprint Covered by a CSR 1000v*

Technology Package	CSR 1000v Features (Software 3.17 Release)
IP Base (Routing)	Basic networking: BGP, OSPF, EIGRP, RIP, IS-IS, IPv6, GRE, VRF-LITE, NTP, QoS
	Multicast: IGMP, PIM
	High availability: HSRP, VRRP, GLBP
	Addressing: 802.1Q VLAN, EVC, NAT, DHCP, DNS
	Basic security: ACL, AAA, RADIUS, TACACS+
	Management: IOS-XE CLI, SSH, Flexible NetFlow, SNMP, EEM, NETCONF
Security (Routing + Security)	IP Base features plus the following:
	Advanced security: ZBFW, IPsec, VPN, EZVPN, DMVPN, FlexVPN, SSLVPN
APPX/APP	IP Base features plus the following:
	Advanced networking: L2TPv3, BFD, MPLS, VRF, VXLAN
	Application experience: WCCPv2, APPXNAV, NBAR2, AVC, IP SLA
	Hybrid cloud connectivity: LISP, OTV, VPLS, EoMPLS
	Subscriber management: PTA, LNS, ISG
AX (Routing + Security + APPX + Hybrid Cloud)	Security features plus the following:
	Advanced networking: L2TPv3, BFD, MPLS, VRF, VXLAN
	Application experience: WCCPv2, APPXNAV, NBAR2, AVC, IP SLA
	Hybrid cloud connectivity: LISP, OTV, VPLS, EoMPLS
	Subscriber management: PTA, LNS, ISG

Note   Use the Cisco feature navigator tool, at www.cisco.com/go/fn, to see the latest features available with the CSR 1000v.

Service Reflection Feature

Service reflection is a multicast feature that provides a translation service for multicast traffic. It allows you to translate externally received multicast or unicast destination addresses to multicast or unicast addresses. This feature offers the advantage of completely isolating the external multicast source information. The end receivers in the destination network can receive identical feeds from two ingress points in the network. The end host can then subscribe to two different multicast feeds that have identical information. The ability to select a particular multicast stream is dependent on the capability of the host, but provides a solution for highly available multicast.

Use Case 1: Multicast-to-Multicast Destination Conversion

Cisco multicast service reflection runs on Cisco IOS software that processes packets forwarded by Cisco IOS software to the Vif1 interface. The Vif1 interface is similar to a loopback interface; it is a logical IP interface that is always up when the router is active. The Vif1 interface has its own unique subnet, which must be advertised in the routing protocol. The Vif1 interface provides private-to-public mgroup mapping and the source of the translated packet. The Vif1 interface is key to the functionality of service reflections. Unlike IP Multicast Network Address Translation (NAT), which only translates the source IP address, service reflection translates both source and destination addresses. Figure 2-6 illustrates a multicast-to-multicast destination conversion use case.

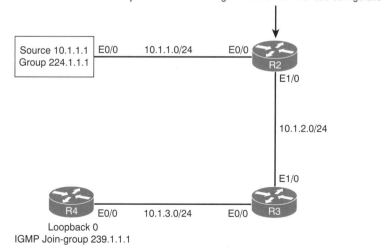

Figure 2-6   *Multicast-to-Multicast Destination Conversion*

Figure 2-6 shows the lab setup for a multicast-to-multicast destination conversion use case. In Figure 2-6, R2 converts the multicast stream from 224.1.1.1 to 239.1.1.1. The virtual interface (VIF) configuration at R2 (for service reflection) has a static Internet Group Management Protocol (IGMP) join for 224.1.1.1 to attract the multicast flow to the VIF (Example 2-1). In converting the stream from 224.1.1.1 to 239.1.1.1, the source for the multicast stream is changed to 10.5.1.2.

Example 2-1   *VIF Configuration at R2*

```
R2# show run interface vif1
Building configuration...


Current configuration : 203 bytes
!
interface Vif1
 ip address 10.5.1.1 255.255.255.0
 ip service reflect Ethernet0/0 destination 224.1.1.1 to 239.1.1.1 mask-len 32
   source 10.5.1.2
 ip pim sparse-mode
 ip igmp static-group 224.1.1.1
end
```

Prior to enabling the multicast source, the output at R4 (with the IGMP join group configuration for 239.1.1.1) is as shown in Example 2-2.

Example 2-2   show ip mroute *Output at R4*

```
R4# show ip mroute
IP Multicast Routing Table
Flags: D - Dense, S - Sparse, B - Bidir Group, s - SSM Group, C - Connected,
       L - Local, P - Pruned, R - RP-bit set, F - Register flag,
       T - SPT-bit set, J - Join SPT, M - MSDP created entry, E - Extranet,
       X - Proxy Join Timer Running, A - Candidate for MSDP Advertisement,
       U - URD, I - Received Source Specific Host Report,
       Z - Multicast Tunnel, z - MDT-data group sender,
       Y - Joined MDT-data group, y - Sending to MDT-data group,
       G - Received BGP C-Mroute, g - Sent BGP C-Mroute,
       N - Received BGP Shared-Tree Prune, n - BGP C-Mroute suppressed,
       Q - Received BGP S-A Route, q - Sent BGP S-A Route,
       V - RD & Vector, v - Vector, p - PIM Joins on route,
       x - VxLAN group
Outgoing interface flags: H - Hardware switched, A - Assert winner, p - PIM Join
 Timers: Uptime/Expires
 Interface state: Interface, Next-Hop or VCD, State/Mode
```

```
(*, 239.1.1.1), 03:04:11/00:02:53, RP 192.168.2.2, flags: SJCL
  Incoming interface: Ethernet0/0, RPF nbr 10.1.3.1
  Outgoing interface list:
    Loopback0, Forward/Sparse, 03:04:10/00:02:53

(*, 224.0.1.40), 03:04:11/00:02:53, RP 192.168.2.2, flags: SJCL
  Incoming interface: Ethernet0/0, RPF nbr 10.1.3.1
  Outgoing interface list:
    Loopback0, Forward/Sparse, 03:04:10/00:02:53
```

There is no (S, G) entry for 239.1.1.1 multicast flow. After multicast has been enabled, traffic is captured between the source and R2 to verify the packet flow, as shown in Example 2-3.

Example 2-3   *Packet Capture of the Multicast Stream Before Conversion*

```
================================================================================
15:52:55.622 PST Thu Jan 5 2017                 Relative Time: 1.697999
Packet 17 of 148                                In: Ethernet0/0

Ethernet Packet:  298 bytes
      Dest Addr: 0100.5E01.0101,   Source Addr: AABB.CC00.0100
      Protocol: 0x0800

IP    Version: 0x4,  HdrLen: 0x5,  TOS: 0x00
      Length: 284,   ID: 0x0000,   Flags-Offset: 0x0000
      TTL: 60,   Protocol: 17 (UDP),   Checksum: 0xE4A8 (OK)
      Source: 10.1.1.1,      Dest: 224.1.1.1

UDP   Src Port: 0 (Reserved),   Dest Port: 0 (Reserved)
      Length: 264,   Checksum: 0x64B5 (OK)

Data:
Output removed for brevity…
```

By using the **show ip mroute** command output at R2, the 224.1.1.1 stream is converted with service reflection to 239.1.1.1, and the incoming interface (IIF) for 239.1.1.1 is the VIF, as shown in Example 2-4.

Example 2-4   show ip mroute *at R2*

```
R2# show ip mroute
IP Multicast Routing Table
Flags: D - Dense, S - Sparse, B - Bidir Group, s - SSM Group, C - Connected,
       L - Local, P - Pruned, R - RP-bit set, F - Register flag,
       T - SPT-bit set, J - Join SPT, M - MSDP created entry, E - Extranet,
       X - Proxy Join Timer Running, A - Candidate for MSDP Advertisement,
       U - URD, I - Received Source Specific Host Report,
       Z - Multicast Tunnel, z - MDT-data group sender,
       Y - Joined MDT-data group, y - Sending to MDT-data group,
       G - Received BGP C-Mroute, g - Sent BGP C-Mroute,
       N - Received BGP Shared-Tree Prune, n - BGP C-Mroute suppressed,
       Q - Received BGP S-A Route, q - Sent BGP S-A Route,
       V - RD & Vector, v - Vector, p - PIM Joins on route,
       x - VxLAN group
Outgoing interface flags: H - Hardware switched, A - Assert winner, p - PIM Join
 Timers: Uptime/Expires
 Interface state: Interface, Next-Hop or VCD, State/Mode

(*, 239.1.1.1), 02:53:55/stopped, RP 192.168.1.1, flags: SF
  Incoming interface: Ethernet0/0, RPF nbr 10.1.1.1
  Outgoing interface list:
    Ethernet1/0, Forward/Sparse, 02:53:36/00:03:05

(10.5.1.2, 239.1.1.1), 00:00:07/00:02:52, flags: FT
  Incoming interface: Vif1, RPF nbr 0.0.0.0, flags: FT
  Outgoing interface list:
    Ethernet1/0, Forward/Sparse, 00:00:07/00:03:22

(*, 224.1.1.1), 02:47:27/stopped, RP 192.168.2.2, flags: SJCF
  Incoming interface: Ethernet0/0, RPF nbr 10.1.1.1
  Outgoing interface list:
    Vif1, Forward/Sparse, 02:47:27/00:02:47


(10.1.1.1, 224.1.1.1), 00:00:47/00:02:12, flags: FT
  Incoming interface: Ethernet0/0, RPF nbr 10.1.1.1
  Outgoing interface list:
    Vif1, Forward/Sparse, 00:00:47/00:02:12


(*, 224.0.1.40), 02:54:26/00:03:09, RP 192.168.2.2, flags: SJCL
  Incoming interface: Ethernet0/0, RPF nbr 10.1.1.1
  Outgoing interface list:
    Ethernet1/0, Forward/Sparse, 02:53:41/00:03:09
    Loopback0, Forward/Sparse, 02:54:25/00:02:39
```

The output clearly shows R2 receiving the flow 224.1.1.1, and the new stream for 239.1.1.1 is sourced from 10.5.1.2, the VIF interface (that is, the service reflection interface address local to R2).

At R4, the (S, G) route value for 239.1.1.1 is seen with source IP address 10.5.1.2, as shown in Example 2-5.

Example 2-5   show ip mroute *at R4*

```
R4# show ip mroute
IP Multicast Routing Table
Flags: D - Dense, S - Sparse, B - Bidir Group, s - SSM Group, C - Connected,
       L - Local, P - Pruned, R - RP-bit set, F - Register flag,
       T - SPT-bit set, 'J - Join SPT, M - MSDP created entry, E - Extranet,
       X - Proxy Join Timer Running, A - Candidate for MSDP Advertisement,
       U - URD, I - Received Source Specific Host Report,
       Z - Multicast Tunnel, z - MDT-data group sender,
       Y - Joined MDT-data group, y - Sending to MDT-data group,
       G - Received BGP C-Mroute, g - Sent BGP C-Mroute,
       N - Received BGP Shared-Tree Prune, n - BGP C-Mroute suppressed,
       Q - Received BGP S-A Route, q - Sent BGP S-A Route,
       V - RD & Vector, v - Vector, p - PIM Joins on route,
       x - VxLAN group
Outgoing interface flags: H - Hardware switched, A - Assert winner, p - PIM Join
 Timers: Uptime/Expires
 Interface state: Interface, Next-Hop or VCD, State/Mode

(*, 239.1.1.1), 03:08:06/stopped, RP 192.168.2.2, flags: SJCL
  Incoming interface: Ethernet0/0, RPF nbr 10.1.3.1
  Outgoing interface list:
    Loopback0, Forward/Sparse, 03:08:05/00:01:59

(10.5.1.2, 239.1.1.1), 00:00:17/00:02:42, flags: LJT
  Incoming interface: Ethernet0/0, RPF nbr 10.1.3.1
  Outgoing interface list:
    Loopback0, Forward/Sparse, 00:00:17/00:02:42
```

Use Case 2: Unicast-to-Multicast Destination Conversion

Figure 2-7 shows an example of a unicast-to-multicast conversation use case.

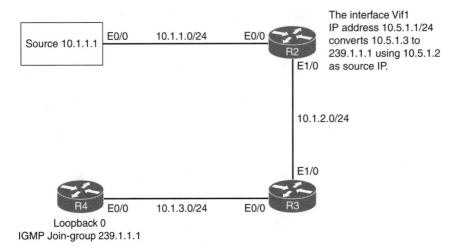

Figure 2-7   *Unicast-to-Multicast Destination Conversion*

Example 2-6 shows the unicast flow 10.5.1.3 converted to multicast flow 239.1.1.1 at R2. The VIF interface configuration at R2 (for service reflection) with the same subnet as 10.5.1.x redirects the packet to the VIF interface. At the VIF interface, 10.5.1.3 is converted to 239.1.1.1 and sourced from 10.5.1.2.

Example 2-6   show interface vif1 *at R2*

```
R2# show run int vif1
Building configuration...


Current configuration : 203 bytes
!
interface Vif1
 ip address 10.5.1.1 255.255.255.0
 ip service reflect Ethernet0/0 destination 10.5.1.3 to 239.1.1.1 mask-len 32
   source 10.5.1.2
 ip pim sparse-mode
end
```

Prior to enabling the multicast source, you need to use the IGMP join group configuration for 239.1.1.1 to ensure that R4 has no (S, G) for 239.1.1.1 by using **show ip mroute** (see Example 2-7).

Example 2-7   show ip mroute *at R4*

```
R4# show ip mroute
IP Multicast Routing Table
Flags: D - Dense, S - Sparse, B - Bidir Group, s - SSM Group, C - Connected,
       L - Local, P - Pruned, R - RP-bit set, F - Register flag,
```

```
        T - SPT-bit set, J - Join SPT, M - MSDP created entry, E - Extranet,
        X - Proxy Join Timer Running, A - Candidate for MSDP Advertisement,
        U - URD, I - Received Source Specific Host Report,
        Z - Multicast Tunnel, z - MDT-data group sender,
        Y - Joined MDT-data group, y - Sending to MDT-data group,
        G - Received BGP C-Mroute, g - Sent BGP C-Mroute,
        N - Received BGP Shared-Tree Prune, n - BGP C-Mroute suppressed,
        Q - Received BGP S-A Route, q - Sent BGP S-A Route,
        V - RD & Vector, v - Vector, p - PIM Joins on route,
        x - VxLAN group
Outgoing interface flags: H - Hardware switched, A - Assert winner, p - PIM Join
 Timers: Uptime/Expires
 Interface state: Interface, Next-Hop or VCD, State/Mode

 (*, 239.1.1.1), 00:00:02/00:02:57, RP 192.168.2.2, flags: SJCL
   Incoming interface: Ethernet0/0, RPF nbr 10.1.3.1
   Outgoing interface list:
     Loopback0, Forward/Sparse, 00:00:02/00:02:57

 (*, 224.0.1.40), 00:00:02/00:02:57, RP 192.168.2.2, flags: SJCL
   Incoming interface: Ethernet0/0, RPF nbr 10.1.3.1
   Outgoing interface list:
     Loopback0, Forward/Sparse, 00:00:02/00:02:57
```

There is no (S, G) entry for the multicast flow of 239.1.1.1 at R4.

Next, you enable the unicast stream from 10.1.1.1 and check the sniffer between the source (10.1.1.1) and R2, as shown in Example 2-8. The unicast stream is generated via an Internet Control Message Protocol (ICMP) ping.

Example 2-8   *Sniffer Capture of the Unicast Stream Before Conversion*

```
===============================================================================
22:38:22.425 PST Thu Jan 5 2017                    Relative Time: 27.684999
Packet 31 of 76                                    In: Ethernet0/0

Ethernet Packet:  114 bytes
      Dest Addr: AABB.CC00.0200,   Source Addr: AABB.CC00.0100
      Protocol: 0x0800

IP    Version: 0x4,  HdrLen: 0x5,  TOS: 0x00
      Length: 100,   ID: 0x0024,  Flags-Offset: 0x0000
      TTL: 255,   Protocol: 1 (ICMP),   Checksum: 0xA56B (OK)
      Source: 10.1.1.1,     Dest: 10.5.1.3
```

```
ICMP   Type: 8,    Code: 0   (Echo Request)
        Checksum: 0x6D42 (OK)
        Identifier: 000C,   Sequence: 0003
Echo Data:
    0 : 0000 0000 0177 0F82 ABCD ABCD ABCD ABCD ABCD ABCD    ..................
   20 : ABCD ABCD ABCD ABCD ABCD ABCD ABCD ABCD ABCD ABCD    ..................
   40 : ABCD ABCD ABCD ABCD ABCD ABCD ABCD ABCD ABCD ABCD    ..................
   60 : ABCD ABCD ABCD ABCD ABCD ABCD                        ............
```

The **show ip mroute** command output at R2 shows that the 239.1.1.1 source entry with
IIF has the Vif1 interface. The VIF interface converts the 10.1.1.1 unicast stream into a
multicast stream with group address 239.1.1.1, as shown in Example 2-9.

Example 2-9   show ip mroute *at R2*

```
R2# show ip mroute
IP Multicast Routing Table
Flags: D - Dense, S - Sparse, B - Bidir Group, s - SSM Group, C - Connected,
       L - Local, P - Pruned, R - RP-bit set, F - Register flag,
       T - SPT-bit set, J - Join SPT, M - MSDP created entry, E - Extranet,
       X - Proxy Join Timer Running, A - Candidate for MSDP Advertisement,
       U - URD, I - Received Source Specific Host Report,
       Z - Multicast Tunnel, z - MDT-data group sender,
       Y - Joined MDT-data group, y - Sending to MDT-data group,
       G - Received BGP C-Mroute, g - Sent BGP C-Mroute,
       N - Received BGP Shared-Tree Prune, n - BGP C-Mroute suppressed,
       Q - Received BGP S-A Route, q - Sent BGP S-A Route,
       V - RD & Vector, v - Vector, p - PIM Joins on route,
       x - VxLAN group
Outgoing interface flags: H - Hardware switched, A - Assert winner, p - PIM Join
 Timers: Uptime/Expires
 Interface state: Interface, Next-Hop or VCD, State/Mode

(*, 239.1.1.1), 06:51:31/00:03:26, RP 192.168.2.2, flags: SF
  Incoming interface: Ethernet0/0, RPF nbr 10.1.1.1
  Outgoing interface list:
    Ethernet1/0, Forward/Sparse, 06:51:12/00:03:26


(10.5.1.2, 239.1.1.1), 00:02:35/00:00:58, flags: FT
  Incoming interface: Vif1, RPF nbr 0.0.0.0
  Outgoing interface list:
    Ethernet1/0, Forward/Sparse, 00:02:35/00:03:26
```

The unicast stream destined to 10.5.1.3 is converted into multicast 239.1.1.1 and sourced from the 10.5.1.2 VIF (that is, the service reflection interface address local to R2). The incoming interface is the Vif1 that is generating this translation, and the outgoing interface is toward the downstream receiver Ethernet1/0.

At R4, now the (S, G) route value for 239.1.1.1 has source IP address 10.5.1.2, as shown in Example 2-10.

Example 2-10   show ip mroute *at R4*

```
R4# show ip mroute 239.1.1.1
IP Multicast Routing Table
Flags: D - Dense, S - Sparse, B - Bidir Group, s - SSM Group, C - Connected,
       L - Local, P - Pruned, R - RP-bit set, F - Register flag,
       T - SPT-bit set, J - Join SPT, M - MSDP created entry, E - Extranet,
       X - Proxy Join Timer Running, A - Candidate for MSDP Advertisement,
       U - URD, I - Received Source Specific Host Report,
       Z - Multicast Tunnel, z - MDT-data group sender,
       Y - Joined MDT-data group, y - Sending to MDT-data group,
       G - Received BGP C-Mroute, g - Sent BGP C-Mroute,
       N - Received BGP Shared-Tree Prune, n - BGP C-Mroute suppressed,
       Q - Received BGP S-A Route, q - Sent BGP S-A Route,
       V - RD & Vector, v - Vector, p - PIM Joins on route,
       x - VxLAN group
Outgoing interface flags: H - Hardware switched, A - Assert winner, p - PIM Join
 Timers: Uptime/Expires
 Interface state: Interface, Next-Hop or VCD, State/Mode

(*, 239.1.1.1), 00:01:54/stopped, RP 192.168.2.2, flags: SJCL
  Incoming interface: Ethernet0/0, RPF nbr 10.1.3.1
  Outgoing interface list:
    Loopback0, Forward/Sparse, 00:01:54/00:02:09

(10.5.1.2, 239.1.1.1), 00:00:52/00:02:07, flags: LJT
  Incoming interface: Ethernet0/0, RPF nbr 10.1.3.1
  Outgoing interface list:
    Loopback0, Forward/Sparse, 00:00:52/00:02:09
```

Use Case 3: Multicast-to-Unicast Destination Conversion

Figure 2-8 illustrates the topology for a multicast-to-unicast conversion.

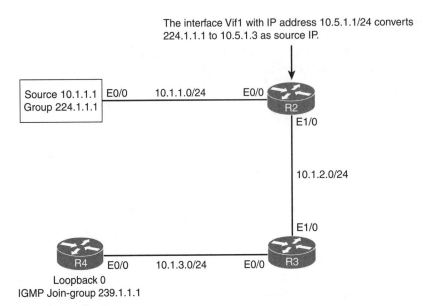

Figure 2-8 *Multicast-to-Unicast Destination Conversion*

Example 2-11 converts the multicast flow of 224.1.1.1 to a unicast flow from 10.1.3.2 at R2. The VIF interface configuration at R2 (for service reflection) has a static join for 224.1.1.1 on the VIF interface, and the multicast packets for 224.1.1.1 are converted into a unicast UDP stream sourced from 10.5.1.2, with destination 10.1.3.2 (the Ethernet0/0 interface of R4).

Example 2-11 show int vif1 *at R2*

```
R2# show run int vif1
Building configuration...


Current configuration : 203 bytes
!
interface Vif1
 ip address 10.5.1.1 255.255.255.0
 ip service reflect Ethernet0/0 destination 224.1.1.1 to 10.1.3.2 mask-len 32 source
  10.5.1.2
 ip pim sparse-mode
 ip igmp static-group 224.1.1.1
```

In Example 2-12, the packet capture between source and R2 shows the multicast flow for 224.1.1.1 sourced from 10.1.1.1.

Example 2-12   *Sniffer Capture Before the Conversion*

```
==============================================================================
22:49:43.470 PST Thu Jan 5 2017              Relative Time: 11:48.729999
Packet 1534 of 4447                          In: Ethernet0/0

Ethernet Packet:  298 bytes
      Dest Addr: 0100.5E01.0101,    Source Addr: AABB.CC00.0100
      Protocol: 0x0800

IP    Version: 0x4,  HdrLen: 0x5,  TOS: 0x00
      Length: 284,   ID: 0x0000,   Flags-Offset: 0x0000
      TTL: 60,   Protocol: 17 (UDP),   Checksum: 0xE4A8 (OK)
      Source: 10.1.1.1,    Dest: 224.1.1.1

UDP   Src Port: 0 (Reserved),   Dest Port: 0 (Reserved)
      Length: 264,   Checksum: 0x64B5 (OK)

Data:
    0 : 0000 0000 0000 0000 0000 0000 0000 0000 0000 0000   ...................
   20 : 0000 0000 0000 0000 0000 0000 0000 0000 0000 0000   ...................
   40 : 0000 0000 0000 0000 0000 0000 0000 0000 0000 0000   ...................
   60 : 0000 0000 0000 0000 0000 0000 0000 0000 0000 0000   ...................
   80 : 0000 0000 0000 0000 0000 0000 0000 0000 0000 0000   ...................
  100 : 0000 0000 0000 0000 0000 0000 0000 0000 0000 0000   ...................
  120 : 0000 0000 0000 0000 0000 0000 0000 0000 0000 0000   ...................
  140 : 0000 0000 0000 0000 0000 0000 0000 0000 0000 0000   ...................
  160 : 0000 0000 0000 0000 0000 0000 0000 0000 0000 0000   ...................
  180 : 0000 0000 0000 0000 0000 0000 0000 0000 0000 0000   ...................
  200 : 0000 0000 0000 0000 0000 0000 0000 0000 0000 0000   ...................
  220 : 0000 0000 0000 0000 0000 0000 0000 0000 0000 0000   ...................
  240 : 0000 0000 0000 0000 0000 0000 0000 0000            ...............
```

In Example 2-13, the current multicast state at R2 shows the (*, G) and (S, G) entries for the 224.1.1.1 multicast group.

Example 2-13   show ip mroute *at R2*

```
R2# show ip mroute
IP Multicast Routing Table
Flags: D - Dense, S - Sparse, B - Bidir Group, s - SSM Group, C - Connected,
       L - Local, P - Pruned, R - RP-bit set, F - Register flag,
       T - SPT-bit set, J - Join SPT, M - MSDP created entry, E - Extranet,
       X - Proxy Join Timer Running, A - Candidate for MSDP Advertisement,
       U - URD, I - Received Source Specific Host Report,
```

```
           Z - Multicast Tunnel, z - MDT-data group sender,
           Y - Joined MDT-data group, y - Sending to MDT-data group,
           G - Received BGP C-Mroute, g - Sent BGP C-Mroute,
           N - Received BGP Shared-Tree Prune, n - BGP C-Mroute suppressed,
           Q - Received BGP S-A Route, q - Sent BGP S-A Route,
           V - RD & Vector, v - Vector, p - PIM Joins on route,
           x - VxLAN group
Outgoing interface flags: H - Hardware switched, A - Assert winner, p - PIM Join
 Timers: Uptime/Expires
 Interface state: Interface, Next-Hop or VCD, State/Mode

(*, 224.1.1.1), 07:02:08/stopped, RP 192.168.1.1, flags: SJCF
  Incoming interface: Ethernet0/0, RPF nbr 10.1.1.1
  Outgoing interface list:
    Vif1, Forward/Sparse, 07:02:08/00:00:06

(10.1.1.1, 224.1.1.1), 00:10:15/00:02:44, flags: FTJ
  Incoming interface: Ethernet0/0, RPF nbr 10.1.1.1
  Outgoing interface list:
    Vif1, Forward/Sparse, 00:10:15/00:01:44
```

In Example 2-14, a packet capture between R3 and R4 shows the unicast stream UDP sourced from 10.5.1.2 and destination 10.1.3.2 (R4 Ethernet0/0 interface).

Example 2-14   *Sniffer Output After the Conversion*

```
================================================================================
22:55:11.710 PST Thu Jan 5 2017            Relative Time: 1.945999
Packet 23 of 262                           In: Ethernet0/0


Ethernet Packet:  298 bytes
        Dest Addr: AABB.CC00.0301,   Source Addr: AABB.CC00.0201
        Protocol: 0x0800


IP     Version: 0x4,  HdrLen: 0x5,  TOS: 0x00
       Length: 284,   ID: 0x0000,   Flags-Offset: 0x0000
       TTL: 58,   Protocol: 17 (UDP),   Checksum: 0x67C8 (OK)
       Source: 10.5.1.2,      Dest: 10.1.3.2


UDP    Src Port: 0 (Reserved),   Dest Port: 0 (Reserved)
       Length: 264,   Checksum: 0xE5D4 (OK)


Data:
    0 : 0000 0000 0000 0000 0000 0000 0000 0000 0000 0000   ...................
   20 : 0000 0000 0000 0000 0000 0000 0000 0000 0000 0000   ...................
```

```
 40 : 0000 0000 0000 0000 0000 0000 0000 0000 0000 0000   ...................
 60 : 0000 0000 0000 0000 0000 0000 0000 0000 0000 0000   ...................
 80 : 0000 0000 0000 0000 0000 0000 0000 0000 0000 0000   ...................
100 : 0000 0000 0000 0000 0000 0000 0000 0000 0000 0000   ...................
120 : 0000 0000 0000 0000 0000 0000 0000 0000 0000 0000   ...................
140 : 0000 0000 0000 0000 0000 0000 0000 0000 0000 0000   ...................
160 : 0000 0000 0000 0000 0000 0000 0000 0000 0000 0000   ...................
180 : 0000 0000 0000 0000 0000 0000 0000 0000 0000 0000   ...................
200 : 0000 0000 0000 0000 0000 0000 0000 0000 0000 0000   ...................
220 : 0000 0000 0000 0000 0000 0000 0000 0000 0000 0000   ...................
240 : 0000 0000 0000 0000 0000 0000 0000 0000            ................
```

Multicast Traffic Engineering

IP Multicast, Volume 1, Chapter 5, "IP Multicast Design Considerations and Implementation," provides a good overview of various methods of multicast traffic engineering, including the following:

- Multipath feature

- **ip mroute** statements or MBGP for multicast path selections

- Multicast via tunnels

Table 2-2 presents a summary of these features.

Table 2-2   *Multicast Features for Traffic Engineering*

Feature	Usage
Multipath feature	Say that multiple unicast paths exist between two routers, and the administrator wants to load-split the multicast traffic. (The default behavior of RPF is to choose the highest IP address as next hop for all the (S, G) flow entries.) Configuring load splitting with the **ip multicast multipath** command causes the system to load-split multicast traffic across multiple equal-cost paths based on the source address, using the S-hash algorithm. This feature load-splits the traffic and does not load-balance the traffic. Based on the S-hash algorithm, the multicast stream from a source uses only one path. The PIM joins are distributed over the different equal-cost multipath (ECMP) links based on a hash of the source address. This enables streams to be divided across different network paths. The S-hash method is used to achieve a diverse path for multicast data flow that is split between two multicast groups to achieve redundancy in transport of the real-time packets. The redundant flow for the same data stream is achieved using an intelligent application that encapsulates the same data in two separate multicast streams.

Feature	Usage
ip mroute statements or MBGP for multicast path selections	Say that two equal-cost paths exist between two routers, and the administrator wishes to force the multicast traffic through one path. The administrator can use a static **ip mroute** statement to force the Reverse Path Forwarding (RPF) check through an interface of choice.
	In a large network with redundant links, to achieve the separation of the multicast traffic from the unicast, a dynamic way is more desirable. This is achieved by using the Border Gateway Protocol (BGP) multicast address family. With BGP address families, the multicast network needs to be advertised, and the next-hop prefix needs to be resolved via a recursive lookup in the Interior Gateway Protocol (IGP) to find the upstream RPF interface.
Multicast via tunnels	Multicast support using a tunnel overlay infrastructure can be used to add a non-enterprise-controlled network segment that does not support multicast.

Multicast within the tunnel infrastructure is a key feature in current cloud deployments to support multicast features over non-enterprise segments. Multicast across point-to-point GRE tunnels is simple, and the only consideration is the RPF interface. The selection for the MRIB interface should be the tunnel interface. The other overlay solution is Dynamic Multipoint VPN (DMVPN).

DMVPN is a Cisco IOS software solution for building scalable IPsec VPNs. DMVPN uses a centralized architecture to provide easier implementation and management for deployments that require granular access controls for diverse user communities, including mobile workers, telecommuters, and extranet users. The use of multipoint generic routing encapsulation (mGRE) tunnels with Next Hop Resolution Protocol (NHRP) creates an overlay solution that can be used for adding various features such as encryption, policy-based routing (PBR), and quality of service (QoS). The use of the NHRP feature with mGRE allows for direct spoke-to-spoke communication, which is useful for voice over IP traffic or any other communication except multicast. With the DMVPN overlay solution, the multicast communication must pass through the hub, which manages replication for the spokes. The replication at the hub is a design consideration that needs to be contemplated for multicast designs on an overlay network. For example, if the multicast stream needs to be transmitted to 100 spokes and the stream size is 200MB, the collective multicast stream after replication is 200MB × 100 spokes, which is 2GB. In this case, the outbound WAN link needs to accommodate 2GB multicast, and the platform at the hub should be able to replicate those multicast flows. The WAN link also needs to accommodate the replicated multicast stream, and this should be considered during the capacity planning stage. Figure 2-9 illustrates the considerations.

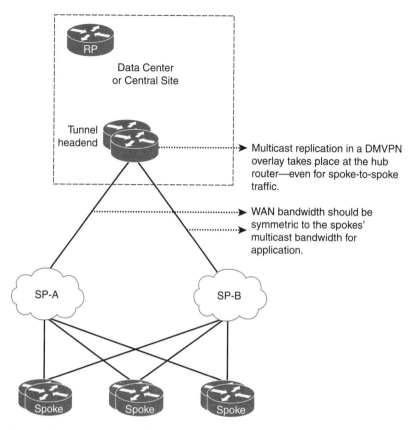

Figure 2-9   *Overview of DMVPN Multicast Considerations*

To spread the load of multicast replication at the hub routers, the design could involve multiple tunnel headend routers that take care of specific spoke routers. They would be tied to the replication processing of the platform, based on the number of spokes. This model can be used for dual hub sites.

Figure 2-10 shows a global deployment of an overlay solution where the customer wants to leverage local carrier-neutral facilities and host multicast services at the regional locations. The customer also wants the flexibility of host spoke-to-spoke tunnels across the different regions, which requires a regional solution with multicast tied to the global multicast solution.

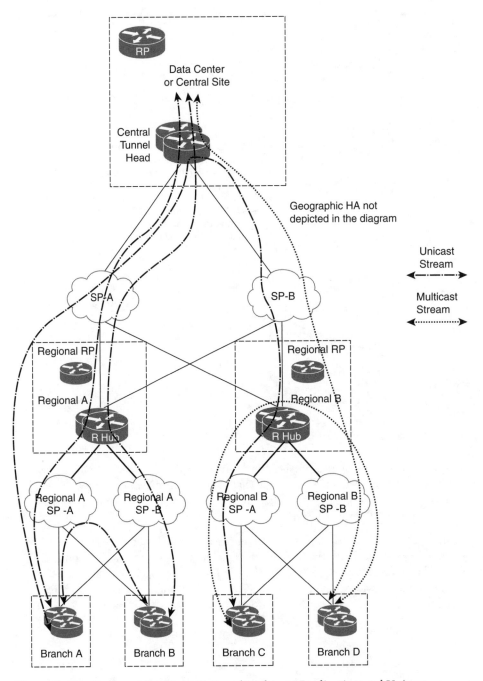

Figure 2-10 *Design to Facilitate Regional Multicast Replication and Unicast Interregional Direct Communication*

The expected communication in this scenario includes the following:

- Unicast (applicable to all branches in the region):

    - Branch A can communicate directly to Branch B (direct spoke-to-spoke communication within the region)

    - Branch A can communicate directly to Branch C without going through the hub (direct spoke-to-spoke interregional communication)

    - Branch A can directly communicate with the hub (regional spoke communication with the central data center connected to the hub)

- Multicast (applicable to all branches in the region):

    - Branch C can send or receive multicast (region-specific multicast) to Branch D (localized replication at a regional hub)

    - Branches A and C can send or receive multicast but must traverse through the central hub and can be part of the global multicast (interregional multicast communication via the DMVPN hub)

    - Branches A, B, C, and D can receive global multicast from the hub (with a data center connected to the global hub then to a regional hub for multicast communication)

Figure 2-11 provides a configuration example of this DMVPN's overlay design.

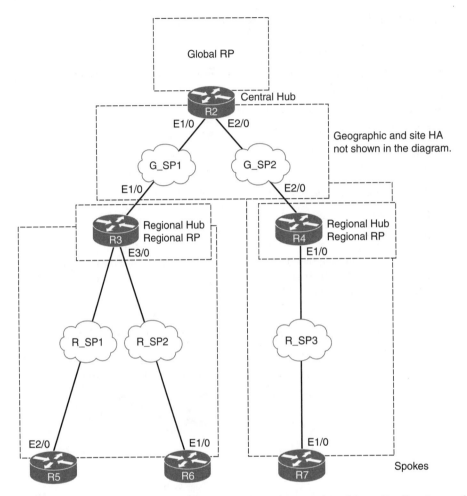

Figure 2-11 *Lab Topology Design to Facilitate Regional Multicast Replication and Unicast Spoke-to-Spoke Communication*

Highlights of the design include the following:

- R2 is the hub for the single NHRP domain (Domain 1). High availability (HA) to R2 is not shown in the topology.

- R3 and R4 are part of the NHRP domain (Domain 1) for Region A and Region B, respectively. HA for the regional hub is not shown.

- The regional hub in the same NHRP domain has two tunnel connections: one toward the central hub (R2) and the other toward the spoke. The loopback sourcing this tunnel should be separate for each tunnel. This is important and provides the regional capability of replicating multicast streams.

- The rendezvous points (RPs) at the central hub represent the global RP and at the regional hubs represent regional RPs.

■ The routing protocol and RP design should be aligned to general best practices not covered in these configurations.

Example 2-15 illustrates the configuration of DMVPN with multicast at hub R2.

Example 2-15 *Configuration Snapshot from Hub R2*

```
interface Loopback0
 ip address 192.168.2.2 255.255.255.255
!
interface Loopback100
 ip address 10.0.100.100 255.255.255.255
 ip pim sparse-mode
!
interface Tunnel1
bandwidth 1000
 ip address 10.0.0.1 255.255.255.0
 no ip redirects
 ip mtu 1400
 no ip split-horizon eigrp 1
 ip pim nbma-mode
 ip pim sparse-mode
 ip nhrp map multicast dynamic
 ip nhrp network-id 1
 ip nhrp holdtime 360
 ip nhrp shortcut
 ip nhrp redirect
 tunnel source Loopback0
 tunnel mode gre multipoint
 tunnel key 1
 hold-queue 4096 in
 hold-queue 4096 out
!
ip pim rp-address 10.0.100.100 2
!
!
!
access-list 2 permit 239.1.1.1
```

Note The configuration does not include crypto or routing configurations.

Example 2-16 gives the configuration for DMVPN with multicast at the regional hub R3.

Example 2-16   *Configuration Snapshot of Regional Hub R3*

```
interface Loopback0
 ip address 192.168.3.3 255.255.255.255
!
interface Loopback1
 ip address 192.168.3.33 255.255.255.255
 ip pim sparse-mode
!
interface Loopback100
 ip address 10.0.100.103 255.255.255.255
 ip pim sparse-mode
!
interface Tunnel1
bandwidth 1000
 ip address 10.0.0.3 255.255.255.0
 no ip redirects
 ip mtu 1400
 ip pim sparse-mode
 ip nhrp map 10.0.0.1 192.168.2.2
 ip nhrp map multicast 192.168.2.2
 ip nhrp network-id 1
 ip nhrp nhs 10.0.0.1
 ip nhrp shortcut
 tunnel source Loopback0
 tunnel mode gre multipoint
 tunnel key 1
 hold-queue 4096 in
 hold-queue 4096 out
!
interface Tunnel3
 bandwidth 1000
 ip address 10.0.1.3 255.255.255.0
 no ip redirects
 ip mtu 1400
 no ip split-horizon eigrp 1
 ip pim nbma-mode
 ip pim sparse-mode
 ip nhrp map multicast dynamic
 ip nhrp network-id 1
 ip nhrp holdtime 360
 ip nhrp shortcut
 ip nhrp redirect
 tunnel source Loopback1
```

```
 tunnel mode gre multipoint
 tunnel key 1
 hold-queue 4096 in
 hold-queue 4096 out
!
ip pim rp-address 10.0.100.103 1
ip pim rp-address 10.0.100.100 2
!
!
!
access-list 1 permit 239.192.0.0 0.0.255.255
access-list 2 permit 239.1.1.1
```

As highlighted in Example 2-17, the regional spoke has two DMVPN tunnel domains sourced from two separate loopbacks (loopbacks 0 and 1). The NHRP and tunnel key for both the DMVPN tunnels have the same ID. This is an important configuration that creates multicast local replication for regional multicast traffic and keeps the unicast traffic spoke to spoke (interregional or intra-regional).

The DMVPN with multicast configuration at the regional spoke R6 is shown in Example 2-17.

Example 2-17 *Configuration Snapshot of Regional Spoke R6*

```
interface Loopback0
 ip address 192.168.6.6 255.255.255.255
!
interface Loopback100
 ip address 10.0.100.102 255.255.255.255
 ip pim sparse-mode
 ip igmp join-group 239.192.1.1
!
interface Tunnel3
 bandwidth 1000
 ip address 10.0.1.6 255.255.255.0
 no ip redirects
 ip mtu 1400
 ip pim sparse-mode
 ip nhrp network-id 1
 ip nhrp nhs 10.0.1.3 nbma 192.168.3.33 multicast
 ip nhrp shortcut
 tunnel source Loopback0
 tunnel mode gre multipoint
```

```
tunnel key 1
 hold-queue 4096 in
 hold-queue 4096 out
!
ip pim rp-address 10.0.100.103 1
ip pim rp-address 10.0.100.100 2
!
!
!
access-list 1 permit 239.192.0.0 0.0.255.255
access-list 2 permit 239.1.1.1
```

Unicast Spoke-to-Spoke Intra-regional Communication

To show unicast spoke-to-spoke intra-regional communication, this section reviews the NHRP configuration at the regional hub. The NHRP mapping shows regional hub 10.0.1.3. (10.0.1.3 is the tunnel IP address at R3 and is the next-hop server.) Example 2-18 uses the **show ip nhrp** command on R5 to reveal the spoke-to-spoke communication stats.

Example 2-18   show ip nhrp *on R5*

```
R5# show ip nhrp
10.0.1.3/32 via 10.0.1.3
    Tunnel3 created 3d09h, never expire
    Type: static, Flags: used
    NBMA address: 192.168.3.33
```

To create the tunnel, as shown in Example 2-19, ping R6 (IP loopback 100 10.0.100.102) from R5 to verify that a dynamic tunnel is created for the unicast flow between R5 and R6.

Example 2-19   ping *from R5 to R6*

```
R5# ping 10.0.100.102 source lo100
Type escape sequence to abort.
Sending 5, 100-byte ICMP Echos to 10.0.100.102, timeout is 2 seconds:
Packet sent with a source address of 10.0.100.101
!!!!!
Success rate is 100 percent (5/5), round-trip min/avg/max = 1/1/1 ms
```

The highlighted part of Example 2-20 shows the creation of the dynamic tunnel between the R5 and R6 spokes for unicast communication within the region. The IP address 10.0.1.6 is the interface for R6, and the route entry 10.0.100.102/32 points to this interface.

The transport for the data path shows a creation of dynamic tunnel DT1 to 192.168.6.6 (the loopback address of R6) through tunnel interface 10.0.1.6 at R6. This dynamic tunnel creation is a result of spoke-to-spoke communication within the region. Issuing the **show ip nhrp** command again reveals the change in the next-hop route, as shown on R5 in Example 2-20.

Example 2-20 *Issuing* **show ip nhrp** *on R5 Again*

```
R5# show ip nhrp
10.0.1.3/32 via 10.0.1.3
   Tunnel3 created 3d09h, never expire
   Type: static, Flags: used
   NBMA address: 192.168.3.33
10.0.1.6/32 via 10.0.1.6
   Tunnel3 created 00:00:04, expire 01:59:55
   Type: dynamic, Flags: router used nhop rib
   NBMA address: 192.168.6.6
10.0.100.101/32 via 10.0.1.5
   Tunnel3 created 00:00:04, expire 01:59:55
   Type: dynamic, Flags: router unique local
   NBMA address: 192.168.5.5
     (no-socket)
10.0.100.102/32 via 10.0.1.6
   Tunnel3 created 00:00:04, expire 01:59:55
   Type: dynamic, Flags: router rib nho
   NBMA address: 192.168.6.6
R5# show dmvpn
Legend: Attrb --> S - Static, D - Dynamic, I - Incomplete
        N - NATed, L - Local, X - No Socket
        T1 - Route Installed, T2 - Nexthop-override
        C - CTS Capable
        # Ent --> Number of NHRP entries with same NBMA peer
        NHS Status: E --> Expecting Replies, R --> Responding, W --> Waiting
        UpDn Time --> Up or Down Time for a Tunnel
==========================================================================
Interface: Tunnel3, IPv4 NHRP Details
Type:Spoke, NHRP Peers:2,
 # Ent  Peer NBMA Addr Peer Tunnel Add State  UpDn Tm Attrb
 ----- -------------- --------------- ----- -------- -----
     1 192.168.3.33         10.0.1.3   UP    3d07h     S
     2 192.168.6.6          10.0.1.6   UP 00:00:09   DT1
                            10.0.1.6   UP 00:00:09   DT2
```

Unicast Spoke-to-Spoke Interregional Communication

In Example 2-21, R7 (located in another region) initiates a ping to R5 (where loopback 100 at R5 is 10.0.100.101). Observe the dynamic tunnel created for spoke-to-spoke communication.

Example 2-21   *Dynamic Tunnel Creation on R7*

```
R7# ping 10.0.100.101 source lo100
Type escape sequence to abort.
Sending 5, 100-byte ICMP Echos to 10.0.100.101, timeout is 2 seconds:
Packet sent with a source address of 10.2.100.102
!!!!!
Success rate is 100 percent (5/5), round-trip min/avg/max = 1/1/1 ms


R7# show dmvpn
Legend: Attrb --> S - Static, D - Dynamic, I - Incomplete
        N - NATed, L - Local, X - No Socket
R7# show dmvpn
Legend: Attrb --> S - Static, D - Dynamic, I - Incomplete
        N - NATed, L - Local, X - No Socket

 T1 - Route Installed, T2 - Nexthop-override
        C - CTS Capable
        # Ent --> Number of NHRP entries with same NBMA peer
        NHS Status: E --> Expecting Replies, R --> Responding, W --> Waiting
        UpDn Time --> Up or Down Time for a Tunnel
==========================================================================


Interface: Tunnel4, IPv4 NHRP Details
Type:Spoke, NHRP Peers:2,

# Ent  Peer NBMA Addr Peer Tunnel Add State  UpDn Tm Attrb
----- --------------- --------------- ----- -------- -----
    1 192.168.5.5          10.0.1.5   UP 00:00:22    D
    1 192.168.4.44         10.0.2.4   UP 08:41:12    S
```

After the ping is initiated, a dynamic tunnel is created from R7 to R5, as shown in the highlighted output. For **show dmvpn**, 192.168.5.5 (loopback 0 at R5) is the dynamic tunnel (D) associated to the physical WAN interface of R5 (10.0.1.5). This is a result of a ping test from R7 that created a need for a data path and hence created this dynamic spoke-to-spoke tunnel relationship.

Unicast Spoke-to-Central Hub Communication

From R5, a ping to 10.0.100.100 (loopback 100 at R2) shows a region communicating with the central hub through a dynamic tunnel created within to the same NHRP domain.

The highlighted output in Example 2-22 shows the creation of the dynamic tunnel for the unicast flow. 10.0.0.1 is the tunnel IP address at R2, 10.0.1.3 is the tunnel IP address at R3, 10.0.1.5 is the tunnel IP address at R5, and 10.0.1.6 is the tunnel IP address at R6.

Example 2-22 *Dynamic Tunnel Usage*

```
R5# ping 10.0.100.100 source lo 100
Type escape sequence to abort.
Sending 5, 100-byte ICMP Echos to 10.0.100.100, timeout is 2 seconds:
Packet sent with a source address of 10.0.100.101
!!!!!
Success rate is 100 percent (5/5), round-trip min/avg/max = 1/1/1 ms
R5# show ip nhrp
10.0.0.1/32 via 10.0.0.1
   Tunnel3 created 00:00:02, expire 00:05:57
   Type: dynamic, Flags: router nhop rib
   NBMA address: 192.168.2.2
10.0.1.3/32 via 10.0.1.3
   Tunnel3 created 3d09h, never expire
   Type: static, Flags: used
   NBMA address: 192.168.3.33
10.0.1.6/32 via 10.0.1.6
   Tunnel3 created 00:04:20, expire 01:55:39
   Type: dynamic, Flags: router used nhop rib
   NBMA address: 192.168.6.6
10.0.100.100/32 via 10.0.0.1
   Tunnel3 created 00:00:02, expire 00:05:57
   Type: dynamic, Flags: router rib nho
   NBMA address: 192.168.2.2
10.0.100.101/32 via 10.0.1.5
   Tunnel3 created 00:04:20, expire 01:55:39
   Type: dynamic, Flags: router unique local
   NBMA address: 192.168.5.5
    (no-socket)
10.0.100.102/32 via 10.0.1.6
   Tunnel3 created 00:04:20, expire 01:55:39
   Type: dynamic, Flags: router rib nho
   NBMA address: 192.168.6.6
```

Traffic Path of a Multicast Stream Sourced at the Central Hub

The source from the central hub transmits a multicast stream (239.1.1.1), and the receiver for this flow is at R5 (a regional spoke router). In Example 2-23, the **show ip mroute** command shows R5 receiving the multicast flow from the hub.

Example 2-23   *R5 Receiving the Flow*

```
R5# show ip mroute 239.1.1.1
IP Multicast Routing Table
Flags: D - Dense, S - Sparse, B - Bidir Group, s - SSM Group, C - Connected,
       L - Local, P - Pruned, R - RP-bit set, F - Register flag,
       T - SPT-bit set, J - Join SPT, M - MSDP created entry, E - Extranet,
       X - Proxy Join Timer Running, A - Candidate for MSDP Advertisement,
       U - URD, I - Received Source Specific Host Report,
       Z - Multicast Tunnel, z - MDT-data group sender,
       Y - Joined MDT-data group, y - Sending to MDT-data group,
       G - Received BGP C-Mroute, g - Sent BGP C-Mroute,
       N - Received BGP Shared-Tree Prune, n - BGP C-Mroute suppressed,
       Q - Received BGP S-A Route, q - Sent BGP S-A Route,
       V - RD & Vector, v - Vector, p - PIM Joins on route,
       x - VxLAN group
Outgoing interface flags: H - Hardware switched, A - Assert winner, p - PIM Join
 Timers: Uptime/Expires
 Interface state: Interface, Next-Hop or VCD, State/Mode

(*, 239.1.1.1), 00:01:23/stopped, RP 10.0.100.100, flags: SJCL
  Incoming interface: Tunnel3, RPF nbr 10.0.1.3
  Outgoing interface list:
    Loopback100, Forward/Sparse, 00:01:23/00:02:17

(10.0.100.100, 239.1.1.1), 00:01:21/00:01:38, flags: LJT
  Incoming interface: Tunnel3, RPF nbr 10.0.1.3
  Outgoing interface list:
    Loopback100, Forward/Sparse, 00:01:21/00:02:17
```

Intra-regional Multicast Flow Between Two Spokes

Looking at the multicast stream from the source at R5 (239.192.1.1) to the receiver at
R6, the **show ip mroute** command at R6 shows the formation of (*, G) and (S, G) states.
Example 2-24 shows the output of R6.

Example 2-24   *R6 mroute Table*

```
R6# show ip mroute 239.192.1.1
IP Multicast Routing Table
Flags: D - Dense, S - Sparse, B - Bidir Group, s - SSM Group, C - Connected,
       L - Local, P - Pruned, R - RP-bit set, F - Register flag,
       T - SPT-bit set, J - Join SPT, M - MSDP created entry, E - Extranet,
       X - Proxy Join Timer Running, A - Candidate for MSDP Advertisement,
       U - URD, I - Received Source Specific Host Report,
       Z - Multicast Tunnel, z - MDT-data group sender,
```

```
            Y - Joined MDT-data group, y - Sending to MDT-data group,
            G - Received BGP C-Mroute, g - Sent BGP C-Mroute,
            N - Received BGP Shared-Tree Prune, n - BGP C-Mroute suppressed,
            Q - Received BGP S-A Route, q - Sent BGP S-A Route,
            V - RD & Vector, v - Vector, p - PIM Joins on route,
            x - VxLAN group
Outgoing interface flags: H - Hardware switched, A - Assert winner, p - PIM Join
 Timers: Uptime/Expires
 Interface state: Interface, Next-Hop or VCD, State/Mode
(*, 239.192.1.1), 4d03h/stopped, RP 10.0.100.103, flags: SJCLF
  Incoming interface: Tunnel3, RPF nbr 10.0.1.3
  Outgoing interface list:
    Loopback100, Forward/Sparse, 4d03h/00:02:44

(10.0.100.101, 239.192.1.1), 00:00:10/00:02:49, flags: LJT
  Incoming interface: Tunnel3, RPF nbr 10.0.1.3
  Outgoing interface list:
    Loopback100, Forward/Sparse, 00:00:10/00:02:49

(10.0.1.5, 239.192.1.1), 00:00:10/00:02:49, flags: LFT
  Incoming interface: Tunnel3, RPF nbr 0.0.0.0
  Outgoing interface list:
    Loopback100, Forward/Sparse, 00:00:10/00:02:49
```

The output at the R3 hub shows that the replication of the multicast stream 239.192.1.1 is at the regional hub (R3), as shown in Example 2-25. The design provides localization of the regional multicast stream and localized replication. The **show ip mroute** command provides the state information. Note that the incoming interface list (IIF) and outgoing interface list (OIF) interfaces for (S, G) flow through Tunnel3.

Example 2-25 *Stream Replication at R3*

```
R3# show ip mroute 239.192.1.1
IP Multicast Routing Table
Flags: D - Dense, S - Sparse, B - Bidir Group, s - SSM Group, C - Connected,
       L - Local, P - Pruned, R - RP-bit set, F - Register flag,
       T - SPT-bit set, J - Join SPT, M - MSDP created entry, E - Extranet,
       X - Proxy Join Timer Running, A - Candidate for MSDP Advertisement,
       U - URD, I - Received Source Specific Host Report,
       Z - Multicast Tunnel, z - MDT-data group sender,
       Y - Joined MDT-data group, y - Sending to MDT-data group,
       G - Received BGP C-Mroute, g - Sent BGP C-Mroute,
       N - Received BGP Shared-Tree Prune, n - BGP C-Mroute suppressed,
       Q - Received BGP S-A Route, q - Sent BGP S-A Route,
       V - RD & Vector, v - Vector, p - PIM Joins on route,
       x - VxLAN group
```

```
Outgoing interface flags: H - Hardware switched, A - Assert winner, p - PIM Join
 Timers: Uptime/Expires
 Interface state: Interface, Next-Hop or VCD, State/Mode
(*, 239.192.1.1), 3d07h/00:03:26, RP 10.0.100.103, flags: S
  Incoming interface: Null, RPF nbr 0.0.0.0
  Outgoing interface list:
    Tunnel3, 10.0.1.6, Forward/Sparse, 14:05:23/00:03:26


(10.0.100.101, 239.192.1.1), 00:00:03/00:02:56, flags:
  Incoming interface: Tunnel3, RPF nbr 10.0.1.5
  Outgoing interface list:
    Tunnel3, 10.0.1.6, Forward/Sparse, 00:00:03/00:03:26
```

The regional stream output at R2, at the central hub, does not have any significance. As shown in Example 2-26, the **show ip mroute** command does not provide any multicast state output.

Example 2-26   show ip mroute *at R2*

```
R2-CH# show ip mroute  239.192.1.1
Group 239.192.1.1 not found
R2-CH#
```

R2 does not have the regional stream 239.192.1.1; rather, replication takes place at R3, the regional hub.

One of the best ways to implement QoS in an overlay infrastructure is with DMVPN. With DMVPN, you can do traffic shaping at the hub interface on a per-spoke or per-spoke-group basis. Using dynamic QoS policies, you can configure multiple branch locations in one QoS template from the hub. The application of the policy to the spoke is dynamic when the spoke comes up.

Note   This book does not aim to review the details of the current or future DMVPN implementations. Instead, it provides an introduction to mGRE, which simplifies administration on the hub or spoke tunnels.

Enabling Multicast to the CSP Use Case 1

This section reviews how to enable multicast in a cloud service with a cloud broker. Figure 2-12 shows the first use case.

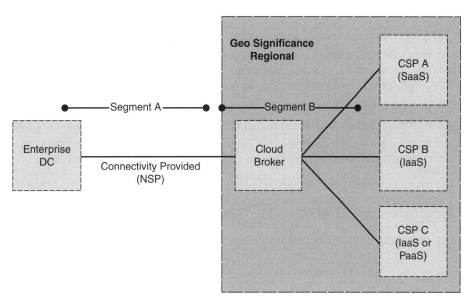

Figure 2-12 *Enabling Multicast to the CSP Use Case 1*

To review the design options available to deploy multicast, let's divide the enterprise access to the cloud service provider into two segments, A and B, as shown in Figure 2-12.

Segment A covers the data center connectivity to the cloud broker. Multiple choices are available for this, as discussed earlier in this chapter: point-to-point virtual circuit (VC) provided by the network service provider (NSP) and MPLS Layer 3 VPN services for the NSP.

Point-to-Point VC Provided by the NSP

With direct VC (dedicated circuit point-to-point provided by the NSP), it is very simple to enable multicast. Segment A needs to terminate at the colocation (COLO) facility provided at the carrier-neutral facility. The termination is in the COLO facility, where the enterprise hosts network devices that offer enterprise-class features.

Segment B provides the transport of multicast from the COLO facility to the CSP. Multicast feature support is not available in the CSP network. In this case, the design engineer uses the service reflection feature and converts the multicast stream to a unicast stream.

MPLS Layer 3 VPN Services for the NSP

Instead of using a direct VC connection, the customer may leverage the SP-provided MPLS Layer 3 VPN service. Multicast support with the MPLS-VPN SP needs to be verified. If it is supported, the customer can leverage the MPLS-VPN SP for transporting multicast traffic. Segment A needs to terminate at the COLO facility provided at the carrier-neutral location. The termination is in the COLO facility where the enterprise hosts network devices for providing enterprise-class features. The termination is based on IP features that extend the connection to the MPLS-VPN cloud with control plane features such as QoS and routing protocols.

Segment B controls the transport of multicast traffic from the COLO facility to the CSP. Multicast feature support is generally not available in the CSP. A similar design principle of using the service reflection feature to convert multicast to a unicast stream can be used here.

Enabling Multicast to the CSP Use Case 2

In this use case, the enterprise data center does not have connectivity to a cloud broker. The connectivity to the CSP is direct via an NSP. Connectivity for Segment A has two options: direct VC access and Internet access. Figure 2-13 illustrates this use case.

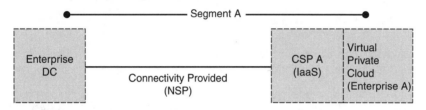

Figure 2-13   *Enabling Multicast to the CSP Use Case 2*

With direct VC access, the enterprise requires network services hosted in the virtual private cloud (VPC). This is accomplished by using a VNF routing instance (such as a CSR 1000v). The enterprise can either buy these instances or rent them from the CSP. Here are two options for the transport of multicast across the NSP:

- Conversion of multicast to unicast can be done at the enterprise data center, using the service reflection feature. In this case, VNF in the cloud is not necessary for multicast.

- GRE tunnels can be used to transport multicast from the enterprise data center to the CSR 1000v hosted in the VPC. At the CSR 1000v, the administrator can use the service reflection feature to convert multicast to unicast. Using CSR 1000v provides visibility and support of enterprise-centric features.

Note   There's a third, non-Cisco-specific option, which is not scalable. It is possible to terminate GRE on the compute instance at both ends. For example, Linux supports GRE tunnels directly in the AWS VPC. However, with this solution, you lose visibility of and support for enterprise-centric features.

The connectivity for Segment A from the enterprise to the CSP is via the Internet. Multicast support is possible through two options:

- Create an overlay GRE network from the data center to the enterprise VPC located at the CSP. The tunnel endpoints are between a data center router and a CSR 1000v hosted at the enterprise VPC. Once the traffic hits the VPC, the administrator can use the multicast service reflection feature to convert the multicast feed to unicast.

- If the enterprise does not host a CSR 1000v instance at the VPC, the conversion of multicast to unicast is done at the enterprise data center router.

Summary

Enterprises are more and more adopting the use of public cloud services. It is therefore important to understand the techniques and considerations involved in transporting multicast to and from a cloud service provider—especially when the cloud service providers do not support native multicast. This chapter reviews different cloud models that an enterprise may use (including SaaS, IaaS, and PaaS) and the various network access types to the cloud. Service reflection is an important feature used to convert multicast to a unicast stream or vice versa. Using NFV with a CSR 1000v is a powerful way for an enterprise to provide enterprise network features in an IaaS public cloud environment. Because multicast functionality is currently not supported in public cloud, it is important to understand cloud network access types and how to use NFV or physical hardware with enterprise features such as service reflection and DMVPN to help provide multicast service in the public IaaS environment.

Chapter 3

Multicast MPLS VPNs

The ability to logically separate traffic on the same physical infrastructure has been possible for many years. Most service providers (SPs) and many enterprise customers implement Multiprotocol Label Switching (MPLS) in order to be able to separate or isolate traffic into logical domains or groups, generally referred to as a virtual private network (VPN). A VPN can separate traffic by customer, job function, security level, and so on. MPLS uses an underlying protocol called Label Distribution Protocol (LDP) to encapsulate messages destined for a particular VPN. A VPN can be made up of several types of devices, including switches, routers, and firewalls. Isolating messages on a switch creates a virtual local area network (VLAN); on a router, Virtual Routing and Forwarding (VRF) instances are used; and a firewall separates traffic by using virtual contexts. The litmus test for virtualization really boils down to one simple question: Do you have the ability to support overlapping IP address space?

This chapter discusses the function of multicast in an MPLS VPN environment, focusing on routing or VRF. In order to establish a foundation, a clear definition of terms is necessary:

- A provider (P) device is also referred to as a label-switched router (LSR). A P device runs an Interior Gateway Protocol (IGP) and Label Distribution Protocol (LDP). You may also find the term P device used regarding the provider signaling in the core of a network.

- A provider edge (PE) device is also referred to as an edge LSR (eLSR). A PE device not only runs IGP and LDP but also runs Multiprotocol Border Gateway Protocol (MP-BGP). A PE device imposes, removes, and/or swaps MPLS labels.

- A customer edge (CE) device is a Layer 3 (L3) element that connects to a PE device for routing information exchange between the customer and the provider.

- Customer (C) or overlay refers to the customer network, messages, traffic flows, and so on. C also refers to customer signaling.

> **Note**   Tag Distribution Protocol (TDP) is not covered in this chapter as it has not been the protocol of choice for many years.

> **Note**   For additional information on LDP, see RFC 5036, "LDP Specification."

Figure 3-1 shows how these elements are connected. It is used throughout the chapter to explain the concepts of multicast VPNs.

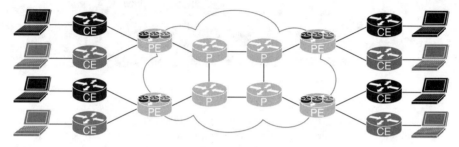

Figure 3-1   *MPLS VPN Network Devices*

The similarly shaded CE devices in Figure 3-1 represent a single overlay or customer network. These devices operate using only the global routing table. The PE devices use MPLS to separate traffic and maintain multiple VRF instances or multiple unique routing tables, one for each customer. Finally, the P devices perform label switching and IP routing to send messages to the appropriate destination PE router.

> **Note**   For additional information, see RFC 4364, "BGP/MPLS IP Virtual Private Networks (VPNs)."

Multicast in an MPLS VPN Network

In order for the routers within a VRF instance to send and receive multicast messages, there must be some type of underlying transport mechanism. The transport mechanism must have the capability of supporting multiple VRF instances, potentially with overlapping IP unicast and multicast address space. In addition, the multicast implementation should have the ability to minimize the impact of the P routers by not overburdening them with too many multicast routes.

The network core must have the capability of transporting multicast messages for each VRF instance. This is accomplished in three ways:

- Using generic routing encapsulation (GRE)

- Transporting multicast by using labels, which is called Multicast Label Distribution Protocol (MLDP), using headend replication, which sends the multicast message using unicast

- Using LDP

Note You will find MLDP has two definitions. Multicast Label Distribution Protocol and Multipoint Label Distribution Protocol. Cisco documentation generally uses the term multicast and RFCs will generally use the term multipoint with a lowercase "m" (mLDP). They are the same.

Multicast Distribution Tree (MDT)

The first method developed for transporting multicast messages within an MPLS VPN network was GRE, which is widely used in current multicast deployments. Eric Rosen along with several others developed this strategy for transporting multicast messages over a unicast MPLS VPN infrastructure. Today, the Rosen method encompasses two fundamental techniques for multicast transport, the first using GRE and the second using MLDP. What differentiates the Rosen methodology is the concept of a default multicast distribution tree (MDT) and a data MDT. What defines the Rosen method is the use of an overlay to provide multicast over multicast. This method is also referred to as *default MDT*, *default MDT-GRE*, the *Rosen model*, the *draft Rosen model*, and *Profile 0*. (We like to keep things confusing as it adds to job security.)

Note For additional information, see "Cisco Systems' Solution for Multicast in MPLS/BGP IP VPNs" (https://tools.ietf.org/html/draft-rosen-vpn-mcast-15). Also see RFC 7441, "Encoding Multipoint LDP Forwarding Equivalence Classes (FECs) in the NLRI of BGP MCAST-VPN Routes."

Default MDT

The default MDT includes all the PE routers that participate in a specific VPN. This is accomplished by using the same route distinguisher (RD) or through the use of importing and exporting routes with a route target (RT). If a group of routers within a VPN are exchanging unicast routing information, they are also in the same default MDT, and all receive the same unicast messages.

The default MDT is used as a mechanism for the PE routers within a VPN to exchange multicast messages with each other. For this to occur, the underlying infrastructure, which includes the IGP, MP-BGP, and Protocol Independent Multicast (PIM), must all be functioning correctly. CE equipment uses the default MDT to exchange multicast control messages. Messages are encapsulated over the core network using IP in IP with a GRE header, as shown in Figure 3-2, when using the default MDT.

Layer 2 Header **Core Network**		Layer 3 Header **Core Network**		GRE Header **Core Network**	Layer 3 Header **Customer Network**	
SRC: AABB.CC00.0920	DST: 0100.5E00.0001	SRC: 10.1.1.5	DST: 10.2.2.5	0x0800	SRC: 172.16.12.20	DST: 224.1.1.20

Figure 3-2 *Default MDT Header Information*

> **Note**   Example 3-12 shows the packet capture and provides additional detail.

Consider the default MDT as full-mesh or as a Multipoint-to-Multipoint (MP2MP) tree. When the default MDT has been configured, it is in an active state, or always operational, and is used to transmit PIM control messages (hello, join, and prune) between routers. Any time a multicast message is sent to the default MDT, all multicast routers participating in that VPN receive that message, as shown in Figure 3-3.

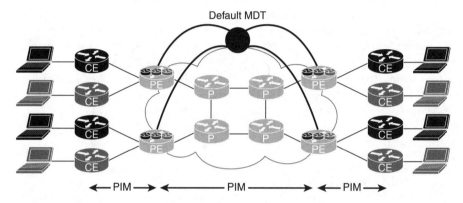

Figure 3-3   *Default MDT MP2MP Tree*

As you can imagine, this is not the most effective use of network bandwidth, and the challenge is addressed later in this chapter. For now, let's take a look at how to configure a router to support the default MDT.

Example 3-1 is a configuration snippet from a router using IOS-XE. Notice that the RD 65000:1 is used for the VRF RED as well as the RT. The command **mdt default 232.0.0.1** assigns a specific multicast address to the VRF. All routers participating in the default MDT must have the same multicast address assigned. (Do not forget to enable multicast routing for each VRF instance.)

The default PIM Source-Specific Multicast (PIM-SSM) range 232/8 is used for ease of configuration. If you plan to exchange multicast routing information with the Internet, however, best practice dictates using the 239/8 network.

> **Note**   This chapter provides a substantial amount of configuration information. Please verify these parameters with the specific code you are using in your environment. These commands are provided for reference only.

Multicast routing and the MDT data in the VRF instance must be configured. Example 3-1 illustrates a configuration for IOS-XE.

Example 3-1 *Default MDT Basic Configuration Using IOS-XE*

```
ip multicast-routing vrf RED
!
vrf definition RED
 rd 65000:1
 !
 address-family ipv4
  mdt default 232.0.0.1
  route-target export 65000:1
  route-target import 65000:1
 exit-address-family
```

Example 3-2 show the IOS-XR commands.

Example 3-2 *Default MDT Basic Configuration Using IOS-XR*

```
router pim
 vrf RED
  address-family ipv4
   interface GigabitEthernet0/0/0/2
   !
  !
 !
!
multicast-routing
 address-family ipv4
  interface Loopback0
   enable
  !
  interface GigabitEthernet0/0/0/0
   enable
  !
  mdt source Loopback0
 !
 vrf RED
  address-family ipv4
   interface all enable
   mdt default ipv4 232.0.0.1
   mdt data 254
   mdt data 232.0.1.0/24
  !
 !
!
```

> **Note**   The term *VPN* refers to a group of devices that exchange routing information and forward messages as part of a unique group. *VRF instance* refers to the routing instance that has be instantiated on a particular L3 device.

Data MDT

The Data MDT is the mechanism used to eliminate multicast data messages from being sent to every PE that participates in a specific VPN; instead, only those PE routers interested in the multicast forwarding tree for the specific group receive those multicast messages. Consider the data MDT as a Point-to-Multipoint (P2MP) tree with the source or root of the tree at the ingress PE device (that is, the PE router closest to the source of the multicast stream generated from the customer network).

The data MDT is not a unique or standalone multicast implementation mechanism but is a subset of the default MDT. As shown in Figure 3-4, the multicast sender is in the top-right corner, and the receiver is near the bottom-right side of the diagram. The data MDT establishes a separate tunnel from PE source to PE receiver(s) in the fashion that you would expect from a proper multicast implementation. In addition, replication of the multicast stream can also occur on a P device.

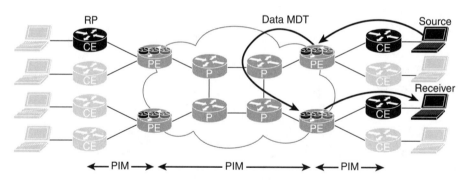

Figure 3-4   *Data MDT*

To configure a VRF instance for the data MDT, use following command set for IOS-XE:

mdt data group-address-range wildcard-bits [*threshold kb/s*] [*list access-list*]

group-address-range and **wildcard-bits** define the size of the pool. The first flow takes the first address from the pool, the second flow takes the second address from the pool, and so on, until the pool is depleted. Once the pool has been depleted, the router reuses addresses from the pool. In this event, you may have routers receiving messages that are not of interest and should be dropped. When selecting the pool size, attempt to minimize overlap for the most efficient transport of multicast messages. The threshold option is configurable from 1 to 4294967 and is used to determine when a multicast stream switches from the default MDT to the data MDT. Finally, the optional **[list access-list]** is used to define the (S, G) entries that are allowed to be used by the pool.

Note When configuring IOS-XR, use **mdt data [maximum number of MDTs]** and **mdt data [IPv4 multicast address range]** to specify the number of multicast groups and the address range for the VPN.

Example 3-3 shows a configuration using IOS-XE. The address range 232.0.1.0 is used with the wildcard bits 0.0.0.255. In addition, the threshold is configured to switch to the data MDT when the multicast stream meets or exceeds 2 Kbps, as shown in Example 3-4.

Example 3-3 *IOS-XE Configuration for Data MDT*

```
vrf definition RED
 rd 65000:1
 !
 address-family ipv4
  mdt default 232.0.0.1
  mdt data 232.0.1.0 0.0.0.255 threshold 2
  mdt data threshold 2
  route-target export 65000:1
  route-target import 65000:1
 exit-address-family
```

Example 3-4 *IOS-XR Configuration for Data MDT*

```
multicast-routing
 vrf RED
  address-family ipv4
   interface all enable
   mdt default ipv4 232.0.0.1
   mdt data 254
   mdt data 232.0.1.0/24 threshold 2
  !
 !
!
```

Note The data MDT is not required but highly recommended unless there are very few multicast streams and they are low-bandwidth.

Multicast Tunnel Interface (MTI)

The MTI is the tunnel interface that is automatically created for each multicast VPN. With the GRE MDT model, multicast traffic within each VPN is transported using a GRE tunnel. As shown in Example 3-5, when you use the **show vrf RED** command for

IOS-XE, two GRE tunnels are created. In this case, one is for the default MDT and the other for the data MDT. (The Data MDT is within the defined threshold.)

Example 3-5   *Multicast Tunnel Interface Using IOS-XE*

```
R4# show vrf RED
  Name                           Default RD          Protocols   Interfaces
  RED                            65000:1             ipv4,ipv6   Et0/2
                                                                 Tu1
                                                                 Tu2
```

With IOS-XR, you can view the tunnel interface by using the **show mfib vrf RED interface** command. Example 3-6 shows the output from R4.

Example 3-6   show mfib *Command Output*

```
RP/0/0/CPU0:R4# show mfib vrf RED interface
Wed Feb 15 23:50:00.358 UTC

Interface : GigabitEthernet0/0/0/2 (Enabled)
SW Mcast pkts in : 23982, SW Mcast pkts out : 11376
TTL Threshold : 0
Ref Count : 6


Interface : mdtRED (Enabled)
SW Mcast pkts in : 0, SW Mcast pkts out : 0
TTL Threshold : 0
Ref Count : 11
```

For IOS-XR, the tunnel interface is **mdtRED** or **mdt[VRF name]**.

Multicast Signaling in the Core

Both the default MDT and the data MDT require that the provider network transport multicast messages. Three options can be used to build PIM in the provider network:

■ PIM Sparse-Mode (PIM-SM)

■ Bidirectional PIM (Bidir-PIM)

■ PIM Source-Specific Multicast (PIM-SSM) or just SSM

This book only covers the configuration of PIM-SSM, which is the recommended method. PIM-SM and Bidir-PIM are explained in detail in *IP Multicast, Volume 1*.

You may recall that the requirement for PIM-SSM is that all the clients must use Internet Group Management Protocol version 3 (IGMPv3) and that there are no requirements for a rendezvous point (RP). Fortunately, all Cisco devices that support MPLS also support IGMPv3. Implementing PIM-SSM is very simple when multicast routing is enabled, as shown in the following configurations.

On IOS-XE devices, use the following command: **ip pim ssm default**

Example 3-7 is a sample configuration using IOS-XR. SSM is enabled by default for the 232.0.0.0/8 range. You may choose to specify a range by using an access control list (ACL), as shown.

Example 3-7 *SSM Configuration Example*

```
router pim
address-family ipv4
 ssm range SSS-RANGE
 !

ipv4 access-list SSM-RANGE
 10 permit ipv4 232.0.0.0/8 any
```

What could be easier? No RP propagation mechanism, and you do not have even have to build in RP high availability! Remember that you must enable PIM-SSM on all P and PE devices in the network.

SSM is the only one of the three methods that does not have the ability to auto-discover the PIM neighbors in the default MDT using PIM. Therefore, you need to use another auto-discovery mechanism: the Border Gateway Protocol (BGP) address family MDT subsequent address family identifiers (MDT-SAFI). After the neighbors have been discovered, SSM can then be used to send PIM messages to those devices. This is configured under **router bgp**, using the MDT address family as shown in Example 3-8, which is for IOS-XE.

Example 3-8 *BGP MDT Address Family*

```
router bgp 65000
!
 address-family ipv4 mdt
  neighbor 192.168.0.1 activate
  neighbor 192.168.0.1 send-community both
  neighbor 192.168.0.2 activate
  neighbor 192.168.0.2 send-community both
 exit-address-family
```

Example 3-9 shows the same configuration using IOS-XR. Neighbor groups and session groups are used here for configuration simplicity, and only pertinent information is shown. Remember also that a route policy must be configured in order to send or receive BGP information.

Example 3-9   *BGP MDT Configuration Using IOS-XR*

```
route-policy ALLOW-ALL
  pass
end-policy
 !
router bgp 65000
 bgp router-id 192.168.0.4
 address-family ipv4 unicast
 !
 address-family vpnv4 unicast
 !
 address-family ipv4 mdt
 !
 session-group AS65000
  remote-as 65000
  update-source Loopback0
 !
 neighbor-group AS65000
  use session-group AS65000
  address-family ipv4 unicast
   route-policy ALLOW-ALL in
   route-policy ALLOW-ALL out
  !
  address-family vpnv4 unicast
   route-policy ALLOW-ALL in
   route-policy ALLOW-ALL out
  !
  address-family ipv4 mdt
   route-policy ALLOW-ALL in
   route-policy ALLOW-ALL out
  !
 neighbor 192.168.0.1
  use neighbor-group AS65000
 !
 neighbor 192.168.0.2
  use neighbor-group AS65000
```

Because route reflectors are used in this network, R4 (ingress PE connected to the receiver) only needs to establish an adjacency to those devices.

You verify the BGP adjacency within a specific VRF by using the **show ip bgp ipv4 mdt vrf RED** command, as shown for IOS-XE in Example 3-10.

Example 3-10 *Verifying MDT BGP Adjacency Using IOS-XE*

```
R4# show ip bgp ipv4 mdt vrf RED
BGP table version is 9, local router ID is 192.168.0.4
Status codes: s suppressed, d damped, h history, * valid, > best, i - internal,
              r RIB-failure, S Stale, m multipath, b backup-path, f RT-Filter,
              x best-external, a additional-path, c RIB-compressed,
Origin codes: i - IGP, e - EGP, ? - incomplete
RPKI validation codes: V valid, I invalid, N Not found

     Network          Next Hop          Metric LocPrf Weight Path
Route Distinguisher: 65000:1 (default for vrf RED)
 * i 192.168.0.3/32   192.168.0.3            0    100      0 ?
 *>i                  192.168.0.3            0    100      0 ?
 *>  192.168.0.4/32   0.0.0.0                              0 ?
 * i 192.168.0.5/32   192.168.0.5            0    100      0 ?
 *>i                  192.168.0.5            0    100      0 ?
 * i 192.168.0.6/32   192.168.0.6            0    100      0 ?
 *>i                  192.168.0.6            0    100      0 ?
```

For IOS-XR, you use the **show bgp ipv4 mdt vrf RED** command, as shown in Example 3-11.

Example 3-11 *Verifying MDT BGP Adjacency Using IOS-XR*

```
RP/0/0/CPU0:R4# show bgp ipv4 mdt vrf RED
Thu Feb 16 00:13:50.290 UTC
BGP router identifier 192.168.0.4, local AS number 65000
BGP generic scan interval 60 secs
Non-stop routing is enabled
BGP table state: Active
Table ID: 0xe0000000   RD version: 8
BGP main routing table version 8
BGP NSR Initial initsync version 2 (Reached)
BGP NSR/ISSU Sync-Group versions 0/0
BGP scan interval 60 secs

Status codes: s suppressed, d damped, h history, * valid, > best
              i - internal, r RIB-failure, S stale, N Nexthop-discard
Origin codes: i - IGP, e - EGP, ? - incomplete
   Network          Next Hop          Metric LocPrf Weight Path
Route Distinguisher: 65000:1
*>i192.168.0.3/96    192.168.0.3                 100      0 i
* i                 192.168.0.3                 100      0 i
*>  192.168.0.4/96   0.0.0.0                              0 i
```

```
*>i192.168.0.5/96      192.168.0.5               100     0 i
* i                    192.168.0.5               100     0 i
*>i192.168.0.6/96      192.168.0.6               100     0 i
* i                    192.168.0.6               100     0 i


Processed 4 prefixes, 7 paths
```

Because the previous command was executed on R4, notice the loopback addresses of the other routers within the RED VPN.

Default MDT in Action

Figure 3-5 provides a better understanding of the interaction between devices and the behavior of multicast in an MPLS environment.

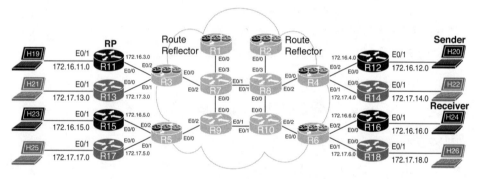

Figure 3-5   *Default MDT in Action*

In order to replicate a typical network and eliminate the need to configure full-mesh MP-BGP, two route reflectors, R1 and R2, were added to the sample network. In this scenario, notice the behavior of multicast messages in the RED VRF. Host 20 (H20) is the multicast sender, H24 is the receiver, and R11 is the RP. The RED VRF is configured to use Auto-RP using sparse mode. This means that all the PE routers with the RED VRF running must use the **ip pim vrf RED autorp listener** command, and routers within the RED network must be configured with the **ip pim autorp listener** command. IOS-XR supports this functionality by default, and no additional configuration is required.

Data MDT Traffic Flow

The IP address of H20 (sender) is 172.16.12.20, the IP address of H24 (receiver) is 172.16.16.24, and the RP has an IP address in R11 of 172.16.3.11. H20 is sending a multicast stream to 224.1.1.20 at about 75 packets per second.

The sender (H20) begins to send traffic to the multicast group 224.1.1.20, but in this example, no receivers have registered to accept the stream. The gateway router (R12) forwards a special register message to the RP, registering the (*, G) and the gateway as a leaf in the tree. When H24 requests the multicast stream of 224.1.1.20, R16 sends a join message to the RP (R11). After a series of multicast messages, the tree switches to the source tree (S, G) (172.16.12.20, 224.1.1.20).

Note   Refer to Chapter 3, "IP Multicast at Layer 3," in *IP Multicast, Volume 1* for a detailed description of the shared-to-source tree process.

All the previous communication from the RED VPN occurs over the default MDT, which is sent to every PE device in the RED VPN.

Multicast traffic is now being sent from R4, the ingress router, to all PE devices in the RED VPN. The ingress device (R4) monitors the rate of the session. When the preconfigured threshold is crossed, the ingress router (R4) sends a PIM messages to all PE routers in the RED VPN, indicating the (S, G) (C-(S, G)) entry and the provider (S, G) (P-(S, G)) entry. The egress PE routers in the RED VPN that are interested in receiving the multicast stream send a join message to the ingress PE (R4). R4 then switches to the data MDT in three seconds unless it is configured for an immediate switchover.

Default MDT Example

To observe the behavior of the default MDT, this section shows how to reconfigure R4 to switch over to the data MDT at the highest configurable rate by using the **mdt data threshold 4294967** command, as shown for IOS-XE in Example 3-12 and IOS-XR in Example 3-13.

Example 3-12   *MDT Data Threshold Configuration Example Using IOS-XE*

```
vrf definition RED
 rd 65000:1
 !
 address-family ipv4
  mdt default 232.0.0.1
  mdt data 232.0.1.0 0.0.0.255 threshold 4294967
  mdt data threshold 4294967
  route-target export 65000:1
  route-target import 65000:1
 exit-address-family
```

Example 3-13   *MDT Data Threshold Configuration Example Using IOS-XR*

```
route-policy PIM-Default
  set core-tree pim-default
end-policy

 vrf RED
  address-family ipv4
   rpf topology route-policy PIM-Default
   interface GigabitEthernet0/0/0/2

multicast-routing
 vrf RED
  address-family ipv4
   interface all enable
   mdt default ipv4 232.0.0.1
   mdt data 232.0.1.0/24 threshold 4294967
  !
 !
!
```

This keeps all multicast streams in the default MDT, unless of course a stream exceeds the threshold of 4,294,967 Kbps, which is not likely in this environment. You could also remove the **mdt data** commands altogether as an alternative solution.

As shown in Figure 3-3, all routers in the same VPN are connected using the same default MDT. You can observe this behavior by using the **show ip pim vrf RED neighbor** command for IOS-XE, as shown in Example 3-14.

Example 3-14   *Showing the PIM Neighbor for VRF RED Using IOS-XE*

```
R4# show ip pim vrf RED neighbor
PIM Neighbor Table
Mode: B - Bidir Capable, DR - Designated Router, N - Default DR Priority,
      P - Proxy Capable, S - State Refresh Capable, G - GenID Capable,
      L - DR Load-balancing Capable
Neighbor          Interface               Uptime/Expires     Ver   DR
Address                                                            Prio/Mode
172.16.4.12       Ethernet0/2             00:21:10/00:01:43 v2    1 / DR S P G
192.168.0.3       Tunnel1                 00:20:19/00:01:35 v2    1 / S P G
192.168.0.6       Tunnel1                 00:20:19/00:01:38 v2    1 / DR S P G
192.168.0.5       Tunnel1                 00:20:19/00:01:37 v2    1 / S P G
```

The equivalent command for IOS-XR is **show pim vrf RED neighbor**, as shown in Example 3-15.

Example 3-15 *Showing the PIM Neighbor for VRF RED Using IOS-XE*

```
RP/0/0/CPU0:R4# show pim vrf RED neighbor
Thu Feb 16 00:26:01.310 UTC


PIM neighbors in VRF RED
Flag: B - Bidir capable, P - Proxy capable, DR - Designated Router,
      E - ECMP Redirect capable
      * indicates the neighbor created for this router


Neighbor Address            Interface             Uptime    Expires  DR pri
  Flags

172.16.4.4*                 GigabitEthernet0/0/0/2 3d23h     00:01:19 1  B E
172.16.4.12                 GigabitEthernet0/0/0/2 3d00h     00:01:22 1 (DR) P
192.168.0.3                 mdtRED                 3d23h     00:01:24 1
192.168.0.4*                mdtRED                 3d23h     00:01:40 1
192.168.0.5                 mdtRED                 3d23h     00:01:32 1
192.168.0.6                 mdtRED                 3d23h     00:01:31 1 (DR)
```

From the output in Examples 3-14 and 3-15, notice that R3, R5, and R6 are PIM adjacent neighbors over **Tunnel 1** for IOS-XE and **mdtRED** for IOS-XR, and there is also a PIM neighbor on the VRF RED interface, which is CE router R12.

You can look at a traffic capture between R5 and R9, as shown in Example 3-16, to get a tremendous amount of information about this exchange.

Example 3-16 *Packet Capture on the Link Between R5 and R9*

```
Ethernet Packet:  578 bytes
      Dest Addr: 0100.5E00.0001,   Source Addr: AABB.CC00.0920
      Protocol: 0x0800


IP    Version: 0x4,  HdrLen: 0x5,  TOS: 0x00
      Length: 564,   ID: 0xCA86,  Flags-Offset: 0x0000
      TTL: 252,   Protocol: 47,  Checksum: 0x4966 (OK)
      Source: 192.168.0.4,    Dest: 232.0.0.1


GRE   Present: 0x0 ( Chksum:0, Rsrvd:0, Key:0, SeqNum:0 )
      Reserved0: 0x000,  Version: 0x0,  Protocol: 0x0800


IP    Version: 0x4,  HdrLen: 0x5,  TOS: 0x00
      Length: 540,   ID: 0x0000,  Flags-Offset: 0x0000
      TTL: 58,    Protocol: 17 (UDP),  Checksum: 0xE593 (OK).
      Source: 172.16.12.20,    Dest: 224.1.1.20
```

```
UDP   Src Port: 37777,   Dest Port: 7050
      Length: 520,   Checksum: 0xB384 ERROR: F071


Data: *removed for brevity*
```

The first item to note is that R5 is not in the receiving path between H20 and H24. Why is R5 even seeing the multicast stream? The behavior of the default MDT is to send multicast messages to every PE in the VPN.

Starting at the top, notice that the L2 destination address is 0100.5E00.0001. This L2 multicast address maps to the default MDT multicast IP address 232.0.0.1. The IP header shows the source IP address 192.168.0.4, which is the loopback IP address of R4. In the next section is a GRE header, and below that is the original IP Multicast message. The encapsulated IP datagram shows the source address 172.16.12.20 (H20), destined to the multicast IP address 224.1.1.20. Finally, the UDP section shows the source port 37777 and the destination port 7050.

Very simply, the IP Multicast traffic from the RED VRF is encapsulated using the configured default MDT for VRF RED, hence the GRE tunnel.

MTI Example

You can determine what MTI the multicast stream is using by checking the state of the multicast routing table in the RED VRF for 224.1.1.20 by using the **show ip mroute** command for IOS-XE. Example 3-17 displays this output for VRF RED on R4.

Example 3-17   *Verifying MTI Using IOS-XE*

```
R4# show ip mroute vrf RED 224.1.1.20
IP Multicast Routing Table
Flags: D - Dense, S - Sparse, B - Bidir Group, s - SSM Group, C - Connected,
       L - Local, P - Pruned, R - RP-bit set, F - Register flag,
       T - SPT-bit set, J - Join SPT, M - MSDP created entry, E - Extranet,
       X - Proxy Join Timer Running, A - Candidate for MSDP Advertisement,
       U - URD, I - Received Source Specific Host Report,
       Z - Multicast Tunnel, z - MDT-data group sender,
       Y - Joined MDT-data group, y - Sending to MDT-data group,
       G - Received BGP C-Mroute, g - Sent BGP C-Mroute,
       N - Received BGP Shared-Tree Prune, n - BGP C-Mroute suppressed,
       Q - Received BGP S-A Route, q - Sent BGP S-A Route,
       V - RD & Vector, v - Vector, p - PIM Joins on route,
       x - VxLAN group
Outgoing interface flags: H - Hardware switched, A - Assert winner, p - PIM Join
 Timers: Uptime/Expires
 Interface state: Interface, Next-Hop or VCD, State/Mode
```

```
(*, 224.1.1.20), 01:05:53/stopped, RP 172.16.3.11, flags: SP
  Incoming interface: Tunnel1, RPF nbr 192.168.0.3
  Outgoing interface list: Null

(172.16.12.20, 224.1.1.20), 00:00:39/00:02:20, flags: T
  Incoming interface: Ethernet0/2, RPF nbr 172.16.4.12
  Outgoing interface list:
    Tunnel1, Forward/Sparse, 00:00:39/00:02:55
```

In the output in Example 3-17, notice that the multicast stream (S, G) in (172.16.12.20, 224.1.1.20) is incoming on Ethernet0/2 and outgoing on Tunnel 1.

You can look at the MTI of R4 by using the **show interfaces tunnel 1** command and compare that with the previous packet capture. The tunnel source IP address matches with 192.168.0.4, the tunnel in multi-GRE/IP. Notice that the five-minute output rate also matches. Example 3-18 shows this output.

Example 3-18   *Verifying MTI Details with* show interfaces tunnel

```
R4# show interfaces tunnel 1
Tunnel1 is up, line protocol is up
  Hardware is Tunnel
  Interface is unnumbered. Using address of Loopback0 (192.168.0.4)
  MTU 17916 bytes, BW 100 Kbit/sec, DLY 50000 usec,
     reliability 255/255, txload 255/255, rxload 1/255
  Encapsulation TUNNEL, loopback not set
  Keepalive not set
  Tunnel linestate evaluation up
  Tunnel source 192.168.0.4 (Loopback0)
   Tunnel Subblocks:
      src-track:
         Tunnel1 source tracking subblock associated with Loopback0
          Set of tunnels with source Loopback0, 2 members (includes iterators), on
          interface <OK>
  Tunnel protocol/transport multi-GRE/IP
    Key disabled, sequencing disabled
    Checksumming of packets disabled
  Tunnel TTL 255, Fast tunneling enabled
  Tunnel transport MTU 1476 bytes
  Tunnel transmit bandwidth 8000 (kbps)
  Tunnel receive bandwidth 8000 (kbps)
  Last input 00:00:02, output 00:00:05, output hang never
  Last clearing of "show interface" counters 1d02h
  Input queue: 0/75/0/0 (size/max/drops/flushes); Total output drops: 0
  Queueing strategy: fifo
  Output queue: 0/0 (size/max)
```

```
5 minute input rate 0 bits/sec, 0 packets/sec
5 minute output rate 337000 bits/sec, 75 packets/sec
   39021 packets input, 3028900 bytes, 0 no buffer
   Received 0 broadcasts (3221 IP multicasts)
   0 runts, 0 giants, 0 throttles
   0 input errors, 0 CRC, 0 frame, 0 overrun, 0 ignored, 0 abort
   183556 packets output, 99558146 bytes, 0 underruns
   0 output errors, 0 collisions, 0 interface resets
   0 unknown protocol drops
   0 output buffer failures, 0 output buffers swapped out
```

You can use the **show pim vrf RED mdt interface** and **show pim vrf RED mdt interface** commands for IOS-XR as shown in Example 3-19.

Example 3-19 *Verifying MTI Using IOS-XR*

```
RP/0/0/CPU0:R4# show pim vrf RED mdt interface
Fri Feb 17 23:04:12.788 UTC


GroupAddress    Interface                 Source     Vrf

232.0.0.1       mdtRED                    Loopback0  RED



RP/0/0/CPU0:R4# show mrib vrf RED route 224.1.1.20
Fri Feb 17 23:01:10.460 UTC


IP Multicast Routing Information Base
Entry flags: L - Domain-Local Source, E - External Source to the Domain,
    C - Directly-Connected Check, S - Signal, IA - Inherit Accept,
    IF - Inherit From, D - Drop, ME - MDT Encap, EID - Encap ID,
    MD - MDT Decap, MT - MDT Threshold Crossed, MH - MDT interface handle
    CD - Conditional Decap, MPLS - MPLS Decap, EX - Extranet
    MoFE - MoFRR Enabled, MoFS - MoFRR State, MoFP - MoFRR Primary
    MoFB - MoFRR Backup, RPFID - RPF ID Set, X - VXLAN
Interface flags: F - Forward, A - Accept, IC - Internal Copy,
    NS - Negate Signal, DP - Don't Preserve, SP - Signal Present,
    II - Internal Interest, ID - Internal Disinterest, LI - Local Interest,
    LD - Local Disinterest, DI - Decapsulation Interface
    EI - Encapsulation Interface, MI - MDT Interface, LVIF - MPLS Encap,
    EX - Extranet, A2 - Secondary Accept, MT - MDT Threshold Crossed,
    MA - Data MDT Assigned, LMI - mLDP MDT Interface, TMI - P2MP-TE MDT Interface
    IRMI - IR MDT Interface
```

```
(172.16.12.20,224.1.1.20) RPF nbr: 172.16.4.12 Flags: RPF
  Up: 00:37:02
  Incoming Interface List
    GigabitEthernet0/0/0/2 Flags: A, Up: 00:37:02
  Outgoing Interface List
    mdtRED Flags: F NS MI, Up: 00:37:02
```

The F flag indicates that multicast traffic is being forwarded, the NS flag is used with PIM-SM to indicate a shortest-path tree (SPT) switchover, and the MI flag indicates that it is an MDT interface.

Data MDT Example

This section examines the behavior of the data MDT, using the same example shown in Figure 3-4. R11 is the RP, H20 is the sender, and H24 is the receiver for multicast group 224.1.1.20. In this scenario, H20 is sending traffic to group 224.1.1.20. Just as in any PIM-SM configuration, R12 registers with the RP (R12). Because there are currently no receivers interested in the traffic, R12 does not forward any multicast messages. When H24 joins the 224.1.1.20 group, it sends the join message to the RP (R12). With an interested receiver, R12 begins to forward the traffic to R4 (PE).

R4 sends multicast messages to the default MDT. This means that every router participating in the RED multicast VPN receives the message, including R3, R5, and R6. Both R3 and R5 drop the traffic because they do not have any receivers interested in the multicast stream. R6, on the other hand, has an interested receiver downstream, which is H24. R6 sends a join message to R4, as shown by the packet capture between R6 and R10. Also note that this is not a GRE encapsulated packet but is sent natively, as shown in Example 3-20.

Example 3-20 *Native Default MDT*

```
Ethernet Packet:  68 bytes
      Dest Addr: 0100.5E00.000D,   Source Addr: AABB.CC00.0600
      Protocol: 0x0800

IP    Version: 0x4,  HdrLen: 0x5,  TOS: 0xC0 (Prec=Internet Contrl)
      Length: 54,   ID: 0x9913,   Flags-Offset: 0x0000
      TTL: 1,   Protocol: 103 (PIM),   Checksum: 0x14D2 (OK)
      Source: 192.168.106.6,    Dest: 224.0.0.13

PIM   Ver:2 , Type:Join/Prune , Reserved: 0 , Checksum : 0x008B (OK)
      Addr Family: IP , Enc Type: 0 , Uni Address: 192.168.106.10
      Reserved: 0 , Num Groups: 1 , HoldTime: 210
      Addr Family: IP , Enc Type: 0 , Reserved: 0 , Mask Len: 32
      Group Address:232.0.1.0
      Num Joined Sources: 1 ,   Num Pruned Sources: 0
      Joined/Pruned Srcs:     Addr Family: IP , Enc Type: 0 , Reserved: 0
      S: 1 , W: 0, R:0,  Mask Len: 32
      Source Address:192.168.0.4
```

R4 continues to send multicast messages to the default MDT (232.0.0.1) until the threshold is reached, at which time it moves the stream from the default MDT to the data MDT, which in this example is the multicast address 232.0.1.0.

It is important to understand that there are two multicast operations happening simultaneously:

- The CE overlay
- The P/PE underlay

Example 3-21 provides some practical configuration, debugging information, and packet captures that assist in explaining the process in greater detail. In order to switch to the data MDT, you need to reconfigure R4 to switch over to the data MDT at a lower rate. As shown in Example 3-21, which uses IOS-XE, you can use 2 Kbps and configure R4 with the **mdt data threshold 2** command.

Example 3-21 *Configuring the Data MDT Threshold Using IOS-XE*

```
vrf definition RED
 rd 65000:1
 !
 address-family ipv4
  mdt default 232.0.0.1
  mdt data 232.0.1.0 0.0.0.255 threshold 2
  mdt data threshold 2
```

Example 3-22 shows the same configuration using IOS-XR.

Example 3-22 *Configuring the Data MDT Threshold Using IOS-XR*

```
multicast-routing
 !
 vrf RED
  address-family ipv4
   interface all enable
   mdt default ipv4 232.0.0.1
   mdt data 232.0.1.0/24 threshold 2
```

The expectation now is that the multicast stream sent from H20 will use the following path: R12, R4, R8, R10, R6, R16, H24. The switchover process takes three seconds.

You can verify the existence of the default MDT with the **show ip pim vrf RED mdt** command on R4, as shown in Example 3-23, which uses IOS-XE. In this example, the * implies the default MDT.

Example 3-23   *PIM Default MDT with IOS-XE*

```
R4# show ip pim vrf RED mdt
  * implies mdt is the default MDT, # is (*,*) Wildcard,
  > is non-(*,*) Wildcard
  MDT Group/Num   Interface   Source          VRF
* 232.0.0.1       Tunnel1     Loopback0       RED
```

Example 3-24 shows the cache entries for the default MDT for IOS-XE, using the **show pim vrf RED mdt cache** command.

Example 3-24   *PIM Default MDT Cache*

```
RP/0/0/CPU0:R4# show pim vrf RED mdt cache
Fri Feb 17 21:41:52.136 UTC

Core Source      Cust (Source, Group)           Core Data      Expires
192.168.0.4      (172.16.12.20, 224.1.1.20)     232.0.1.0      00:02:20
```

With IOS-XR, you use the **show mrib vrf RED mdt-interface detail** command, as shown in Example 3-25.

Example 3-25   *MRIB VRF RED*

```
RP/0/0/CPU0:R4# show mrib vrf RED mdt-interface detail
Fri Feb 17 23:06:39.648 UTC
IP Multicast MRIB MDT ifhandle Interface DB
MH - Handle update count, I - Intranet route count, EX - Extranet route count, Up -
  Uptime
0x90(mdtRED)   TID:0xe0000012  MH:1  I:3  EX:0  Up:01:28:17
   MDT route forward-reference DB:
   (172.16.3.11,224.0.1.39/32) [tid:0xe0000012] recollapse: FALSE
   (172.16.3.11,224.0.1.40/32) [tid:0xe0000012] recollapse: FALSE
   (172.16.12.20,224.1.1.20/32) [tid:0xe0000012] recollapse: FALSE
```

To validate that the data MDT is in use, use the **show ip pim vrf RED mdt send** command on R4, as shown in Example 3-26 for IOS-XR. The (S, G) of (172.16.12.20, 224.1.1.20) is now part of the data MDT.

Example 3-26   *PIM VRF Data MDT Send*

```
R4# show ip pim vrf RED mdt send

MDT-data send list for VRF: RED
  (source, group)                 MDT-data group/num   ref_count
  (172.16.12.20, 224.1.1.20)      232.0.1.0            1
```

The data MDT is 232.0.1.0, as shown in Example 3-26.

Using a similar command with IOS-XR, **show pim vrf RED mdt cache**, Example 3-27 shows that the data MDT is 232.0.1.6.

Example 3-27   *PIM VRF Data MDT IP Address*

```
RP/0/0/CPU0:R4# show pim vrf RED mdt cache
Fri Feb 17 23:10:08.583 UTC


Core Source      Cust (Source, Group)              Core Data       Expires
192.168.0.4      (172.16.12.20, 224.1.1.20)        232.0.1.6       00:02:56
```

Now that the SPT has been established, there is optimal multicast traffic flow from source to receiver. Looking at a packet capture between R6 and R10 with the IOS-XE example, you verify that the data MDT is in operation, as shown in Example 3-28.

Example 3-28   *Data MDT in Operation*

```
Ethernet Packet:   578 bytes
      Dest Addr: 0100.5E00.0100,    Source Addr: AABB.CC00.0A20
      Protocol: 0x0800


IP    Version: 0x4,  HdrLen: 0x5,  TOS: 0x00
      Length: 564,    ID: 0x4447,   Flags-Offset: 0x0000
      TTL: 253,   Protocol: 47,   Checksum: 0xCDA6 (OK)
      Source: 192.168.0.4,    Dest: 232.0.1.0


GRE   Present: 0x0 ( Chksum:0, Rsrvd:0, Key:0, SeqNum:0 )
      Reserved0: 0x000,  Version: 0x0,  Protocol: 0x0800


IP    Version: 0x4,  HdrLen: 0x5,  TOS: 0x00
      Length: 540,    ID: 0x0000,   Flags-Offset: 0x0000
      TTL: 58,   Protocol: 17 (UDP),   Checksum: 0xE593 (OK)
      Source: 172.16.12.20,    Dest: 224.1.1.20


UDP   Src Port: 37777,   Dest Port: 7050
      Length: 520,   Checksum: 0xB384 ERROR: EF72


Data: *removed for brevity*
```

From the packet capture, you can see that the destination IP address is 232.0.1.0, which is the first multicast IP address defined in the pool. Also notice the GRE information and the encapsulated IP Multicast header that is part of VRF RED. Remember that the data MDT is now using SPT for optimal routing.

You can use yet another IOS-XE command to view the functionality of the default MDT and the data MDT with the command **show ip mfib vrf RED 224.1.1.20**, as shown in Example 3-29.

Example 3-29 *Data MDT Packet Count Using IOS-XE*

```
R4# show ip mfib vrf RED 224.1.1.20
Entry Flags:     C - Directly Connected, S - Signal, IA - Inherit A flag,
                 ET - Data Rate Exceeds Threshold, K - Keepalive
                 DDE - Data Driven Event, HW - Hardware Installed
                 ME - MoFRR ECMP entry, MNE - MoFRR Non-ECMP entry, MP - MFIB
                 MoFRR Primary, RP - MRIB MoFRR Primary, P - MoFRR Primary
                 MS - MoFRR  Entry in Sync, MC - MoFRR entry in MoFRR Client.
I/O Item Flags: IC - Internal Copy, NP - Not platform switched,
                 NS - Negate Signalling, SP - Signal Present,
                 A - Accept, F - Forward, RA - MRIB Accept, RF - MRIB Forward,
                 MA - MFIB Accept, A2 - Accept backup,
                 RA2 - MRIB Accept backup, MA2 - MFIB Accept backup

Forwarding Counts: Pkt Count/Pkts per second/Avg Pkt Size/Kbits per second
Other counts:      Total/RPF failed/Other drops
I/O Item Counts:   FS Pkt Count/PS Pkt Count
VRF RED
 (*,224.1.1.20) Flags: C
   SW Forwarding: 0/0/0/0, Other: 0/0/0
   Tunnel1, MDT/232.0.0.1 Flags: A
 (172.16.12.20,224.1.1.20) Flags: ET
   SW Forwarding: 5547/77/540/328, Other: 0/0/0
   Ethernet0/2 Flags: A
   Tunnel1, MDT/232.0.1.0 Flags: F NS
     Pkts: 4784/0
```

With IOS-XR the equivalent command is **show mfib vrf RED route 224.1.1.20**, as shown in Example 3-30.

Example 3-30 *Data MDT Packet Count Using IOS-XR*

```
RP/0/0/CPU0:R4# show mfib vrf RED route 224.1.1.20
Thu Feb 16 00:47:58.929 UTC


IP Multicast Forwarding Information Base
Entry flags: C - Directly-Connected Check, S - Signal, D - Drop,
  IA - Inherit Accept, IF - Inherit From, EID - Encap ID,
  ME - MDT Encap, MD - MDT Decap, MT - MDT Threshold Crossed,
  MH - MDT interface handle, CD - Conditional Decap,
  DT - MDT Decap True, EX - Extranet, RPFID - RPF ID Set,
  MoFE - MoFRR Enabled, MoFS - MoFRR State, X - VXLAN
```

```
Interface flags: F - Forward, A - Accept, IC - Internal Copy,
  NS - Negate Signal, DP - Don't Preserve, SP - Signal Present,
  EG - Egress, EI - Encapsulation Interface, MI - MDT Interface,
  EX - Extranet, A2 - Secondary Accept
Forwarding/Replication Counts: Packets in/Packets out/Bytes out
Failure Counts: RPF / TTL / Empty Olist / Encap RL / Other

(172.16.12.20,224.1.1.20),  Flags:
  Up: 01:09:21
  Last Used: 00:00:00
  SW Forwarding Counts: 165863/165863/89566020
  SW Replication Counts: 165863/0/0
  SW Failure Counts: 0/0/0/0/0
  mdtRED Flags:  F NS MI, Up:00:34:52
  GigabitEthernet0/0/0/2 Flags:  A, Up:00:34:52
```

The commands in the preceding examples provide a wealth of information for trouble-shooting, such as the packet count and the specific tunnel interface.

Multicast LDP (MLDP)

MLDP is an extension to LDP used to facilitate the transportation of multicast messages in an MPLS network. MLDP supports P2MP and MP2MP label-switched paths (LSPs). With MLDP, you can use the same encapsulation method as with the unicast messages, which reduces the complexity of the network. MLDP is a true pull-model implementation in that the PE closest to the receiver is the device to initiate the LSP.

Figure 3-6 illustrates the MLDP topology. Receivers send traffic upstream, toward the root, and the source sends traffic downstream.

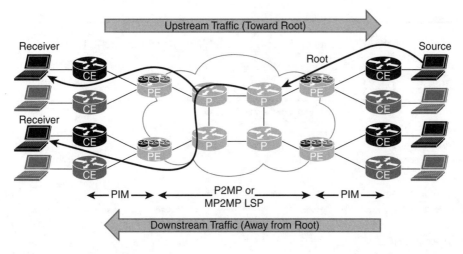

Figure 3-6 *MLDP Topology*

Every time there is a new receiver, a multipoint LSP (MP-LSP) is either created or joined. Every MP-LSP must have a root (in the MPLS core). MLDP uses downstream on-demand label allocation, with labels allocated by the downstream PE (closest to the receiver) toward the upstream PE (closest to the root). The ingress router is the PE closest to the multicast source, and the flow away from the root toward the receiver is called the downstream traffic. The egress router in this case is the PE closest to the receiver. Both the ingress and egress devices (PEs) participate in the native IP Multicast domain (PIM) on the customer side and also the MPLS domain (MLDP) on the provider side.

How did LDP get the capability to support multicast signaling and Reverse Path Forwarding (RPF)? LDP does not have any mechanism to support multicast capabilities or signaling. The draft standard has been proposed (see https://tools.ietf.org/html/draft-ietf-mpls-ldp-capabilities-02), and it provides guidelines for advertising the type-length-value (TLV) capability at the beginning of the session after LDP is established. Three capability TLVs are defined in the implementation of MLDP:

- **P2MP:** TLV 0x0508

- **MP2MP:** TLV 0x0509

- **Make Before Break (MBB):** TLV 0x050A

Cisco does not currently support MBB.

FEC Elements

The Forwarding Equivalence Class (FEC) describes a set of packets with a similar characteristic for forwarding and that are bound to the same outbound MPLS label. With MLDP, the multicast information is transmitted for the control plane to function correctly. MLDP uses the label mapping message to create the MP-LSP hop-by-hop to the root ingress PE device. This path is established using IGP to find the most efficient path to the root, using the appropriate routing metrics. The label mapping message carries additional information known as TLVs. The FEC TLV contains FEC elements, which actually define the set of packets that will use the LSP. This FEC TLV for multicast contains the following information:

- **Tree type:** Point-to-point or bidirectional tree

- **Address family:** The type of stream (IPv4 or IPv6) the tree is replicating, which defines the root address type.

- **Address length:** The length of the root address.

- **Root node address:** The actual root address of the MP-LSP within the MPLS core (IPv4 or IPv6).

- **Opaque value:** The stream information that uniquely identifies this tree to the root. The opaque value contains additional information that defines the (S, G), PIM-SSM Transit, or it can be an LSP identifier to define the default/data MDTs in a multicast VPN (MVPN) application. Currently, four multicast mechanisms are supported, each with a unique opaque value:

  - **IPv4 PIM-SSM transit:** This allows global PIM-SSM streams to be transported across the MPLS core. The opaque value contains the actual (S, G), which reside in the **global mroute** table of the ingress and egress PE routers.

  - **IPv6 PIM-SSM transit:** This is similar to IPv4 PIM-SSM but for IPv6 streams in the global table.

  - **Multicast VPN:** This allows VPNv4 traffic to be transported across the default MDT or the data MDT using label switching. The current method is to use mGRE tunneling (which is reviewed earlier in this chapter). Use MLDP to replace the mGRE tunnel with an MP-LSP tunnel. Multicast VPN is independent of the underlying tunnel mechanism.

  - **Direct MDT or VPNv4 transit:** This opaque value allows VPNv4 streams to be directly built without the need for the default MDT to exist. This is useful for high-bandwidth streams with selective PEs requiring the multicast stream. Currently, this is not a supported feature.

In-Band Signaling Operation

In-band signaling uses opaque LSAs directly between the ingress PE and the egress PE with MLDP. Figure 3-7 shows the operation, which is as follows:

Step 1.   PE3 (egress PE) receives an IGMP join from a receiver. In this example, the receiver is directly connected to the PE. In a real-life scenario, the CE sends a PIM (*, G) join toward the PE. PE3 creates a label-mapping message with FEC TLV with the opaque value. The root address in the FEC element is derived from the BGP next hop or source.

Note   All PEs connected to the receiver create the same FEC element.

Step 2.   Once the source begins transmitting, PE3 builds an MP-LSP toward PE1 (considered the root of the tree). At each hop along the way, the P routers use the same FEC element and associate a local label map, which will be label swapped. Finally, when the packet is received, the ingress PE parses the opaque value to extract the multicast stream information.

Step 3.   When the ingress PE receives the multicast stream, it forwards it on to the correct interface to which the receiver is connected.

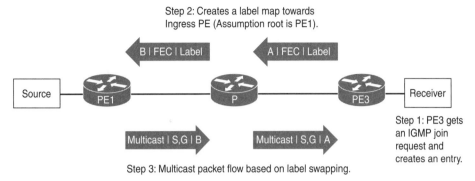

Figure 3-7   *In-Band Signaling Operation*

Out-of-Band (Overlay) Signaling Operation

The other signaling method used to build MLDP is out-of-band signaling.

Figure 3-8 illustrates this procedure, which is as follows:

Step 1.   PE3 (egress PE) receives an IGMP join from a receiver.

Step 2.   PE3 (egress PE) creates an FEC and then builds the multicast LSP hop-by-hop to the root, based on the FEC information using overlay signaling.

Step 3.   PE3 (egress PE) builds the multicast LSP hop-by-hop to the root, based on the FEC information, using the overlay signaling mechanism. (The overlay creates a unique FEC value that is used to forward the multicast stream from PE1 to PE3.)

Step 4.   Multicast messages are transmitted from PE1 to PE3, using the labels created from the out-of-band signaling.

The common overlay signaling model used to build the out-of-band (overlay) signaling includes PIM and the BGP address family.

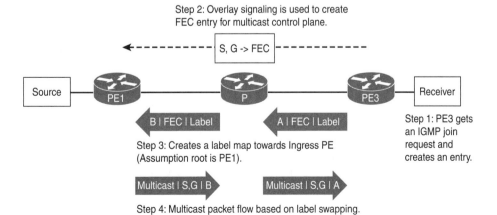

Figure 3-8   *Out-of-Band Signaling Operation*

Default MDT MLDP

The default MDT-GRE, examined earlier in this chapter, uses IP-in-IP with a GRE header to establish connectivity between all PE devices within a VPN. This section builds on the concept of the default MDT and the data MDT, but in this situation, MLDP is used as the transport mechanism.

The default MDT uses an MP2MP bidirectional tree to send multicast hello, join, and prune messages to all the PE routers participating in a particular MVPN. Much as when using the default MDT with GRE, all devices must be aware and able to send and receive multicast messages to all the peers in the VPN. With MLDP, you can take advantage of the underlying LSPs to transport multicast messages, which eliminates the need to run PIM in the core of the network. PIM configured on the customer side of the PE device is still required to establish connectivity with those devices.

The default MDT MLDP is one of the most popular options when implementing MLDP as it offers an easy transition to MLDP compared to some of the other methods. MDT MLDP is also sometimes referred to as Multidirectional Inclusive Provider Multicast Service Interface (MI-PMSI) or Profile 1. (Profiles are explained later in this chapter.)

The first step is to enable PIM MPLS on all P and PE devices in the network by using the **ip pim mpls source Loopback0** command. The P devices must also understand the multicast labels as they may have to preform multicast packet replication. The second step is to create a VPN ID by using the **vpn id** command. The VPN ID must be consistent across all PE device in the same VPN. This command is the equivalent of the MDT group address used on the default MDT GRE.

> **Note**   In this example, the same VPN ID as the RD is used, but this is not a requirement.

Finally, you need to configure at least one device as the root of the MP2MP tree by using the **mdt default mpls mldp [IP_Address]** IOS-XE command or the **mdt default mldp ipv4 [IP_Address]** IOS-XR command. The root of the MDT tree must be configured on all PE devices within a VPN. This is statically configured as there is not an automatic discovery method today. When selecting the root, be sure to choose a device that has the capability to accommodate the additional load. This means you should avoid using a route reflector as the root as may adversely affect the control plane and consequently take down your entire network.

Default MDT MLDP Root High Availability

If only one root is configured, what happens when that device fails? No multicast messages flow across the network. There are two options to address this. The first is to use anycast root node redundancy (RNR). This is accomplished by configuring a primary root and a backup root, which involves creating an additional loopback on the primary root and the backup root that advertise the same IP address. The difference is that the IP address of the primary root advertises the route with a longer mask. For example, refer-ring to Figure 3-5, you could add a loopback address to R8 as 192.168.0.254 with subnet mask 255.255.255.255 (/32) and also add a loopback address to R9 with the same address 192.168.0.254, but with the shorter subnet mask 255.255.255.254 (/31).

Remember that routes are chosen by longest match first. This makes R8 the root, and in the event of a failure, R9 takes over. The issue with this implementation is that when R8 fails, you have to wait for IGP to reconverge to make R9 the new root.

An alternative solution is to configure two devices as the root. Figure 3-9 shows an example in which R8 and R9 are chosen as the root. The upside to this implementation is that immediate failover occurs in the event that the root is unavailable, but the downside is that it creates additional MLDP state in the core of the network. As the network archi-tect, you need to determine if the additional overhead is worth the reduced failover time.

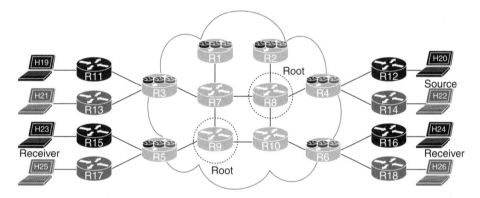

Figure 3-9   *MLDP Root High Availability*

MLDP in Action

This section shows how to configure VRF BLU for MLDP, with R8 and R9 as the root of the tree. In this example, VRF BLU is configured for auto-RP, using R13 as the RP. H22 (172.17.14.22) is configured to send traffic to multicast address 224.2.2.22. H25 and H26 are set up as receivers, as shown in Figure 3-9.

Default MDT MLDP Example

As shown in Examples 3-31 and 3-32, PIM MPLS is configured for Loopback0, the VPN ID is 65000:2, and two roots are configured for high availability: R8 (192.168.0.8) and R9 (192.168.0.9).

Note   All core devices must also be configured to support MPLS MLDP.

Example 3-31 *Default MDT MLDP Configuration Using IOS-XE*

```
PE routers#
vrf definition BLU
 rd 65000:2
 vpn id 65000:2
 !
 address-family ipv4
  mdt default mpls mldp 192.168.0.8
  mdt default mpls mldp 192.168.0.9
  route-target export 65000:2
  route-target import 65000:2
 exit-address-family
```

Example 3-32 *Default MDT MLDP Configuration Using IOS-XR*

```
PE routers#
mpls ldp
 mldp
 !
vrf BLU
 vpn id 65000:2
 address-family ipv4 unicast
   import route-target
    65000:2
   export route-target
    65000:2
 !
route-policy Data-MDT-mLDP
  set core-tree mldp
end-policy
!
multicast-routing
 vrf BLU
  address-family ipv4
   interface all enable
   mdt default mldp ipv4 192.168.0.8
   mdt default mldp ipv4 192.168.0.9
   !
router pim
 vrf BLU
  address-family ipv4
   rpf topology route-policy Data-MDT-mLDP
   interface GigabitEthernet0/0/0/1
```

You need to verify MLDP neighbor relationships by using the **show mpls mldp neighbors** command, as shown in Examples 3-33 and 3-34, from R7. This is one of the few commands that are consistent across IOS-XE and IOS-XR.

Example 3-33   *MPLS MLDP Neighbors Using IOS-XE*

```
R7# show mpls mldp neighbors

 MLDP peer ID    : 192.168.0.1:0, uptime 1w2d Up,
  Target Adj     : No
  Session hndl   : 1
  Upstream count : 0
  Branch count   : 0
  Path count     : 1
  Path(s)        : 192.168.71.1      LDP Ethernet0/3
  Nhop count     : 0


 MLDP peer ID    : 192.168.0.8:0, uptime 1w2d Up,
  Target Adj     : No
  Session hndl   : 3
  Upstream count : 1
  Branch count   : 0
  Path count     : 1
  Path(s)        : 192.168.87.8      LDP Ethernet0/1
  Nhop count     : 1
  Nhop list      : 192.168.87.8


 MLDP peer ID    : 192.168.0.9:0, uptime 1w2d Up,
  Target Adj     : No
  Session hndl   : 4
  Upstream count : 1
  Branch count   : 0
  Path count     : 1
  Path(s)        : 192.168.97.9      LDP Ethernet0/0
  Nhop count     : 1
  Nhop list      : 192.168.97.9


 MLDP peer ID    : 192.168.0.3:0, uptime 5d21h Up,
  Target Adj     : No
  Session hndl   : 6
  Upstream count : 0
  Branch count   : 2
  Path count     : 1
  Path(s)        : 192.168.73.3      LDP Ethernet0/2
  Nhop count     : 0
```

Example 3-34 *MPLS MLDP Neighbors Using IOS-XR*

```
RP/0/0/CPU0:R7# show mpls mldp neighbors
Sat Feb 18 22:26:00.867 UTC
mLDP neighbor database
 MLDP peer ID      : 192.168.0.1:0, uptime 00:31:53 Up,
  Capabilities     : Typed Wildcard FEC, P2MP, MP2MP
  Target Adj       : No
  Upstream count   : 0
  Branch count     : 0
  Label map timer  : never
  Policy filter in :
  Path count       : 1
  Path(s)          : 192.168.71.1      GigabitEthernet0/0/0/3 LDP
  Adj list         : 192.168.71.1      GigabitEthernet0/0/0/3
  Peer addr list   : 192.168.71.1
                   : 192.168.0.1

 MLDP peer ID      : 192.168.0.3:0, uptime 00:31:53 Up,
  Capabilities     : Typed Wildcard FEC, P2MP, MP2MP
  Target Adj       : No
  Upstream count   : 0
  Branch count     : 2
  Label map timer  : never
  Policy filter in :
  Path count       : 1
  Path(s)          : 192.168.73.3      GigabitEthernet0/0/0/2 LDP
  Adj list         : 192.168.73.3      GigabitEthernet0/0/0/2
  Peer addr list   : 192.168.73.3
                   : 192.168.0.3

 MLDP peer ID      : 192.168.0.8:0, uptime 00:31:53 Up,
  Capabilities     : Typed Wildcard FEC, P2MP, MP2MP
  Target Adj       : No
  Upstream count   : 1
  Branch count     : 1
  Label map timer  : never
  Policy filter in :
  Path count       : 1
  Path(s)          : 192.168.87.8      GigabitEthernet0/0/0/1 LDP
  Adj list         : 192.168.87.8      GigabitEthernet0/0/0/1
  Peer addr listw  : 192.168.108.8
                   : 192.168.87.8
                   : 192.168.84.8
```

```
                        : 192.168.82.8

                        : 192.168.0.8

MLDP peer ID            : 192.168.0.9:0, uptime 00:31:53 Up,

 Capabilities           : Typed Wildcard FEC, P2MP, MP2MP

 Target Adj             : No

 Upstream count         : 1

 Branch count           : 1

 Label map timer        : never

 Policy filter in       :

 Path count             : 1

 Path(s)                : 192.168.97.9        GigabitEthernet0/0/0/0 LDP

 Adj list               : 192.168.97.9        GigabitEthernet0/0/0/0

 Peer addr list         : 192.168.97.9

                        : 192.168.109.9

                        : 192.168.95.9

                        : 192.168.0.9
```

The output in Examples 3-33 and 3-34 shows that R7 has established an MLDP neighbor relationships. You can run the **show mpls mldp neighbors** command from any P or PE device to determine the appropriate neighbors.

You also need to verify that the root of the default MDT trees are established by using the **show mpls mldp root** command for both IOS-XE and IOS-XR, as shown in Examples 3-35 and 3-36.

Example 3-35 *MPLS MLDP Root Using IOS-XE*

```
R7# show mpls mldp root
 Root node     : 192.168.0.8
  Metric       : 11
  Distance     : 110
  Interface    : Ethernet0/1 (via unicast RT)
  FEC count    : 1
  Path count   : 1
  Path(s)      : 192.168.87.8    LDP nbr: 192.168.0.8:0    Ethernet0/1

 Root node     : 192.168.0.9
  Metric       : 11
  Distance     : 110
  Interface    : Ethernet0/0 (via unicast RT)
  FEC count    : 1
  Path count   : 1
  Path(s)      : 192.168.97.9    LDP nbr: 192.168.0.9:0    Ethernet0/0
```

Example 3-36   *MPLS MLDP Root Using IOS-XR*

```
RP/0/0/CPU0:R7# show mpls mldp root
Sat Feb 18 22:27:11.592 UTC
mLDP root database
 Root node    : 192.168.0.8
  Metric      : 11
  Distance    : 110
  FEC count   : 1
  Path count  : 1
  Path(s)     : 192.168.87.8     LDP nbr: 192.168.0.8:0

 Root node    : 192.168.0.9
  Metric      : 11
  Distance    : 110
  FEC count   : 1
  Path count  : 1
  Path(s)     : 192.168.97.9     LDP nbr: 192.168.0.9:0
```

One item that is interesting to note is that the P devices are all aware of where the roots are in the tree. The output in Example 3-36 is from R7, one of the P devices.

With the command **show mpls mldp bindings**, you can view the labels associated with the MP2MP trees, as shown in Examples 3-37 and 3-38.

Example 3-37   *MPLS MLDP Bindings Using IOS-XE*

```
R7# show mpls mldp bindings
System ID: 7
Type: MP2MP, Root Node: 192.168.0.8, Opaque Len: 14
Opaque value: [mdt 65000:2 0]
lsr: 192.168.0.8:0, remote binding[U]: 32, local binding[D]: 32 active
lsr: 192.168.0.3:0, local binding[U]: 31, remote binding[D]: 38

System ID: 8
Type: MP2MP, Root Node: 192.168.0.9, Opaque Len: 14
Opaque value: [mdt 65000:2 0]
lsr: 192.168.0.9:0, remote binding[U]: 35, local binding[D]: 34 active
lsr: 192.168.0.3:0, local binding[U]: 33, remote binding[D]: 39
```

Example 3-38 *MPLS MLDP Bindings Using IOS-XR*

```
RP/0/0/CPU0:R7# show mpls mldp bindings
Sat Feb 18 22:42:44.968 UTC
mLDP MPLS Bindings database


LSP-ID: 0x00001 Paths: 3 Flags:
 0x00001 MP2MP  192.168.0.9 [mdt 65000:2 0]
   Local Label: 24017 Remote: 24018 NH: 192.168.97.9 Inft: GigabitEthernet0/0/0/0
     Active
   Local Label: 24015 Remote: 24023 NH: 192.168.73.3 Inft: GigabitEthernet0/0/0/2
   Local Label: 24019 Remote: 24018 NH: 192.168.87.8 Inft: GigabitEthernet0/0/0/1


LSP-ID: 0x00002 Paths: 3 Flags:
 0x00002 MP2MP  192.168.0.8 [mdt 65000:2 0]
   Local Label: 24018 Remote: 24017 NH: 192.168.87.8 Inft: GigabitEthernet0/0/0/1
     Active
   Local Label: 24016 Remote: 24022 NH: 192.168.73.3 Inft: GigabitEthernet0/0/0/2
   Local Label: 24020 Remote: 24019 NH: 192.168.97.9 Inft: GigabitEthernet0/0/0/0
```

Traffic is being generated from the sender, H22 (172.17.14.22), to the multicast address
224.2.2.22, with source port 7060 and destination port 38888. There are two receivers,
H25 and H26. On R4 there are both (*, G) and (S, G) entries, using the **show ip mroute
vrf BLU 224.2.2.22** IOS-XE command, as shown in Example 3-39.

Example 3-39 *MPLS MLDP Bindings Using IOS-XE*

```
R4# show ip mroute vrf BLU 224.2.2.22
IP Multicast Routing Table
Flags: D - Dense, S - Sparse, B - Bidir Group, s - SSM Group, C - Connected,
       L - Local, P - Pruned, R - RP-bit set, F - Register flag,
       T - SPT-bit set, J - Join SPT, M - MSDP created entry, E - Extranet,
       X - Proxy Join Timer Running, A - Candidate for MSDP Advertisement,
       U - URD, I - Received Source Specific Host Report,
       Z - Multicast Tunnel, z - MDT-data group sender,
       Y - Joined MDT-data group, y - Sending to MDT-data group,
       G - Received BGP C-Mroute, g - Sent BGP C-Mroute,
       N - Received BGP Shared-Tree Prune, n - BGP C-Mroute suppressed,
       Q - Received BGP S-A Route, q - Sent BGP S-A Route,
       V - RD & Vector, v - Vector, p - PIM Joins on route,
       x - VxLAN group
Outgoing interface flags: H - Hardware switched, A - Assert winner, p - PIM Join
 Timers: Uptime/Expires
```

```
Interface state: Interface, Next-Hop or VCD, State/Mode

(*, 224.2.2.22), 00:06:38/stopped, RP 172.17.3.13, flags: SP
  Incoming interface: Lspvif1, RPF nbr 192.168.0.3
  Outgoing interface list: Null

(172.17.14.22, 224.2.2.22), 00:03:04/00:03:25, flags: T
  Incoming interface: Ethernet0/1, RPF nbr 172.17.4.14
  Outgoing interface list:
    Lspvif1, Forward/Sparse, 00:03:04/00:03:10
```

Notice that the (*, G) entry has a null outgoing interface list, which is expected because it is in a pruned state. The (S, G) outgoing interface entry is using Lspvif1, which is an LSP virtual interface (LSP-VIF).

For IOS-XR, you use the **show mrib vrf BLU route 224.2.2.22** command, as shown in Example 3-40.

Example 3-40   *MPLS MLDP Bindings Using IOS-XR*

```
RP/0/0/CPU0:R4# show mrib vrf BLU route 224.2.2.22
Sat Feb 18 22:59:50.937 UTC

IP Multicast Routing Information Base
Entry flags: L - Domain-Local Source, E - External Source to the Domain,
    C - Directly-Connected Check, S - Signal, IA - Inherit Accept,
    IF - Inherit From, D - Drop, ME - MDT Encap, EID - Encap ID,
    MD - MDT Decap, MT - MDT Threshold Crossed, MH - MDT interface handle
    CD - Conditional Decap, MPLS - MPLS Decap, EX - Extranet
    MoFE - MoFRR Enabled, MoFS - MoFRR State, MoFP - MoFRR Primary
    MoFB - MoFRR Backup, RPFID - RPF ID Set, X - VXLAN
Interface flags: F - Forward, A - Accept, IC - Internal Copy,
    NS - Negate Signal, DP - Don't Preserve, SP - Signal Present,
    II - Internal Interest, ID - Internal Disinterest, LI - Local Interest,
    LD - Local Disinterest, DI - Decapsulation Interface
    EI - Encapsulation Interface, MI - MDT Interface, LVIF - MPLS Encap,
    EX - Extranet, A2 - Secondary Accept, MT - MDT Threshold Crossed,
    MA - Data MDT Assigned, LMI - mLDP MDT Interface, TMI - P2MP-TE MDT Interface
    IRMI - IR MDT Interface

(172.17.14.22,224.2.2.22) RPF nbr: 172.17.4.14 Flags: RPF
  Up: 00:40:17
  Incoming Interface List
    GigabitEthernet0/0/0/1 Flags: A, Up: 00:40:17
  Outgoing Interface List
    LmdtBLU Flags: F NS LMI, Up: 00:40:17
```

With the output shown in Example 3-40, only the (S, G) entry is listed with the outgoing interface LmdtBLU.

To determine the MPLS labels assigned the data MDT entries, you use the IOS-XE **show mpls mldp database** command, as shown in Example 3-41.

Example 3-41 *MPLS MLDP Database Using IOS-XE*

```
R4# show mpls mldp database
 * Indicates MLDP recursive forwarding is enabled

LSM ID : 1 (RNR LSM ID: 2)   Type: MP2MP   Uptime : 1w2d
  FEC Root            : 192.168.0.8
  Opaque decoded      : [mdt 65000:2 0]
  Opaque length       : 11 bytes
  Opaque value        : 02 000B 0650000000000200000000
  RNR active LSP       : (this entry)
  Candidate RNR ID(s): 6
  Upstream client(s) :
    192.168.0.8:0    [Active]
      Expires        : Never        Path Set ID  : 1
      Out Label (U)  : 31           Interface    : Ethernet0/0*
      Local Label (D): 38           Next Hop     : 192.168.84.8
  Replication client(s):
    MDT  (VRF BLU)
      Uptime         : 1w2d         Path Set ID  : 2
      Interface      : Lspvif1

LSM ID : 6 (RNR LSM ID: 2)   Type: MP2MP   Uptime : 02:01:58
  FEC Root            : 192.168.0.9
  Opaque decoded      : [mdt 65000:2 0]
  Opaque length       : 11 bytes
  Opaque value        : 02 000B 0650000000000200000000
  RNR active LSP      : 1 (root: 192.168.0.8)
  Upstream client(s) :
    192.168.0.8:0    [Active]
      Expires        : Never        Path Set ID  : 6
      Out Label (U)  : 34           Interface    : Ethernet0/0*
      Local Label (D): 39           Next Hop     : 192.168.84.8
  Replication client(s):
    MDT  (VRF BLU)
      Uptime         : 02:01:58     Path Set ID  : 7
      Interface      : Lspvif1
```

The output shown in Example 3-41 also shows that the active RNR is R8 (192.168.0.8). The Out Label (U), which is upstream toward the root, has the label 31 assigned, and the (D) downstream label, away from the root, has the value 38.

You can validate that multicast traffic is using the upstream label with the **show mpls forwarding-table labels 31** command, as shown with Example 3-42 on R8.

Example 3-42   *MPLS Forwarding Table Using IOS-XE*

```
R8# show mpls forwarding-table labels 31
Local      Outgoing   Prefix          Bytes Label   Outgoing    Next Hop
Label      Label      or Tunnel Id    Switched      interface
31         33         [mdt 65000:2 0] 16652686      Et0/0       192.168.108.10
           32         [mdt 65000:2 0] 16652686      Et0/1       192.168.87.7
```

From the output in Example 3-42, notice that the number of label-switched bytes is 16,652,686 and that the multicast stream is being replicated to R7 through Et0/1 and R10 through Et0/0. Because R8 is a P device, multicast replication is occurring in the core.

For IOS-XR, you use a series of commands to validate the behavior, starting with the **show mpls mldp database** command in Example 3-43.

Example 3-43   *MPLS MLDP Database Using IOS-XR*

```
RP/0/0/CPU0:R4# show mpls mldp database
Sat Feb 18 23:07:07.917 UTC
mLDP database
LSM-ID: 0x00001  (RNR LSM-ID: 0x00002)  Type: MP2MP  Uptime: 01:31:35
  FEC Root           : 192.168.0.8
  Opaque decoded     : [mdt 65000:2 0]
  RNR active LSP     : (this entry)
  Candidate RNR ID(s): 00000003
  Upstream neighbor(s) :
    192.168.0.8:0 [Active] Uptime: 01:29:54
      Next Hop     : 192.168.84.8
      Interface    : GigabitEthernet0/0/0/0
      Local Label (D) : 24024           Remote Label (U): 24016
  Downstream  client(s):
    PIM MDT          Uptime: 01:31:35
      Egress intf  : LmdtBLU
      Table ID     : IPv4: 0xe0000011 IPv6: 0xe0800011
      HLI          : 0x00002
      RPF ID       : 1
      Local Label  : 24000 (internal)
```

```
LSM-ID: 0x00003  (RNR LSM-ID: 0x00002)  Type: MP2MP  Uptime: 01:31:35
 FEC Root           : 192.168.0.9
 Opaque decoded     : [mdt 65000:2 0]
 RNR active LSP     : LSM-ID: 0x00001 (root: 192.168.0.8)
 Candidate RNR ID(s):  00000003
 Upstream neighbor(s) :
   192.168.0.8:0 [Active] Uptime: 01:29:54
     Next Hop         : 192.168.84.8
     Interface        : GigabitEthernet0/0/0/0
     Local Label (D) : 24025              Remote Label (U) : 24015
 Downstream  client(s):
   PIM MDT            Uptime: 01:31:35
     Egress intf      : LmdtBLU
     Table ID         : IPv4: 0xe0000011 IPv6: 0xe0800011
     RPF ID           : 1
     Local Label      : 24001 (internal)
     RPF ID           : 1
     Local Label      : 24001 (internal)
```

Notice that the multicast type is MP2MP, which is indicative of the default MDT, and you can see the labels associated. Use the command **show mpls mldp database root 192.168.0.8** to show only the trees that have been rooted on R4.

The **show mpls mldp bindings** IOS-XR command verifies the label associated with each tree, as shown in Example 3-44.

Example 3-44 *MPLS MLDP Bindings Using IOS-XR*

```
RP/0/0/CPU0:R4# show mpls mldp bindings
Sat Feb 18 23:32:34.197 UTC
mLDP MPLS Bindings database

LSP-ID: 0x00001 Paths: 2 Flags: Pk
 0x00001 MP2MP  192.168.0.8 [mdt 65000:2 0]
   Local Label: 24020 Remote: 24016 NH: 192.168.84.8 Inft: GigabitEthernet0/0/0/0
     Active
   Local Label: 24000 Remote: 1048577 Inft: LmdtBLU RPF-ID: 1 TIDv4/v6:
     0xE0000011/0xE0800011

LSP-ID: 0x00003 Paths: 2 Flags: Pk
 0x00003 MP2MP  192.168.0.9 [mdt 65000:2 0]
   Local Label: 24021 Remote: 24015 NH: 192.168.84.8 Inft: GigabitEthernet0/0/0/0
     Active
   Local Label: 24001 Remote: 1048577 Inft: LmdtBLU RPF-ID: 1 TIDv4/v6:
     0xE0000011/0xE0800011
```

Yes, everything is working as expected—but not very efficiently because multicast messages are being sent to every PE in the VPN. If you look at a packet capture between R7 and R3, where there are not any multicast receivers, you see the multicast messages shown in Example 3-45.

Example 3-45   *MPLS MLDP Packet Capture*

```
Ethernet Packet:  558 bytes
      Dest Addr: AABB.CC00.0300,    Source Addr: AABB.CC00.0720
      Protocol : 0x8847


MPLS   Label: 38,  CoS: 0,  Bottom: 1,   TTL: 56


IP     Version: 0x4,  HdrLen: 0x5,  TOS: 0x00
       Length: 540,   ID: 0x0000,   Flags-Offset: 0x0000
       TTL: 58,   Protocol: 17 (UDP),   Checksum: 0xE291 (OK)
       Source: 172.17.14.22,    Dest: 224.2.2.22


UDP    Src Port: 38888,   Dest Port: 7060
       Length: 520,   Checksum: 0xAC21 (OK)


Data: *removed for brevity*
```

Data MDT MLDP Example

The multicast everywhere problem can be solved with the data MDT by using MLDP. In Figure 3-10 the commands from Example 3-46 for IOS-XE and Example 3-47 for IOS-XR are added to every PE router that participates in the BLU VPN. The goal is to build the most efficient multicast transport method.

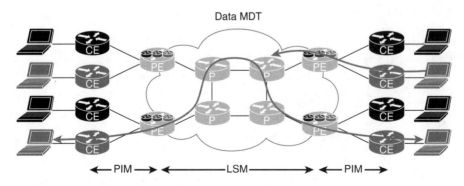

Data MDT

←— PIM —→ ←———LSM———→ ←— PIM —→

Figure 3-10   *Data MDT MLDP*

Example 3-46 *MPLS MLDP Threshold Using IOS-XE*

```
vrf definition BLU
 rd 65000:2
 vpn id 65000:2
 !
 address-family ipv4
  mdt preference mldp
  mdt default mpls mldp 192.168.0.8
  mdt default mpls mldp 192.168.0.9
  mdt data mpls mldp 64
  mdt data threshold 1
  route-target export 65000:2
  route-target import 65000:2
 exit-address-family
```

Example 3-47 *MPLS MLDP Threshold Using IOS-XR*

```
multicast-routing
 vrf BLU
  address-family ipv4
   interface all enable
   mdt default mldp ipv4 192.168.0.8
   mdt default mldp ipv4 192.168.0.9
   mdt data 254 threshold 1
```

The **mdt data mpls mldp** command for IOS-XE and the **mdt data 254 threshold 2** command for IOS-XR set the maximum number of data MDTs that are allow to be created until they are reused. The **threshold** command determines how large the multicast stream must be before it is moved to the data MDT. Here, it is 2 Kbps.

After configuring all the PE devices with the data MDT commands, you can take a look at the output of the **show mpls mldp database** IOS-XE command, as shown in Example 3-48.

Example 3-48 *MPLS MLDP Database Using IOS-XE*

```
R4# show mpls mldp database
  * Indicates MLDP recursive forwarding is enabled

LSM ID : 7   Type: P2MP   Uptime : 00:04:15
  FEC Root           : 192.168.0.4 (we are the root)
  Opaque decoded     : [mdt 65000:2 1]
  Opaque length      : 11 bytes
  Opaque value       : 02 000B 0650000000000200000001
```

```
  Upstream client(s) :
    None
      Expires        : N/A          Path Set ID  : 8
  Replication client(s):
    MDT  (VRF BLU)
      Uptime         : 00:04:15     Path Set ID  : None
      Interface      : Lspvif1
    192.168.0.8:0
      Uptime         : 00:04:15     Path Set ID  : None
      Out label (D)  : 36           Interface    : Ethernet0/0*
      Local label (U): None         Next Hop     : 192.168.84.8


LSM ID : 1 (RNR LSM ID: 2)   Type: MP2MP   Uptime : 1w2d
  FEC Root             : 192.168.0.8
  Opaque decoded       : [mdt 65000:2 0]
  Opaque length        : 11 bytes
  Opaque value         : 02 000B 0650000000000200000000
  RNR active LSP       : (this entry)
  Candidate RNR ID(s): 6
  Upstream client(s) :
    192.168.0.8:0    [Active]
      Expires        : Never        Path Set ID  : 1
      Out Label (U)  : 31           Interface    : Ethernet0/0*
      Local Label (D): 38           Next Hop     : 192.168.84.8
  Replication client(s):
    MDT  (VRF BLU)
      Uptime         : 1w2d         Path Set ID  : 2
      Interface      : Lspvif1


LSM ID : 6 (RNR LSM ID: 2)   Type: MP2MP   Uptime : 03:38:05
  FEC Root             : 192.168.0.9
  Opaque decoded       : [mdt 65000:2 0]
  Opaque length        : 11 bytes
  Opaque value         : 02 000B 0650000000000200000000
  RNR active LSP       : 1 (root: 192.168.0.8)
  Upstream client(s) :
    192.168.0.8:0    [Active]
      Expires        : Never        Path Set ID  : 6
      Out Label (U)  : 34           Interface    : Ethernet0/0*
      Local Label (D): 39           Next Hop     : 192.168.84.8
  Replication client(s):
    MDT  (VRF BLU)
      Uptime         : 03:38:05     Path Set ID  : 7
      Interface      : Lspvif1
```

The output in Example 3-48 shows some very valuable information. The tree type is P2MP, and the FEC root shows that R4 is the root of the tree. This is as it should be because R4 is originating the multicast stream. Notice that the Opaque decoded value is [mdt 65000:2 1]. The last value in the string is a 1, which indicates the change from the default MDT to the data MDT. Finally, the Out label (D) value is 36. The downstream (from a multicast perspective) router R8 shows that the incoming label is 36, and the outgoing labels are 35 and 38 because H25 and H26 are both receivers.

As shown in Example 3-49, you can use the **show mpls forwarding-table labels 36** IOS-XE command to see the associated labels for the P2MP interface.

Example 3-49 *MPLS MLDP P2MP Using IOS-XE*

```
R8# show mpls forwarding-table labels 36
Local      Outgoing   Prefix          Bytes Label   Outgoing    Next Hop
Label      Label      or Tunnel Id    Switched      interface
36         38         [mdt 65000:2 1]  63819576     Et0/0       192.168.108.10
           35         [mdt 65000:2 1]  63819576     Et0/1       192.168.87.7
```

With IOS-XR, you get a similar output with the **show mpls mldp database p2mp root 192.168.0.4** command, as shown in Example 3-50.

Example 3-50 *MPLS MLDP P2MP Using IOS-XR*

```
RP/0/0/CPU0:R4# show mpls mldp database p2mp root 192.168.0.4
Sun Feb 19 00:17:56.420 UTC
mLDP database
LSM-ID: 0x00004  Type: P2MP  Uptime: 00:08:50
  FEC Root           : 192.168.0.4 (we are the root)
  Opaque decoded     : [mdt 65000:2 1]
  Upstream neighbor(s) :
    None
  Downstream  client(s):
    LDP 192.168.0.8:0  Uptime: 00:08:50
      Next Hop         : 192.168.84.8
      Interface        : GigabitEthernet0/0/0/0
      Remote label (D) : 24022
    PIM MDT            Uptime: 00:08:50
      Egress intf      : LmdtBLU
      Table ID         : IPv4: 0xe0000011 IPv6: 0xe0800011
      HLI              : 0x00004
      RPF ID           : 1
      Ingress          : Yes
      Local Label      : 24026 (internal)
```

You can see the label bindings in IOS-XR with the **show mpls mldp bindings** command, as shown in Example 3-51.

Example 3-51 *MPLS MLDP Bindings Using IOS-XR*

```
RP/0/0/CPU0:R4# show mpls mldp bindings
Sun Feb 19 00:22:42.951 UTC
mLDP MPLS Bindings database


LSP-ID: 0x00001 Paths: 2 Flags: Pk
 0x00001 MP2MP  192.168.0.8 [mdt 65000:2 0]
   Local Label: 24020 Remote: 24016 NH: 192.168.84.8 Inft: GigabitEthernet0/0/0/0
     Active
   Local Label: 24000 Remote: 1048577 Inft: LmdtBLU RPF-ID: 1 TIDv4/v6:
     0xE0000011/0xE0800011


LSP-ID: 0x00003 Paths: 2 Flags: Pk
 0x00003 MP2MP  192.168.0.9 [mdt 65000:2 0]
   Local Label: 24021 Remote: 24015 NH: 192.168.84.8 Inft: GigabitEthernet0/0/0/0
     Active
   Local Label: 24001 Remote: 1048577 Inft: LmdtBLU RPF-ID: 1 TIDv4/v6:
     0xE0000011/0xE0800011


LSP-ID: 0x00008 Paths: 2 Flags:
 0x00008 P2MP   192.168.0.3 [mdt 65000:2 2]
   Local Label: 24029 Active
   Remote Label: 1048577 Inft: LmdtBLU RPF-ID: 1 TIDv4/v6: 0xE0000011/0xE0800011


LSP-ID: 0x00004 Paths: 2 Flags:
 0x00004 P2MP   192.168.0.4 [mdt 65000:2 1]
   Local Label: 24026 Remote: 1048577 Inft: LmdtBLU RPF-ID: 1 TIDv4/v6:
     0xE0000011/0xE0800011
   Remote Label: 24022 NH: 192.168.84.8 Inft: GigabitEthernet0/0/0/0


LSP-ID: 0x00007 Paths: 2 Flags:
 0x00007 P2MP   192.168.0.3 [mdt 65000:2 1]
   Local Label: 24028 Active
   Remote Label: 1048577 Inft: LmdtBLU RPF-ID: 1 TIDv4/v6: 0xE0000011/0xE0800011
```

To verify the number of clients, you can use the **show mpls mldp database summary** command in IOS-XE, as shown in Example 3-52.

Example 3-52 *MPLS MLDP Database Summary Using IOS-XE*

```
R4# show mpls mldp database summary


LSM ID     Type    Root           Decoded Opaque Value        Client Cnt.
7          P2MP    192.168.0.4    [mdt 65000:2 1]             2
1          MP2MP   192.168.0.8    [mdt 65000:2 0]             1
6          MP2MP   192.168.0.9    [mdt 65000:2 0]             1
```

The output from R4 in Example 3-52 appears to clients in the data MDT.

A very similar command is used for IOS-XR, as shown in Example 3-53.

Example 3-53 *MPLS MLDP Database Brief Using IOS-XR*

```
RP/0/0/CPU0:R4# show mpls mldp database brief
Sun Feb 19 00:23:21.638 UTC


LSM ID    Type    Root              Up Down Decoded Opaque Value
0x00007   P2MP    192.168.0.3       1  1    [mdt 65000:2 1]
0x00004   P2MP    192.168.0.4       0  2    [mdt 65000:2 1]
0x00008   P2MP    192.168.0.3       1  1    [mdt 65000:2 2]
0x00001   MP2MP   192.168.0.8       1  1    [mdt 65000:2 0]
0x00003   MP2MP   192.168.0.9       1  1    [mdt 65000:2 0]
```

You can look at R7 to validate that multicast messages are going only to the correct locations. The **show mpls mldp database summary** IOS-XE command reveals only one client, as shown in Example 3-54.

Example 3-54 *MPLS MLDP Database Summary Validation Using IOS-XR*

```
R7# show mpls mldp database summary
LSM ID     Type     Root           Decoded Opaque Value      Client Cnt.
9          P2MP     192.168.0.4    [mdt 65000:2 1]           1
7          MP2MP    192.168.0.8    [mdt 65000:2 0]           1
8          MP2MP    192.168.0.9    [mdt 65000:2 0]           1
```

You can validate the outgoing interface on R7 with the **show mpls forwarding-table | include 65000:2 1** IOS-XE command, as shown in Example 3-55.

Example 3-55 *MPLS Forwarding Table Using IOS-XE*

```
R7# show mpls forwarding-table | inc 65000:2 1
35         37         [mdt 65000:2 1]   85357260      Et0/0       192.168.97.9
```

The only outgoing interface for the multicast stream is R9 (192.168.97.9), which is in the downstream direction, toward H25. It is no longer flooding multicast to every PE in the BLU VPN. Traffic is flowing according to Figure 3-5. Mission accomplished!

Profiles

Profiles are essentially the different methods to implement MVPN. Each profile provides unique capabilities, whether they are core transport or signaling methods or how the interaction with the customer is accomplished. Using profile numbers is much easier than having to say, "I am implementing partitioned MDT with MLDP and MP2MP transport using BGP-AD in the core with BGP C-multicast signaling" when you could just say "I am using Profile 14."

Currently you can select from 27 different profiles. Previous sections of this chapter mention only 2 of these implementation strategies. As you can imagine, it is well beyond the scope of this book to explain them all, but here is a list of the available options:

- Profile 0 Default MDT - GRE - PIM C-mcast Signaling
- Profile 1 Default MDT - MLDP MP2MP PIM C-mcast Signaling
- Profile 2 Partitioned MDT - MLDP MP2MP - PIM C-mcast Signaling
- Profile 3 Default MDT - GRE - BGP-AD - PIM C-mcast Signaling
- Profile 4 Partitioned MDT - MLDP MP2MP - BGP-AD - PIM C-mcast Signaling
- Profile 5 Partitioned MDT - MLDP P2MP - BGP-AD - PIM C-mcast Signaling
- Profile 6 VRF MLDP - In-band Signaling
- Profile 7 Global MLDP In-band Signaling
- Profile 8 Global Static - P2MP-TE
- Profile 9 Default MDT - MLDP - MP2MP - BGP-AD - PIM C-mcast Signaling
- Profile 10 VRF Static - P2MP TE - BGP-AD
- Profile 11 Default MDT - GRE - BGP-AD - BGP C-mcast Signaling
- Profile 12 Default MDT - MLDP - P2MP - BGP-AD - BGP C-mcast Signaling
- Profile 13 Default MDT - MLDP - MP2MP - BGP-AD - BGP C-mcast Signaling
- Profile 14 Partitioned MDT - MLDP P2MP - BGP-AD - BGP C-mast Signaling
- Profile 15 Partitioned MDT - MLDP MP2MP - BGP-AD - BGP C-mast Signaling
- Profile 16 Default MDT Static - P2MP TE - BGP-AD - BGP C-mcast Signaling
- Profile 17 Default MDT - MLDP - P2MP - BGP-AD - PIM C-mcast Signaling
- Profile 18 Default Static MDT - P2MP TE - BGP-AD - PIM C-mcast Signaling
- Profile 19 Default MDT - IR - BGP-AD - PIM C-mcast Signaling
- Profile 20 Default MDT - P2MP-TE - BGP-AD - PIM - C-mcast Signaling
- Profile 21 Default MDT - IR - BGP-AD - BGP - C-mcast Signaling
- Profile 22 Default MDT - P2MP-TE - BGP-AD BGP - C-mcast Signaling
- Profile 23 Partitioned MDT - IR - BGP-AD - PIM C-mcast Signaling
- Profile 24 Partitioned MDT - P2MP-TE - BGP-AD - PIM C-mcast Signaling
- Profile 25 Partitioned MDT - IR - BGP-AD - BGP C-mcast Signaling
- Profile 26 Partitioned MDT - P2MP TE - BGP-AD - BGP C-mcast Signaling

Note Where do you start looking for information on all these profiles? The Cisco website is a good place to find information on each profile: www.cisco.com/c/en/us/support/docs/ip/multicast/118985-configure-mcast-00.html.

Another implementation that is worth noting is partitioned MDT, which is a more efficient method of multicast communication across the provider network than using the default MDT method. The partitioned MDT technique does not require the use of the default MDT, which means a reduction in the amount of unwanted multicast traffic sent to PE devices within a VPN. Today, Profile 2 is only supported using IOS-XR, but if you have both IOS-XE and IOS-XR devices in your network, you can use Profile 4, which uses BGP-Auto Discovery (AD) for signaling.

Luc De Ghein from Cisco TAC created an overview framework that really helps with understanding the different profiles (see Figure 3-11).

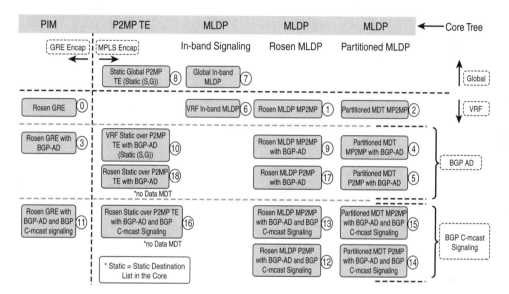

Figure 3-11 *MPLS Profiles*

When you're determining which profile to implement, you first need to think about which operating systems are being used in the network. It all boils down to the least common denominator. For example, if you are using NX-OS in your network, you are limited to Profile 0, and the decision is easy. Table 3-1 provides details on the profiles supported in each operating system as of this writing. You can also see the current version of the release notes to verify support of your specific hardware and software platforms.

Table 3-1 *MVPN Operating System Support Matrix*

Profile	NX-OS	IOS-XE	IOS-XR
0	IPv4 only	X	X
1		X	X
2			X
3			X
4			X
5			X

Profile	NX-OS	IOS-XE	IOS-XR
6		X	X
7		X	X
8		X	X
9		X	X
10			X
11		X	X
12		X	X
13		X	X
14		X	X
15			X
16			X
17		X	X
18			X
19			X
20			X
21			X
22			X
23			X
24			X
25			X
26			X

Next, you need to determine what you need to accomplish and the available resources. Items to consider include the following:

- Core and customer multicast requirements

- Scalability—that is, how many core and customer routes will be needed

- Hardware limitations

- Operational experience, which may determine which requirements you can support

- High-availability requirements

If one of your requirements is high availability, consider using a profile that supports MLDP. With this implementation, you can take advantage of Loop-Free Alternate (LFA) routing and minimize the complexity of traffic engineering tunnels.

After you have made a decision on which profile to implement, you should build a lab and test, test, test to become familiar with the operation and troubleshooting of your particular environment.

Migrating Between Profiles

With IOS-XE, you can configure support for multiple profiles within the address family of the VRF definition. In Example 3-56, both Profile 0 and Profile 1 are supported simultaneously, but Profile 0 is preferred unless the **mdt preference mldp** command is configured, in which case Profile 1 is selected. Using two profiles at once certainly helps to ease the migration from some profiles, but the capabilities are limited.

Example 3-56 *Migrating Between Profiles Using IOS-XE*

```
vrf definition RED
 rd 65000:1
 vpn id 65000:1
 !
 address-family ipv4
  mdt preference mldp
  mdt default mpls mldp 192.168.0.8
  mdt default mpls mldp 192.168.0.9
  mdt default 232.0.0.1
  mdt data 232.0.1.0 0.0.0.255 threshold 2
  mdt data threshold 2
 exit-address-family
```

IOS-XR, on the other hand, allows you to map individual flows to a unique profile by using route policy language (RPL). This is a very powerful feature, as shown in Example 3-57.

Example 3-57 *Migrating Between Profiles Using IOS-XR and RPL*

```
RP/0/0/CPU0:R4#
route-policy MCast-Policy-RED
  if source in (172.16.12.20/32) then
    set core-tree pim-default
  endif
  if destination in (224.1.3.0/24) then
    set core-tree mldp
  else
    set core-tree mldp-partitioned-mp2mp
  endif
end-policy
```

In the command set shown in Example 3-57, the first if statement looks at the source address. A match to 172.16.12.20 means Profile 0, or data MDT with GRE, is used. The second if statement looks for a destination match. If the destination multicast address falls in the subnet range 224.1.3.0/24, MLDP, or Profile 1, is used. The final else statement is a catch-all that means the partitioned MLDP, or Profile 2, is used. The capabilities are almost endless.

Be sure to apply the statement as shown in Example 3-58.

Example 3-58   *Applying Profiles Using IOS-XR and RPL*

```
router pim
 vrf RED
  address-family ipv4
   rpf topology route-policy MCast-Policy-RED
```

Provider (P) Multicast Transport

Transporting multicast traffic flows across the provider network is accomplished using any one of or a combination of these three methods:

- **PIM:** With PIM in the core, customer multicast messages are mapped to provider multicast messages using IP in IP with a GRE header, as shown in Example 3-3 with Profile 0.

- **MLDP:** Both P2MP and MP2MP transport are supported.

- **TE tunnels:** Profiles 8, 10, and 18 use traffic engineering (TE) tunnels. Profile 8 is unique in that it does not send traffic through a VPN but rather uses the global routing table.

PE–CE Multicast Routing

Multicast routing between multiple customer (C) locations requires the integration of the provider edge (PE) and customer edge (CE) equipment. The universal requirement is to have PIM enabled and functional between the PE and the CE, as shown in Figure 3-12.

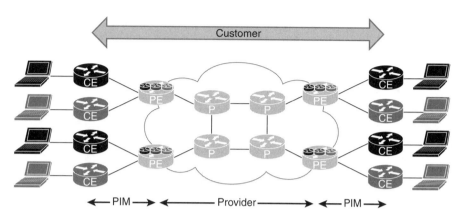

Figure 3-12 *PE–CE Multicast Routing*

Previous examples in this chapter use PIM-SM or Any-Source Multicast (ASM) on the customer network. The integration between the PE and the CE means that the provider network is an extension of the customer network. For example, if a CE router is used as the RP, any source or receiver would register with the RP over the provider network, and only one RP is required for the entire VPN. The propagation of (*, G) or (S, G) multicast messages is handled "transparently" from the customer's perspective.

CE–CE Multicast Routing

With ASM, an RP is required. The placement of the RP and how it is connected does provide some options. In previous examples, one of the CE devices was configured as an RP for the entire VPN, but there are two more options. The first option is to use a PE device as the RP (in the case of a self-managed MPLS solution). High availability can be configured using Anycast RP. The second solution is to build an RP at each CE location and connect the RPs using MSDP. This solution adds a tremendous amount of configuration overhead. It would be a good choice if the environment has an SP-managed MPLS Layer 3 VPN solution.

PE–PE Ingress Replication

PE–PE ingress replication enables you to create a P2MP tree where ingress devices replicate the multicast packets, encapsulate the packets in a unicast tunnel, and send the packets to egress devices. PE–PE ingress replication is a great tool to have in the tool-box, but it's not one that should be used all the time or even very often. PE–PE ingress replication works well when the core of the network does not support any type of multicast routing. For example, you might have equipment in the core that will not support multicast, or you may be integrating with another provider that does not allow multicast. Whatever the reason, PE–PE ingress replication is a workaround solution, and using it really defeats the purpose of multicast in the first place because it involves converting multicast streams to unicast so they can be propagated over the core network.

In Figure 3-13, the PE router in the top-right corner of the diagram is receiving multicast traffic from the sender, converting it into two unicast flows, and sending it across the network.

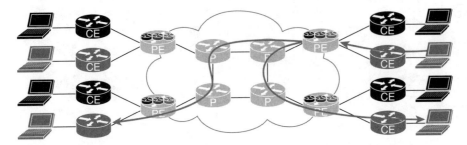

Figure 3-13   *PE–PE Ingress Replication*

At the time of this writing, the Cisco CSR 1000v is the only IOS-XE device that supports ingress replication. (This topic is explained in detail in Chapter 2, "Multicast Scalability and Transport Diversification.") With IOS-XR, you have the capability to configure PE–PE ingress replication. Example 3-59 is a configuration snippet.

Example 3-59   *PE–PE Ingress Replication Using IOS-XR*

```
RP/0/0/CPU0:R4#
route-policy IR-Default
  set core-tree ingress-replication-default
end-policy

multicast-routing
 !
 vrf BLU
  address-family ipv4
   interface all enable
   bgp auto-discovery ingress-replication
   !
   mdt default ingress-replication
   mdt data ingress-replication

router pim
 !
 vrf BLU
  address-family ipv4
   rpf topology route-policy IR-Default
   mdt c-multicast-routing bgp
   !
    !
   !
  !
```

You can look at the MRIB table by using the **show mrib vrf BLU route 224.2.2.22** command. The interface list in Example 3-60 shows IRmdtBLU, which indicates that it is using ingress replication.

Example 3-60 *IRmdtBLU Ingress Replication Using IOS-XR*

```
RP/0/0/CPU0:R4# show mrib vrf BLU route 224.2.2.22
Fri Feb 24 23:08:26.136 UTC


IP Multicast Routing Information Base
Entry flags: L - Domain-Local Source, E - External Source to the Domain,
    C - Directly-Connected Check, S - Signal, IA - Inherit Accept,
    IF - Inherit From, D - Drop, ME - MDT Encap, EID - Encap ID,
    MD - MDT Decap, MT - MDT Threshold Crossed, MH - MDT interface handle
    CD - Conditional Decap, MPLS - MPLS Decap, EX - Extranet
    MoFE - MoFRR Enabled, MoFS - MoFRR State, MoFP - MoFRR Primary
    MoFB - MoFRR Backup, RPFID - RPF ID Set, X - VXLAN
Interface flags: F - Forward, A - Accept, IC - Internal Copy,
    NS - Negate Signal, DP - Don't Preserve, SP - Signal Present,
    II - Internal Interest, ID - Internal Disinterest, LI - Local Interest,
    LD - Local Disinterest, DI - Decapsulation Interface
    EI - Encapsulation Interface, MI - MDT Interface, LVIF - MPLS Encap,
    EX - Extranet, A2 - Secondary Accept, MT - MDT Threshold Crossed,
    MA - Data MDT Assigned, LMI - mLDP MDT Interface, TMI - P2MP-TE MDT Interface
    IRMI - IR MDT Interface

(172.19.14.22,224.2.2.22) RPF nbr: 172.19.4.4 Flags: RPF
  Up: 00:02:06
  Incoming Interface List
    IRmdtBLU Flags: A IRMI, Up: 00:02:06
```

To verify the PE devices that are participating in the BLU MVPN, you use the **show mvpn vrf BLU pe** command, as shown in Example 3-61.

Example 3-61 *MVPN VRF PEs Using IOS-XR*

```
RP/0/0/CPU0:R4# show mvpn vrf BLU pe
Sat Feb 25 23:03:16.548 UTC


MVPN Provider Edge Router information


VRF : BLU


PE Address : 192.168.0.3 (0x12be134c)
  RD: 65000:2 (valid), RIB_HLI 0, RPF-ID 9, Remote RPF-ID 0, State: 1, S-PMSI: 0
```

```
PPMP_LABEL: 0, MS_PMSI_HLI: 0x00000, Bidir_PMSI_HLI: 0x00000, MLDP-added:
[RD 0, ID 0, Bidir ID 0, Remote Bidir ID 0], Counts(SHR/SRC/DM/DEF-MD): 0, 1, 0,
0, Bidir: GRE RP Count 0, MPLS RP Count 0RSVP-TE added: [Leg 0, Ctrl Leg 0, Part
tail 0 Def Tail 0, IR added: [Def Leg 0, Ctrl Leg 0, Part Leg 0, Part tail 0,
Part IR Tail Label 0

bgp_i_pmsi: 0,0/0 , bgp_ms_pmsi/Leaf-ad: 0/0, bgp_bidir_pmsi: 0, remote_bgp_bidir_
pmsi: 0, PMSIs: I 0x0, 0x0, MS 0x0, Bidir Local: 0x0, Remote: 0x0, BSR/Leaf-ad
0x0/0, Autorp-disc/Leaf-ad 0x0/0, Autorp-ann/Leaf-ad 0x0/0

IIDs: I/6: 0x0/0x0, B/R: 0x0/0x0, MS: 0x0, B/A/A: 0x0/0x0/0x0


Bidir RPF-ID: 10, Remote Bidir RPF-ID: 0

I-PMSI:  (0x0)

I-PMSI rem:  (0x0)

MS-PMSI:  (0x0)

Bidir-PMSI:  (0x0)

Remote Bidir-PMSI:  (0x0)

BSR-PMSI:  (0x0)

A-Disc-PMSI:  (0x0)

A-Ann-PMSI:  (0x0)

RIB Dependency List: 0x121696a4

Bidir RIB Dependency List: 0x0

  Sources: 1, RPs: 0, Bidir RPs: 0


PE Address : 192.168.0.5 (0x12c9f7a0)

RD: 0:0:0 (null), RIB_HLI 0, RPF-ID 11, Remote RPF-ID 0, State: 0, S-PMSI: 0

PPMP_LABEL: 0, MS_PMSI_HLI: 0x00000, Bidir_PMSI_HLI: 0x00000, MLDP-added:
[RD 0, ID 0, Bidir ID 0, Remote Bidir ID 0], Counts(SHR/SRC/DM/DEF-MD): 0, 0, 0,
0, Bidir: GRE RP Count 0, MPLS RP Count 0RSVP-TE added: [Leg 0, Ctrl Leg 0,
Part tail 0 Def Tail 0, IR added: [Def Leg 0, Ctrl Leg 0, Part Leg 0, Part tail 0,
Part IR Tail Label 0

bgp_i_pmsi: 1,0/0 , bgp_ms_pmsi/Leaf-ad: 0/0, bgp_bidir_pmsi: 0, remote_bgp_bidir_
pmsi: 0, PMSIs: I 0x12897d48, 0x0, MS 0x0, Bidir Local: 0x0, Remote: 0x0, BSR/
Leaf-ad 0x0/0, Autorp-disc/Leaf-ad 0x0/0, Autorp-ann/Leaf-ad 0x0/0

IIDs: I/6: 0x1/0x0, B/R: 0x0/0x0, MS: 0x0, B/A/A: 0x0/0x0/0x0


Bidir RPF-ID: 12, Remote Bidir RPF-ID: 0

I-PMSI:   Unknown/None (0x12897d48)


I-PMSI rem:  (0x0)

MS-PMSI:  (0x0)

Bidir-PMSI:  (0x0)

Remote Bidir-PMSI:  (0x0)

BSR-PMSI:  (0x0)

A-Disc-PMSI:  (0x0)

A-Ann-PMSI:  (0x0)

RIB Dependency List: 0x0

Bidir RIB Dependency List: 0x0

  Sources: 0, RPs: 0, Bidir RPs: 0
```

```
PE Address : 192.168.0.6 (0x12be86e0)

 RD: 0:0:0 (null), RIB_HLI 0, RPF-ID 1, Remote RPF-ID 0, State: 0, S-PMSI: 0

 PPMP_LABEL: 0, MS_PMSI_HLI: 0x00000, Bidir_PMSI_HLI: 0x00000, MLDP-added: [RD
 0, ID 0, Bidir ID 0, Remote Bidir ID 0], Counts(SHR/SRC/DM/DEF-MD): 0, 0, 0, 0,
 Bidir: GRE RP Count 0, MPLS RP Count 0RSVP-TE added: [Leg 0, Ctrl Leg 0, Part tail
 0 Def Tail 0, IR added: [Def Leg 1, Ctrl Leg 0, Part Leg 0, Part tail 0, Part IR
 Tail Label 0

 bgp_i_pmsi: 1,0/0 , bgp_ms_pmsi/Leaf-ad: 0/0, bgp_bidir_pmsi: 0, remote_bgp_bidir_
 pmsi: 0, PMSIs: I 0x12b06580, 0x0, MS 0x0, Bidir Local: 0x0, Remote: 0x0, BSR/
 Leaf-ad 0x0/0, Autorp-disc/Leaf-ad 0x0/0, Autorp-ann/Leaf-ad 0x0/0

 IIDs: I/6: 0x1/0x0, B/R: 0x0/0x0, MS: 0x0, B/A/A: 0x0/0x0/0x0


 Bidir RPF-ID: 2, Remote Bidir RPF-ID: 0
 I-PMSI:   (0x12b06580)
 I-PMSI rem:  (0x0)
 MS-PMSI:   (0x0)
 Bidir-PMSI:  (0x0)
 Remote Bidir-PMSI:  (0x0)
 BSR-PMSI:  (0x0)
 A-Disc-PMSI:  (0x0)
 A-Ann-PMSI:  (0x0)
 RIB Dependency List: 0x0
 Bidir RIB Dependency List: 0x0
   Sources: 0, RPs: 0, Bidir RPs: 0
```

The highlighted IP addresses in Example 3-61 are the PEs that are participating in the BLU VPN.

One final command in Example 3-62, **show mvpn vrf BLU ipv4 database ingress-replication**, shows the PEs that have valid receivers and the unique labels associated with each of them.

Example 3-62 *MVPN VRF Valid Receivers Using IOS-XR*

```
RP/0/0/CPU0:R4# show mvpn vrf BLU ipv4 database ingress-replication
Sun Feb 26 20:14:25.693 UTC
Tunnel/MDT Type          Core        Head Local     Leg      Head
Label                    Source        Label       Count    LSM-ID


Default IR MDT        192.168.0.4      24028         2      0x80001
  I-PMSI Leg(out label):  192.168.0.5(24024)
                         192.168.0.6(24023)
Partition IR MDT        0.0.0.0          0           0      0x0
Control IR MDT          0.0.0.0          0           0      0x0
```

Multicast Extranet VPNs

Most service providers do not generally allow multicast from one customer network into another customer network. An extranet VPN or inter-VRF multicast is useful when a customer is deploying a self-managed MPLS VPN network. This feature allows multicast messages to flow from one VRF to another. An example of a use case is a customer that has a VPN for video cameras and wants to protect those resources from attack by placing them into a unique VPN, but it wants other departments, groups, or organizations to be able to view multicast video streams from the cameras. Several options can be used, including the following:

- Route leaking

- VRF fallback

- VRF select

- Fusion router

- VRF-Aware Service Infrastructure (VASI)

Route Leaking

Although route leaking is a possible solution, it not one that is recommended. With route leaking, routes from one VRF are imported/exported into another VRF, as shown in Figure 3-14.

RT Import/Export

172.16.1.2   172.17.1.2

Figure 3-14 *Route Leaking*

The configuration for route leaking using IOS-XR is shown in Example 3-63.

Example 3-63 *Route Leaking Using IOS-XR*

```
vrf BLU
 address-family ipv4 unicast
  import route-target
   65000:1
   65000:2
  !
  export route-target
   65000:1
   65000:2
  !
 !
vrf RED
 address-family ipv4 unicast
  import route-target
   65000:1
   65000:2
  !
  export route-target
   65000:1
   65000:2

router bgp 65000
 bgp router-id 192.168.0.4
 address-family ipv4 unicast
 !
 address-family ipv4 multicast
!
 address-family vpnv4 unicast
 !
 address-family ipv6 unicast
 !
 address-family vpnv6 unicast
 !
 address-family ipv4 mdt
 !
 session-group AS65000
  remote-as 65000
  update-source Loopback0
 !
 neighbor-group AS65000
  use session-group AS65000
  address-family ipv4 unicast
   route-policy ALLOW-ALL in
```

```
    route-policy ALLOW-ALL out
   !
   address-family ipv4 multicast
    route-policy ALLOW-ALL in
    route-policy ALLOW-ALL out
   !
   address-family vpnv4 unicast
    route-policy ALLOW-ALL in
    route-policy ALLOW-ALL out
   !
   address-family ipv6 unicast
    route-policy ALLOW-ALL in
    route-policy ALLOW-ALL out
   !
   address-family vpnv6 unicast
    route-policy ALLOW-ALL in
    route-policy ALLOW-ALL out
   !
   address-family ipv4 mdt
    route-policy ALLOW-ALL in
    route-policy ALLOW-ALL out
   !
  !

multicast-routing
 !
 vrf BLU
  address-family ipv4
   mdt source Loopback0
   interface all enable
   mdt default ipv4 232.0.0.2
   mdt data 232.0.2.0/24 threshold 2
 !
 vrf RED
  address-family ipv4
   mdt source Loopback0
   interface all enable
   mdt default ipv4 232.0.0.1
   mdt data 232.0.1.0/24 threshold 2
  !
 !
!

router pim
 !
```

```
vrf BLU
 address-family ipv4
  interface GigabitEthernet0/0/0/1
  !
 !
!
vrf RED
 address-family ipv4
  !
  interface GigabitEthernet0/0/0/2
  !
 !
 !
!
```

The primary challenge with this solution is that you have limited control over the traffic flow, and it works only if you do not have overlapping address space. You are essentially making one VRF instance out of two, and this completely invalidates the need for multiple VRF instances.

VRF Fallback

When all else fails, you can use a static route! VRF fallback gives you the ability to configure a static multicast route that directs multicast messages to another VRF or the global routing table. As shown in Figure 3-15, there are three VRF instances: SVCS, RED, and BLU. The RP is in the SVCS VRF with IP address 10.0.0.5, and you want the RED and BLU VRF instances to be able to access the sender in the SVCS VRF.

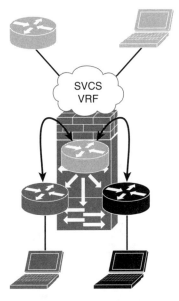

Figure 3-15   *VRF Fallback*

Example 3-64 shows the IOS-XE commands used to configure VRF fallback.

Example 3-64   *VRF Fallback Using IOS-XE*

```
vrf definition BLU
 address-family ipv4
!
vrf definition RED
 address-family ipv4
!
vrf definition SVCS
 address-family ipv4
!
interface Ethernet0/0
 vrf forwarding SVCS
 ip address 10.0.0.2 255.255.255.0
 ip pim sparse-mode
!
interface Ethernet0/1
 vrf forwarding BLU
 ip address 172.17.2.2 255.255.255.0
 ip pim sparse-mode
!
interface Ethernet0/2
vrf forwarding RED
 ip address 172.16.2.2 255.255.255.0
 ip pim sparse-mode
!
ip multicast-routing vrf BLU
ip multicast-routing vrf RED
ip multicast-routing vrf SVCS
ip pim vrf BLU rp-address 10.0.0.5
ip pim vrf RED rp-address 10.0.0.5
ip pim vrf SVCS rp-address 10.0.0.5
ip mroute vrf BLU 10.0.0.0 255.255.255.0 fallback-lookup vrf SVCS
ip mroute vrf RED 10.0.0.0 255.255.255.0 fallback-lookup vrf SVCS
```

Using the **show ip mroute vrf SVCS 224.1.1.1** command, you can verify the extranet receivers in the RED and BLU VRF instances, as shown in Example 3-65.

Example 3-65   *VRF Fallback Verification Using IOS-XE*

```
S1# show ip mroute vrf SVCS 224.1.1.1
IP Multicast Routing Table
Flags: D - Dense, S - Sparse, B - Bidir Group, s - SSM Group, C - Connected,
       L - Local, P - Pruned, R - RP-bit set, F - Register flag,
       T - SPT-bit set, J - Join SPT, M - MSDP created entry, E - Extranet,
       X - Proxy Join Timer Running, A - Candidate for MSDP Advertisement,
       U - URD, I - Received Source Specific Host Report,
       Z - Multicast Tunnel, z - MDT-data group sender,
       Y - Joined MDT-data group, y - Sending to MDT-data group,
       V - RD & Vector, v - Vector
Outgoing interface flags: H - Hardware switched, A - Assert winner
 Timers: Uptime/Expires
 Interface state: Interface, Next-Hop or VCD, State/Mode
(*, 224.1.1.1), 00:10:24/stopped, RP 10.0.0.5, flags: SJCE
  Incoming interface: Ethernet0/0, RPF nbr 10.0.0.5
  Outgoing interface list: Null
  Extranet receivers in vrf BLU:
(*, 224.1.1.1), 00:10:58/stopped, RP 10.0.0.5, OIF count: 1, flags: SJC
  Extranet receivers in vrf RED:
(*, 224.1.1.1), 00:10:48/stopped, RP 10.0.0.5, OIF count: 1, flags: SJC
(10.0.0.1, 224.1.1.1), 00:10:24/00:02:24, flags: TE
  Incoming interface: Ethernet0/0, RPF nbr 0.0.0.0
  Outgoing interface list: Null
  Extranet receivers in vrf BLU:
  (10.0.0.1, 224.1.1.1), 00:02:58/stopped, OIF count: 1, flags: T
  Extranet receivers in vrf RED:
  (10.0.0.1, 224.1.1.1), 00:08:39/stopped, OIF count: 1, flags: T
```

The **show ip mroute vrf RED 224.1.1.1** and the **show ip mroute vrf BLU 224.1.1.1** commands in Example 3-66 both show the incoming interface as Ethernet0/0, which is from VRF SVCS.

Example 3-66   *VRF Fallback Interface Using IOS-XE*

```
S1# show ip mroute vrf RED 224.1.1.1
IP Multicast Routing Table
Outgoing interface flags: H - Hardware switched, A - Assert winner
 Timers: Uptime/Expires
 Interface state: Interface, Next-Hop or VCD, State/Mode
(*, 224.1.1.1), 00:15:42/stopped, RP 10.0.0.5, flags: SJC
  Incoming interface: Ethernet0/0, RPF nbr 10.0.0.5, using vrf SVCS
  Outgoing interface list:
    Ethernet0/2, Forward/Sparse, 00:14:48/00:03:25
```

```
(10.0.0.1, 224.1.1.1), 00:02:43/stopped, flags: T
  Incoming interface: Ethernet0/0, RPF nbr 0.0.0.0, using vrf SVCS
  Outgoing interface list:
    Ethernet0/2, Forward/Sparse, 00:02:43/00:03:25


S1# show ip mroute vrf BLU 224.1.1.1
IP Multicast Routing Table
Outgoing interface flags: H - Hardware switched, A - Assert winner
 Timers: Uptime/Expires
 Interface state: Interface, Next-Hop or VCD, State/Mode
(*, 224.1.1.1), 00:15:57/stopped, RP 10.0.0.5, flags: SJC
  Incoming interface: Ethernet0/0, RPF nbr 10.0.0.5, using vrf SVCS
  Outgoing interface list:
    Ethernet0/1, Forward/Sparse, 00:15:02/00:03:11
(10.0.0.1, 224.1.1.1), 00:03:03/stopped, flags: T
  Incoming interface: Ethernet0/0, RPF nbr 0.0.0.0, using vrf SVCS
  Outgoing interface list:
    Ethernet0/1, Forward/Sparse, 00:03:03/00:03:11
```

Finally, the **show ip rpf vrf RED 10.0.0.1** and **show ip rpf vrf BLU 10.0.0.1** commands show that the extranet RPF rule is in use, as indicated by the highlighted output in Example 3-67.

Example 3-67   *Extranet RPF Rule Using IOS-XE*

```
S1# show ip rpf vrf RED 10.0.0.1
RPF information for ? (10.0.0.1)
  RPF interface: Ethernet0/0
  RPF neighbor: ? (10.0.0.1) - directly connected
  RPF route/mask: 10.0.0.0/24
  RPF type: multicast (connected)
  Doing distance-preferred lookups across tables
  Using Extranet RPF Rule: Static Fallback Lookup, RPF VRF: SVCS
  RPF topology: ipv4 multicast base

S1# show ip rpf vrf BLU 10.0.0.1
RPF information for ? (10.0.0.1)
  RPF interface: Ethernet0/0
  RPF neighbor: ? (10.0.0.1) - directly connected
  RPF route/mask: 10.0.0.0/24
  RPF type: multicast (connected)
  Doing distance-preferred lookups across tables
  Using Extranet RPF Rule: Static Fallback Lookup, RPF VRF: SVCS
  RPF topology: ipv4 multicast base
```

VRF Select

The VRF select feature is similar to VRF fallback except that with VRF select, the multi-cast address can be specified. This feature provides additional security because you can easily limit the multicast groups. The IOS-XE configuration is shown in Example 3-68.

Example 3-68 *VRF Select Using IOS-XE*

```
ip mroute vrf BLU 10.0.0.0 255.255.255.0 fallback-lookup vrf SVCS
ip mroute vrf RED 10.0.0.0 255.255.255.0 fallback-lookup vrf SVCS
ip multicast vrf BLU rpf select vrf SVCS group-list 1
ip multicast vrf RED rpf select vrf SVCS group-list 1
!
access-list 1 permit 224.1.1.1
```

Using the **show ip mroute vrf SVCS 224.1.1.1** command, validate the extranet receivers in the RED and BLU VRF instances, as shown in Example 3-69.

Example 3-69 *VRF Select Validation Using IOS-XE*

```
S1# show ip mroute vrf SVCS 224.1.1.1
IP Multicast Routing Table
Outgoing interface flags: H - Hardware switched, A - Assert winner
 Timers: Uptime/Expires
 Interface state: Interface, Next-Hop or VCD, State/Mode
(*, 224.1.1.1), 00:20:42/stopped, RP 10.0.0.5, flags: SJCE
Incoming interface: Ethernet0/0, RPF nbr 10.0.0.5
  Outgoing interface list: Null
  Extranet receivers in vrf BLU:
(*, 224.1.1.1), 01:08:40/stopped, RP 10.0.0.5, OIF count: 1, flags: SJC
  Extranet receivers in vrf RED:
(*, 224.1.1.1), 01:08:31/stopped, RP 10.0.0.5, OIF count: 1, flags: SJC
(10.0.0.1, 224.1.1.1), 00:20:42/00:02:03, flags: TE
  Incoming interface: Ethernet0/0, RPF nbr 0.0.0.0
  Outgoing interface list: Null
  Extranet receivers in vrf BLU:
  (10.0.0.1, 224.1.1.1), 00:15:15/stopped, OIF count: 1, flags: T
  Extranet receivers in vrf RED:
  (10.0.0.1, 224.1.1.1), 00:55:31/stopped, OIF count: 1, flags: T
```

Fusion Router

A fusion router acts as a fusion or connector point for multiple VPNs. It is fundamentally an L3 device where all VPNs connect. This design has several benefits, such as better control of routing and multicast routing and the ability to perform Network Address

Translation (NAT) functionality in the event of overlapping IP addresses. In addition, a fusion router can act as a central RP for all the VPNs, as shown in Figure 3-16.

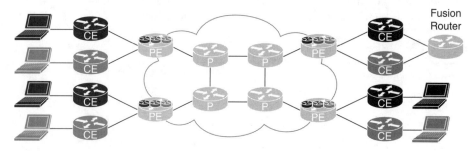

Figure 3-16   *Fusion Router*

Additional fusion routers configured as the RP can be used for a high availability solution. By assigning the RP functionality to a loopback address, you can implement the Anycast RP model for high availability.

Many customers choose to implement firewalls between the edge CE and the firewall for additional protection and inspection of traffic. Depending on the capabilities of the firewall, you may consider implementing fusion routers in transparent or L2 mode to minimize the impact on multicast control plane traffic and multicast flows, as shown in Figure 3-17.

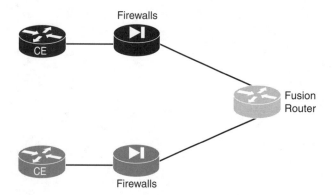

Figure 3-17   *Fusion Router with Firewalls*

VRF-Aware Service Infrastructure (VASI)

VASI is essentially a software cable that connects VRF instances. It supports NAT, firewalling, IPsec, IPv4, IPv6, multiple routing protocols, and IPv4 and IPv6 multicast. This design is very similar to the fusion routers concept except that the CE routing and fusion capability happens all in the same device, as shown in Figure 3-18.

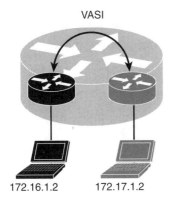

VASI

172.16.1.2   172.17.1.2

Figure 3-18 *VASI*

Configuring VASI is a simple task, as shown in Example 3-70.

Example 3-70 *VASI Configuration Using IOS-XE*

```
vrf definition BLU
 address-family ipv4
!
vrf definition RED
 address-family ipv4
!
interface GigabitEthernet0/0/0
 vrf forwarding RED
 ip address 172.16.1.1 255.255.255.0
!
interface GigabitEthernet0/0/1
 vrf forwarding BLU
 ip address 172.17.1.1 255.255.255.0
!
interface vasileft1
 vrf forwarding RED
 ip address 192.168.0.1 255.255.255.0
!
interface vasiright1
 vrf forwarding BLU
 ip address 192.168.0.2 255.255.255.0
!
ip route vrf BLU 172.16.0.0 255.255.0.0 vasiright1
ip route vrf RED 172.17.0.0 255.255.0.0 vasileft1
```

In this example, VRF RED connects to vasileft1, and VRF BLU connect to vasiright1, essentially building a logical wire between the RED and BLU VRF instances. Additional features and functionality can now be applied to the VASI interface to meet security, NAT, or other requirements.

IPv6 MVPN

Fortunately, making the transition to IPv6 is easy when comes to MVPNs. Most of the features and functionality you have already learned about in this chapter apply to IPv6. (Check the latest documentation for current feature support.)

Just as you would enable address families for IPv4, you can do this for IPv6, as shown in the following snippet from IOS-XR:

```
address-family ipv6 unicast
!
address-family vpnv6 unicast
!
address-family ipv4 mvpn
!
address-family ipv6 mvpn
```

Bit Index Explicit Replication (BIER)

BIER is a new development in multicast transport. It does not require any of the traditional methods of tree building and takes an innovative approach to propagating multicast messages. When a multicast data packet enters the domain, the ingress router determines the set of egress routers to which the packet needs to be sent. The ingress router encapsulates the packet in a BIER header, which contains a bitstring in which each bit represents exactly one egress router in the domain; to forward the packet to a given set of egress routers, the bits corresponding to those routers are set in the BIER header. The multicast forwarding state is created using link-state protocols such as OSPF or IS-IS. Each bit-forwarding router (BFR) is identified as a single bit in the BIER header. When a message is to be sent to multiple BIER nodes, the bits in the bitstring that identifies those particular nodes are set by the ingress BIER node. As the BIER message moves through the network, the packet can be replicated out multiple interfaces by a BIER node to maintain the shortest path to the destination. In an MPLS environment, BIER labels are assigned to MPLS labels; this is called BIER MPLS. The BIER solution eliminates the per-flow state and the explicit tree-building protocols, which results in considerable simplification.

BIER addresses the problems associated with current multicast solutions reviewed earlier in this chapter:

■ Explicit tree building protocols are the core of multicast transport. The tree-building process requires memory to build up state in every node in the routing domains. This also impacts multicast convergence in the large routing domain.

■ Using RPF to build the trees toward the root could result in different paths between the same endpoints in a topology with multiple paths.

■ Control plane aggregation of the flows is not possible in the current multicast solutions. Optimal delivery for every flow has two states maintained in the RIB.

■ Maintaining and troubleshooting multicast networks can be very difficult. The need to understand the multicast control plane that overlays the unicast control plane increases the operational overhead for solution management.

The BIER concept is as follows:

Step 1.   The router assigns a unique bit position mask to each router in the domain.

Step 2.   Each edge router floods the bit position to ID mapping within IGP (OSPF or IS-IS). A new LSA type is used to exchange this new information.

Step 3.   All the routers in the unicast domain for BIER calculate the best path for each of the BFR indexes. In addition, the bit positions are OR'd (Boolean function) for the bitmask for each BFR neighbor. This constitutes the bit forwarding table.

Step 4.   The multicast packets are forwarded based on the bit forwarding table using a logical AND operation of the multicast flow bit.

The bit index table is tied to ECMP for multiple paths from each node, where applicable. The ECMP paths taking parallel interfaces to a single neighbor are noted as a single bitmask. If the ECMP for multiple paths is seen for different neighbors, it is noted as a separate bitmask. BIER also has a concept of sets, whereby you can group a set of routers in a single group (similar to an area). The forwarding behavior is based on the packets' set ID, as illustrated in Figure 3-19.

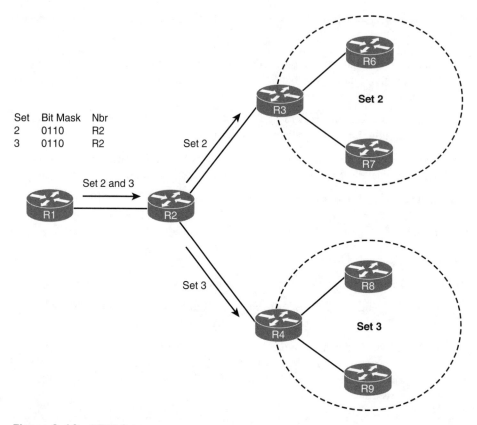

Figure 3-19 *BIER Sets*

The receiver information (egress router for multicast flow) is learned via an overlay mechanism. The current deployment of BIER in IOS-XR is via BGP overlay for receiver learning. Once the receiver is known within the domain, the forwarding is simple, using the bitmask index. This is different from PIM domains, where the forwarding and signaling are maintained in the multicast state table at the same time. In BIER, multicast forwarding is kept separate from the signaling.

Figure 3-20 provides a high-level overview of packet flow in BIER:

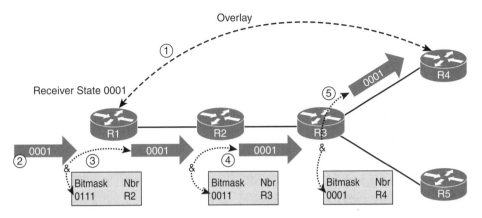

Figure 3-20 *Multicast Forwarding of Packets in BIER*

- Before the multicast exchange, all the routers in the BIER domain exchange bitmask information by using IGP (OSPF in this case). All the routers in the unicast domain for BIER calculate the best path for each of the BFR indexes.

- The overlay control plane (in this case BGP) transmits the receiver information and the BIER nodes in the domain, as in the step above.

- The multicast data plane from the source connected to R1 is propagated to R4 through the bit index Boolean AND function, as in steps 2 through 4.

BIER, which is relatively new, is available only in IOS-XR at this writing. With this innovative solution, there is no need for an explicit multicast signaling protocol in the network. With BIER there is no need to run PIM, MLDP, or P2MP MPLS traffic engineering in the network to signal multicast state at every router in the multicast domain. With BIER, the multicast forwarding state created in the network is driven by advertisements through the link state protocols OSPF or IS-IS. This forwarding state is not per (*, G) or (S, G), but per egress router. Each egress router for multicast is identified by a bit index. Each BIER router must have one unique bit in a bitstring. This bitstring is also found in the multicast packets that need to be forwarded through a BIER network.

Summary

MPLS VPN has been around for many years, implemented by service providers and enterprise customers because it provides the ability to logically separate traffic using one physical infrastructure. The capability of supporting multicast in an MPLS VPN environment has been available using default MDT. As technology has evolved, so has the capability of supporting multicast in an MPLS network. Today you can still use the traditional default MDT method, but there are now also 26 other profiles to choose from—from IP/GRE encapsulation using PIM, to traffic engineering tunnels, to MLDP, to BIER.

The requirements for extranet MVPNs, or the capability of sharing multicast messages between VPNs, has also brought about development of new capabilities, such as VRF fallback, VRF select, and VASI. The combinations of solutions are almost endless, and this chapter was specifically written to provide a taste of the different solutions and capabilities. Please do not stop here; a search engine can help you make your way through the mass of information available online to continue your education.

References

"Configure mVPN Profiles Within Cisco IOS," www.cisco.com/c/en/us/support/docs/ip/multicast/118985-configure-mcast-00.html

RFC 2365, "Administratively Scoped IP Multicast"

RFC 6037, "Cisco Systems' Solution for Multicast in BGP/MPLS IP VPNs"

RFC 6514, "BGP Encodings and Procedures for Multicast in MPLS/BGP IP VPNs"

RFC 6516, "IPv6 Multicast VPN (MVPN) Support Using PIM Control Plane and Selective Provider Multicast Service Interface (S-PMSI) Join Messages"

RFC 7358, "Label Advertisement Discipline for LDP Forwarding Equivalence Classes (FECs)"

RFC 7441, "Encoding Multipoint LDP (mLDP) Forwarding Equivalence Classes (FECs) in the NLRI of BGP MCAST-VPN Routes"

"Encapsulating MPLS in IP or GRE," https://tools.ietf.org/html/draft-rosen-mpls-in-ip-or-gre-00

"Encapsulation for Bit Index Explicit Replication in MPLS and non-MPLS Networks," https://tools.ietf.org/html/draft-ietf-bier-mpls-encapsulation-06

Chapter 4

Multicast in Data Center Environments

Most of this book discusses multicast in LANs and WANs, but one of the most critical components of any organization is its data center. Understanding the nuances of how multicast functions in myriad solutions is extremely critical to the success of an organization. The goal of this chapter is to provide insight into the operation of multicast, using the most popular methods for data center implementation, including virtual port channel (VPC), Virtual Extensible LAN (VXLAN), and Application Centric Infrastructure (ACI).

Multicast in a VPC Environment

VPC is a technology that allows two Ethernet switches to appear as a single L2 entity to downstream devices, consequently minimizing the impact of blocked ports from spanning tree. Although the two VPC switches appear as a single device, they are managed independently. The benefits of VPC are that it provides Layer 2 redundancy without requiring the use of spanning-tree knobs, the convergence of a port channel is faster for link recovery, and the topology is loop free because no ports are in the spanning-tree blocking state. Figure 4-1 shows a conceptual representation of VPC.

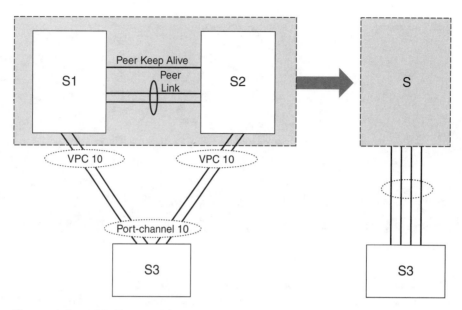

Figure 4-1   *VPC Conceptual Design*

In Figure 4-1, the S1 and S2 switches are mapped to a single switch identity for all the downstream switches (S3). VPC covers combined port channel between the VPC peer device and downstream devices. VPC topology uses all port-channel links that are part of the VPC for forwarding traffic. If a link fails, local hashing of the port channel redirects the traffic to the remaining links. If one of the peer switches fails, the other peer switch has the capability to take in the traffic with minimal impact. In VPC, each peer switch runs its own control plane, and both devices work independently. (Control plane issues are localized to each peer switch.) S1 and S2 are VPC peer switches; they are connected by a special port channel known as a *VPC peer link*. In the peer switch configuration, one device is selected as primary, and the other device is a secondary device. The port channel (peer link) carries control traffic between two VPC switches and also carries multicast and broadcast traffic. In a few failure scenarios, unicast traffic also passes through the peer link (though that topic is beyond the scope of this book). Because of the heavy use of this link, a best practice is to use this link in dedicated rate mode proportional to southbound and northbound interface bandwidth. The VPC domain represents VPC peer devices, the VPC peer keepalive link, and all the port channels in the VPC connected to the downstream devices. The peer keepalive link is used to monitor the VPC peer switch. The periodic keepalive messages between VPC peer devices are sent via this link. No data or synchronization traffic moves over the VPC peer keepalive link. Interfaces that belong to the VPC are classified as VPC member ports. (Interfaces that are not part of VPC and have single attached receivers are called *orphan ports*.)

Multicast Flow over a VPC

Consider the example in Figure 4-2, in which the source is connected to the L3 network (upstream router via router A), and the receiver is connected to the VPC environment (downstream). Figure 4-2 shows the control-plane flow, which involves the following steps:

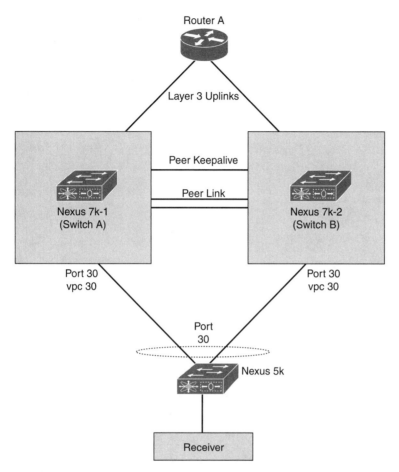

Figure 4-2 *Control-Plane Flow*

Step 1. The receiver sends an Internet Group Management Protocol (IGMP) membership join to the designated router (DR), and the flow gets hashed from the access switch connected to the core (port-channel hash). In this case, if the flow transits Switch B, then Switch B creates a snooping entry and the (*, G) mroute state with the VPC VLAN as the outgoing interface list (OIL):

```
SwitchB# show ip igmp groups vlan 100
IGMP Connected Group Membership for Interface "Vlan100" - 1 total
entries
Type: S - Static, D - Dynamic, L - Local, T - SSM Translated
Group Address    Type Interface    Uptime    Expires   Last Reporter
239.1.1.1        D    Vlan100      00:00:31  00:04:11  10.100.100.10
SwitchB# show ip mroute
IP Multicast Routing Table for VRF "default"
(*, 239.1.1.1/32), uptime: 00:00:39, igmp ip pim
```

```
        Incoming interface: port-channel30, RPF nbr: 10.1.1.1
        Outgoing interface list: (count: 1)
          Vlan100, uptime: 00:00:39, igmp
```

Step 2.   Switch B sends an IGMP packet to switch A, and this packet is encapsulated using Cisco Fabric Services (CFS). This creates an identical control plane state in Switch A:

```
SwitchB# show ip mroute
IP Multicast Routing Table for VRF "default"
(*, 239.1.1.1/32), uptime: 00:01:48, pim ip
  Incoming interface: loopback2, RPF nbr: 10.20.0.20
  Outgoing interface list: (count: 1)
    port-channel30, uptime: 00:01:48, pim


SwitchA# show ip mroute
IP Multicast Routing Table for VRF "default"
(*, 239.1.1.1/32), uptime: 00:02:02, pim ip
  Incoming interface: loopback2, RPF nbr: 10.20.0.20
  Outgoing interface list: (count: 1)
    port-channel1, uptime: 00:02:02, pim
```

Step 3.   Now each of the two switches sends a control plane join toward the rendezvous point (RP).

Step 4.   The source communicates to the first-hope router (FHR) and builds the control plane with the RP (connected through Router A upstream).

Step 5.   One or both of the VPC peers receive the (S, G) join. The multicast flow state depends on the upstream routing.

Step 6.   The VPC pair negotiates which peer takes on the forwarder role. CFS messages are exchanged between peers during this negotiation. The switches use the best routing metric in conjunction with VPC role as a tiebreaker. In most cases, the VPC primary becomes the forwarder because the VPC Layer 3 uses an equal-cost route toward the upstream router.

Step 7.   Only the elected forwarder responds to the (S, G) state toward the source and adds the relative state changes to (S, G) entry:

```
SwitchA# show ip mroute
IP Multicast Routing Table for VRF "default"
(10.20.0.10/32, 239.1.1.1/32), uptime: 00:00:55, ip pim
  Incoming interface: Vlan100, RPF nbr: 10.20.0.20
  Outgoing interface list: (count: 1)
    port-channel30, uptime: 00:00:49, pim


SwitchB# show ip mroute
IP Multicast Routing Table for VRF "default"
(10.20.0.10/32, 239.1.1.1/32), uptime: 00:01:12, ip pim
```

```
Incoming interface: Vlan100, RPF nbr: 10.20.0.20
Outgoing interface list: (count: 0)
```

Switch A is the VPC primary and VPC role is used as tiebreaker for multicast forwarding path (source is connected to the upstream).

Step 8.   Data flows down the source to the forwarding VPC peer.

VXLAN

VXLAN provides an overlay network to transport L2 packets on an L3 network. VXLAN uses MAC-in-UDP encapsulation, which extends Layer 2 segments. MAC-in-UDP encapsulation is illustrated in Figure 4-3.

Outer MAC Header (14 Bytes)	Outer IP Header (20 Bytes)	UDP Header (8 Bytes)	VXLAN Header (8 Bytes)	Layer 2 Frame (Original)	FCS

Figure 4-3   *MAC-in-UDP Encapsulation in VXLAN*

VTEP

The IP encapsulation of an L2 frame is accomplished with VXLAN, which uses VXLAN Tunnel Endpoints (VTEPs) to map a tenant's end devices to VXLAN segments and to perform VXLAN encapsulation and de-encapsulation. A VTEP has two functions: It is a switch interface on the local LAN segment to support local endpoint communication via bridging, and it is also an IP interface to the transport IP network toward the remote endpoint. The VTEP IP interface identifies the VTEP on the transport IP network. The VTEPs use this IP address to encapsulate Ethernet frames as shown in Figure 4-4.

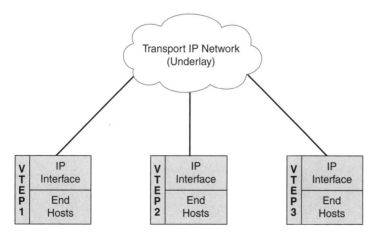

Figure 4-4   *VTEP*

Between the VTEPs, tunnel encapsulation provides the overlay services. Regarding VXLAN, these services are distinctively identified with a Virtual Network Identifier (VNI), which significantly expands the ability to accommodate a much larger scale of broadcast domains within the network. VNI interfaces are similar to VLANs. They keep the L2 traffic separate by using separate tagging. VNI interfaces can be aligned to network or security segmentation. Note that all VNI interfaces are associated with the same VTEP interface. Figure 4-5 is a representation of the VNI/VTEP relationship and tunnel encapsulation.

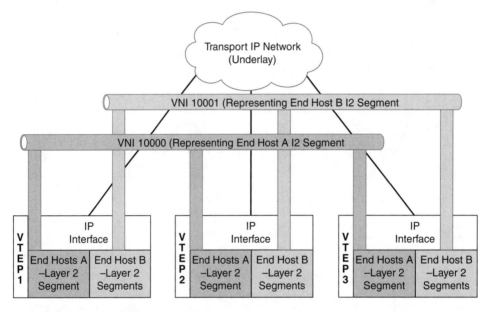

Figure 4-5   *VNI/VTEP Relationship*

A VTEP device holds the VXLAN forwarding table, which maps a destination MAC address to a remote VTEP IP address where the destination MAC is located, and also a local table that contains the VLAN-to-VXLAN map. As shown in Figure 4-6, the data plane is represented by the VNI interface (NVE).

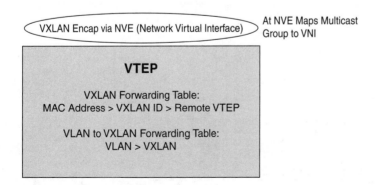

Figure 4-6   *VTEP Mapping*

Now that you understand the basic building blocks of VXLAN, you're ready to look at the these VXLAN deployment types:

■ VXLAN flood and learn

■ VXLAN with EVPN

VXLAN Flood and Learn

In flood and learn mode, the source and destination frames are encapsulated with the VTEP source and destination IP addresses. The source IP address is the IP address of the encapsulating VTEP, and the destination IP address is either a multicast or unicast address of the remote VTEP that hosts the destination. VXLAN uses VTEPs to map tenants' end devices to VXLAN segments. The communication between VTEPs depends on whether the end host address is known to the remote VTEP connected to the source; this is maintained in the VXLAN forwarding table. If the destination is known, the process leverages unicast data plane overlay communication between the VTEPs, as shown in Figure 4-7. The communication of the unicast data plane occurs when the VTEP receives an ARP reply from a connected system and knows the destination MAC address, thanks to local MAC-A-to-IP mapping to determine the IP address of the destination VTEP connected to the destination host. The original packet is encapsulated in a unicast tunnel using User Datagram Protocol (UDP), with the source IP address of the local VTEP and the destination IP address of the remote VTEP.

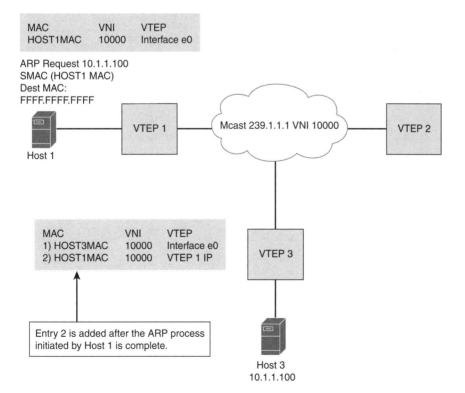

Figure 4-7 *VXLAN Flood and Learn*

For unknown unicast, broadcast, or multicast traffic (BUM), in VXLAN flood and learn mode, multicast is used in the underlay for learning. To illustrate this flow, say that Host 1 in Figure 4-7 sends a message to Host 3. Host 1 needs to resolve the IP/MAC binding for Host 3. Host 1 sends out an ARP request with DMAC=FFFF.FFFF.FFFF. VTEP 1 receives the ARP and verifies whether the binding is available in its local table. If it is not available, VTEP 1 sends a multidestination frame to all the member VTEPs of the corresponding VNI (for example, VNI 1000). This message is encapsulated in the multi-cast frame source IP of VTEP 1 and the destination of the multicast group (for example, 239.1.1.1). The VTEP members of VNI 1000 are the receivers of the multicast group. The remote VTEP 3 connected to Host 3 creates a control plane response to VTEP 1 after the multidestination frame is de-encapsulated. The multidestination traffic is flooded over the VXLAN between VTEPs to learn about the host MACs located behind the VTEPs so that subsequent traffic can be sent via unicast. This same mechanism is used for broadcast or multicast data frames that need to be sent via the overlay.

To understand the configuration better, Figure 4-8 shows a use of VXLAN.

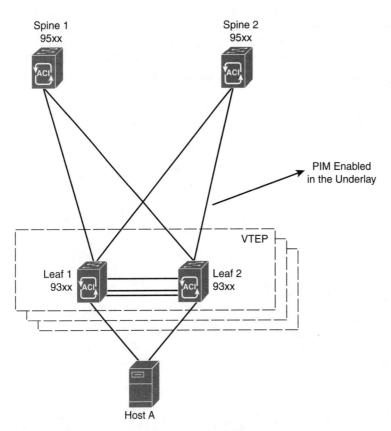

Figure 4-8 *VXLAN Flood and Learn Configuration*

Let's review the leaf configuration for VXLAN leaves. The following steps provide an overview of the configuration needed for a VXLAN leaf to flood and learn:

Step 1. Enable the relevant protocols needed for the leaf:

```
feature ospf
feature pim
feature nv overlay
feature vn-segment-vlan-based
```

Step 2. Enable the IGP for the underlay:

```
router ospf 1
router-id 100.100.100.1
```

Step 3. Enable multicast (with Anycast RP configuration at the spine):

```
ip pim rp-address 10.100.1.1 group-list 224.0.0.0/4
```

Step 4. Enable loopback 0 (used as a common VTEP IP address between two VPC peers configured at the leaf 10.50.1.1/32):

```
interface loopback0
 ip address 10.20.1.1/32
 ip address 10.50.1.1/32  secondary
 ip router ospf 1 area 0.0.0.0
 ip pim sparse-mode
  <.. Uplinks should be layer 3 interfaces..>
```

Step 5. Configure nve1 and downstream host VLANs:

```
interface nve1
no shutdown
source-interface loopback0
 member vni 10000 mcast-group 239.1.1.1

vlan 2901
 vn-segment 2901
```

Note In flood and learn, the spine only needs to support routing paths between the leafs. The RPs (pim sparse-mode, Anycast RP distribution) need to be added to the spine configuration.

Example 4-1 shows the **show** commands you can use to verify that the NVE peers are using multicast.

Example 4-1 *Leaf VTEP 1:* **show nve peers** *Command Output*

```
VTEP-1# show nve peers
Interface Peer-IP          State LearnType Uptime    Router-Mac
--------- --------------- ----- --------- -------- ----------------
nve1      10.50.1.1        Up    DP         00:05:09 n/a

VTEP-1# show nve vni
Codes: CP - Control Plane      DP - Data Plane
       UC - Unconfigured       SA - Suppress ARP


Interface VNI      Multicast-group   State Mode Type [BD/VRF]      Flags
--------- -------- ----------------- ----- ---- ----------------- -----
nve1      2901     239.1.1.1         Up    DP   L2 [2901]




VTEP-1# show ip mroute
IP Multicast Routing Table for VRF "default"

(*, 232.0.0.0/8), uptime: 5d10h, pim ip
  Incoming interface: Null, RPF nbr: 0.0.0.0, uptime: 5d10h
  Outgoing interface list: (count: 0)


(*, 239.1.1.1/32), uptime: 00:05:18, nve ip pim
  Incoming interface: Ethernet1/58, RPF nbr: 10.19.9.2, uptime: 00:05:18
  Outgoing interface list: (count: 1)
    nve1, uptime: 00:05:18, nve


(10.11.2.2/32, 239.1.1.1/32), uptime: 00:05:18, nve ip mrib pim
  Incoming interface: loopback0, RPF nbr: 10.11.2.2, uptime: 00:05:18
  Outgoing interface list: (count: 1)
    Ethernet1/58, uptime: 00:02:34, pim


(10.50.1.1/32, 239.1.1.1/32), uptime: 00:02:26, ip mrib pim nve
  Incoming interface: Ethernet1/59, RPF nbr: 10.19.10.2, uptime: 00:02:21
  Outgoing interface list: (count: 1)
    nve1, uptime: 00:02:26, nve
```

VXLAN with EVPN

Using Border Gateway Protocol (BGP) and Ethernet virtual private networks (EVPNs) with VXLAN reduces the problems related to learning via flooding (which is applicable in scalable environments). VXLAN optimizes learning of MAC addresses of all hosts in the VXLAN fabric without flood behavior. BGP is a standardized protocol for Network Layer Reachability Information (NLRI) to exchange host-to-host reachability and learning within the fabric. BGP NLRI provides complete visibility of all the MAC and IP address combinations of the hosts behind the VTEP in order to complete VXLAN fabric connectivity by providing the MAC/IP info to all VTEPs. The EVPN extensions that are part of BGP (or Multiprotocol BGP MBGP) add enough information within these to standardize the control plane for communication. Through integrated routing and switching, BGP EVPN facilitates transport for both L2 and L3, using known workload addresses present within the VXLAN network. This is particularly useful in multitenant environments as MAC address and IP information can be separated by BGP NLRI for individual tenants. Figure 4-9 shows this VXLAN capability.

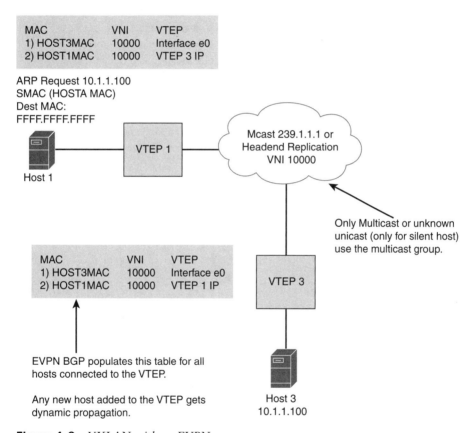

Figure 4-9   *VXLAN with an EVPN*

The EVPN address family allows the host MAC, IP, network, Virtual Route Forwarding (VRF), and VTEP information to be carried over MBGP. In this way, within the fabric, the VTEP learns about hosts connected using BGP EVPN. BGP EVPN does not eliminate the need for flooding for BUM traffic, but unknown unicast is eliminated (sparing silent hosts). However, broadcast and multicast data communication between the hosts still needs to be transported. The transportation is implemented by multicast underlay, which is similar to flood and learn, but the multicast traffic is optimized because all hosts' IP/MAC addresses are learned via BGP EVPN. The only exception is silent hosts. In BGP EVPN or flood and learn mode, the multicast deployments are either Any-Source Multicast (ASM) (using

Anycast) or bidirectional (with a phantom RP). With ASM, the multicast design uses the spine as the RP for the underlay traffic traversal. Multicast implementation involves one group to manage a set of VNIs (grouped under a category that is tied to multitenancy, user groups, and so on). This reduces the multicast state table in the underlay.

You can also have each VNI tied to a separate multicast group; this is adequate for a small deployment, but you should not consider it for larger deployments that have scale constraints due to the number of multicast group entries mapped with each VNI. VXLAN supports up to 16 million logical L2 segments, using the 24-bit VNID field in the header. With one-to-one mapping between VXLAN segments and IP Multicast groups, an increase in the number of VXLAN segments causes a parallel increase in the required multicast address space and some forwarding states on the core network devices. Packets forwarded to the multicast group for one tenant are sent to the VTEPs of other tenants that are sharing the same multicast group. This communication is inefficient utilization of multicast data plane resources. Therefore, the solution is a trade-off between control plane scalability and data plane efficiency.

To understand the configuration of VXLAN with BGP EVPN, let's review the use case of BGP EVPN with a multicast underlay configuration. The diagram in Figure 4-10 illustrates eBGP established between spine and leaf, using Nexus 9000 devices.

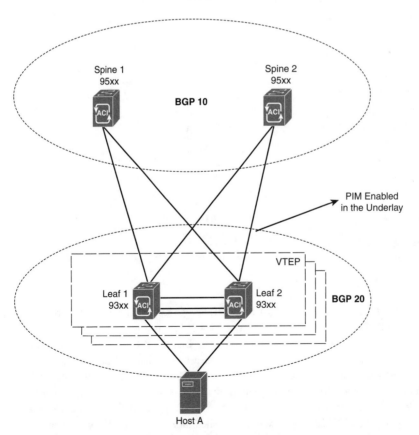

Figure 4-10 *VXLAN with eBGP Between Leaf and Spine*

Spine 1 Configuration

The spine configuration with EVPN VXLAN occurs as follows:

Step 1. Enable the EVPN control plane:

```
nv overlay evpn
```

Step 2. Enable the relevant protocols needed for the spine:

```
feature bgp
feature pim
```

(In this case, BGP is used for the underlay and overlay.)

Step 3. Configure loopback for the local VTEP IP, the BGP peer relationship (loopback 0), and anycast (loopback 1):

```
interface loopback0
  ip address 10.10.1.1/32
  ip pim sparse-mode
interface loopback1
  ip address 10.100.1.1/32
  ip pim sparse-mode
```

Step 4. Configure Anycast RP:

```
ip pim rp-address 10.100.1.1 group-list 225.0.0.0/8
ip pim rp-candidate loopback1 group-list 225.0.0.0/8
ip pim log-neighbor-changes
ip pim anycast-rp 10.100.1.1 10.10.1.1
ip pim anycast-rp 100.1.1.1 10.20.1.1
```

Step 5. Configure the route map used by eBGP at the spine:

```
route-map permitANY permit 10
  set ip next-hop unchanged
```

Note   Interfaces between the spine and leaf are Layer 3 interfaces with PIM sparse mode. If the underlay is BGP, use the interfaces to establish peer relationships.

Step 6. Configure the BGP overlay for the EVPN address family:

```
router bgp 10
  router-id 10.10.1.1
  address-family l2vpn evpn
    nexthop route-map permitANY
    retain route-target all
  neighbor 10.30.1.1 remote-as 20
    update-source loopback0
```

```
      ebgp-multihop 3
      address-family l2vpn evpn
        disable-peer-as-check
        send-community extended
        route-map permitANY out
  neighbor 10.40.1.1 remote-as 20
    update-source loopback0
    ebgp-multihop 3
    address-family l2vpn evpn
      disable-peer-as-check
      send-community extended
      route-map permitANY out
```

Step 7.   Specify the BGP underlay configurations (with the direct IP address of the interface between the spine and leaf):

```
neighbor 172.16.1.2 remote-as 20
    address-family ipv4 unicast
        allowas-in
disable-peer-as-check
<..>
```

Leaf Configuration

The leaf configuration with EVPN VXLAN is as follows:

> **Note**   Interfaces between the spine and leaf are Layer 3 interfaces with PIM sparse mode. If the underlay is BGP, use the interfaces to establish peer relationships.

Step 1.   Enable the EVPN control plane:

```
nv overlay evpn
```

Step 2.   Enable the relevant features:

```
feature bgp
feature pim
feature interface-vlan
feature dhcp
feature vn-segment-vlan-based
feature nv overlay
fabric forwarding anycast-gateway-mac 0000.2222.3333
```

Step 3.   Enable PIM RP:

```
ip pim rp-address 10.100.1.1 group-list 225.0.0.0/8
```

Step 4.   Configure the loopback for BGP and configure the loopback for the local
VTEP IP:

```
interface loopback0
  ip address 10.30.1.1/32
  ip address 10.30.50.1/32 secondary


  ip pim sparse-mode
```

Because the leaf device has a VPC configuration, use the same IP address
(secondary) for both the VPC peers, including the NVE connection source.

Step 5.   Create the VRF overlay VLAN and configure the vn-segment:

```
vlan 101
  vn-segment 1001
```

Step 6.   Configure the VRF overlay VLAN/SVI for the VRF:

```
interface Vlan101
  no shutdown
  vrf member vxlan-red
```

Step 7.   Create the VLAN and provide mapping to VXLAN (with the user VLAN segment to which you have downstream hosts):

```
vlan 2901
  vn-segment 2901
```

Step 8.   Create the VRF and configure the VNI:

```
vrf context vxlan-red
  vni 1001
  rd auto
  address-family ipv4 unicast
    route-target import 65535:100 evpn
    route-target export 65535:100 evpn
    route-target import 65535:100
    route-target export 65535:100
```

Step 9.   Create the server-facing SVI and enable distributed anycast-gateway:

```
interface Vlan2901
  no shutdown
  vrf member vxlan-red
  ip address 192.168.4.1/24
  fabric forwarding mode anycast-gateway
```

Step 10.   Create the NVE interface 239.1.1.1:

```
interface nve1
  no shutdown
  source-interface loopback1
  host-reachability protocol bgp
  member vni 10001 associate-vrf
  member vni 2901
    suppress-arp
    mcast-group 239.1.1.1
```

Step 11.   Configure BGP for the underlay and overlay (EVPN):

```
router bgp 20
router-id 10.30.1.1
  neighbor 10.10.1.1 remote-as 10
    update-source loopback0
    ebgp-multihop 3
      allowas-in
      send-community extended
    address-family l2vpn evpn
      allowas-in
      send-community extended
  neighbor 10.20.1.1 remote-as 100
    update-source loopback0
    ebgp-multihop 3
      allowas-in
      send-community extended
    address-family l2vpn evpn
      allowas-in
      send-community extended
  vrf vxlan-red
      advertise l2vpn evpn
<.. single tenant VRF Red..>
evpn
  vni 2901 l2
    rd auto
    route-target import auto
    route-target export auto
<.. add other user VNIs..>
```

Then view the nve peers using the **show nve peers** command:

```
show nve peers
9396-B# show nve peers
```

```
Interface  Peer-IP          Peer-State
---------  ---------------  ----------
nve1       10.30.1.1        Up
```

To verify the status of the VNI use the show nve vni command:

```
show nve vni
9396-B# show nve vni
Codes: CP - Control Plane      DP - Data Plane
       UC - Unconfigured       SA - Suppress ARP


Interface VNI     Multicast-group   State Mode Type [BD/VRF]         Flags
--------- ------- ----------------- ----- ---- ------------------    -----
nve1      1001    n/a               Up    CP   L3   [vxlan-red]
nve1      2901    239.1.1.1         Up    CP   L2   [2901]           SA
```

The control plane for the VNI is built and can be viewed by show ip mroute
at the VTEP (leaf), see the highlighted flags to shows the nve control state:

```
VTEP-1# sh ip mroute
IP Multicast Routing Table for VRF "default"

(*, 232.0.0.0/8), uptime: 5d10h, pim ip
  Incoming interface: Null, RPF nbr: 0.0.0.0, uptime: 5d10h
  Outgoing interface list: (count: 0)


(*, 239.1.1.1/32), uptime: 00:05:18, nve ip pim
  Incoming interface: Ethernet1/58, RPF nbr: 10.19.9.2, uptime: 00:05:18
  Outgoing interface list: (count: 1)
    nve1, uptime: 00:05:18, nve


(10.11.2.2/32, 239.1.1.1/32), uptime: 00:05:18, nve ip mrib pim
  Incoming interface: loopback0, RPF nbr: 10.11.2.2, uptime: 00:05:18
  Outgoing interface list: (count: 1)
    Ethernet1/58, uptime: 00:02:34, pim


(10.50.1.1/32, 239.1.1.1/32), uptime: 00:02:26, ip mrib pim nve
  Incoming interface: Ethernet1/59, RPF nbr: 10.19.10.2, uptime: 00:02:21
  Outgoing interface list: (count: 1)
    nve1, uptime: 00:02:26, nve
```

Ingress Replication

In this case, the BUM traffic is not sent via the multicast underlay. Instead, data packets are replicated by the ingress VTEP to other neighboring VTEPs that are part of the same VNI. The resources the ingress VTEP needs to allocate for BUM traffic are tied to the number of VTEPs associated with the VNI in the fabric. The ingress replication method can also be applied to BGP EVPN and VXLAN flood and learn, as shown in Example 4-2 (using the topology from Figure 4-10).

Example 4-2   *Leaf Configuration for nve1 for Ingress Replication*

```
interface nve1
  no shutdown
  source-interface loopback0
  host-reachability protocol bgp
  member vni 2901
    suppress-arp
    ingress-replication protocol static
      peer-ip 10.50.1.1
  member vni 900001 associate-vrf
```

Example 4-3 shows the command to verify ingress replication.

Example 4-3   *Verifying Ingress Replication*

```
VTEP-1# show nve vni ingress-replication
Interface VNI      Replication List  Source  Up Time
--------- -------- ----------------- ------- -------

nve1      2901     10.50.1.1         CLI     00:00:33
VTEP-1#
```

The spine and leaf need not have multicast configuration with ingress replication. Leaf IP address 10.50.1.1 (loopback 0 for remote VTEP identification) is mentioned in this configuration. The example shows only two VTEPs participating in the fabric. The ingress replication IP address is equal to the total number of leafs in the fabric and must be replicated to all the VNI segments in the leaf.

Host-to-Host Multicast Communication in VXLAN

In VXLAN, there are two types of multicast host-to-host communication:

■ Layer 2 communication within the boundary of the VNI

■ Layer 3 multicast communication

Layer 2 Communication Within the Boundary of the VNI

Enabling IGMP snooping helps achieve communication to hosts in the VNI that are interested in multicast traffic. With standard IGMP snooping, the VTEP interface is added to the outgoing interface list for multicast traffic. Then, even if no receiver is connected to the VTEP, the VTEP receives the traffic and drops it. The way to optimize this behavior for only the VTEP with multicast receivers in the L2 VNI is by adding the configuration shown in Example 4-4 (under the bridge domain).

Example 4-4 *Configuration to Optimize IGMP Snooping for VLXAN*

```
VTEP-2(config)# ip igmp snooping vxlan
VTEP-2 (config)# int vlan 01
VTEP-2 (config-if)# ip igmp snooping disable-nve-static-router-port
VTEP-2 (config)#
```

You can configure **ip igmp snooping disable-nve-static-router-port** globally or per VLAN to learn snooping states dynamically, as show in Figure 4-11.

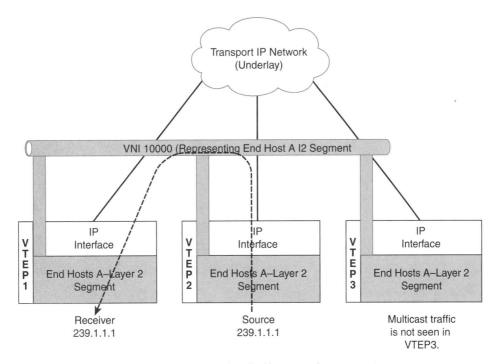

With ip igmp snooping disable-nve-static-router-port

Figure 4-11 *L2 Communication Within the Boundary of the VNI*

Using this command, the VTEP interface to the multicast group is added to the Layer 2 outgoing interface, based on the availability of the receiver. In Figure 4-11 the multicast source is connected to VTEP2. The traffic does not get flooded to all the VTEPs where the VNI has an instance. Instead, communication is optimized between VTEP2 and VTEP1, and VTEP 3 does not get the traffic because no receiver is connected to VTEP3 for the multicast traffic 239.1.1.1.

Layer 3 Multicast Communication

The routed multicast capability over VXLAN fabric is achieved by extending the bridge domain over VXLAN to the edge router. A per-tenant pairing needs to be configured to establish a Protocol Independent Multicast (PIM) relationship within the L3 environments. Unfortunately, this per-tenant peering is not efficient.

Figure 4-12 shows a centralized model of a multicast control plane for a VXLAN fabric. The VXLAN fabric leverages an external router. This method is similar to using Layer 2 multicast in a given bridge domain sent to an external router. All bridge domain instances are present in the router. The default gateway for the VXLAN is still through the unicast distributed anycast gateways. The designated router for PIM is at the external router, outside the VXLAN fabric. Incoming packets will need to pass the Reverse Path Forwarding (RPF) checks on the external router. The external router knows all the sources or receivers in the fabric and is the conduit to exchange unicast RIB information with the L3 environment outside the fabric. However, with this approach, you need a dedicated external router infrastructure to support multicast. A future VXLAN solution with multicast may evolve with more distributed approaches for Layer 3 deployment.

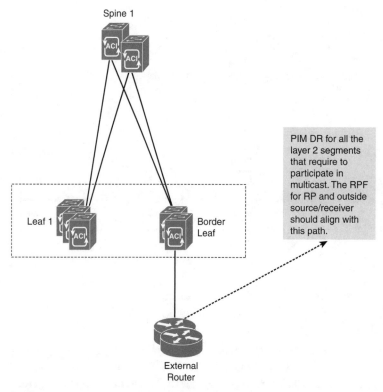

Figure 4-12 *VXLAN Fabric*

Multicast in ACI Data Center Networks

Application Centric Infrastructure (ACI) is a software-defined networking (SDN) solution developed by Cisco to run and control data center networks, with a special emphasis on multitenancy. ACI uses a spine/leaf topology, much like the VXLAN topology shown in the previous section. The major difference between a typical VXLAN fabric and ACI is that the underlying fabric is constructed and deployed by the central controller, the Application Policy Infrastructure Controller (APIC).

The switches in the fabric are the same Nexus 9300s, the fabric still uses IS-IS and VXLAN for provisioning, and each switch performs forwarding in the same independent manner. The APIC is merely a configuration and collection entity that uses specific constructs to create isolated networks that overlay on the VXLAN fabric, much as an architect designs. Segmentation is derived from common policy elements and is based on either application requirements (in which case it's called application-centric), or network requirements (in which case it's called network-centric). IP Multicast is then deployed within these overlay segments. Figure 4-13 depicts an ACI fabric topology with external L3 routing.

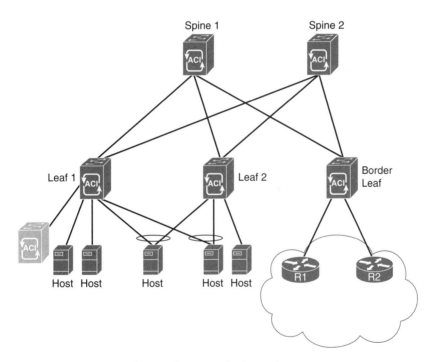

Figure 4-13   *ACI Fabric with External L3 Routing*

Each of the leaf and border leaf switches in the ACI topology is acting as a VTEP. Thus, many of the same rules for multicast routing over VXLAN apply. The major differences in an ACI deployment are related to the way the network handles network overlay elements. These elements include endpoint groups (EPGs), bridge domains (BDs), policies, and Virtual Route Forwarding (VRF) instances. These elements allow ACI to isolate tenants, networks, and applications within the underlying VXLAN fabric. All these elements are configured with the APIC, like the one shown in Figure 4-13.

Regardless of the virtual network topologies overlaid on the fabric, ACI uses a specific forwarding model for all multidestination traffic that is a little unique. All multidestination traffic in an ACI fabric is encapsulated in a IP Multicast packet. These packets then follow a forwarding tag (FTAG) tree, which is built between leafs and fabric spines so that traffic is load balanced over all available bandwidth. The idea is that if the leaf must send all traffic north, regardless of its east–west or north–south path, load splitting traffic between the spines improves the overall efficiency of the fabric. FTAGs are built into the MAC address of each packet that uses the tree. The spine switches manage the tree and then forward the packets to any VTEPs in the tree that need the packet. Each FTAG has one FTAG tree associated with it. Between any two switches, only one link forwards per FTAG. Because there are multiple FTAGs, parallel links are used, with each FTAG choosing a different link for forwarding. A larger number of FTAG trees in the fabric means better load balancing potential. The ACI fabric supports up to 12 FTAGs. Figure 4-14 depicts the FTAG tunneling matrix for a two-spine, three-leaf fabric.

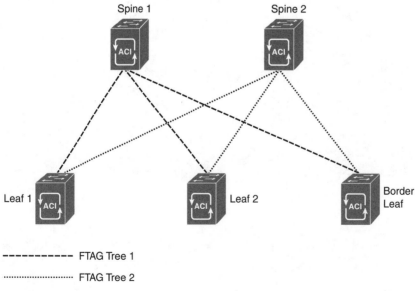

Figure 4-14 *FTAG Tree Forwarding*

ACI Fabrics and Overlay Elements

In order to understand the unique differences of a multicast implementation, it is helpful to quickly review the ACI fabric and how traffic is driven by policy across the network. This is not intended to be a thorough review of ACI technology but rather an introduction to the elements relevant to moving multicast across the ACI fabric. For information about the configuration of ACI, the APIC, and design elements, refer to the ACI configuration guides available at www.cisco.com.

ACI uses a database of elements to construct a network overlay configuration that resides on top of the VXLAN infrastructure. These elements do not necessarily correspond to traditional network design elements. For example, the APIC can be configured to use VPCs for physical packet transport across the fabric. In this case, a VPC is a fabric construct used to determine packet flow between leaf switches and connected hosts.

A VLAN is an example of a traditional network element that is used differently in ACI than in conventional networks. The APIC uses VLAN numbers to segment traffic inbound or outbound from the fabric, but VLAN tagging isn't necessary to create segmentation within the fabric, nor are VLANs required for forwarding between segments.

Instead, ACI segregates traffic based on VRFs, EPGs, and bridge domains. An EPG is quite simply a defined collection of interfaces (physical access ports or virtual access ports, like those of a virtual server). Ports are gathered into EPGs so that policy is applied across all the ports in a similar manner. Using default configurations, IP hosts within an EPG are able to communicate with each other (which means there is an explicit default trust policy between hosts inside an EPG).

A bridge domain is a Layer 2 construct, similar in purpose to a VLAN, but it does not use a VLAN tag. The purpose of a bridge domain is to provide logical segmentation at Layer 2 within the EPG. An ACI VRF is essentially the same as any Layer 3 VRF and serves the same purpose as the bridge domain except at Layer 3. Thus, loopback addresses, IP routing, and L3 functions for a specific purpose are configured under a VRF.

An EPG can have multiple bridge domains and VRFs, but it is not a requirement as there is a default bridge domain and a default VRF for each EPG. There must be one of each to fully operate at each layer (Layers 2 and 3). Hosts connected to ports in different EPGs cannot, by default, communicate with each other. Instead, specific policies must be applied to allow inter-host communication between EPGs. Policies are unidirectional forwarding rules that allow specific traffic, like a firewall whitelist. This includes potential Layer 3 hosts, such as routers and firewalls, that are outside the ACI fabric. For this purpose, a specific type of policy, an L3 Out policy, is provided to route IP traffic beyond the fabric. Figure 4-15 shows a visualization of these elements overlaid on the fabric from Figure 4-13.

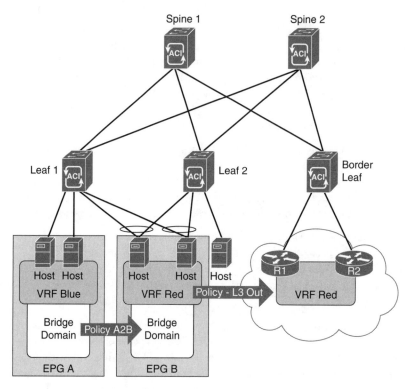

Figure 4-15 *ACI Fabric with Overlay Elements*

In this network design, two hosts are added to EPG A, and two hosts are added to
EPG B. A fifth host is a bare metal server with no EPG assignment. Each EPG has one
bridge domain and one VRF. In order for the hosts in EPG A to communicate with the
hosts in EPG B, a specific policy—in this case Policy A2B—must explicitly allow it.
Without a policy in the return direction, the hosts in EPG B cannot respond to EPG A.
In addition, a host without an EPG is isolated from the other hosts in this diagram,
including the routers (R1 and R2) that are connected to the border leaf switch. Finally,
an L3 Out policy is applied to EPG B to allow IP traffic to move toward routers R1 and
R2 and outside the fabric.

Note The diagram depicts the policies in this way to make clear how ACI forwarding
occurs. This is not a recommended ACI design. An in-depth discussion of ACI is beyond
the scope of this text. For more information on ACI operations and configurations, please
refer to ACI design guides available at www.cisco.com.

Layer 2 IGMP Snooping in ACI

ACI supports IGMP snooping by enabling an IGMP router function in software. The IGMP router function is enabled first within a bridge domain and is used to discover EPG ports that have attached hosts that are multicast clients. ACI uses the port information obtained through IGMP snooping to reduce bandwidth consumption in a multi-access bridge domain environment. If the leaf switch knows where the clients are located, there is no need to flood multicast flows across the entire bridge domain. Instead, only leaf ports with attached subscribers receive multicast flow packets for a given flow. IGMP snooping is enabled on each bridge domain by default.

When IGMP snooping is enabled, the leaf switch snoops the IGMP membership reports and leave messages as they enter the fabric from attached hosts. The leaf switch records the group subscriptions and then forwards them to the IGMP router function—only if L3 processing is required. Figure 4-16 shows the IGMP router function and IGMP snooping functions both enabled on an ACI leaf switch.

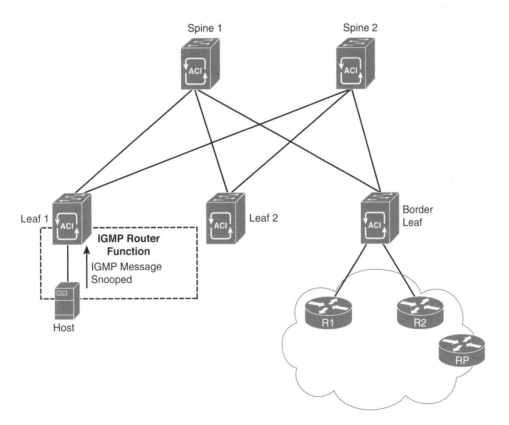

Figure 4-16   *ACI IGMP Snooping*

When VRFs are deployed in the overlay, IGMP snooping can also be configured on the VRF. If no VRF is configured, the default VRF (which is enabled with IGMP snooping) is used for all bridge domains. The VRF is the recommended location to control IGMP snooping when necessary. Do not disable snooping on the bridge domains so that multicast efficiency is still achieved for flows that are intra-bridge domain. This also prevents overflooding of multicast packets in those scenarios.

ACI supports IGMP snooping for all three versions of IGMP and the corresponding unique messages of each version. Additional IGMP snooping features available on within an ACI overlay include the following:

- Source filtering that allows forwarding of multicast packets based on destination and source IP addresses

- Multicast forwarding based on IP addresses rather than the MAC address

- Multicast forwarding based on the MAC address

For more information on these specific features, see the ACI Layer 2 IGMP snooping configuration guide at www.cisco.com.

The following section takes a closer look at how ACI handles multicast flows within a Layer 3 overlay network.

Layer 3 Multicast in ACI

ACI is an advanced data center networking platform that uses SDN. ACI, therefore, supports both Layer 2 and Layer 3 multicast configurations within the configurable virtual network overlays. PIM is supported in these constructs; however, it is important to understand the following:

- **PIM-enabled interfaces:** The border leaf switches run the full PIM protocol. This allows the ACI fabric to peer with other PIM neighbors outside the fabric.

- **Passive mode PIM-enabled interfaces:** The PIM-enabled interfaces do not peer with any PIM router outside the fabric. This is configured on all non-border leaf interfaces.

- **The fabric interface:** This interface is used within the fabric for multicast routing. This interface is a software representation of a segment/node in ACI fabric for multicast routing. The interface is similar to a tunnel interface with the destination being GIPo (Group IP Outer Address). VRF GIPo is allocated implicitly based on the configuration of the APIC. There is one GIPo for the VRF and one GIPo for every bridge domain under that VRF. Each interface is tied to a separate multitenant domain (VRF) in the same node. Within the fabric, if the border leaf has an outgoing interface for multicast group 239.1.1.1, the fabric interface is tied to the VRFs. This is accomplished by using a unique loopback address on each border leaf on each VRF that enables multicast routing. Figure 4-17 gives a quick depiction of how the logical fabric interfaces are viewed by the leaf switches.

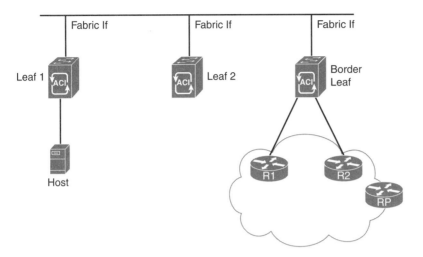

Figure 4-17 *ACI Fabric Interface for Multicast*

To enable multicast in a fabric, you need to configure a VRF, an L3 Out (for the respective VRF), and a bridge domain. The bridge domains must be enabled to participate in multicast; otherwise, even if the VRF is configured with multicast, the bridge domain is not seen. Multicast-enabled pervasive bridge domains are stubs for multicast routing. The Switched Virtual Interface (SVI) of the bridge domain is considered the DR of anything that is connected southbound.

Note   In data center networking, the traffic entering and exiting the data center is typically referred to as north–south traffic, while traffic that spans the data center is called east–west traffic. In the explanation above, southbound refers to traffic entering the data center and moving toward the hosts (that is, moving south).

It is very important to have all three logical constructs enabled for multicast traffic to flow. While configuring the L3 Out port, use individual ports or subinterfaces (the only interfaces that currently support multicast). Because SVIs are not supported by multicast PIM, these interfaces cannot be enabled in any L3 Out with VPC configuration.

The border leaf configuration for multicast is key because the outgoing interface list (OIF) from the fabric within a VRF points to the border leaf. The border leaf is also the designated forwarder for attracting the traffic from the external network. To avoid duplication of multicast traffic within the fabric, the border leafs elect the responsible border leaf for a multicast group to attract the traffic into the fabric on behalf of the receivers. This is tied to a VRF tenant election on the border leaf for the multicast group. The designated border leaf forwarder for group information is exchanged among all the border leafs.

Figure 4-18 shows a sample network design using these principles. In ACI, only the border leaf switches run a full PIM process. Leaf switches that are not borders run PIM in a type of passive mode, encompassing any multicast-enabled interfaces. These switches do not peer with any other PIM routers. Border leaf switches are configured to peer with the PIM routers, R1 and R2, connected to them over L3 Outs. If additional border switches are configured on this network, there is also a PIM relationship between them. RP functions in this network are located in the external L3 domain but could be moved closer to the ACI fabric.

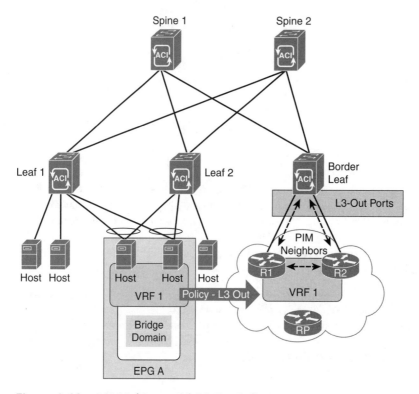

Figure 4-18 *ACI Multicast with L3 Out Policy*

What is passive mode PIM on the non-border-leaf switches? For ACI, Cisco has developed a new passive probe that only sends PIM hello packets but does not process received hellos. This passive mode runs on all non-border-leaf fabric interfaces and on any pervasive bridge domain SVIs. The switch does not expect to see PIM neighbors on these interfaces, and no relationship is required to add them to the PIM forwarding tree. Remember that it is assumed that all non-local PIM destinations for a flow must first flow through the spine switches. This simplifies the tree-building process and makes PIM more efficient on the leaf switches.

However, on fabric interfaces, PIM receives and processes the following PIM packets:

■ **PIM hellos:** These are used to track the active border leaf list on the fabric interface and on the pervasive BD interfaces. This list is used to raise faults.

■ **PIM BSR, Auto-RP advertisements:** These are received on the fabric interface and are used to create any necessary group-range mappings because you still need an RP mapping for sparse-mode network overlays.

In case of an event, such as removal or addition of a border leaf, rehashing of a multicast group takes place. Based on the rehashing, a newly elected border leaf builds the PIM relationship outside the fabric for a specific multicast group and is the designated forwarder for that group within the fabric. This rehashing is optimized by using the fast convergence mode for multicast in ACI. This rehashing within the border leafs and programming of the new designated forwarder border leaf for the fabric with the right RPF interface is achieved by fast convergence mode in ACI. The only disadvantage in fast convergence mode—not only for the winner of the border leaf but also for the other (non-elected) border leafs—is that all the switches attract the traffic for the fabric on the external interface for a particular group. This increases multicast data plane utilization for the fabric external links because the multicast traffic is forwarded to all border leafs. The elected border leaf forwards the traffic for the group, whereas the non-elected border leafs drop the traffic. The convergence is fast; however, the multicast utilization within the fabric is still optimized, with a single elected border leaf acting as designated forwarder. In a normal scenario, without the fast convergence, the other border leaf not elected for the group does not participate in the L3 PIM message for the specific multicast group on the egress L3 links, thereby optimizing multicast traffic.

Note   This section is by no means a comprehensive explanation of all things ACI, or even of multicast in ACI. As of this writing, ACI is a fairly new technology that continues to evolve. The goal of this section is to review the most fundamental elements of a multicast-enabled ACI deployment. Check www.cisco.com for the latest configuration and deployment guides for ACI.

Summary

There are numerous network architecture solutions in the data center, and each of them includes a unique method to support multicast. A solution may be as simple as VPC, which uses a hashing method to determine the path that messages use to traverse the network. Another solution is VXLAN, which uses an underlay to encapsulate messages and propagate those messages across the fabric. Finally, ACI also takes advantage of VXLAN for extensibility but also adds functionality to specifically control traffic flow based on the application.

Applications within the data center (server to server) and those used to support the customers (client to server) may have unique multicast requirements. It is best practice to delve deeply into those multicast technologies and the applications that are most critical to the success of your organization.

Chapter 5

Multicast Design Solutions

The previous chapters of this book discuss some rather advanced types of multicast networks. Typically, as the requirements of a network grow in complexity, so do the number and type of protocols needed to meet those requirements. The chapters so far in this book and *IP Multicast, Volume 1* have provided the tools needed to meet most of these requirements. However, there are some additional elements to consider when designing complex multicast networks.

Items to cogitate include desired replication points, multitenancy and virtualization properties, and scalability of the multicast overlay in relation to the unicast network. In addition, every network architect must be concerned with the redundancy, reliability, and resiliency of a network topology. Multicast network design must consider these elements as well. The best way to discuss these elements of multicast design is through the examination of specific network archetypes that employ good design principles.

This chapter examines several archetypical network design models. These models might represent a specific network strategy that meets a specific commercial purpose, such as a trade floor. The examined model may also be a general design for a specific industry, such as the deployment of multicast in a hospital environment. The intent is to provide a baseline for each type of design, while providing examples of best practices for multicast deployments.

This chapter looks at the following design models:

- Multicast-enabled hospital networks, with an emphasis on multicast in wireless access networks

- Multicast multitenancy data centers

- Software-defined networks with multicast

- Multicast applications in utility networks

- Multicast-enabled market applications and trade floors

- Multicast service provider networks

Note   The information provided in this chapter is not intended to be a comprehensive list of everything an architect needs to know about a particular design type, nor is it meant to be an exercise in configuration of these elements. Rather, this chapter provides a baseline of best practices and principles for specific types of networks. Before completing a network implementation, consult the most current design documents for multicast networks at www.cisco.com.

Multicast-Enabled Clinical Networks

A large hospital network design is very similar to most large campus network designs. Campus networks typically focus on providing services to users. A proper campus network design may be very familiar to long-time Cisco networking veterans who studied the three-tier (access/distribution/core) network hierarchy. Figure 5-1 shows an archetype of the three-tier model.

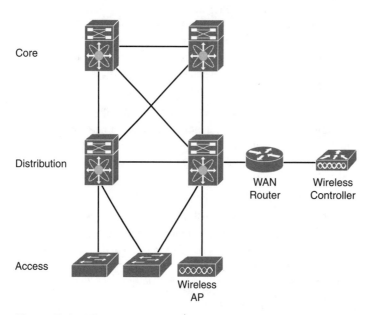

Figure 5-1   *Three-Tier Network Hierarchy*

Some newcomers to networking may be unacquainted with the access/distribution/core design model. Modern network devices and protocols allow architects to collapse much of the three-tier hierarchy into segments or, in many cases, single devices. For most campuses, even if the physical segmentation between the layers does not exist, there is at minimum a logical segmentation between the access and distribution/core layers of the design. For example, there is a routing and switching layer at the collapsed distribution/ core of the network. Additional resources connect to this collapsed core, including data center or WAN connections. Figure 5-2 shows a basic campus network with collapsed distribution and core layers.

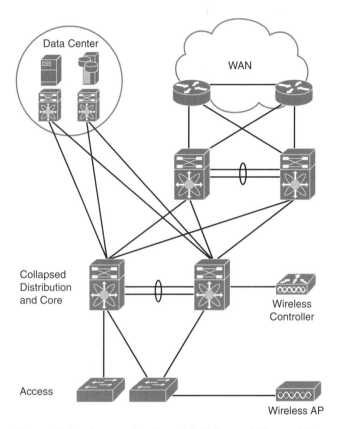

Figure 5-2   *Campus Design with Collapsed Network Core*

> **Note**   The ramifications of this hierarchy discussion and the effects on campus design are beyond the scope of this text but provide context for discussing design models as the parlance has not changed. For more information on this topic and full campus design, see the latest network design guides at www.cisco.com.

Because network access can be obtained by a myriad of device types, the access layer design usually includes a very robust wireless and wired infrastructure. Most isolation and segmentation in the access layer is provided by virtual local area network (VLAN) segmentation on Layer 2 switches. Layer 3 distribution routers provide inter-VLAN routing, virtual private network (VPN) services, and transit to centralized resources. Campus core switches and routers move traffic across all segments of the network quickly and efficiently.

In addition, many elements of hospital network design are completely unique. A typical campus network provides employees access to resources such as Internet services, centralized employee services (print, file, voice, and so on), bring-your-own-device (BYOD) services, and some minor guest services. A hospital network needs to deliver these to employees as well. However, the main purpose of a hospital is to provide services to patients and guests. Therefore, a hospital network needs to accommodate devices that service patients. Devices in a hospital network include badge systems, medical monitors, interpersonal communications, media services, and biomedical equipment. Data generated by these devices needs to be stored locally and remotely, and other data center type services are required as well. In addition, the hospital is likely to have extensive guest services, mostly focused on providing wireless guest Internet access.

Keeping all these devices secure and properly securing and segmenting data paths is critical. Government regulations, such as the well-known Health Insurance Portability and Accountability Act (HIPAA) in the United States, require that these security measures be comprehensive and auditable. This means hospital devices must be segregated from both users and personnel networks.

All these unique elements make network design very complex. For this reason, there is a great deal of variability in hospital network deployments. Regardless of this variability, almost every hospital network offers some level of multicast service. Most medical devices and intercommunications media can be configured with IP Multicast to make service delivery and data collection more efficient. Providing medical device and intercommunications services is the primary focus of this design discussion.

Accommodating Medical Device Communications Through Multicast

If you have ever been to a hospital, it is likely that you have noticed that many medical devices are used by doctors and staff to treat and monitor patients. What you may not have realized is that many of these devices are connected to the hospital campus network. These devices can include anything from a smart pump, to a heart monitor, to imaging equipment such as x-ray machines.

The benefits of connecting these devices to the network are enormous. The most important benefit is that data generated by these devices can be accessed remotely and, in many cases, in real time. In addition, network-connected biomedical devices—as well as non-medical devices such as badges—can be moved to any room on the hospital campus. When connected to a wireless network, these devices can be small and follow staff and patients about the hospital as required.

Note   Badge systems in hospitals are critical infrastructure. Because of the intense security requirements of human care and regulations such as HIPAA, hospitals need to know where patients are, where staff are, and where each person should be. Badge systems also control access to medical devices, medication, and data. This not only secures the devices, medication, and data but protects patients from their own curiosity.

Generally, the way in which these devices communicate is largely controlled by the device manufacturer. However, most modern hospital devices can at a minimum communicate using Layer 2 Ethernet, and many communicate using Internet Protocol (IP) at Layer 3. Most medical devices of a particular kind need to connect to a centralized controller or database that also needs access to the same network resources.

Manufacturers use three prototypical communication models to accomplish this:

- Layer 2 only
- Layer 2 and Layer 3 hybrid
- Layer 3 only

The first type of model uses Layer 2 connections only. In this model, it may be a requirement that all devices be on the same Layer 2 domain (segment). In an Ethernet network, this means they must be on the same VLAN. Centralized device controllers and data collectors may also need to be on the same segment. Some manufacturers require that the same wireless network, identified by the same Service Set Identification (SSID), be used for the monitors and controllers alike. Figure 5-2 depicts this type of model, with all the networked devices and their centralized resources connected to the same SSID (OneHospital) and VLAN (VLAN 10).

> **Note** In Figure 5-3, the campus distribution/core switch is more than a single switch. In a modern network, the collapsed core is typically made of at least one pair of switches, acting as a singular switch. For example, this might be Cisco's Virtual Switching System (VSS) running on a pair of Cisco Catalyst 6800 switches.

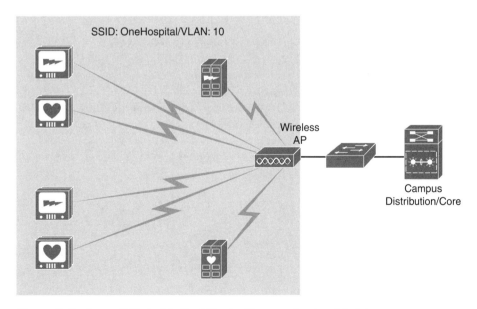

Figure 5-3 *Layer 2 Only Medical Device Communication Model*

The second communications model uses a hybrid of Layer 2 and Layer 3 communications. In this case, devices may be on separate VLANs and may be able to function within a small routed domain. However, a specific device type and its corresponding controller or central station may need to connect to the same VLAN. The controllers might provide communications and data outside the VLAN to remote resources, such as either a local or remote data center. They may also have no Layer 3 capabilities. A wireless LAN controller (WLC) is likely needed to accommodate inter-VLAN or Layer 3 communication at scale in this model. Figure 5-4 shows such a hybrid communications model.

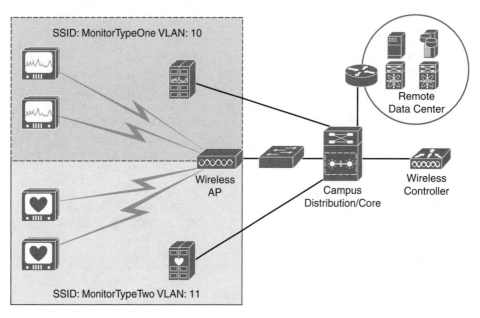

Figure 5-4   *Layer 2 and Layer 3 Hybrid Device Communications Model*

Finally, some devices are capable of fully routed Layer 3 IP communications. Controllers and central stations may be located remotely, or they may be centralized on the hospital campus. Devices may roam the network but are likely segmented for security. Figure 5-5 shows an example of this communications model. In this example, the devices use IP to speak to controllers in a localized data center. The device controller servers share this data with local and remote data center resources across the network.

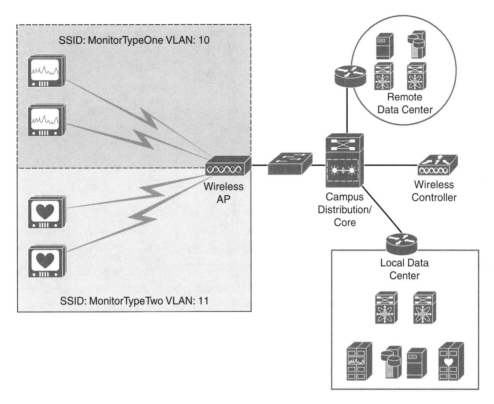

Figure 5-5 *Layer 3 Only Communications Model*

Even though there are three distinct models, you cannot assume that all devices fit neatly within one model—or even within the examples as they are shown here. They are, after all, only models. It is also likely that a hospital campus network has to accommodate all three models simultaneously to connect all medical devices.

Medical devices that make full use of IP networking and multicast communications are very similar to other network devices. They need to obtain an IP address, usually via Dynamic Host Configuration Protocol (DHCP), and have a default gateway to communicate outside their local VLAN. One major difference, as shown in the models in this section, is that medical devices typically connect to some type of controller or station. This is where multicast becomes very practical: allowing these devices to communicate with the central station in a very efficient manner, as there are many devices that connect to a single controller. In these scenarios, either the central station or the device (or both) may be the multicast source. This is a typical many-to-many multicast setup. Figure 5-6 shows this communication in action for the Layer 3 model shown in Figure 5-5.

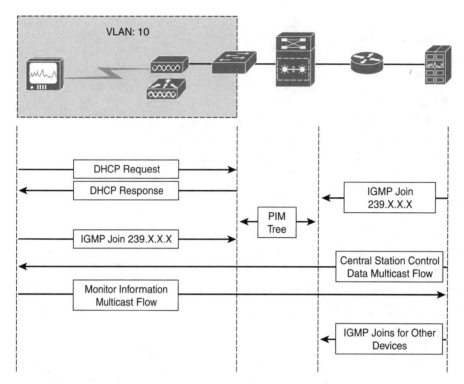

Figure 5-6   *Medical Device Communication Flow Example*

There are many devices connected to a hospital network—many more than in a typical campus network. Multicasting eases the operational burden on network resources, including access switching resources. There are a number of things to consider in the multicast design of the campus to accommodate the communication shown in Figure 5-6.

The first decision that must be made corresponds to the type of communication model in place. If all the devices are using a Layer 2 only communications model, then a complex multicast overlay design may not be required. In this case, the local network access points (APs) and switches may only need to support basic Internet Group Management Protocol (IGMP) and IGMP snooping to accommodate localized multicast inside the same Layer 2 domain. If Layer 3 services are required, Protocol Independent Multicast (PIM) must also be used.

The second decision to make involves the type of PIM implementation to deploy across the network. If there are many sources and many receivers (many-to-many multicast, a likely scenario at a hospital), it may be wise to consider deploying Bidirectional PIM (Bidir-PIM). Using Bidir-PIM dramatically improves network device resource consumption by eliminating steps in the source tree building process, as all source packets are forwarded from the source toward the rendezvous point (RP). It also makes multicast traffic more predictable. However, Bidir-PIM inevitably causes path selection that may not be ideal, and it may cause overconsumption of centralized resources, potentially including precious bandwidth at the distribution/core of the network (depending on RP placement).

Many medical devices use both multicast and unicast communications—but for different functions. Each function may have different security and routing requirements. These networks may require that an RP exist at each segment, with no centralized RP services so that domain security is tightly controlled. Bidir-PIM could be a poor choice in an environment where severe segmentation at both Layer 2 and Layer 3 are required. When multiple RPs need to coexist, a standard PIM Sparse-Mode (PIM-SM) implementation may be a better choice. This is essentially a multidomain configuration. If interdomain multicast forwarding is required, PIM-SM with Multicast Source Discovery Protocol (MSDP), and perhaps Border Gate Protocol (BGP), is ideal.

PIM Source-Specific Multicast (SSM) provides the benefits of both Bidir-PIM and PIM-SM without the need for a complex interdomain or multidomain design. SSM does not require an RP for pathing, nor does it require additional protocols for interdomain communications. The biggest drawback to using SSM is that many medical devices, especially those that are antiquated, may not support IGMPv3. Recall from *IP Multicast, Volume 1* that IGMPv3 subscribes a host to a specific source/group combination and is required for the last-hop router (LHR) to join the appropriate source-based tree. In addition, SSM may not be able to scale with a very large many-to-many design.

Selecting the best PIM implementation for a hospital campus is an exercise in comparing the advantages and disadvantages of each with the capabilities of both the network devices and the devices connecting to the campus network. It is very likely that no single implementation will perfectly address all the needs of the network. Table 5-1 compares some of the advantages and disadvantages of the different PIM implementations in a hospital network.

Table 5-1 *Comparison for PIM Implementation Selection for Hospital Networks*

Issue	Bidir-PIM	PIM-SM	PIM-SSM
Improved switch and router resource efficiency	Yes	No	No
Bandwidth conservation and optimum flow of traffic	No	Yes	Yes
Interdomain support	Yes (as long as Phantom RP is not used)	Yes	Not required
Better for RP centralization	Yes	No	Not required
Many-to-many efficiency	Yes	No	No
Universal support on network equipment	No	Yes	Yes
Universal support on medical devices (IGMP version)	Yes	Yes	No
Universal wireless network support	Unlikely	Yes	Unlikely
More complex to deploy	No	Yes	No

This table is useful for any campus design but considers the specific needs of a hospital campus. It is very likely that the deployment of more than one implementation is the best choice. For example, localized medical device multicast that does not leave the local VLANs can use a simple Bidir-PIM implementation with a centralized Phantom RP. VLANs with devices that need fully routed IP Multicast with possible interdomain communication can use a single Anycast RP solution, with PIM-SM providing the tree building. Core network services may use an SSM implementation to improve the reliability of the infrastructure by eliminating the need for RPs. All three PIM implementations can coexist within the same campus if properly configured as separate, overlapping, or intersecting domains. PIM-SM and PIM-SSM can be configured on the same router interfaces, whereas PIM-SM and Bidir-PIM are mutually exclusive.

This brings up an important point: When purchasing network equipment for a medical campus, make sure it optimizes support for these implementations. Whenever possible, select routers, switches, APs, WLCs, and other infrastructure that support the following:

- All versions of IGMP (versions 1, 2, and 3)

- The appropriate scale of IGMP joins and IGMP snooping for the number of expected devices (This is the most basic requirement at the edge of the network.)

- The appropriate PIM implementation(s) (Bidir-PIM, PIM-SM, and PIM-SSM)

- Optimal packet replication techniques to improve throughput and resource consumption

- Simplified multicast configuration and troubleshooting

- Multicast path optimization features, such as multipath multicast and spanning-tree optimization, or elimination, for all traffic flows

- Ability to secure multicast devices and domains

- Ability to provide quality of service (QoS) to multicast flows, including rate-limiting and/or storm control to limit overconsumption of resources by malfunctioning devices

Multicast Considerations for Wireless Networks

For wired switches, multicast is rudimentary, a basic component of Layers 2 and 3. A wired switch uses IGMP snooping, and each VLAN is configured with at least one routed interface that supports IGMP and multicast forwarding. This ensures that the devices connected to the switch port have access to the larger campus multicast overlay. Wireless Ethernet functions in a similar manner but introduces additional concerns. Ensuring that the wireless network efficiently and effectively transports all traffic is perhaps the most important consideration in designing multicast in a medical campus.

The first point to understand when considering multicast data transmission in wireless networking is that wireless networks use IP Multicast in the wireless management plane. A campus network is likely to have many APs. To ensure that these APs function in sync with one another, one or more WLCs are used. A WLC acts very much like the medical device central station discussed in the previous section. It connects to and oversees the configuration of the APs in the network. To enable multicast within the management plane, the switched management network must be properly configured for a multicast overlay. This may very well be an MVPN using multicast Virtual Route Forwarding (VRF) instances, as discussed in Chapter 3, "Multicast MPLS VPNs."

More important is the flow of multicast traffic to and from wireless LAN (WLAN) connected devices. This is especially relevant when sources and receivers are connected via either the wired or wireless infrastructure and they must be able to complete a forwarding tree, regardless of the connection type or location. Cisco WLANs must work seamlessly with the physical wired LAN. Another way of saying this is that a campus WLAN must be a functional extension of the VLAN, making the two functionally equivalent.

In an archetypical campus, each SSID is equivalent to a VLAN and is essentially configured as such. The VLAN may only be delivered wirelessly, or it could be accessible through both the wireless and the wired infrastructure. Figure 5-4 (shown earlier) illustrates just such a network, where patient heart monitors and the central station for these monitors are all part of the same VLAN, VLAN 11. SSID MonitorTypeTwo extends the VLAN to the individual wireless client monitors.

This design works well in environments where multicast is rarely forwarded past the local VLAN and where individual monitor functions need to be on the same Layer 2 domain. However, many modern hospitals use segmentation that is based on the patient's location rather than the type of device deployed. Figure 5-7 shows a design that uses a room grouping (perhaps based on the hospital floor, or even the type of room) to divide VLANs and SSIDs. In this design, the central monitor stations are part of the same VLAN, terminated on the access layer switches of the hospital.

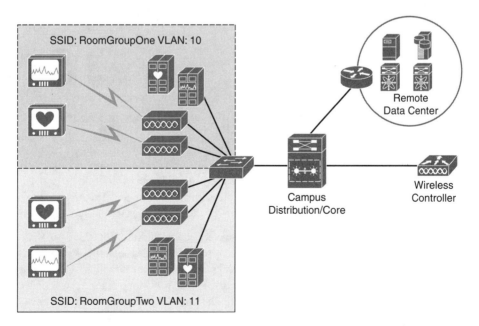

Figure 5-7 *SSIDs Deployed by Room Groups with Local Control Stations*

It is also possible that a routed network separates the monitoring station servers, which are then accessed by hospital staff through an application. These stations are generally centralized in a local data center to prevent WAN failures from causing service interruption. Figure 5-8 depicts the same room grouping design, with centralized control stations. Wireless APs provide access to the monitors, while a fully routed Layer 3 network extends between the monitor devices and the data center, crossing the collapsed campus core.

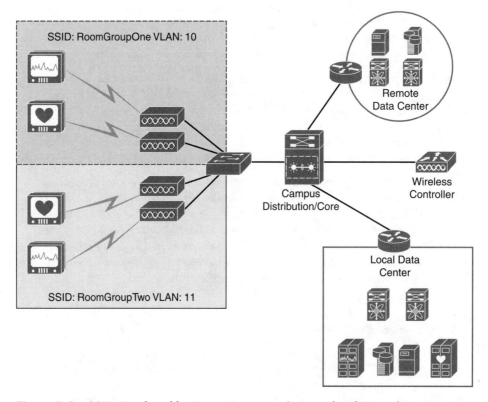

Figure 5-8   *SSIDs Deployed by Room Groups with Centralized Central Stations*

Regardless of how the SSIDs are deployed, how does the AP know what to do with the multicast packets sourced from either the wireless clients or other sources on the network? This question is especially relevant in a Layer 2 and 3 hybrid design or in a fully routed Layer 3 device communications model, like the one shown in Figure 5-8. The APs need to be able to replicate and forward packets upstream to where Layer 3 is terminated.

Wireless networks are, of course, more than just a collection of APs, SSIDs, and VLANs. Campus WLANs also use WLCs to manage the APs and SSIDs of the network. WLCs in a hospital campus almost always function as local management, meaning that APs are not only configured by the WLC but also tunnel traffic to the WLC for advanced switching capabilities, such as multicast packet replication. The tunneling mechanism used in this type of campus is the IETF standard Control and Provisioning of Wireless Access Points

(CAPWAP), as defined by IETF RFC 5415. Figure 5-9 shows this relationship between the APs and the WLC(s) in a campus with a fully routed Layer 3 device communications model.

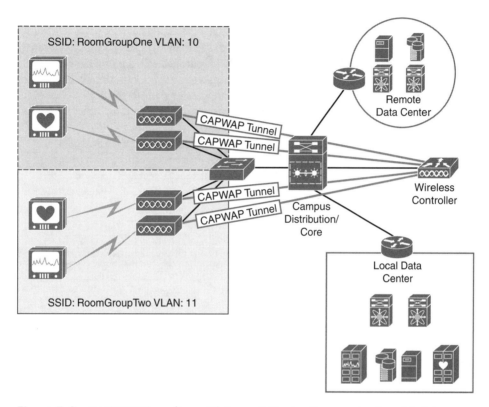

Figure 5-9   *CAPWAP Tunneling with Layer 3 Device Communications Model*

Note   This section provides only a rudimentary discussion of basic WLAN principles. It assumes that you have a working knowledge of WLAN technology and Cisco's implementation of wireless Ethernet at the campus. For more information on wireless network theory and wireless campus design, refer to documentation at www.cisco.com.

Some years ago, Cisco introduced a new architecture called Unified Access (UA) for deploying wireless in general but especially for multicast and broadcast traffic. While not all UA features are adopted in every network, this book uses UA as the de facto standard for this discussion. Before UA was implemented in Cisco wireless APs and WLCs, multicast packets were forwarded by a WLC encapsulated inside unicast packets. The WLC sent these unicast packets to each AP that had clients subscribed to the group instead of performing proper multicast replication, potentially including an AP from where the source was connected. This is not particularly efficient, nor does it control packet looping—one of the primary functions of multicast forwarding in modern networks. Cisco UA instead supports multicast forwarding across the APs and WLCs. Let's examine how this works.

A Cisco UA-capable WLAN controller appears to the routed network as a router joined to the multicast groups of downstream clients. When the controller receives a multicast packet from the network, it examines the group to see if any wireless clients are currently subscribed. If there are subscribed clients, the WLC encapsulates the original multicast packet inside a CAPWAP multicast packet that uses a specific group. APs are subscribed to this group, making the WLAN controller the source and the APs the clients. The WLC then sends a single multicast toward the routed network for standard multicast replication and forwarding. The APs receive the CAPWAP-encapsulated multicast via the network, strip the CAPWAP headers, and then forward the original multicast packet. The packet must be transmitted on all radios servicing an SSID. There is no other way to transmit a local wireless multicast. As with a Layer 2 switch, if the AP receives unassociated multicast packets, it sends those packets to the bit bucket. Figure 5-10 visualizes this multicast flow.

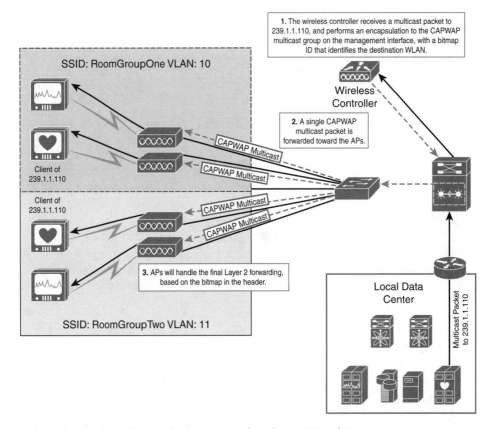

Figure 5-10 *CAPWAP Multicast Forwarding from a Wired Source*

To summarize, when a multicast packet is received from the routed network, there are three main steps in the forwarding process, as outlined in Figure 5-10:

Step 1.   The WLC receives a multicast packet from the routed network and encapsulates the packet in a CAPWAP multicast packet. APs have already joined the CAPWAP group, acting as clients. A bitmap is created to map SSIDs to CAPWAP packets. CAPWAP multicast packets are forwarded using the management interface.

Step 2.   The multicast-enabled network receives the CAPWAP multicast from the management interface and forwards the packet to the APs through the multicast overlay. This relieves the WLC of the burden of replication.

Step 3.   APs receive the CAPWAP multicast packet and read the WLC-assigned bitmap for the packet, indicating the SSID for which the original multicast is intended. The AP then strips the outer header and broadcasts on the corresponding SSID. APs may receive other multicast packets, but they will forward only one copy of the multicast packet received from its primary WLC. An AP drops all other packets.

Note   All radios associated with the SSID must transmit the packet, even if a radio has no subscribed clients. For example, WLAN RoomGroupOne, VLAN 10 in Figure 5-10, may have both 802.11b/g/n radios and 802.11a radios servicing clients. Even if there are no clients on the 802.11a spectrum, the AP must assume that the flooding of the multicast needs to be complete.

When a wireless client is the source of the multicast stream, the packet flow is slightly different. First, unlike a Layer 2 switch, the AP does not replicate the packet locally. Instead, it must forward all multicast packets up the unicast CAPWAP tunnel to the WLC. The WLC handles the multicast from there. Remember that clients for a group may be located on the wired LAN, on the routed network, or on the same WLAN. The WLC needs to service all these paths. You can add an additional two steps to the forwarding process when this happens, as shown in Figure 5-11:

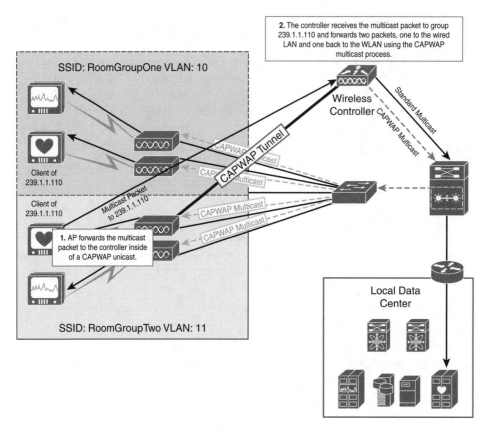

Figure 5-11   *CAPWAP Multicast Forwarding from a Wireless Source*

Step 1.   The AP receives a multicast packet from a wireless client—in this case, for group 239.1.1.110. The AP encapsulates the original multicast packet inside the CAPWAP unicast tunnel and forwards it to the WLC. This is the same process for any packet that needs additional routing in a wireless CAPWAP network.

Step 2.   The WLC receives the packet, strips the unicast CAPWAP header, and forwards the original multicast packet upstream, toward the routed network. The standard routed multicast overlay ensures that the packets are forwarded toward any wired subscribed clients, regardless of their location (assuming that a complete multicast tree can be built). The WLAN controller also replicates the original multicast packet, encapsulates it inside a single CAPWAP multicast packet with the appropriate bitmap ID, and sends it toward the routed network. From there, the process is the same as when the packet comes from a wired client, eventually being forwarded to the appropriate APs and then to the SSID. This means the originating SSID, including the originating client, gets a copy of the same packet. Wireless multicast clients are designed to account for this phenomenon and should not process the replicated packet.

One of the primary uses of a multicast design in a hospital is to enable a hospital badging system. Clinical badge systems are not like the standard swipe card badge systems that many users are familiar with. Badge systems for hospitals, such as those provided by system manufacturer Vocera, are more forward thinking. They use IP integration and Voice over IP (VoIP) to establish communications between badge users and other hospital systems and applications, much like the futuristic badges used on your favorite sci-fi TV series.

Clinical badge systems allow hospital staff to communicate quickly and efficiently across specific teams, hospital wards, or other organizations. Many have unique paging features and are also used to track the locations of wearers. This location tracking is integrated into hospital security systems for quick access to specific areas of the hospital. Other medical badge systems can be used to track location for system lockdowns, like those used to monitor infant location and prevent infants from leaving the wards to which they are assigned. If you have ever been to a hospital, you may have seen badge systems like these.

Because badges are worn by hospital staff, it is critical that wireless infrastructure be fast, resilient, and reliable. Medical devices also need similar network resiliency. That is the primary reason that WLCs are installed locally at the distribution or access layer of the network and use CAPWAP tunnels instead of remotely deployed WLCs. As mentioned earlier, these badge systems rely on multicast as well. This means the multicast infrastructure should also be fast, resilient, and reliable. Achieving this means that designing a robust Layer 2 and Layer 3 multicast implementation is critical; the implementation must follow the best practices described in *IP Multicast, Volume 1*.

In addition, for PIM-SM networks, the placement of the RP is a critical consideration. If the RP is located on a remote WAN separated segment, or if there are too many failure points between the WLC and the RP, there will likely be outages for multicast clients and sources. To reduce the number of failures, place the WLCs and RPs close to each other and near the multicast network, with few failure points between.

Two typical multicast domain models are used to deploy RPs:

- **Domain model 1:** The first model is used for isolated domains that do not extend beyond specific geographic locations. In this model, RPs are placed locally in each domain. Often the nearest Layer 3 switch that is acting as the first-hop router (FHR) and last-hop router (LHR) is also configured as the RP. This limits the failure scope of the domain to that specific Layer 2 or 3 domain.

- **Domain model 2:** The second model is used when multidomain or interdomain communications are required. In this model, multiple redundant RPs may be used, usually placed by domain. This is similar to the first model but with the addition of hospitalwide resources.

Figure 5-12 shows a comparison of the domain setup for the two models. Domain model 1 uses one controller and the distribution/core switch pair as the RP for each group of rooms. The Layer 3 FHR and RP are configured on the appropriate VLAN interfaces. Domain model 2 expands on Domain model 1 by adding a hospitalwide domain with Anycast RPs and a stack of hospitalwide WLCs in the local hospital data center.

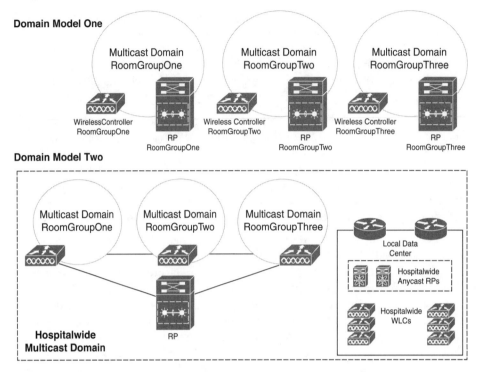

Figure 5-12 *Multicast Domain Models*

Note   Remember that the example using a RoomGroup for VLAN and WLAN assignment is simply one option for device grouping. The domains in each model can be organized in any logical way, typically based on the requirements of the application. The grouping used in this chapter simply makes the design elements easier to consume. In addition, a larger Layer 3 PIM-SM model can link domains together by using MSDP and/or BGP to provide the ability to forward between multicast domains. In addition, more intense segmentation may exist within the hospital, and multicast VRF instances may be a requirement that must also be met in the design.

No matter what domain model is used, domains must be secured and segmented properly. Wireless and multicast architects should be well versed in the operation of these networks and should design clinical multicast with resiliency and reliability as key foundational elements. They need to ensure that clinical staff do not experience interruptions to service, which produces a superior patient experience.

Multicast in Multitenant Data Centers

Chapter 3 discusses the ability of networks using MPLS VPNs to provide multicast over the VPN overlay. These VPNs allow service providers to provide private IP service to customers over a single Layer 3 network. Chapter 4, "Multicast in Data Center Environments," also examines the ability of Cisco data center networks to provide multicast services to and from data center resources. A multitenant data center combines these two concepts, creating multiple customer overlays on a single topology. This allows service providers that offer infrastructure as a service (IaaS) to reduce the cost of implementation and operation of the underlying data center network.

In a multitenant data center, each customer overlay network is referred to as a *tenant*. The tenant concept is flexible, meaning that a single customer may have multiple tenant overlays. If you are familiar with Cisco Application Centric Infrastructure (ACI), discussed in Chapter 4, you will be familiar with this concept. If properly designed, IaaS providers can offer multicast as part of the service of each overlay network in a multitenant data center.

To understand multitenant multicast deployments, this section first briefly reviews how tenant overlays are implemented. The primary design model in this discussion uses segmentation and policy elements to segregate customers. An example of this type of design is defined in Cisco's Virtualized Multi-Tenant Data Center (VMDC) architecture. VMDC outlines how to construct and segment each tenant virtual network. Cisco's ACI is another example. A quick review of the design elements of VMDC and ACI helps lay the foundation for understanding multitenant multicast.

Note   VMDC is a Cisco Validated Design (CVD). CVDs provide network architects with standardized design recommendations, based on common usage and best practices. CVDs are comprehensively tested by Cisco engineers to ensure faster, more reliable network deployments at scale. Readers can learn more about VMDC and other CVDs from Cisco's Design Zone, at www.cisco.com/c/en/us/solutions/design-zone.html. This is not a comprehensive explanation of VMDC. Refer to the published design guides and version updates to fully explore the architectural elements. Other data center–focused CVDs are related to the concepts in this chapter. VMDC was updated in version 2.0 to include multicast as part of the standardized deployment model. The latest versions of VMDC also include the ability to incorporate ACI into the topology.

VMDC uses standard Cisco virtual port channel (VPC) or Virtual Extensible LAN (VXLAN) networking for building the underlay infrastructure. It then breaks a tenant overlay into reproducible building blocks that can be adjusted or enhanced to fit the service level requirements of each customer. These blocks consist of segmentation and policy elements that can be virtualized within the underlay. For example, a Silver-level service, as defined by VMDC, incorporates virtual firewall (VFW) and load balancing (LB) services and segmentation through the use of VRF instances, VLANs, firewall contexts, and Layer 3 routing policies. Figure 5-13 shows the service levels possible in a VMDC network, with the virtualized segmentation and policy elements used in each service level.

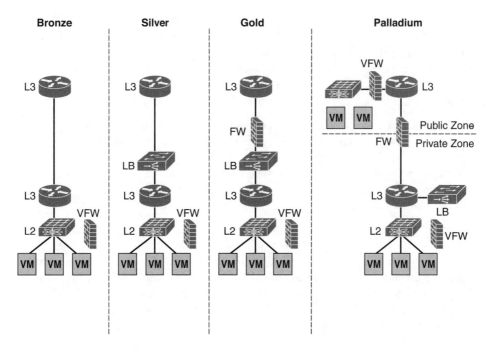

Figure 5-13   *VMDC Tenant Service Levels*

Most data center designs, even private single-tenant data centers, further segment compute and application resources that reside on physical and virtual servers into zones. The concept of zones is also depicted in Figure 5-13, on the Palladium service level, which shows a separation between public and private zones. Zones may also be front-end zones (that is, application or user facing) or back-end zones (that is, intersystem and usually non-accessible to outside networks). Firewalls (physical and virtual) are critical to segmenting between zones, especially where public and private zones meet. Finally, public zone segmentation can be extended beyond the data center and into the public network by using VRF instances and MPLS VPNs.

A multitenant data center's main function is to isolate, segment, and secure individual applications, services, and customers from each other to the extent required. This, in turn, drives the fundamental design elements and requirements when enabling multicast within each customer overlay. Any of Cisco's multitenant-capable systems are capable of offering multicast. When deploying multicast, a data center architect needs to consider the function and policies of each zone/end point group (EPG) and design segmented multicast domains accordingly.

To put this more simply, the multicast domain, including the placement of the RP, must match the capabilities of each zone. If a zone is designed to offer a public shared service, then a public, shared multicast domain with a shared RP is required to accommodate that service. If the domain is private and restricted to a back-end zone, the domain must be private and restricted by configuration to the switches and routers providing L2 and L3 services to that zone. Such a zone may not require an RP but may need IGMP snooping support on all L2 switches (physical or virtual) deployed in that zone. Finally, if the zone is public, or if it is a front-end zone that communicates with both private and public infrastructure, the design must include proper RP placement and multicast support on all firewalls.

In per-tenant overlays, multiple zones and multicast domains are likely to be required. Hybrid-domain and multidomain multicast designs are appropriate for these networks. Consider the network design in Figure 5-14, which is based on an implementation of multiple multicast domains within a Palladium service level container on a VMDC architecture.

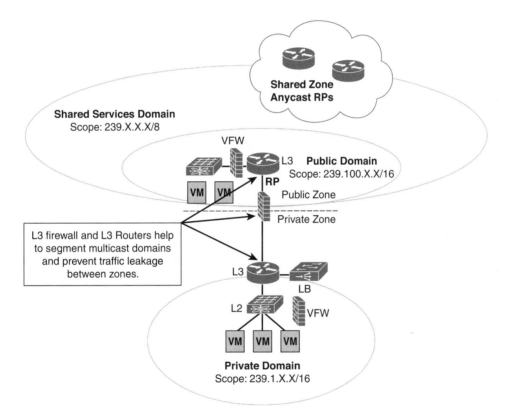

Figure 5-14   *Palladium Service with Hybrid Multicast Domain Design*

The tenant of Figure 5-14 wishes to use a private multicast domain within the private zone of the network for back-end services. The L2 switch is enabled with IGMP snooping, and the domain is scoped to groups in the 239.1.0.0/16 range. This is a private range and can overlap with any range in the public or shared-public zones, as the domain ends at the inside L3 router.

In addition, the public zone with Layer 3 services offers multicast content on the front end to internal entities outside the DC. A public domain, scoped to 239.100.0.0/16, will suffice. The top L3 router supplies RP services, configured inside a corresponding tenant VRF.

Finally, a shared services domain is offered to other datacenter tenants. The shared public zone has a global multicast scope of 239.0.0.0/8. The tenant uses the L3 FW and L3 routers to carve out any services needed in the shared zone and segments them from the public front-end zone. The overlapping scope of the shared services zone needs to be managed by the configuration of the RP mapping on the public domain RP such that it is mapped as RP for any 239.100.0.0 groups and the shared service Anycast RPs are automatically mapped to all other groups. Additional segmentation and firewall rule sets are applied on the public L3 router and VFW to further secure each multicast domain, based on the rules of the zones in which they are configured.

Best practice to achieve this level of domain scoping is to use PIM-SM throughout the multitenant DC. There may be issues running PIM-SSM if there are overlapping domains in the model. When scoping domains for multitenancy, select one of the four following models:

- Use a single RP for all domains with a global scope for each data center

- Use local scoping per multitenant zone with a single RP for each domain (may not require firewall multicast transport)

- Use a global scope for each DC with one RP and local scoping within multitenant domains and one RP for all domains and zones (requires firewall transport)

- A hybrid between per-DC and per-tenant designs, using firewalls and L3 routers to segment domains

Remember that the resources shown in Figure 5-14 could be virtual or physical. Any multitenant design that offers per-tenant multicast services may need to support multiple domain deployment models, depending on the customer service level offerings. For example, the architect needs to deploy hardware and software routers that provide RPs and multicast group mappings on a per-tenant basis. The virtual and physical firewalls need to not only be capable of forwarding IP Multicast traffic but also need multicast-specific policy features, such as access control lists (ACLs), that support multicast. Newer software-defined networking (SDN) technologies, such as Cisco's ACI, help ease the burden of segmentation in per-tenant multicast designs.

ACI Multitenant Multicast

Cisco ACI enhances the segmentation capabilities of multitenancy. ACI, as you learned in Chapter 4, is an SDN data center technology that allows administrators to deconstruct the segmentation and policy elements of a typical multitenant implementation and deploy them as an overlay to an automated Layer 2/Layer 3 underlay based on VXLAN. All principal policy elements in ACI, including VRF instances, bridge domains (BDs), endpoint groups (EPGs), and subnets, are containerized within a hierarchical policy container called a tenant. Consequently, multitenancy is an essential foundation for ACI networks. Figure 5-15 shows the relationship between these overlay policy elements.

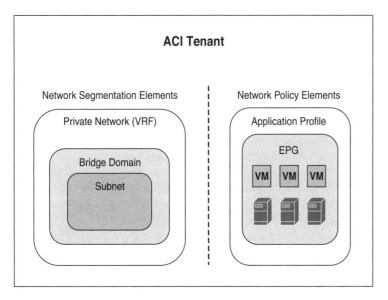

ACI Tenant

Network Segmentation Elements

Private Network (VRF)

Bridge Domain

Subnet

Network Policy Elements

Application Profile

EPG

VM   VM   VM

Figure 5-15   *ACI Overlay Policy Elements*

Note   It is important to understand that while *tenant* is a universally understood term as defined by National Institute of Standards and Technology (NIST) standards, its usage in ACI is very loose. A tenant can be any grouping of policy and segmentation elements that is needed. This grouping is used to control intertenant communication as well as access to administration and configuration. A single customer may use a single tenant, or it may have multiple tenants, depending on the customer's needs. EPGs within the tenant can also be deployed in a very flexible manner. An architect should ensure that the deployment matches the needs of the customer and provides the appropriate segmentation and policy to keep customer resources segregated.

An EPG is conceptually very similar to a zone in the VMDC architecture. Some EPGs do not allow any inter-EPG communication. Others may be private to the tenant but allow inter-EPG routing. Still others may be public facing through the use of a Layer 3 Out policy. Segmentation between zones is provided natively by the whitelist firewall nature of port assignments within an EPG. Without specific policy—namely contracts—inter-EPG communication is denied by default. EPGs can then align to private and public zones and can be designated as front-end or back-end zones by the policies and contracts applied to the application profile in which the EPG resides.

When using non-routed L3 multicast within a zone, the BD that is related to the EPG natively floods multicasts across the BD, much as a switched VLAN behaves. Remember from Chapter 4 that the default VRF is enabled with IGMP snooping by default, and all BDs flood the multicast packets on the appropriate ports with members. Link-local multicast, group range 224.0.0.X, is flooded to all ports in the BD GIPo (Group IP outer), along with one of the FTAG (forwarding tag) trees.

ACI segmentation and policy elements can be configured to support multicast routing, as covered in Chapter 4. For east–west traffic, border leafs act as either the FHR or LHR when PIM is configured on the L3 Out or VRF instance. Border leafs and spines cannot currently act as RPs. Thus, the real question to answer for ACI multitenancy is the same as for VMDC architectures: What is the scope of the domain? The answer to this question drives the placement of the RP.

Because the segmentation in ACI is cleaner than with standard segmentation techniques, architects can use a single RP model for an entire tenant. Any domains are secured by switching VRF instances on or off from multicast or by applying specific multicast contracts at the EPG level. Firewall transport of L3 multicast may not be a concern in these environments. A data center–wide RP domain for shared services can also be used with ACI, as long as the RP is outside the fabric as well. Segmenting between a shared public zone and a tenant public or private zone using different domains and RPs is achieved with VRF instances on the outside L3 router that correspond to internal ACI VRF instances. EPG contracts further secure each domain and prevent message leakage, especially if EPG contracts encompass integrated L3 firewall policies.

Multicast and Software-Defined Networking

Cisco Digital Network Architecture (DNA) includes three key fabrics from an infrastructure standpoint that need to be understood to comprehend the functioning of multicast. As shown in Figure 5-16, the fabrics defined are SD-Access for campus, ACI for software-defined data center (SD-DC), and software-defined WAN (SD-WAN). The principles of Cisco DNA provide a transformational shift in building and managing campus network, data center, and WAN fabrics in a faster, easier way and with improved business efficiency.

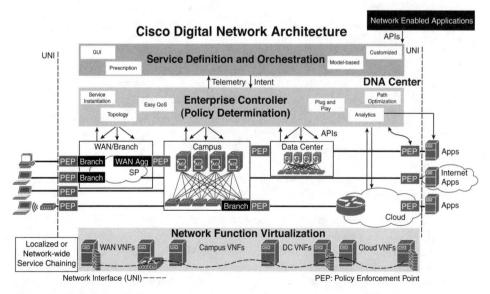

Figure 5-16 *Cisco DNA*

The salient features to achieve this transition are as follows:

■ End-to-end segmentation

■ Simple, automated workflow design

■ Intelligent network fabric

This chapter has already reviewed SD-DC with ACI and the implication of multicast in DC multitenancy. Chapter 4 explores VXLAN and its design implications with multicast. SD-WAN uses the principles of Layer 3 VPNs for segmentation.

The hub replication for the overlay solution must be considered while selecting the SD-WAN location, which is tied to Dynamic Multipoint VPN (DMVPN) or a Cisco Viptela-based solution. A Cisco Viptela SD-WAN–based solution provides options for the designer to select the headend multicast replication node, which includes the following options:

■ The replication headend for each individual multicast group

■ The replication headend aligned to each VPN (assuming that the deployment is segmented)

Splitting the multicast VPN replication reduces the load from the headend routers and helps in localization of traffic based on regional transit points in a global enterprise network.

Within SD-WAN technology are two Cisco solutions: Intelligent WAN (IWAN) and Viptela. There are plans to converge these two SD-WAN solutions with unified hardware and feature support.

In terms of multicast, the following are the key considerations to keep in mind for SD-DC and SD-WAN:

■ PIM mode needs to be supported in the fabric.

■ Replication and convergence are required within the fabric.

■ For simplicity, it is best to keep the RP outside the fabric. (Note that in some fabrics, it is recommended, based on availability of feature support, to keep the multicast RP outside the fabric.)

As of this writing, SD-Access is the fabric most recently added to the Cisco DNA portfolio. This fabric covers the enterprise campus to provide the following functions:

■ Helps ensure policy consistency

■ Provides faster service enablement

■ Significantly improves issue resolution times and reduces operational expenses

SDA includes the following elements:

- Identity-based segmentation on the network allows various security domains to coexist on the same network infrastructure while keeping their policies for segmentation intact.

- Security is provided by Cisco TrustSec infrastructure (Security Group Tags [SGTs], Security Group Access Control Lists [SGACLs]) and Cisco segmentation capabilities (Cisco Locator/ID Separation Protocol [LISP], Virtual Extensible LAN [VXLAN], and Virtual Route Forwarding [VRF]). Cisco DNA Center aligns all these functions to solutions and abstracts them from users.

- Identity context for users and devices, including authentication, posture validation, and device profiling, is provided by the Cisco Identity Services Engine (ISE).

- Assurance visibility helps operations with proactive and predictive data to help provide health to the fabric.

- The Network Data Platform (NDP) efficiently categorizes and correlates vast amounts of data into business intelligence and actionable insights.

- Complete network visibility is provided through simple management of a LAN, WLAN, and WAN as a single entity for simplified provisioning, consistent policy, and management across wired and wireless networks.

- Cisco DNA Center software provides single-pane-of-glass network control.

The technical details of data forwarding in the fabric are based on control and data plane elements. It is important to understand that the control plane for the SDA fabric is based on LISP, and LISP forwarding is based on an explicit request. The data plane is established for source and destination communication and uses VXLAN encapsulation. The policy engine for SDA is based on Cisco TrustSec. (The details of the operation of SDA are beyond the scope of this chapter.)

Chapter 4 explains VXLAN and its interaction with multicast. This chapter reviews details about multicast with LISP.

Traditional routing and host addressing models use a single namespace for a host IP address, and this address is sent to every edge layer node for building the protocol control. A very visible and detrimental effect of this single namespace is manifested with the rapid growth of the Internet routing table as a consequence of multihoming, traffic engineering, non-aggregable address allocation, and business events such as mergers and acquisitions: More and more memory is required to handle routing table size, and the requirement to solve end-host mobility with address/security attributes has resulted in the investment of alternative solutions to the traditional control plane model. LISP identifies the end host based on two attributes: host and location address. The control plane build is based on explicit pull, similar to that of Domain Name System (DNS). The use of LISP provides the following advantages over traditional routing protocols:

- **Multi-address family support:** LISP supports IPv4 and IPv6. LISP is added into an IPv6 transition or coexistence strategy to simplify the initial rollout of IPv6 by taking advantage of the LISP mechanisms to encapsulate IPv6 host packets within IPv4 headers (or IPv4 host packets within IPv6 headers).

- **Virtualization support:** Virtualization/multi-tenancy support provides the capability to segment traffic that is mapped to VRF instances while exiting the LISP domain.

- **Host mobility:** VM mobility support provides location flexibility for IP endpoints in the enterprise domain and across the WAN. The location of an asset is masked by the location identification or routing locator (RLOC). When the packet reaches the location, the endpoint identifier (EID) is used to forward the packet to the end host.

- **Site-based policy control without using BGP:** Simplified traffic engineering capabilities provide control and management of traffic entering and exiting a specific location.

LISP addresses, known as EIDs, provide identity to the end host, and RLOCs provide the location where the host resides. Splitting EID and RLOC functions yields several advantages, including improved routing system scalability and improved multihoming efficiency and ingress traffic engineering.

The following is a list of LISP router functions for LISP egress tunnel routers (ETRs) and ingress tunnel routers (ITRs):

- Devices are generally referred to as xTR when ETR and ITR functions are combined on a single device.

- ETR publishes EID-to-RLOC mappings for the site-to-map server and responds to map-request messages.

- ETRs and ITRs de-encapsulate and deliver LISP-encapsulated packets to a local end host within a site.

During operation, an ETR sends periodic map-register messages to all its configured map servers. These messages contain all the EID-to-RLOC entries for the EID-numbered networks that are connected to the ETR's site.

An ITR is responsible for finding EID-to-RLOC mappings for all traffic destined for LISP-capable sites. When a site sends a packet, the ITR receives a packet destined for an EID (IPv4 address in this case); it looks for the EID-to-RLOC mapping in its cache. If the ITR finds a match, it encapsulates the packet inside a LISP header, with one of its RLOCs as the IP source address and one of the RLOCs from the mapping cache entry as the IP destination. If the ITR does not have a match, then the LISP request is sent to the mapping resolver and server.

LISP Map Resolver (MR)/Map Server (MS)

Both map resolvers (MR) and map servers (MS) connect to the LISP topology. The function of the LISP MR is to accept encapsulated map-request messages from ITRs and then de-encapsulate those messages. In many cases, the MR and MS are on the same device. Once the message is de-encapsulated, the MS is responsible for matching the ETR's RLOC is authoritative for the requested EIDs.

An MS maintains the aggregated distributed LISP mapping database; it accepts the original request from the ETR that provides the site RLOC with EID mapping connected to the site. The MS/MR functionality is similar to that of a DNS server.

LISP PETRs/PITRs

A LISP proxy egress tunnel router (PETR) implements ETR functions for non-LISP sites. It sends traffic to non-LISP sites (which are not part of the LISP domain). A PETR is called a *border node* in SDA terminology.

A LISP proxy ingress tunnel router (PITR) implements mapping database lookups used for ITR and LISP encapsulation functions on behalf of non-LISP-capable sites that need to communicate with the LISP-capable site.

Now that you know the basic components of a LISP domain, let's review the simple unicast packet flow in a LISP domain, which will help you visualize the function of each node described. Figure 5-17 shows this flow, which proceeds as follows:

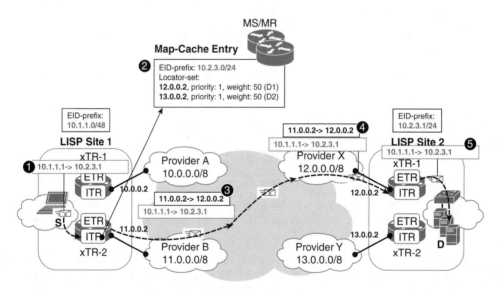

Figure 5-17 *Basic LISP Packet Flow*

Step 1.   Source 10.1.1.1/24 sends a packet to 10.2.3.1. The FHR is the local xTR, and 10.2.3.1 is not in the IP routing table.

Step 2.   The xTR checks its LISP map cache to verify whether the RLOC location for 10.2.3.1 (the previous communication) is cached. If not, it sends a packet to the MS/MR to get the RLOC resolution for 10.2.3.1. Note that the weight attribute advertised by the ETR of LISP site 2 to MS can be changed to influence ingress routing into the site. In this case, it is equal (50).

Step 3.   When the RLOC information is received from MS/MR, the xTR from LISP site 1 encapsulates the packet with the LISP header, using the destination IP address of the RLOC IPs. This directs the packet to LISP site 2.

Step 4.   At LISP site 2, the xTR de-encapsulates the packet from the LISP header and also updates the LISP map cache with 10.1.1.0/24.

Step 5.   The IP packet (10.1.1.1 to 10.2.3.1) is forwarded out the appropriate interface (which could be in a VRF) to the destination.

LISP and Multicast

The LISP multicast feature introduces support for carrying multicast traffic over a LISP overlay. This support currently allows for unicast transport of multicast traffic with head-end replication at the root ITR site.

The implementation of LISP multicast includes the following:

■ At the time of this writing, LISP multicast supports *only* IPv4 EIDs or IPv4 RLOCs.

■ LISP supports only PIM-SM and PIM-SSM at this time.

■ LISP multicast does not support group-to-RP mapping distribution mechanisms, Auto-RP, or Bootstrap Router (BSR). Only Static-RP configuration is supported at the time of this writing.

■ LISP multicast does not support LISP VM mobility deployment at the time of this writing.

In an SDA environment, it is recommended to deploy the RP outside the fabric.

Example 5-1 is a LISP configuration example.

Example 5-1 *LISP Configuration Example*

```
xTR  Config
ip multicast-routing
!
interface LISP0
 ip pim sparse-mode
!
interface e1/0
 ip address 10.1.0.2 255.255.255.0
 ip pim sparse-mode
!
router lisp
 database-mapping 192.168.1.0/24 10.2.0.1 priority 1 weight 100
 ipv4 itr map-resolver 10.140.0.14
 ipv4 itr
```

```
 ipv4 etr map-server 10.140.0.14 key password123
 ipv4 etr
 exit
!
!
Routing protocol config <..>
!
ip pim rp-address 10.1.1.1

MR/MS Config
ip multicast-routing
!
interface e3/0
 ip address 10.140.0.14 255.255.255.0
  ip pim sparse-mode
!
!
router lisp
 site Site-ALAB
  authentication-key password123
  eid-prefix 192.168.0.0/24
  exit
 !
 site Site-B
  authentication-key password123
  eid-prefix 192.168.1.0/24
  exit
 !

 ipv4 map-server
 ipv4 map-resolver
 exit
!
Routing protocol config <..>
!
ip pim rp-address 10.1.1.1
```

In this configuration, the MS/MR is in the data plane path for multicast sources and receivers.

For SDA, the configuration for multicast based on the latest version of DNA Center is automated from the GUI. You do not need to configure interface or PIM modes using the CLI. This configuration is provided just to have an understanding of what is under the hood for multicast configuration using the LISP control plane. For the data plane, you should consider the VXLAN details covered in Chapter 3, and with DNA Center, no CLI configuration is needed for the SDA access data plane.

Multicast in Utility Networks

Before getting into the details of multicast utility design, let's review the design blocks of a utility environment, as shown in Figure 5-18.

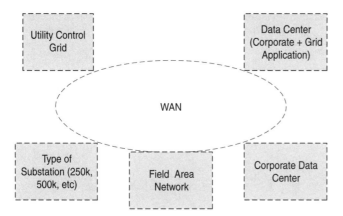

Figure 5-18 *Utility Network Design Blocks*

The WANs of most of utility environments are privately owned. This is one of the reasons for the legacy utility designs to have a WAN infrastructure for corporate function and a separate infrastructure for utility function (such as substations, grid control center, and so on). However, in many modern enterprise networks, it is common to see a Multiprotocol Label Switching (MPLS) Layer 3 VPN or L2 VPN deployed in the WAN block.

The reason for the change in the WAN design is that interconnected power delivery networks require close control of grid operations by increasing the visibility and creating smarter monitoring systems. Increased efficiency is created by using newer Supervisory Control and Data Acquisition (SCADA) measurements—typically every few seconds—to feed command, control, and monitoring systems, which causes an increase in bandwidth utilization. Several power system disturbances and extended outages have shown that the SCADA measurement data is no longer sufficient to provide adequate situational awareness to have visibility into the complexity of the interconnected power delivery networks. The goal in the next-generation power grid monitoring systems is to have visibility to small disturbances in these power delivery systems to improve the efficiency and fault tolerance of the power grid. Thereby, the need for newer measurement systems at different levels has created a requirement to modernize the network.

Field area networks are located at the distribution level and are broken into two tiers:

- **Distribution Level 2 tier:** This is the last "last-mile," also known as the neighborhood area network (NAN) level. Some of the functions of this network service include metering, distribution automation, and public infrastructure for electric vehicle charging.

- **Distribution Level 1 tier:** This tier supports multiple services that aggregate and provide backhaul connectivity directly back to control centers, using system control directly with primary distribution substations. This tier also provides peer-to-peer connectivity for field area networks (FANs).

The deployment of FANs involves IPv6 and Wi-Fi mesh technologies as follows:

- **Substation tier:** A substation level services wide-ranging scenarios—from connecting secondary stations, to complex requirements on primary substations—to provide critical low-latency functions such as teleprotection. Within the substation, networks may comprise from one to three buses (system, process, and multiservice).

Note   The primary distribution substation networks may also include distribution (FAN) aggregation points.

- **Utility control center:** This architecture block covers networks inside utility data centers and control centers. The control centers have very different requirements for security and connections to real-time systems. The use of firewalls at different tiers for regulatory compliance and protection of grid assets creates a requirement for multicast transport across the firewalls.

The data center network, or corporate office, follows the traditional enterprise environments and feature design components. To design multicast in a utility environment, you need to understand a couple key applications that are unique to utility environments, as discussed in the following sections.

PMU

Phasor measurement units (PMUs) allow for granular collection of important operational data to provide high-quality observation and control of the power system as it responds to supply and demand fluctuations. PMU data is useful for early detection of disturbances and needs to be collected at significantly higher frequency (typically 120 to 200 times per second); it requires a high degree of performance collection, aggregation, dissemination, and management. This requires higher bandwidth and data transmission with the least amount of latency. The bandwidth ranges between 1Mb/s and 2Mb/s of continuous streaming, and the latency component can be anywhere between 60 ms to 160 ms.

Most networks in the utility space are not designed or positioned to deal with the explosion of data that PMUs generate. PMU data is a multicast feed that is sourced from sensors and sent to the control grid. The design for PIM-SM or PIM-SSM depends on the number of multicast state entries and the type of IGMP driver supported in the host. The critical design factor to consider is the firewall's support for multicast; most of the sensor data is within the substation domain, which is considered a North American Electric Reliability Corporation (NERC) asset. The control grid is also protected by a firewall infrastructure. For PMU application, multicast transport across the firewall infrastructure is a key design factor.

Radio over IP Design

In the utility environment, the Radio over IP design is a key building block required for communication. The use of multicast needs to be understood based on the design of Radio over IP systems. The communication details are as follows:

■ Individual calls between two radios from different site (Unicast could be a possible communication mechanism.)

■ Group calls from radios from different site (Multicast could be a possible communication mechanism.)

■ Dispatcher calls between different sites

■ Radio to telephone calls, where the radio and the private automatic branch exchange (PABX) are at different sites

Normally, Radio over IP design is considered any-to-any multicast. You are correct if you are thinking about bidirectional multicast design.

In addition, the energy grid application utility infrastructure hosts corporate applications such as music on hold (MoH), wireless multicast, multicast applications for imaging, data center requirements for multicast, and so on. The utility multicast design has requirements of different types of multicast traffic with separate domains. These domains can be virtual and separated by a control plane (MPLS Layer 3 VPNs using MVPNs or other methods) or can be logical, existing in the same control plane and overlapping. This is generally applicable to the utility WAN, control grid, and data center design blocks. It is important to configure multicast applications with a proper multicast addressing plan that can be rolled out enterprisewide.

Multicast-Enabled Markets

The use of multicast in financial environments is very prevalent, and it is extremely important for business application in the trade environment. This section introduces you to multicast design and fundamentals of financial networks. The elements of the financial network are stock exchanges, financial service providers, and brokerages (see Figure 5-19). These domains are not only separate multicast networks, they are separate entities; for example, NASDAQ is an example of a stock exchange, Bloomberg is an example of a financial provider, and JPMorgan is an example of a brokerage.

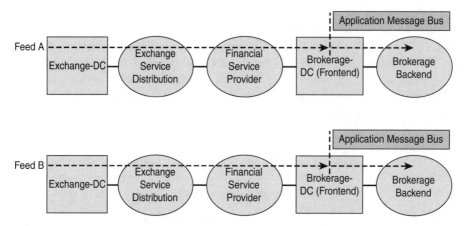

Figure 5-19   *Market Domain Feeds*

As you will see, the multicast applications must function across all these environments to provide a quality end-to-end user experience. Before we review multicast network design, you must understand market data delivery, which consists of two main phases.

- **Phase 1:** The stream is brought from the exchange to the brokerage network. The feeds are terminated at the customer premises. These multicast streams are normalized and republished by feed handlers in the data center.

- **Phase 2:** The second phase involves injecting the normalized data stream into the application messaging bus, which feeds the core infrastructure of the trading applications. The data in the application messaging bus is used by a multitude of applications that use the market data streams for live trades, long-term trending, arbitrage, risk modeling, compliance, and so on. Many of these applications listen to the feeds and then republish their own analytical and derivative information. For example, let's consider a CSCO stock comparison. A brokerage might compare the offered price of CSCO to the option price of CSCO on another exchange and then publish ratings that a different application might monitor to see how far out of sync they are. A complex analytical engine provides traders relevant information related to selling or buying in the market in real time at trade floor stations. The application bus is needed for network designers to understand the system. These data streams are typically delivered over a reliable multicast transport protocol. Traditionally, this has been TIBCO Rendezvous, which operates in a publish-and-subscribe environment. The application has a built-in reliability mechanism by which the market data retransmission is sent using a unicast stream.

Let's review the network components.

- **Exchange network:** An exchange network includes the exchange data center, where the servers process financial orders. The financial orders based on the application are sent as two feeds, feed A and feed B. The service distribution network feeds these transmissions to the edge that connects to the financial service provider. Note that some exchange networks outsource their service distribution network; in such a case, the multicast domain within the exchange network has two domains for control.

- **Financial service provider (FSP):** The FSP is the provider network that extends over a regional or global area. The design of regional and global is tied to the FSP's business model and customers. The network design is similar to that of a traditional enterprise WAN.

  An additional element of the FSP is the service edge network, which includes access points of presence (POPs) to support necessary service policies for positioning services for end brokerage customers. Some FSPs also offer a service that involves normalization of market data feeds to reduce errors (if any) in the transmission by identifying any missing parameters in the ordering process. Such a service is offered by the brokerages themselves or could be tied to a service from the FSPs. The FSPs also provide business-to-business service of market data feeds for brokerages that deal with high volume. This necessitates a network transport system created for differential services.

- **Brokerage network:** This network is divided into two components:

  - **The back-office network:** This network includes trading and security, trading record keeping, trade confirmation, trade settlement, and regulatory compliance, and so on. This network is highly secured and always protected by firewalls.

  - **The front-end brokerage network:** This is where the feeds (A and B) are collapsed by an application (such as TIBCO) in a messaging bus architecture for arbitration. These streams are distributed to the traders.

Multicast Design in a Market Data Environment

This section provides an overview of market data multicast design considerations. For more information, see *IP Multicast, Volume 1* and Chapter 1, "Interdomain Routing and Internet Multicast," Chapter 2, "Multicast Traffic Engineering, Scalability, and Reliability," and Chapter 3, "Multicast MPLS VPNs," of this book. Figure 5-20 illustrates multicast domains from the exchange, FSP, and brokerage environment.

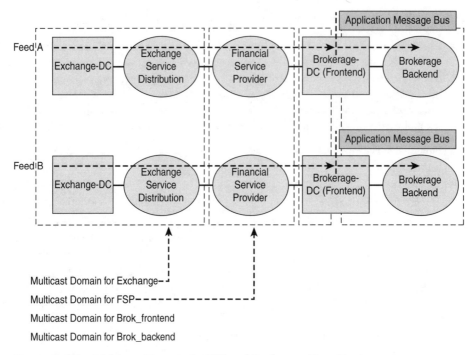

Figure 5-20 *Multicast Domain in FSP and Brokerage Data Environments*

The exchange network produces two live feeds (feeds A and B). The feeds, which are identical, are created for redundancy. The feeds are transported using different source and multicast groups. The multicast and unicast routing information base (RIB) design should ensure path diversity for the feeds. Physical path diversity and node diversity are employed to create the separation. Ideally, for complete redundancy, separate infrastructures with isolated control and data planes provide resiliency and reliability to the transport mechanism. Multicast designs should include separate RPs for multicast routing for different feeds, tied to separate multicast address groups. If platform support is available, Bidir-PIM is recommended for this type of market data distribution. At the FSP exchange points, the **bidir-neighbor-filter** command should be used on the customer-facing interfaces. This ensures that designated forwarder (DF) election occurs, even if the downstream router does not support Bidir-PIM. RP redundancy for Bidir-PIM is created by using the Phantom-RP method.

The exchange between two domains is achieved by using one of the methods for interdomain exchange reviewed in Chapter 1: static or dynamic provisioning between interdomain multicast. Normally, static provisioning methods are used if the FSP requires the feeds constantly. The dynamic provisioning method allows the FSP to manage the feeds based on the bandwidth available and offers more granular bandwidth management. The dynamic method provides more control and is therefore recommended.

FSP Multicast Design

Figure 5-21 provides an overview of the FSP network and connectivity. This is the network on which the multicast domain is overlaid.

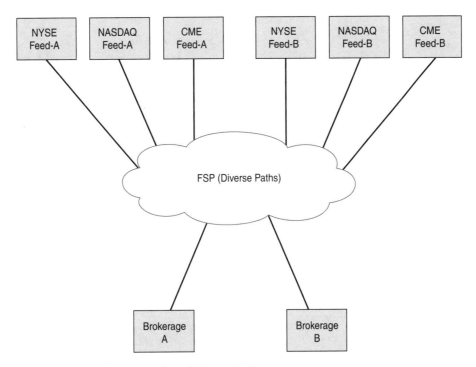

Figure 5-21   *FSP Network and Connectivity*

The design requirements for an FSP are similar to those of a regular service provider. The key difference is that an FSP may require higher reliability and strict latency. The market data streams are typically forwarded statically into the FSP, as noted earlier in this chapter. Path separation for the multicast streams is created by traffic engineering methods, or the FSP can have a dual-core architecture to create complete isolation and separation of the control and data planes. For segmentation of traffic, MPLS VPN service is commonly utilized. Multicast transport schemes applicable to WAN, traffic engineering, and MPLS VPN are applied in the design.

Brokerage Multicast Design

The multicast design of the front-office brokers transports the multicast feed to the application message bus. Each feed terminates at a different data pod infrastructure; this pod consists of a message bus for handling the feeds. The design is simple, but multiple geographic locations or sites for the pod distribution require multicast to be enabled over a WAN or metro network. Generally, Bidir-PIM is best in this scenario. Figure 5-22 illustrates the multicast data feed to a brokerage network. The figure shows the multicast brokerage design.

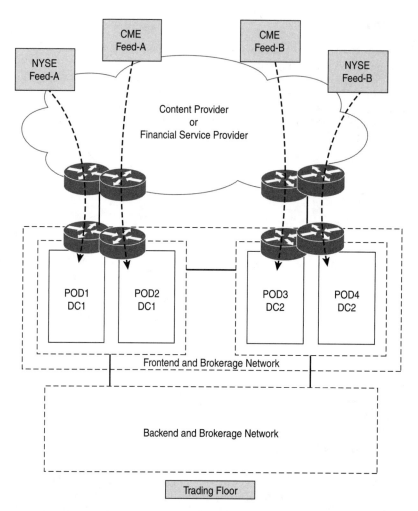

Figure 5-22   *Brokerage Network Multicast Feed*

The back-end office that hosts the traders has separate RPs for the new multicast streams available from the different application handlers and should use Bidir-PIM. Due to network platform restriction, if Bidir-PIM is not a viable option, PIM-SM with shortest path tree (SPT) threshold infinity should be considered. Multiple RPs can be deployed, each tied to a multicast group range based on the application use case.

Service Provider Multicast

Service provider multicast message transport falls into two categories: infrastructure multicast, used for delivering services, and customer multicast packet transport. Multicast that supports the provider infrastructure enables the provider to offer services to customers—such as multicast VPNs (MVPNs) (discussed in Chapter 3) and multitenant data center services (discussed earlier in this chapter and in Chapter 4). The provider infrastructure may also use multicast for content services. Internet multicast services is one example. In addition, many providers use multicast to deliver television content over their networks, where the set-top box is a multicast client, and channel content is delivered over specific groups.

Today, relatively few multicast applications are transported across the Internet natively. Most service providers have yet to embrace the benefits of transporting multicast, primarily due to the complexity and the ability to charge for multicast services. For SPs that have enabled and are using multicast, kudos to you! Chapters 1, 3, and 4 are very helpful for creating multicast-enabled provider infrastructure. In addition, there are a few design elements to consider when deploying multicast services in a provider network, as discussed in the following sections.

Service Provider PIM-Type Selection and RP Placement

The most important decisions that service providers have to make are similar to the decisions required for multitenant data centers: What mode of PIM needs to be selected, and where should RPs be placed? Chapter 3 discusses the numerous options that service providers use to transport multicast messages using MPLS, since using MPLS is currently the preferred method of moving both unicast and multicast messages across a shared service cloud. Remember that to deploy an MPLS service that supports multicast, the provider network needs a multicast-enabled core network that supports multicast data trees (MDTs).

The provider multicast domain that services the MDTs is completely isolated from any customer domains. This means the provider network needs to choose a PIM method (ASM or SSM) and, if necessary, configure RPs for the network. Service provider network architects should consider using SSM as the infrastructure delivery method. It greatly simplifies the multicast deployment at scale. SSM does not require an RP and has a separate and specific multicast range, 232.0.0.0/8, that is easy to scope and manage. Examine the network diagram in Figure 5-23. This network provides an MPLS MVPN service to the customer between Site 1 and Site 2. The customer is using PIM-SM and is providing its own RP on the customer premises equipment router at Site 1. The provider network is using SSM to transport the MDT for the customer VPN with route distinguisher (RD) 100:2.

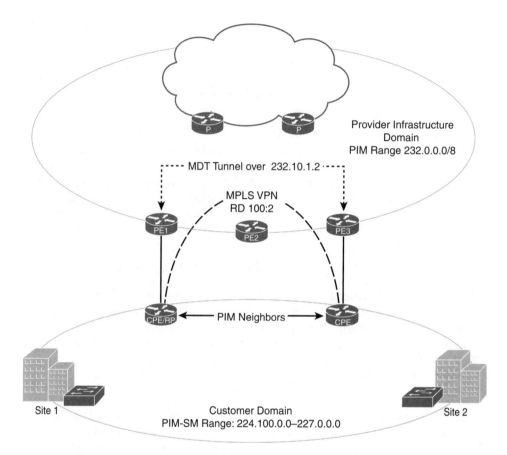

Figure 5-23   *SSM Provider Infrastructure Domain*

Note   The network shown in Figure 5-23 is designed to provide multicast transport to customer VPNs, with customer-configured and -established PIM domains. This is by far the most common deployment model for MVPN. If a provider wishes to provide domain services, such as a centralized RP for PIM-SM, the provider should consider using VRF technology and a separate router, or router pair, to provide separate RP services for each VPN. Configuration information from Chapters 2 and 3 of this book assist with such a design.

Using SSM also simplifies scaling across global networks and eases the burden of converting merged autonomous systems from network acquisitions, as interdomain routing is a natural amenity of SSM. In addition, the same SSM domain can be used to provide content services within the infrastructure. Or, if needed, the SSM domain can coexist with a PIM-SM domain when required.

Remember that to implement SSM, any clients need to support IGMPv3. Cisco IOS-XR service provider software supports SSM delivery for MPLS MVPNs natively. The MVPN configuration requires a specific source and group for MDT. Simply use an SSM group range for MDT configurations and enable the transport interfaces with PIM-SM. Example 5-2 shows the relevant configuration of PE1 from Figure 5-23 to enable SSM and the MDT in IOS-XR.

Example 5-2   *MDT SSM Configuration Using IOS-XR*

```
RP/0/RP0/CPU0:PE1# configure
RP/0/RP0/CPU0:PE1(config)# multicast-routing
RP/0/RP0/CPU0:PE1(config-mcast-ipv4)# interface all enable
RP/0/RP0/CPU0:PE1(config-mcast-ipv4)# mdt source Loopback 0
RP/0/RP0/CPU0:PE1(config-mcast-default-)# vrf Customer
RP/0/RP0/CPU0:PE1(config-mcast-vrf_A-ipv4)# mdt default 232.10.1.1
RP/0/RP0/CPU0:PE1(config-mcast-vrf_A-ipv4)# mdt data 232.10.1.0/24 threshold 1200
RP/0/RP0/CPU0:PE1(config-mcast-ipv4)# exit
RP/0/RP0/CPU0:PE1(config)# router igmp
RP/0/RP0/CPU0:PE1(config-igmp)# version 3
RP/0/RP0/CPU0:PE1(config)# commit
```

For customers interested in these services, purchasing multicast transport from an SP is something of a premium service—that is, service providers usually charge an additional fee. If you are purchasing L2 VPN services that a service provider offers using Virtual Private LAN Service (VPLS), Provider Backbone Bridging combined with Ethernet VPN (PBB-EVPN), or a Pseudowire service, there is a better chance that multicast transport services are offered. The transport of multicast messages is often limited to a certain rate. If more bandwidth is required, you can overcome the limitation by purchasing additional bandwidth or encapsulating multicast messages using some sort of overlay technology, such as MVPN, GRE, and so on.

Service provider networks that want to also provide content services over the same infrastructure may not be able to choose SSM if the set-top box or other clients do not support IGMPv3. In such cases, PIM-SM is the preferred alternative for the provider infrastructure, and the provider network should either use static RP mappings or redundant Anycast RP for added reliability. Figure 5-24 shows the same provider network as Figure 5-23, but this time using PIM-SM.

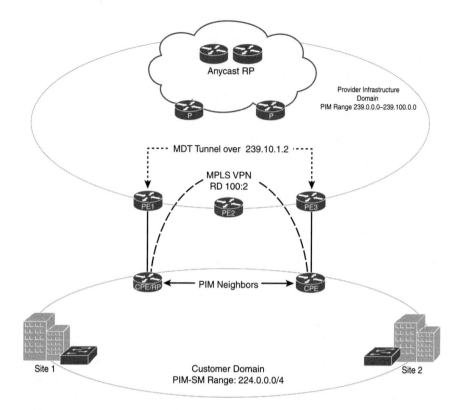

Figure 5-24   *PIM-SM Provider Domain*

When a provider grows beyond the ability to support every customer in a single routed domain, BGP confederations or even multiple public domains are often used to carry traffic. Remember from Chapter 1 that using multiple IGP and BGP domains for unicast requires corresponding multicast domains, with interdomain routing, to complete multicast transport across the network. In such situations, providers should consider nesting RPs, using anycast for redundancy, and building a mesh of MSDP peerings between them. This completes the transport across the provider domain. Figure 5-25 shows a very high-level diagram of this type of provider multicast domain design.

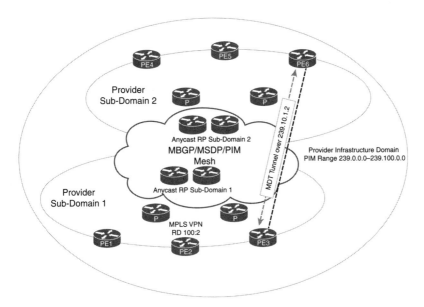

Figure 5-25 *Interdomain Infrastructure Transport*

For networks that also provide multicast services to customers, there are other considerations. In particular, IP Television (IPTV) delivery requires some unique design elements, which are discussed next.

IPTV Delivery over Multicast

Figure 5-26 provides a 10,000-foot view of the components of multicast in the cable environment.

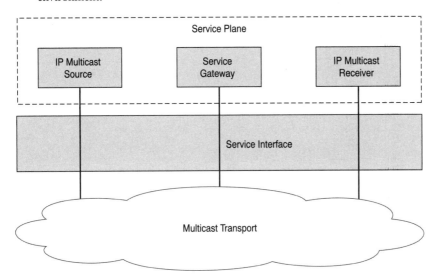

Figure 5-26 *High-Level Cable TV Multicast Network*

There are three main architectural components in an IPTV multicast delivery service:

- **Service plane:** Consists of the IPTV source, IPTV multicast service gateway, and IP Multicast receiver

- **Service interface:** Consists of the signaling mode between the service plane and the network plane

- **Network plane:** Consists of IP network configuration to support multicast (control and data plane), resiliency, and high availability of the network transport

The network consists of a shared platform needed for all services, like QoS (DiffServ or RSVP based on applicability) or QoS-based Call Admission Control (CAC) systems for transport of multiple types of content. IP Multicast gateways consists of ad splicers, converters, and so on.

The choice of multicast transport protocols should determine the service plane communication needs of connected devices. Based on protocol requirements for the content providers, such as CAC, IGMPv3 or v2 support, and application redundancy, the multicast network technology selected for the transport layer should be able to support all required application services. The WAN technology generally consists of an MPLS L3 VPN or L2 VPN solution that connects to the end host access technology. Layer 2 Pseudowire could also be considered using a protected Pseudowire deployment. This provides subsecond convergence by leveraging features such as Fast Reroute (FRR) with RSVP-TE LSPs. It also provides the network operators service level agreement (SLA) guidelines for multicast transport. The items to consider in the design are as follows:

- The need for global, national, or regional content sources

- Fast convergence and availability

- Requirements for different media content

Other factors to keep in mind during the design stage relate to the type of feed. The feed could be any or all of the following:

- **Broadcast feed:** Including static forwarding to a DSLAM

- **Switched digital video:** Static PIM tree to the PE-AGG router

- **Multicast based video:** Dynamic path creation to the end receiver

These three types of video feed are illustrated in Figure 5-27.

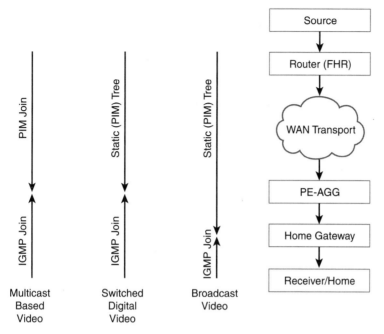

Figure 5-27   *Three Types of Video Feed*

The service interface consideration in this section includes multicast signaling support with IGMPv3, applications built to SLA requirements, and applications built using CAC methods. The PIM-SSM model generally fits this design, with one-to-many communication building on any individual sources. This method is best suited to handling join/prune latency requirements. PIM-SSM will also help with the localization of services based on unicast IP addresses of different host servers using the same multicast group. Techniques using different masks for source IP addresses can be used for redundancy for the source of the multicast service. SSM multicast technology can be aligned with channel feeds, and source IP address spoofing is mitigated based on built-in application support for IGMPv3. The transport design also covers path separation across the WAN transport segment.

It is critical to understand multicast VLAN registration (MVR) and the features in the cable environments. MVR is designed for multicast applications deployed in Ethernet ring-based service provider networks. The broadcast of multiple television channels over a service provider network is one typical example. MVR allows a subscriber on a port to subscribe and unsubscribe to a multicast stream on the networkwide multicast VLAN, thereby enabling a single multicast VLAN to be shared in the network while subscribers (receivers) remain in separate VLANs. It also optimizes stream delivery by providing the ability to send continuous multicast streams in the multicast VLAN rather than send separate streams from the subscriber VLANs.

MVR assumes that subscriber ports subscribe and unsubscribe to these multicast streams by sending IGMPv2 join and leave messages on the VLAN. MVR uses IGMP snooping, but MVR and IGMP snooping can be enabled or disabled without impacting each other. The MVR feature only intercepts the IGMP join and leave messages from multicast groups configured under MVR. The MVR feature has the following functions:

- Categorizes the multicast streams configured under the MVR feature and ties the associated IP Multicast group in the Layer 2 forwarding table

- Modifies the Layer 2 forwarding table to include or exclude the receiver of the multicast stream (not constrained by VLAN boundaries)

The MVR has two port types:

- **Source:** Configures a port that receives and sends multicast data as source ports. Subscribers cannot be directly connected to source ports; all source ports on a switch belong to the single multicast VLAN.

- **Receiver:** Configures a port as a receiver port and only receives multicast data.

Summary

When designing a multicast infrastructure, items to consider are desired replication points, multitenancy, and scalability. In addition, redundancy, reliability, and resiliency are primary design elements.

Transporting multicast messages is critical in health care, wireless networks, data centers, utilities, market exchanges, service provider networks, and, of course, LANs and WANs. The better you understand the different multicast service offerings and the desired outcomes for your organization, the better you will be able to provide a service that is redundant, reliable, and resilient.

References

"Cisco Virtualized Multi-Tenant Data Center Cloud Consumer Models," www.cisco.com/c/en/us/td/docs/solutions/Enterprise/Data_Center/VMDC/2-2/collateral/vmdcConsumerModels.html

RFC 4761, "Virtual Private LAN Service (VPLS) Using BGP for Auto-Discovery and Signaling"

RFC 7623, "Provider Backbone Bridging Combined with Ethernet VPN (PBB-EVPN)"

Chapter 6

Advanced Multicast Troubleshooting

IP Multicast, Volume 1 introduces a basic methodology for troubleshooting IP multicast networks. This methodology concentrates on implementations of Any-Source Multicast (ASM) using PIM Sparse-Mode (PIM-SM). To review quickly, there are three ordered steps in this methodology:

1. Receiver check

2. Source check

3. State verification

These fundamental steps of troubleshooting never change, even in advanced multicast designs. As discussed in this book, there are many new protocols and nuances involved in advanced designs. Cross-domain forwarding of multicast over the Internet is a great example. Interdomain multicast introduces Multicast Source Discovery Protocol (MSDP) and Border Gateway Protocol (BGP) into the multicast design. In addition, source, receiver, and state checks can be complicated if there are multiple domains, some of which are under the control of entities other than your own.

Despite these additional protocols and elements, with troubleshooting, you always start at the beginning. The following is a breakdown of this three-element methodology into high-level steps for troubleshooting multicast in a single domain:

> **Note** Certain protocol and router checks have been added to each of these steps to help identify where the source of the problem exists. These high-level steps are found in *IP Multicast, Volume 1* Chapter 7, "Operating and Troubleshooting IP Multicast Networks."

Step 1. **Receiver check.** Make sure a receiver is subscribed via Internet Group Management Protocol (IGMP) and that a (*, G) to the rendezvous point (RP) exists (if using PIM-SM):

- ✔ Check the group state on the last-hop router (LHR).

- ✔ Check IGMP membership on the last-hop PIM-designated router (DR).

- ✔ Verify the (*, G) state at the LHR and check the RP for the (*, G) entry and Reverse Path Forwarding (RPF).

Step 2. **Source check.** Make sure you have an active source before trying to troubleshoot:

- ✔ Verify that the source is sending the multicast traffic to the first-hop router (FHR).

- ✔ Confirm that the FHR has registered the group with the RP.

- ✔ Determine that the RP is receiving the register messages.

- ✔ Confirm that the multicast state is built on the FHR.

Step 3. **State verification.** Ensure that each router in the path has correct RPF information by using the **show ip rpf <IP_address>** command:

- ✔ Verify the RP and shortest-path tree (SPT) state entries across the path:

  - ○ Check the MSDP summary to verify that peering is operational.

  - ○ Verify the group state at each active RP.

  - ○ Verify SPT changes.

- ✔ Verify the mroute state information for the following elements:

  - ○ Verify that the incoming interface list (IIF) is correct.

  - ○ Verify that the outgoing interface list (OIF) is correct.

  - ○ Ensure that the flags for (*, G) and (S, G) entries are correct and that the RP information is correct.

    - • Does this align with the information in the mroute entry?

    - • Is this what you would expect when looking at the unicast routing table?

It is helpful to examine the troubleshooting steps for some of the different types of advanced designs introduced in this book. As shown here, you need to adjust the steps to include additional checks for the protocols in use with each technology. However, the basic three-step process is always used. This chapter covers these concepts and expands on your knowledge of advanced multicasting protocols, starting with interdomain multicast forwarding.

Troubleshooting Interdomain Multicast Networks

To find and repair trouble in an interdomain network, you can follow the basic three-step methodology and high-level steps with some additional checks to accommodate for interdomain PIM neighborships, proper MSDP source-active (SA) handling, and Multiprotocol BGP (MBGP) state sharing (if present). Remember, first and foremost, you must have at least one active receiver and one active source for a given group, regardless of which domains they are in. Write out the same high-level steps previously mentioned and add these elements:

Step 1.   **Receiver check.** Make sure a receiver is subscribed via IGMP and that a (*, G) to the RP exists before trying to troubleshoot:

   ✔ Check the group state on the LHR.

   ✔ Check IGMP membership on the last-hop PIM DR.

   ✔ Verify the (*, G) state at the LHR and check the RP for the (*, G) entry and RPF.

Step 2.   **Source check.** Make sure you have an active source before trying to troubleshoot (the source will be in a different domain from the receiver):

   ✔ Verify that the source is sending the multicast traffic to the FHR.

   ✔ Confirm that the FHR has registered the group with the RP.

   ✔ Determine whether the source domain RP is receiving the registry messages.

   ✔ Confirm that the multicast state is built on the FHR.

   ✔ Ensure that the RP is running MSDP and is adding the source to the MSDP SA cache.

   ✔ Confirm that the source domain RP is advertising this route to its MSDP neighbor RPs.

Step 3.   **State verification.** Ensure that each router in the path has correct RPF information by using the **show ip rpf <IP_address>** command:

   ✔ Verify RP and SPT state entries across the path at each RP router, starting with the LHR:

      ○ Ensure that each router interface in the path has appropriate PIM neighborships.

      ○ Discover whether the RP local to the LHR is running MSDP and whether it has either an (S, G) entry or an entry in the MSDP SA cache for the (S, G).

      ○ Check the MSDP peerings on each RP for every domain in the path to verify that peering is operational end-to-end.

○ Verify the group state at each active RP.

○ Verify SPT changes at each RP.

○ If MBGP is in use, verify the following:

● Is each MSDP-enabled RP also an MBGP peer, to prevent black-holing?

● Is the MSDP-enabled RP running BGP receiving an NLRI entry that covers the source IP?

● Is the next-hop router in the NLRI entry a PIM neighbor of the local domain?

✔ Verify the mroute state information for the following elements at every router in the path:

○ Verify that the IIF is correct.

○ Verify that the OIF is correct.

○ Ensure that the flags for (*, G) and (S, G) entries are correct and that the RP information is correct.

● Does this align with the information in the mroute entry?

● Is this what you would expect when looking at the unicast routing table?

Let's put the methodology to work, using the example of the final ASM multidomain network from Chapter 1, "Interdomain Routing and Internet Multicast," with a couple problems introduced into the configuration so that you can use the methodology to sniff them out and repair them. Figure 6-1 depicts the high-level ASM network as completed in Chapter 1, and Figure 6-2 shows the interface map for the routers in the path between the source and the client.

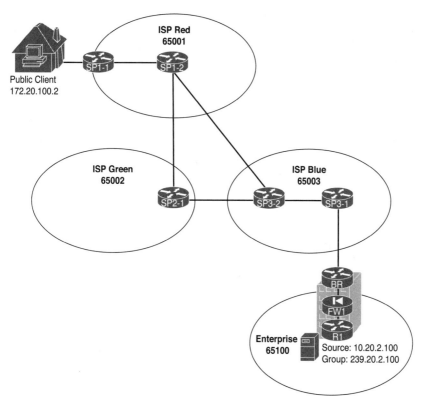

Figure 6-1   *Final Interdomain IP Multicast Design from Chapter 1*

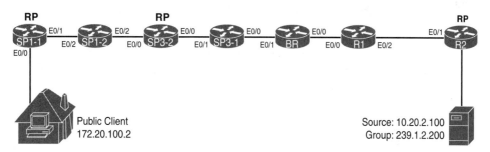

Figure 6-2   *Interdomain IP Multicast Design Interface Map*

Remember that in this design, Enterprise Company is offering up content to clients on the public Internet via group 239.1.2.200. Enterprise Company routers are configured as a single domain, and the BR router has an MSDP and MBGP relationship with router SP3-1 in Internet service provider (ISP) Blue. The ISPs have interconnected multicast domains. At the end of this configuration example, the client at public IP 172.21.100.2 was able to receive multicast packets from the source at 10.20.2.200 (see Example 6-1).

Example 6-1   *Multicast Reachability from Source to Client for 10.20.2.100, 239.1.2.200*

```
Server2# ping 239.1.2.200
Type escape sequence to abort.
Sending 1, 100-byte ICMP Echos to 239.1.2.200, timeout is 2 seconds:


Reply to request 0 from 172.21.100.2, 4 ms
```

Sometime after the completion of this configuration, the client stops receiving multicast. As shown in Example 6-2, a simple ping test indicates that the client is no longer responding to multicast pings.

Example 6-2   *Multicast Reachability Broken from Source to Client for 10.20.2.200*

```
Server2# ping 239.1.2.200
Type escape sequence to abort.
Sending 1, 100-byte ICMP Echos to 239.1.2.200, timeout is 2 seconds:
. . .
```

To figure out what the problem is, you can start with step 1 at the LHR to discover what happened:

Step 1.   **Receiver check.** Make sure a receiver is subscribed via IGMP and that (*, G) to the RP exists before trying to troubleshoot:

   ✔ Check the group state on the LHR.

   ✔ Check IGMP membership on the last-hop PIM DR.

   ✔ Verify the (*, G) state at the LHR and check the RP for the (*, G) entry and RPF.

Use the commands **show ip igmp groups**, **show ip pim rp mapping**, and **show ip mroute 239.1.2.200** on the LHR, SP1-1, to confirm proper receiver joins and proper RP mapping. Example 6-3 shows the output for these commands, issued on SP1-1.

Example 6-3   *Receiver Checking Output on SP1-1*

```
SP1-1# show ip igmp groups
IGMP Connected Group Membership
Group Address     Interface             Uptime    Expires   Last Reporter    Group
Accounted
239.1.2.200       Ethernet0/0           6d00h     00:02:27  172.21.100.2
224.0.1.40        Ethernet0/0           6d00h     00:02:22  172.21.100.1

SP1-1# show ip pim rp mapping
PIM Group-to-RP Mappings

Group(s): 224.0.0.0/4, Static
    RP: 172.21.0.2 (?)
```

```
SP1-1# show ip mroute 239.1.2.200
IP Multicast Routing Table
Flags: D - Dense, S - Sparse, B - Bidir Group, s - SSM Group, C - Connected,
       L - Local, P - Pruned, R - RP-bit set, F - Register flag,
       T - SPT-bit set, J - Join SPT, M - MSDP created entry, E - Extranet,
       X - Proxy Join Timer Running, A - Candidate for MSDP Advertisement,
       U - URD, I - Received Source Specific Host Report,
       Z - Multicast Tunnel, z - MDT-data group sender,
       Y - Joined MDT-data group, y - Sending to MDT-data group,
       G - Received BGP C-Mroute, g - Sent BGP C-Mroute,
       N - Received BGP Shared-Tree Prune, n - BGP C-Mroute suppressed,
       Q - Received BGP S-A Route, q - Sent BGP S-A Route,
       V - RD & Vector, v - Vector, p - PIM Joins on route
Outgoing interface flags: H - Hardware switched, A - Assert winner, p - PIM Join
 Timers: Uptime/Expires
 Interface state: Interface, Next-Hop or VCD, State/Mode
(*, 239.1.2.200), 6d00h/00:02:23, RP 172.21.0.2, flags: SJC
  Incoming interface: Ethernet0/1, RPF nbr 172.21.1.2
  Outgoing interface list:
    Ethernet0/0, Forward/Sparse, 6d00h/00:02:23
```

As you can see in Example 6-3, the receiver is joined via IGMP to the group, and a (*, G)
for the group exists in the mroute table. Next, check the RP in the receiver's domain
for the proper (*, G) state—in this case (*, 239.1.2.200). The RP router for the receiver's
domain, ISP Red, is SP1-2. **show ip mroute 239.1.2.200** confirms that the entry is correct, as shown in Example 6-4.

Example 6-4 *Checking the RP for (*, G)*

```
SP1-2# show ip mroute 239.1.2.200
IP Multicast Routing Table
Flags: D - Dense, S - Sparse, B - Bidir Group, s - SSM Group, C - Connected,
       L - Local, P - Pruned, R - RP-bit set, F - Register flag,
       T - SPT-bit set, J - Join SPT, M - MSDP created entry, E - Extranet,
       X - Proxy Join Timer Running, A - Candidate for MSDP Advertisement,
       U - URD, I - Received Source Specific Host Report,
       Z - Multicast Tunnel, z - MDT-data group sender,
       Y - Joined MDT-data group, y - Sending to MDT-data group,
       G - Received BGP C-Mroute, g - Sent BGP C-Mroute,
       N - Received BGP Shared-Tree Prune, n - BGP C-Mroute suppressed,
       Q - Received BGP S-A Route, q - Sent BGP S-A Route,
       V - RD & Vector, v - Vector, p - PIM Joins on route
Outgoing interface flags: H - Hardware switched, A - Assert winner, p - PIM Join
 Timers: Uptime/Expires
```

```
Interface state: Interface, Next-Hop or VCD, State/Mode
(*, 239.1.2.200), 6d01h/00:02:46, RP 172.21.0.2, flags: S
  Incoming interface: Null, RPF nbr 0.0.0.0
  Outgoing interface list:
    Ethernet0/2, Forward/Sparse, 6d01h/00:02:46
```

Notice that the RP, SP1-2, has the correct entry. Assume that the receiver checks out. However, also note from this entry that the IIF is Null and has no RPF neighbor. You can move to step 2 of the troubleshooting methodology to check the source:

Step 2.   **Source check.** Make sure you have an active source before trying to troubleshoot (the source is in a different domain from the receiver):

   ✔ Verify that the source is sending the multicast traffic to the FHR.

   ✔ Confirm that the FHR registered the group with the RP.

   ✔ Determine whether the source domain RP is receiving the registry messages.

   ✔ Confirm that the multicast state is built on the FHR.

   ✔ Ensure that the RP is running MSDP and is adding the source to the MSDP SA cache.

   ✔ Confirm that the source domain RP is advertising this route to its MSDP neighbor RPs.

In this case, the source is in Enterprise Company's domain. The FHR for the source, 10.20.2.200, is R2. This is where you start. You first check that the source is indeed sending a multicast stream and verify that R2 has the appropriate (S, G) state information for the source and group. You can check both of these items with the simple commands **show ip mroute 239.1.2.200** and **show ip pim rp mapping**. In addition, because R2 is also the RP, you should check for MSDP SA cache entries and peers by using the commands **show ip msdp sa-cache** and **show ip msdp summary**. Example 6-5 shows the outputs for these commands.

Example 6-5   *Checking for Source State and RP Registration on the FHR*

```
R2# show ip mroute 239.1.2.200
IP Multicast Routing Table
Flags: D - Dense, S - Sparse, B - Bidir Group, s - SSM Group, C - Connected,
       L - Local, P - Pruned, R - RP-bit set, F - Register flag,
       T - SPT-bit set, J - Join SPT, M - MSDP created entry, E - Extranet,
       X - Proxy Join Timer Running, A - Candidate for MSDP Advertisement,
       U - URD, I - Received Source Specific Host Report,
```

```
              Z - Multicast Tunnel, z - MDT-data group sender,
              Y - Joined MDT-data group, y - Sending to MDT-data group,
              G - Received BGP C-Mroute, g - Sent BGP C-Mroute,
              N - Received BGP Shared-Tree Prune, n - BGP C-Mroute suppressed,
              Q - Received BGP S-A Route, q - Sent BGP S-A Route,
              V - RD & Vector, v - Vector, p - PIM Joins on route
Outgoing interface flags: H - Hardware switched, A - Assert winner, p - PIM Join
 Timers: Uptime/Expires
 Interface state: Interface, Next-Hop or VCD, State/Mode

(*, 239.1.2.200), 00:00:12/stopped, RP 10.0.0.2, flags: SP
  Incoming interface: Null, RPF nbr 0.0.0.0
  Outgoing interface list: Null

(10.20.2.200, 239.1.2.200), 00:00:12/00:02:47, flags: PTA
  Incoming interface: Ethernet0/0, RPF nbr 0.0.0.0
  Outgoing interface list: Null

R2# show ip pim rp mapping
PIM Group-to-RP Mappings

Group(s): 224.0.0.0/4, Static-Override
    RP: 10.0.0.2 (?)
R2# show ip msdp summary
MSDP Peer Status Summary
Peer Address      AS      State     Uptime/  Reset SA    Peer Name
                                    Downtime Count Count
10.0.0.1          65101 Up          1w0d      0     0     ?
R2# show ip msdp sa-cache
MSDP Source-Active Cache - 1 entries
(10.20.2.200, 239.1.2.200), RP 10.0.0.2, MBGP/AS 65102, 00:03:04/00:05:10
```

Note from the highlighted output in Example 6-5 that source 10.20.2.200 is indeed sending packets to the group 239.1.2.200. This router is the RP for this group, and therefore you know that the source is registered. In addition, MSDP has added the (S, G) as an active SA in the cache and should be sending to any peers, in this case 10.0.0.1. However, there is a problem in the state entry for this (S, G). Can you identify it? (*Hint:* It is in the last line of the highlighted output.)

That's right, there is no valid OIF, as indicated by Null in the output. This means the router does not know of any downstream receivers for this group. What might be causing this issue? There is a good, properly registered source. You can move to step 3 in the process to check the state and configuration of each router in the path between the FHR and the LHR for this scenario:

Step 3.   **State verification.** Ensure that each router in the path has correct RPF information by using the **show ip rpf <IP_address>** command:

   ✔ Verify RP and SPT state entries across the path at each RP router, starting with the LHR:

   ○ Ensure that each router interface in the path has appropriate PIM neighborships.

   ○ Discover whether the RP local to the LHR is running MSDP and whether it has either an (S, G) entry or an entry in the MSDP SA cache for the (S, G).

   ○ Check the MSDP peerings on each RP for every domain in the path to verify that peering is operational end-to-end.

   ○ Verify the group state at each active RP.

   ○ Verify SPT changes at each RP.

   ○ If MBGP is in use, verify the following:

   • Is each MSDP-enabled RP also an MBGP peer, to prevent blackholing?

   • Is the MSDP-enabled RP running BGP receiving an NLRI entry that covers the source IP?

   • Is the next-hop router in the NLRI entry a PIM neighbor of the local domain?

   ✔ Verify the mroute state information for the following elements at every router in the path:

   ○ Verify that the IIF is correct.

   ○ Verify that the OIF is correct.

   ○ Ensure that the flags for (*, G) and (S, G) entries are correct and that the RP information is correct.

   • Does this align with the information in the mroute entry?

   • Is this what you would expect when looking at the unicast routing table?

The first part of step 3 is to ensure that there is a proper PIM neighborship at each interface in the path. Use the **show ip pim neighbor** command at each router, starting with the FHR and moving toward the LHR, as shown in Example 6-6.

Example 6-6 *Checking for PIM Neighborships Along the Path*

```
R2# show ip pim neighbor
PIM Neighbor Table
Mode: B - Bidir Capable, DR - Designated Router, N - Default DR Priority,
      P - Proxy Capable, S - State Refresh Capable, G - GenID Capable
Neighbor           Interface              Uptime/Expires     Ver   DR
Address                                                            Prio/Mode
10.1.2.1           Ethernet0/1            2w4d/00:01:37      v2    1 / S P G

BR# show ip pim neighbor
PIM Neighbor Table
Mode: B - Bidir Capable, DR - Designated Router, N - Default DR Priority,
      P - Proxy Capable, S - State Refresh Capable, G - GenID Capable
Neighbor           Interface              Uptime/Expires     Ver   DR
Address                                                            Prio/Mode
10.1.4.1           Ethernet0/0            1w0d/00:01:43      v2    1 / S P G
```

You don't have to go very far before you find the first problem. The BR router for
Enterprise Company should definitely have more than one neighbor. In this case, remember, the BR is connected to router R1 on E0/0. Where is the PIM connection for the ISP
Blue router SP3-1? You can check the interface configurations on each side to see if there
is an error in the configuration that might cause this problem. In this case, interface E0/1
on the BR connects to interface E0/0 on router SP3-1. The command **show running-
config interface E*X*/*X*** gives you the output needed to analyze the PIM configuration for
each router, as shown in Example 6-7.

Example 6-7 *Checking the PIM Configurations of Each Relevant Interface*

```
BR# show running-config interface e0/1
Building configuration...

Current configuration : 142 bytes
!
interface Ethernet0/1
 description Connection_to_E0/0_SP3-1
 ip address 172.23.31.4 255.255.255.0
 ip access-group 101 in
 ip access-group MCAST_OUT out
 ip pim sparse-mode
SP3-1# show running-config interface e0/0
Building configuration...
```

```
Current configuration : 67 bytes
!
interface Ethernet0/0
 ip address 172.23.31.1 255.255.255.0
```

Well, there is a major problem in the network right there: Someone mistakenly removed the PIM configuration on E0/0 on SP3-1! You can quickly fix this issue and see what happens to the mroute entry on R2. Example 6-8 shows the configuration fix for SP3-1 and the **show ip mroute 239.1.2.200** command issued again on R2. Notice the PIM DR Up console message on SP3-1 that appears immediately after configuration. This will correspond to the highlighted text request in the example.

Example 6-8 *Restoring the PIM Configuration on Router SP3-1*

```
SP3-1(config-if)# ip pim sparse-mode
SP3-1(config-if)#
*Mar 16 23:45:50.205: %PIM-5-NBRCHG: neighbor 172.23.31.4 UP on interface
  Ethernet0/0
*Mar 16 23:45:50.246: %PIM-5-DRCHG: DR change from neighbor 0.0.0.0 to 172.23.31.4
  on interface Ethernet0/0

R2# sh ip mroute 239.1.2.200
IP Multicast Routing Table
Flags: D - Dense, S - Sparse, B - Bidir Group, s - SSM Group, C - Connected,
       L - Local, P - Pruned, R - RP-bit set, F - Register flag,
       T - SPT-bit set, J - Join SPT, M - MSDP created entry, E - Extranet,
       X - Proxy Join Timer Running, A - Candidate for MSDP Advertisement,
       U - URD, I - Received Source Specific Host Report,
       Z - Multicast Tunnel, z - MDT-data group sender,
       Y - Joined MDT-data group, y - Sending to MDT-data group,
       G - Received BGP C-Mroute, g - Sent BGP C-Mroute,
       N - Received BGP Shared-Tree Prune, n - BGP C-Mroute suppressed,
       Q - Received BGP S-A Route, q - Sent BGP S-A Route,
       V - RD & Vector, v - Vector, p - PIM Joins on route
Outgoing interface flags: H - Hardware switched, A - Assert winner, p - PIM Join
 Timers: Uptime/Expires
 Interface state: Interface, Next-Hop or VCD, State/Mode

(*, 239.1.2.200), 00:36:41/stopped, RP 10.0.0.2, flags: SP
  Incoming interface: Null, RPF nbr 0.0.0.0
  Outgoing interface list: Null

(10.20.2.200, 239.1.2.200), 00:36:41/00:02:57, flags: PTA
  Incoming interface: Ethernet0/0, RPF nbr 0.0.0.0
  Outgoing interface list: Null
```

It appears that there is still a problem at the FHR. The OIF still shows Null. You are going to have to keep working through step 3 to hunt down any remaining problems. Step 3 suggests that you check the RP for the LHR to determine if it is running MSDP and if it has an entry in the SA cache for the source/group pair (10.20.2.200, 239.1.2.200). The RP for ISP Red is router SP1-2. Use the **show ip msdp sa-cache** command to check for the entry in question (see Example 6-9).

Example 6-9   *Checking the LHR RP MSDP SA State*

```
SP1-2# show ip msdp sa-cache
MSDP Source-Active Cache - 0 entries
```

That's not correct; the MSDP SA cache on the RP is empty! You need to walk the path back to the FHR MSDP speaker to find if there is a problem with MSDP. You can run **show ip msdp summary** on SP1-2 and then again on each of the RPs in the path. If you combine this with the command **show ip msdp sa-cache** at each of those hops, you may find exactly where the breakdown in MSDP has occurred. Example 6-10 provides the appropriate output.

Note   For this exercise, you already know that the RP/MSDP peer in the path at ISP Blue is SP3-2 and R1 at Enterprise Company. However, this output helps visualize this peering, along with the SA cache entries at each hop.

Example 6-10   *MSDP Peering and SA Check, Hop by Hop*

```
FOR ISP RED:


SP1-2# show ip msdp summary
MSDP Peer Status Summary
Peer Address      AS      State    Uptime/   Reset SA    Peer Name
                                   Downtime  Count Count
172.22.0.1        65002 Up         1w0d      0     0      ?
172.23.0.2        65003 Up         1w0d      0     0      ?



FOR ISP BLUE:
SP3-2# show ip msdp summary
MSDP Peer Status Summary
Peer Address      AS      State    Uptime/   Reset SA    Peer Name
                                   Downtime  Count Count
10.0.0.1          65100 Up         00:06:10  2     0      ?
172.22.0.1        65002 Up         1w0d      0     0      ?
172.21.0.2        65001 Up         1w0d      0     0      ?
```

```
SP3-2# show ip msdp sa-cache
MSDP Source-Active Cache - 0 entries



FOR ENTERPRISE:
R1# show ip msdp summary
MSDP Peer Status Summary
Peer Address      AS      State     Uptime/   Reset SA     Peer Name
                                    Downtime  Count Count
172.23.0.2        65003 Up          1w0d        0     0       ?
10.0.0.2          65102 Up          1w0d        0     1       ?
10.0.0.3          65103 Up          1w0d        0     0       ?


R1# show ip msdp sa-cache
MSDP Source-Active Cache - 1 entries
(10.20.2.200, 239.1.2.200), RP 10.0.0.2, MBGP/AS 65101, 01:00:49/00:05:14,
   Peer 10.0.0.2
```

Notice that SP1-2, SP3-2, and R1 all have the correct MSDP peerings, as highlighted. However, R1 has the appropriate SA cache entry for the (S, G), but SP3-2 does not. You have identified a second problem: The SA entry is not getting installed in each RP in the path!

You need to correct this problem before moving on to the next parts of step 3. Make sure the end-to-end PIM path builds an RPF checked source tree at each domain in the overall network. Without this, you will always have an incomplete source tree at the downstream domains. To discover the trouble, use the **debug ip msdp detail** command at R1 and SP3-2, where the peering and SA cache entries seem to break down. Example 6-11 gives the debug output for a few minutes on each router.

Example 6-11   *Debugging MSDP to Identify the Problem*

```
R1# debug ip msdp detail
MSDP Detail debugging is on
<..>
*Mar 16 23:59:07.535: MSDP(0): Received 3-byte TCP segment from 172.23.0.2
*Mar 17 00:01:28.877: MSDP(0): start_index = 0, sa_cache_index = 0, Qlen = 0
*Mar 17 00:01:28.877: MSDP(0): Sent entire sa-cache, sa_cache_index = 0, Qlen = 0
*Mar 17 00:01:38.956: MSDP(0): Received 20-byte TCP segment from 10.0.0.2
*Mar 17 00:01:38.956: MSDP(0): Append 20 bytes to 0-byte msg 31149 from 10.0.0.2, qs 1
*Mar 17 00:01:38.956: MSDP(0): (10.20.2.200/32, 239.1.2.200), accepted
*Mar 17 00:01:41.954: MSDP(0): start_index = 0, mroute_cache_index = 0, Qlen = 0
*Mar 17 00:01:41.954: MSDP(0): Sent entire mroute table, mroute_cache_index = 0,
   Qlen = 0
*Mar 17 00:01:41.954: MSDP(0): start_index = 0, sa_cache_index = 0, Qlen = 0
*Mar 17 00:01:41.954: MSDP(0): Sent entire sa-cache, sa_cache_index = 0, Qlen = 0
*Mar 17 00:02:08.332: MSDP(0): Received 3-byte TCP segment from 172.23.0.2
```

```
*Mar 17 00:02:08.332: MSDP(0): Append 3 bytes to 0-byte msg 31150 from 172.23.0.2,
  qs 1
*Mar 17 00:00:49.345: MSDP(0): Received 3-byte TCP segment from 172.21.0.2
*Mar 17 00:00:49.345: MSDP(0): Append 3 bytes to 0-byte msg 31737 from 172.21.0.2,
  qs 1
*Mar 17 00:00:50.969: MSDP(0): start_index = 0, mroute_cache_index = 0, Qlen = 0
*Mar 17 00:00:50.969: MSDP(0): Sent entire mroute table, mroute_cache_index = 0,
  Qlen = 0


SP3-2# debug ip msdp detail
MSDP Detail debugging is on
<..>
*Mar 17 00:01:01.006: MSDP(0): start_index = 0, sa_cache_index = 0, Qlen = 0
*Mar 17 00:01:01.006: MSDP(0): Sent entire sa-cache, sa_cache_index = 0, Qlen = 0
*Mar 17 00:01:24.567: MSDP(0): Received 3-byte TCP segment from 172.22.0.1
*Mar 17 00:01:24.567: MSDP(0): Append 3 bytes to 0-byte msg 31738 from 172.22.0.1,
  qs 1
*Mar 17 00:01:28.877: MSDP(0): Received 20-byte TCP segment from 10.0.0.1
*Mar 17 00:01:28.877: MSDP(0): Append 20 bytes to 0-byte msg 31739 from 10.0.0.1, qs 1
*Mar 17 00:01:43.207: MSDP(0): start_index = 0, mroute_cache_index = 0, Qlen = 0
*Mar 17 00:01:43.207: MSDP(0): Sent entire mroute table, mroute_cache_index = 0,
  Qlen = 0
*Mar 17 00:01:43.207: MSDP(0): start_index = 0, sa_cache_index = 0, Qlen = 0
*Mar 17 00:01:43.207: MSDP(0): Sent entire sa-cache, sa_cache_index = 0, Qlen = 0
*Mar 17 00:01:49.652: MSDP(0): Received 3-byte TCP segment from 172.21.0.2
*Mar 17 00:01:49.652: MSDP(0): Append 3 bytes to 0-byte msg 31740 from 172.21.0.2,
  qs 1
*Mar 17 00:01:54.249: MSDP(0): start_index = 0, mroute_cache_index = 0, Qlen = 0
*Mar 17 00:01:54.249: MSDP(0): Sent entire mroute table, mroute_cache_index = 0,
  Qlen = 0
<..>
```

Notice that there are a lot of debug messages for this command, and not all of them are helpful. The important messages to review are highlighted. For example, the high-lighted output from R1 clearly shows that it received an MSDP update from R2. It also shows that the update included an SA entry for (10.20.2.200, 239.1.2.200) and that it was accepted. Accepted is a keyword in MSDP speak; it means that the SA entry was received and installed into the SA cache on the RP. It also means that the MSDP process on R1 will repackage the update and forward it to its peers.

However, look at the highlighted debug output from SP3-2. It also clearly shows that R1 has sent a 20-byte update, a clear indicator that an SA message was received. The SA cache, remember, was still empty. There is also no indication that the SA entry was accepted by SP3-2. You need to find out why. The quickest way to discover if the SA entry was received but rejected is by using the **show ip msdp sa-cache rejected-sa** com-mand. Example 6-12 shows output of this command from router SP3-2.

Example 6-12   *Rejected SA Cache Entries*

```
SP3-2# show ip msdp sa-cache rejected-sa
MSDP Rejected SA Cache
1 rejected SAs received over 00:01:44, cache size: 100 entries
Timestamp (source, group)
638628.861, (10.20.2.200, 239.1.2.200), RP: 10.0.0.2
```

Note   You must first enable caching of rejected entries for this feature to work on operating systems that offer support for rejected SA caching. The command to accomplish this for IOS-XE, the operating system in use for this example, is **ip msdp cache-rejected-sa** *number*, where *number* is the total entries you allow the router to cache.

The MSDP process on RP SP3-2 is rejecting the (10.20.2.200, 239.1.2.200) SA cache entry. If the entry is rejected, it will never be forwarded to the RP/MSDP Peer, SP1-2, in the domain of the LHR. Without that information, neither ISP domain can complete a source tree. You need to check the MSDP configuration on SP3-2 and look for any configuration issues. You can use the **show running-config | begin ip msdp** command to see only the relevant configuration, as shown in Example 6-13.

Example 6-13   *MSDP Configuration Check*

```
SP3-2# show run | begin msdp
ip msdp peer 10.0.0.1 connect-source Loopback0 remote-as 65100
ip msdp sa-filter in 10.0.0.1 route-map MSDP-FILTER
ip msdp peer 172.22.0.1 connect-source Loopback0 remote-as 65002
ip msdp peer 172.21.0.2 connect-source Loopback0 remote-as 65001
ip msdp cache-sa-state
ip msdp cache-rejected-sa 100
ip route 172.23.0.0 255.255.0.0 Null0
!
!
route-map MSDP-FILTER deny 10
!
route-map MSDP-FILTER permit 20
```

Notice from the highlighted text that there is another configuration problem at SP3-2. It looks like ISP Blue is making multicast life difficult! In this case, an MSDP filter was added. The route map used for the filter, however, is misconfigured as the deny statement at place 10 in the route map has no criteria. This causes a "match-all" scenario to occur and denies all SA entries from being installed.

Remove the filter command from SP3-2 and use the **show ip msdp sa-cache** command to see if this resolves this problem. Wait a minute to allow the update from R1 to come in and get accepted. You can also simultaneously run the **debug ip msdp detail** command again to capture when that happens and to look for an "Accept(ed)" for the entry. Example 6-14 shows the relevant output from these commands on SP3-2.

Example 6-14   *Repairing the MSDP SA Cache*

```
SP3-2# config t
Enter configuration commands, one per line.  End with CNTL/Z.
SP3-2(config)#no ip msdp sa-filter in 10.0.0.1 route-map MSDP-FILTER
SP3-2(config)#exit

SP3-2# debug ip msdp detail
*Mar 17 00:54:20.197: MSDP(0): Received 20-byte TCP segment from 10.0.0.1
*Mar 17 00:54:20.197: MSDP(0): Append 20 bytes to 0-byte msg 31899 from 10.0.0.1,
  qs 1
*Mar 17 00:54:20.197: MSDP(0): (10.20.2.200/32, 239.1.2.200) RP 10.0.0.2 Accepted

SP3-2# show ip msdp sa-cache
MSDP Source-Active Cache - 1 entries
(10.20.2.200, 239.1.2.200), RP 10.0.0.2, BGP/AS 65100, 00:00:17/00:05:46, Peer
  10.0.0.1
Learned from peer 10.0.0.1, RPF peer 10.0.0.1,
SAs received: 2, Encapsulated data received: 0
```

The SA is now installed in the SA cache on the RP. SP3-2 forwards this SA in an update to the LHR domain RP, SP1-2. Now that this problem is resolved, you can continue with step 3. Return to SP1-1, the LHR, and check the state information for the group by using the **show ip mroute** command once again. Example 6-15 shows the output of this command.

Example 6-15   *mroute State on the LHR*

```
SP1-1# show ip mroute 239.1.2.200
IP Multicast Routing Table
Flags: D - Dense, S - Sparse, B - Bidir Group, s - SSM Group, C - Connected,
       L - Local, P - Pruned, R - RP-bit set, F - Register flag,
       T - SPT-bit set, J - Join SPT, M - MSDP created entry, E - Extranet,
       X - Proxy Join Timer Running, A - Candidate for MSDP Advertisement,
       U - URD, I - Received Source Specific Host Report,
       Z - Multicast Tunnel, z - MDT-data group sender,
       Y - Joined MDT-data group, y - Sending to MDT-data group,
       G - Received BGP C-Mroute, g - Sent BGP C-Mroute,
       N - Received BGP Shared-Tree Prune, n - BGP C-Mroute suppressed,
       Q - Received BGP S-A Route, q - Sent BGP S-A Route,
       V - RD & Vector, v - Vector, p - PIM Joins on route
```

```
Outgoing interface flags: H - Hardware switched, A - Assert winner, p - PIM Join
 Timers: Uptime/Expires
 Interface state: Interface, Next-Hop or VCD, State/Mode

(*, 239.1.2.200), 1w0d/stopped, RP 172.21.0.2, flags: SJC
  Incoming interface: Ethernet0/1, RPF nbr 172.21.1.2
  Outgoing interface list:
    Ethernet0/0, Forward/Sparse, 1w0d/00:02:00

(10.20.2.200, 239.1.2.200), 00:00:04/00:02:55, flags: JT
  Incoming interface: Ethernet0/1, RPF nbr 172.21.1.2
  Outgoing interface list:
    Ethernet0/0, Forward/Sparse, 00:00:04/00:02:55
```

It looks as though the state for the stream is restored—all the way to the LHR and potentially to the client. You can test from the server to confirm this. A simple ping to the group 239.1.2.200 shows success if you fixed all the problems (see Example 6-16).

Example 6-16 *Successful ping to 239.1.2.200*

```
Server2# ping 239.1.2.200
Type escape sequence to abort.
Sending 1000, 100-byte ICMP Echos to 239.1.2.200, timeout is 2 seconds:
Reply to request 1 from 172.21.100.2, 63 ms
```

You have resolved all the issues in the multicast network, and service is restored. Notice from this scenario that the three main checks for multicast continuity are just as effective in an advanced interdomain deployment as in a basic single-domain deployment. You simply needed to perform additional checks for the additional protocol elements.

Note It is relatively easy to assess and repair trouble that arises in a multicast network with a single domain. Multidomain designs are just as simple if you control the entire design end-to-end (source to receivers). You have a solid methodology for end-to-end troubleshooting, regardless of how large the forwarding trees may be. But what about networks where you do not have control over the entire design, like multicast over the public Internet or a partner network? This adds a purely political layer to the troubleshooting process. You need to work with your ISP or partner networks to perform all three checks. You may not control either the domain with the source or the domain(s) with receivers. You may even be a service provider in between the two, merely providing transit to each domain. However, the steps for troubleshooting do not change: You must always start at step 1 and work through step 3. The key to success is complete information sharing between all parties involved in the transport of the multicast stream.

Assume that it is safe to apply these steps to other advanced designs as well. You may have to adjust some of the steps based on the protocols used in the design, but that is a relatively small component of troubleshooting. It's very simple: You must have a registered receiver, an active source, and a working tree between the two. The following sections examine other complex multicast designs using this same methodology.

Troubleshooting PIM with Traffic Engineering

Chapter 5, "IP Multicast Design Considerations and Implementation," in *IP Multicast, Volume 1* discusses using traffic engineering principles for scenarios in which PIM needs to build a tree over interfaces that do not have natural RPF affinity. This can occur, for example, when there are interfaces in the network that do not support PIM configurations. It could also occur when the Interior Gateway Protocol (IGP) best path for unicast does not align with the desired best path for multicast.

There are different ways to solve traffic engineering problems. For example, you can use GRE tunnels to bypass PIM configuration issues, such as unsupportive interfaces, or physical domain control gaps. In addition, you can use a static method or a dynamic method for giving routers RPF information not obtained by the IP unicast table. This supplemental RPF information allows the router to select a forwarding path that does not necessarily coincide with the preferred unicast path when RPF checking a source. PIM-enabled tunnels or alternative network paths can then be used to direct multicast streams down a specified set of interfaces in the network.

In many Cisco IOS platforms, an **mroute** command statement statically adds RPF information. The dynamic option for traffic engineering is to use MBGP to share prefix data for RPF checking against the chosen path in BGP. Dynamic, BGP-based traffic engineering is the preferred mechanism for alternate path selection in most networks, and it is the method recommended in *IP Multicast, Volume 1*.

When multicast traffic engineering is used, network operations staff need to adjust the standard troubleshooting model to accommodate additional checks on multicast data with additional commands. Because traffic engineering only deals with the building of state along the PIM path, it is not necessary to alter the first two steps of the model (the receiver check and the source check). You can use the following adjusted step 3 in the troubleshooting model to troubleshoot the PIM path for a traffic engineered flow:

Step 3.   State verification. Ensure that each router in the path has correct RPF information by using the **show ip rpf <IP_address>** command:

   ✔ Verify the RP and SPT state entries across the path:

   ○ Ensure that each router interface in the path has appropriate PIM neighborships.

   ○ Check the MSDP summary to verify that peering is operational.

   ○ Verify the group state at each active RP.

   ○ Verify SPT changes.

   ○ Inspect RPF state for the data source (unicast, static, BGP).

✔ Verify the mroute state information for the following elements:

○ Verify that the incoming interface list (IIF) is correct.

○ Verify that the outgoing interface list (OIF) is correct.

○ Ensure that the flags for (*, G) and (S, G) entries are correct and that the RP information is correct.

• Does this align with the information in the mroute entry?

• Is this what you would expect when looking at the unicast routing table? If not, is there a static entry for the (S, G), and does it correctly align with the desired path? Should there be a BGP entry for traffic engineering?

❑ Check the BGP routing information base (RIB) for proper prefix data.

❑ If the prefix is missing, check BGP peering for complete peering and proper state advertisements.

Let's examine a scenario in which traffic engineering is desired to change the path of the multicast data flow. For ease of understanding, the same Enterprise Company example is used from the previous section except that now the multidomain configuration has been removed. The multicast flow in question travels only between Server 2, connected to router R2, and a client connected to router R1. Figure 6-3 shows a network diagram for this configuration.

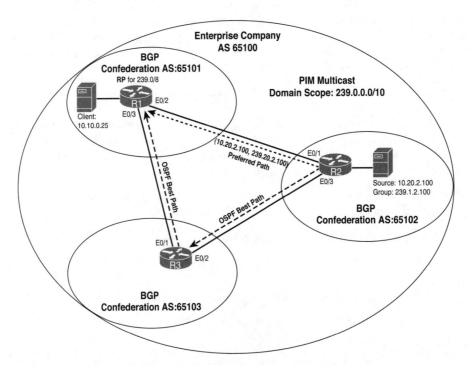

Figure 6-3 *Multicast Traffic Engineering in Enterprise Company*

Notice from the diagram that the core of the network is still using Open Shortest Path First (OSPF) between the routers and a BGP confederation to move end system routes. The network administrators for Enterprise Company do not want the unicast and multicast traffic to travel the same path. The path between R1 and R2 is not as fast as the path R2 to R3 to R1. The network architect has asked that OSPF prefer the R2 to R3 path for unicast traffic and that PIM be disabled along that path to ensure that no multicast passes between R2 and R3. Example 6-17 provides the relevant configuration for this network, excluding the necessary RPF information for transporting multicast.

Example 6-17 *Traffic Engineering Router Configurations*

```
R1
hostname R1
!
ip multicast-routing
ip cef
no ipv6 cef
!
interface Loopback0
 ip address 10.0.0.1 255.255.255.255
 ip pim sparse-mode
!
interface Ethernet0/0
 ip address 10.1.4.1 255.255.255.0
 ip pim sparse-mode
!
interface Ethernet0/1
 ip address 10.10.0.1 255.255.255.0
 ip pim sparse-mode
!
interface Ethernet0/2
 ip address 10.1.2.1 255.255.255.0
 ip pim sparse-mode
 ip ospf cost 1000
!
!
router ospf 10
 network 10.0.0.1 0.0.0.0 area 0
 network 10.1.2.1 0.0.0.0 area 0
 network 10.1.3.1 0.0.0.0 area 0
 network 10.1.4.1 0.0.0.0 area 0
!
router bgp 65101
 bgp router-id 10.0.0.1
 bgp log-neighbor-changes
```

```
bgp confederation identifier 65100
bgp confederation peers 65102 65103
neighbor 10.0.0.2 remote-as 65102
neighbor 10.0.0.2 ebgp-multihop 2
neighbor 10.0.0.2 update-source Loopback0
neighbor 10.0.0.3 remote-as 65103
neighbor 10.0.0.3 ebgp-multihop 2
neighbor 10.0.0.3 update-source Loopback0
neighbor 10.0.0.4 remote-as 65101
neighbor 10.0.0.4 update-source Loopback0
!
address-family ipv4
 network 10.10.0.0 mask 255.255.255.0
 neighbor 10.0.0.2 activate
 neighbor 10.0.0.3 activate
 neighbor 10.0.0.4 activate
exit-address-family
!
address-family ipv4 multicast
 neighbor 10.0.0.2 activate
 neighbor 10.0.0.3 activate
 neighbor 10.0.0.4 activate
exit-address-family
!
ip pim rp-address 10.0.0.1 override
```

```
R2
hostname R2
!
ip multicast-routing
ip cef
no ipv6 cef
!
interface Loopback0
 ip address 10.0.0.2 255.255.255.255
 ip pim sparse-mode
!
interface Ethernet0/0
 ip address 10.20.2.1 255.255.255.0
 ip pim sparse-mode
!
interface Ethernet0/1
 ip address 10.1.2.2 255.255.255.0
 ip pim sparse-mode
 ip ospf cost 1000
!
```

```
interface Ethernet0/2
 no ip address
 ip pim sparse-mode
 ip igmp join-group 239.20.2.100
!
interface Ethernet0/3
 ip address 10.2.3.2 255.255.255.0
 ip ospf cost 1
!
router ospf 10
 network 10.0.0.2 0.0.0.0 area 0
 network 10.1.2.2 0.0.0.0 area 0
 network 10.2.3.2 0.0.0.0 area 0
!
router bgp 65102
 bgp router-id 10.0.0.2
 bgp log-neighbor-changes
 bgp confederation identifier 65100
 bgp confederation peers 65101 65103
 neighbor 10.0.0.1 remote-as 65101
 neighbor 10.0.0.1 ebgp-multihop 2
 neighbor 10.0.0.1 update-source Loopback0
 neighbor 10.0.0.3 remote-as 65103
 neighbor 10.0.0.3 ebgp-multihop 2
 neighbor 10.0.0.3 update-source Loopback0
 !
 address-family ipv4
  network 10.20.2.0 mask 255.255.255.0
  neighbor 10.0.0.1 activate
  neighbor 10.0.0.3 activate
 exit-address-family
 !
 address-family ipv4 multicast
  neighbor 10.0.0.1 activate
  neighbor 10.0.0.3 activate
 exit-address-family
!
ip pim rp-address 10.0.0.1 override
```

```
R3
hostname R3
!
ip multicast-routing
ip cef
no ipv6 cef
!
```

```
interface Loopback0
 ip address 10.0.0.3 255.255.255.255
 ip pim sparse-mode
!
interface Ethernet0/0
 no ip address
 ip pim sparse-mode
!
interface Ethernet0/1
 ip address 10.1.3.3 255.255.255.0
 ip ospf cost 1
!
interface Ethernet0/2
 ip address 10.2.3.3 255.255.255.0
 ip ospf cost 1
!
router ospf 10
 network 10.0.0.3 0.0.0.0 area 0
 network 10.1.3.3 0.0.0.0 area 0
 network 10.2.3.3 0.0.0.0 area 0
!
router bgp 65103
 bgp router-id 10.0.0.3
 bgp log-neighbor-changes
 bgp confederation identifier 65100
 bgp confederation peers 65101 65102
 neighbor 10.0.0.1 remote-as 65101
 neighbor 10.0.0.1 ebgp-multihop 2
 neighbor 10.0.0.1 update-source Loopback0
 neighbor 10.0.0.2 remote-as 65102
 neighbor 10.0.0.2 ebgp-multihop 2
 neighbor 10.0.0.2 update-source Loopback0
 !
 address-family ipv4
  neighbor 10.0.0.1 activate
  neighbor 10.0.0.2 activate
 exit-address-family
 !
 address-family ipv4 multicast
  neighbor 10.0.0.1 activate
  neighbor 10.0.0.2 activate
 exit-address-family
!
ip pim rp-address 10.0.0.1 override
```

Notice from the configuration in Example 6-15 that the network path from R2 to R1 has a configured OSPF cost of 1,000, whereas the cost of the path R2–R3–R1 has a configured cost of 1. This causes the routers to prefer the lower-cost path for all traffic between the BGP distributed networks 10.10.0.0/24 (where the client is located) and 10.20.2.0/24 (where the source is connected). The interfaces in the R2–R3–R1 path do not have any PIM configurations.

This should cause an incomplete tree between the source and the client. You can prove this with a simple ping to the group 239.20.2.100 on Server 2 from the source (10.20.2.100). Example 6-18 shows this ping failing.

Example 6-18 *Failed PIM Path for (10.20.2.100, 239.20.2.100)*

```
Server2# ping 239.20.2.100
Type escape sequence to abort.
Sending 1, 100-byte ICMP Echos to 239.20.2.100, timeout is 2 seconds:
. . .
```

The reason for this break is obvious, but let's apply the troubleshooting elements from step 3 in the model to prove why the break in the stream is occurring. Check the PIM path between the source and client, starting at the router closest to the receiver, R1 (which also happens to be the RP for this network). Then move to R2, the next router in the path, and the one closest to the source. The **show ip mroute** *group* and **show ip rpf** **neighbor** *source* commands are sufficient to meet the checks in step 3. The command output for both routers is shown in Example 6-19.

Example 6-19 *Discovering the Broken Path Between R1 and R2*

```
R1# show ip mroute
IP Multicast Routing Table
Flags: D - Dense, S - Sparse, B - Bidir Group, s - SSM Group, C - Connected,
       L - Local, P - Pruned, R - RP-bit set, F - Register flag,
       T - SPT-bit set, J - Join SPT, M - MSDP created entry, E - Extranet,
       X - Proxy Join Timer Running, A - Candidate for MSDP Advertisement,
       U - URD, I - Received Source Specific Host Report,
       Z - Multicast Tunnel, z - MDT-data group sender,
       Y - Joined MDT-data group, y - Sending to MDT-data group,
       G - Received BGP C-Mroute, g - Sent BGP C-Mroute,
       N - Received BGP Shared-Tree Prune, n - BGP C-Mroute suppressed,
       Q - Received BGP S-A Route, q - Sent BGP S-A Route,
       V - RD & Vector, v - Vector, p - PIM Joins on route
Outgoing interface flags: H - Hardware switched, A - Assert winner, p - PIM Join
 Timers: Uptime/Expires
 Interface state: Interface, Next-Hop or VCD, State/Mode

(*, 239.20.2.100), 00:10:39/stopped, RP 10.0.0.1, flags: SJC
```

```
   Incoming interface: Null, RPF nbr 0.0.0.0
   Outgoing interface list:
     Ethernet0/1, Forward/Sparse, 00:10:39/00:02:02


(10.20.2.100, 239.20.2.100), 00:00:02/00:02:57, flags:
  Incoming interface: Null, RPF nbr 0.0.0.0
  Outgoing interface list:
    Ethernet0/1, Forward/Sparse, 00:00:02/00:02:57



R1#show ip rpf 10.20.2.100
 failed, no route exists


R2# show ip mroute
IP Multicast Routing Table
Flags: D - Dense, S - Sparse, B - Bidir Group, s - SSM Group, C - Connected,
       L - Local, P - Pruned, R - RP-bit set, F - Register flag,
       T - SPT-bit set, J - Join SPT, M - MSDP created entry, E - Extranet,
       X - Proxy Join Timer Running, A - Candidate for MSDP Advertisement,
       U - URD, I - Received Source Specific Host Report,
       Z - Multicast Tunnel, z - MDT-data group sender,
       Y - Joined MDT-data group, y - Sending to MDT-data group,
       G - Received BGP C-Mroute, g - Sent BGP C-Mroute,
       N - Received BGP Shared-Tree Prune, n - BGP C-Mroute suppressed,
       Q - Received BGP S-A Route, q - Sent BGP S-A Route,
       V - RD & Vector, v - Vector, p - PIM Joins on route
Outgoing interface flags: H - Hardware switched, A - Assert winner, p - PIM Join
 Timers: Uptime/Expires
 Interface state: Interface, Next-Hop or VCD, State/Mode


(*, 239.120.1.1), 00:13:05/00:02:57, RP 10.0.0.1, flags: SJC
  Incoming interface: Null, RPF nbr 0.0.0.0
  Outgoing interface list:
    Ethernet0/0, Forward/Sparse, 00:13:05/00:02:57


(*, 239.20.2.100), 00:13:41/stopped, RP 10.0.0.1, flags: SJPLF
  Incoming interface: Null, RPF nbr 0.0.0.0
  Outgoing interface list: Null


(10.20.2.100, 239.20.2.100), 00:02:30/00:00:29, flags: PLFT
  Incoming interface: Ethernet0/0, RPF nbr 0.0.0.0, Registering
  Outgoing interface list: Null
```

```
R2# show ip rpf 10.20.2.100
RPF information for ? (10.20.2.100)
  RPF interface: Ethernet0/0
  RPF neighbor: ? (10.20.2.100) - directly connected
  RPF route/mask: 10.20.2.0/24
  RPF type: multicast (connected)
  Doing distance-preferred lookups across tables
  RPF topology: ipv4 multicast base
```

Notice the highlighted output in Example 6-19. R1 does not have any RPF information for the source, 10.20.2.100, and so has an IIF of Null in the (S, G) entry and a Prune (P) flag. R2 has RPF information for the source because it is directly connected. However, because the RP (R1) does not have the ability to complete the source tree, R2 has pruned the (S, G), as indicated by the P flag in the entry. This causes R2 to have a OIF of Null.

Continue using the checks outlined in the modified step 3 to further expose the problem with the PIM path. The Null paths for the entries on routers R1 and R2 are clearly not working. You need to check whether the unicast table matches the data. Back at R1, execute the **show ip route** *source* and **show ip cef** *source* commands to discover what information the unicast RIB and forwarding information base (FIB) show for the source, 10.20.2.100. Example 6-20 provides this output from router R1.

Note   It is always a good idea to check the RIB and the FIB together when looking for routing information for unicast routes. This is especially true when BGP is in use. The RIB contains the BGP route for the network, but the router has to perform a recursive lookup in the RIB. The recursive lookup allows the router to route traffic toward the BGP next-hop router address learned from the IGP. Running both commands at the same time helps you get a complete look at any recursion in the RIB. In addition, if there are discrepancies between the RIB and the FIB, there are very likely problems in PIM pathing as well. Those discrepancies will likely need to be corrected to resolve discovered path problems with the PIM tree-building process. The command **show ip cef** reveals the FIB in IOS-XE. Refer to OS command references to discover the appropriate commands for other operating systems.

Example 6-20   *R1 Unicast RIB and FIB Entries*

```
R1# show ip route 10.20.2.100
Routing entry for 10.20.2.0/24
  Known via "bgp 65101", distance 200, metric 0
  Tag 65102, type internal
  Last update from 10.0.0.2 00:46:49 ago
```

```
    Routing Descriptor Blocks:
    * 10.0.0.2, from 10.0.0.2, 00:46:49 ago
        Route metric is 0, traffic share count is 1
        AS Hops 0
        Route tag 65102
        MPLS label: none
R1# show ip cef  10.20.2.100
10.20.2.0/24
  nexthop 10.1.3.3 Ethernet0/3
```

R1 clearly has a route to 10.20.2.100. So why is this route not being used for the IIF and RPF check? The unicast BGP RIB is not a valid source for PIM to perform RPF checks on. The route must be learned by the IGP. The Cisco Express Forwarding entry clearly shows interface E0/3 as the preferred path to reach the source. Check the PIM state on this interface. You know from the configuration that PIM is not configured on E0/3, and therefore the source tree has completely failed.

To resolve this problem, add a static mroute to R1 with the appropriate next-hop address for R2, where a PIM neighborship exists. You also need an RPF entry for the RP address on R2, or the RPF check for the shared tree will fail. This should add the necessary RPF information for R1 to complete the tree and for R2 to pick up the shared tree from the RP. As shown in Example 6-21, you can add the mroute on R1 and then perform the same checks from Example 6-18 to discover how the tree information changes. Example 6-21 shows the output, including a ping test on Server 2 to see if the stream is now functional.

Example 6-21   *Adding an IP mroute to R1*

```
R1# config t
R1(config)# ip mroute 10.20.2.0 255.255.255.0 10.1.2.2

R2# config t
R2(config)# ip mroute 10.0.0.1 255.255.255.255 10.1.2.1

R1# show ip mroute 239.20.2.100
IP Multicast Routing Table
Flags: D - Dense, S - Sparse, B - Bidir Group, s - SSM Group, C - Connected,
       L - Local, P - Pruned, R - RP-bit set, F - Register flag,
       T - SPT-bit set, J - Join SPT, M - MSDP created entry, E - Extranet,
       X - Proxy Join Timer Running, A - Candidate for MSDP Advertisement,
       U - URD, I - Received Source Specific Host Report,
       Z - Multicast Tunnel, z - MDT-data group sender,
       Y - Joined MDT-data group, y - Sending to MDT-data group,
       G - Received BGP C-Mroute, g - Sent BGP C-Mroute,
       N - Received BGP Shared-Tree Prune, n - BGP C-Mroute suppressed,
```

```
        Q - Received BGP S-A Route, q - Sent BGP S-A Route,
        V - RD & Vector, v - Vector, p - PIM Joins on route
Outgoing interface flags: H - Hardware switched, A - Assert winner, p - PIM Join
 Timers: Uptime/Expires
 Interface state: Interface, Next-Hop or VCD, State/Mode


(*, 239.20.2.100), 00:42:07/stopped, RP 10.0.0.1, flags: SJC
  Incoming interface: Null, RPF nbr 0.0.0.0
  Outgoing interface list:
    Ethernet0/1, Forward/Sparse, 00:42:07/00:02:33


(10.20.2.100, 239.20.2.100), 00:01:10/00:01:49, flags:
  Incoming interface: Ethernet0/2, RPF nbr 10.1.2.2, Mroute
  Outgoing interface list:
    Ethernet0/1, Forward/Sparse, 00:01:10/00:02:33


R1# show ip rpf 10.20.2.100
RPF information for ? (10.20.2.100)
  RPF interface: Ethernet0/2
  RPF neighbor: ? (10.1.2.2)
  RPF route/mask: 10.20.2.0/24
  RPF type: multicast (static)
  Doing distance-preferred lookups across tables
  RPF topology: ipv4 multicast base


R2# show ip mroute 239.20.2.100
IP Multicast Routing Table
Flags: D - Dense, S - Sparse, B - Bidir Group, s - SSM Group, C - Connected,
       L - Local, P - Pruned, R - RP-bit set, F - Register flag,
       T - SPT-bit set, J - Join SPT, M - MSDP created entry, E - Extranet,
       X - Proxy Join Timer Running, A - Candidate for MSDP Advertisement,
       U - URD, I - Received Source Specific Host Report,
       Z - Multicast Tunnel, z - MDT-data group sender,
       Y - Joined MDT-data group, y - Sending to MDT-data group,
       G - Received BGP C-Mroute, g - Sent BGP C-Mroute,
       N - Received BGP Shared-Tree Prune, n - BGP C-Mroute suppressed,
       Q - Received BGP S-A Route, q - Sent BGP S-A Route,
       V - RD & Vector, v - Vector, p - PIM Joins on route
Outgoing interface flags: H - Hardware switched, A - Assert winner, p - PIM Join
 Timers: Uptime/Expires
 Interface state: Interface, Next-Hop or VCD, State/Mode


(*, 239.20.2.100), 00:02:47/stopped, RP 10.0.0.1, flags: SJPLF
  Incoming interface: Null, RPF nbr 0.0.0.0
  Outgoing interface list: Null
```

```
(10.20.2.100, 239.20.2.100), 00:02:47/00:00:11, flags: LFT
  Incoming interface: Ethernet0/0, RPF nbr 0.0.0.0, Registering
  Outgoing interface list:
    Ethernet0/1, Forward/Sparse, 00:02:47/00:02:39


R2# show ip rpf 10.20.2.100
RPF information for ? (10.20.2.100)
  RPF interface: Ethernet0/0
  RPF neighbor: ? (10.20.2.100) - directly connected
  RPF route/mask: 10.20.2.0/24
  RPF type: multicast (connected)
  Doing distance-preferred lookups across tables
  RPF topology: ipv4 multicast base


Server2# ping 239.20.2.100
Type escape sequence to abort.
Sending 1, 100-byte ICMP Echos to 239.20.2.100, timeout is 2 seconds:

Reply to request 0 from 10.10.0.25, 2 ms
```

R1 now has a complete (S, G) entry with a proper IIF, and R2 has an entry with a complete OIF that uses the appropriate interface, E0/1. R2 has also removed the P flag, and the server can now receive a group ping response from the client. Look closely at the highlighted elements in the output in Example 6-21. The RPF information in the (S, G) entry on R1 clearly shows that the RPF entry is a static mroute entry.

You could also have repaired this problem by using BGP and introducing the network into the IPv4 Multicast address family on R2, as shown in Example 6-22. The mroute removal on R1 and the BGP entry on R2 are also shown for convenience. The output from the command **show ip bgp ipv4 multicast** on R1 is included to highlight the additional RPF information.

Example 6-22   *Adding an mroute to R2 using MBGP*

```
R1# config t
R1(config)# no ip mroute 10.20.2.0 255.255.255.0 10.1.2.2
R2# config t
R2(config)# router bgp 65102
R2(config-router)# address-family ipv4 multicast
R2(config-router-af)# network 10.20.2.0 255.255.255.0


R1# show ip mroute 239.20.2.100
IP Multicast Routing Table
Flags: D - Dense, S - Sparse, B - Bidir Group, s - SSM Group, C - Connected,
       L - Local, P - Pruned, R - RP-bit set, F - Register flag,
       T - SPT-bit set, J - Join SPT, M - MSDP created entry, E - Extranet,
```

```
       X - Proxy Join Timer Running, A - Candidate for MSDP Advertisement,
       U - URD, I - Received Source Specific Host Report,
       Z - Multicast Tunnel, z - MDT-data group sender,
       Y - Joined MDT-data group, y - Sending to MDT-data group,
       G - Received BGP C-Mroute, g - Sent BGP C-Mroute,
       N - Received BGP Shared-Tree Prune, n - BGP C-Mroute suppressed,
       Q - Received BGP S-A Route, q - Sent BGP S-A Route,
       V - RD & Vector, v - Vector, p - PIM Joins on route
Outgoing interface flags: H - Hardware switched, A - Assert winner, p - PIM Join
 Timers: Uptime/Expires
 Interface state: Interface, Next-Hop or VCD, State/Mode

(*, 239.20.2.100), 00:42:07/stopped, RP 10.0.0.1, flags: SJC
  Incoming interface: Null, RPF nbr 0.0.0.0
  Outgoing interface list:
    Ethernet0/1, Forward/Sparse, 00:42:07/00:02:33

(10.20.2.100, 239.20.2.100), 00:01:10/00:01:49, flags:
  Incoming interface: Ethernet0/2, RPF nbr 10.1.2.2, Mbgp
  Outgoing interface list:
    Ethernet0/1, Forward/Sparse, 00:01:10/00:02:33


R1# show ip rpf 10.20.2.100
RPF information for ? (10.20.2.100)
  RPF interface: Ethernet0/2
  RPF neighbor: ? (10.1.2.2)
  RPF route/mask: 10.20.2.0/24
  RPF type: multicast (bgp 65101)
  Doing distance-preferred lookups across tables
  RPF topology: ipv4 multicast base, originated from ipv4 unicast base


R1# show ip bgp ipv4 multi
BGP table version is 10, local router ID is 10.0.0.1
Status codes: s suppressed, d damped, h history, * valid, > best, i - internal,
              r RIB-failure, S Stale, m multipath, b backup-path, f RT-Filter,
              x best-external, a additional-path, c RIB-compressed,
Origin codes: i - IGP, e - EGP, ? - incomplete
RPKI validation codes: V valid, I invalid, N Not found


     Network          Next Hop          Metric LocPrf Weight Path
 *>  10.20.2.0/24     10.0.0.2               0    100      0 (65102) i
```

BGP on R2 is now sharing the multicast prefix for 10.20.2.0/24 with R1. R1 uses this pre-fix as the RPF source (as shown by MBGP in the mroute entry and bgp 65102 in the RPF output) and completes the shared and source trees. This should result in a successful ping.

As you can see, the adjustments given for step 3 in the troubleshooting methodology help identify when and where traffic engineering might be needed or where in the network configured traffic engineering may be broken. Multicast traffic engineering implementations can be very complicated. Some in-depth understand of the protocols is certainly going to make troubleshooting and repair easier. But even without this knowledge, an operator should be able to follow the outlined methodology and make significant progress. The additional checks for static mroute entries and MBGP entries are necessary for identifying where pathing may be breaking down.

You should also be able to see now that the three-step methodology proposed at the beginning of this chapter is universal for all troubleshooting exercises. The more in-depth your understanding of the protocols in use, the more checks you can add to each step. The following sections introduce additional troubleshooting tips for other advanced designs, but only the additional checks and commands for each are provided to avoid repetition. Let's start with multicast VPN (MVPN) designs.

Troubleshooting MVPN

MVPN is significantly more difficult to troubleshoot than traditional ASM networks as there are multiple layers (like an onion or parfait) that rely upon one another to function correctly. The preceding examples have already explained: step 1 (receiver check) and step 2 (source check). Therefore, this section begins at step 3, using the same troubleshooting methodology as before but with additional changes to the checks and substeps.

This example uses the diagram shown in Figure 6-4 (which you might recognize from Chapter 3, "Multicast MPLS VPNs").

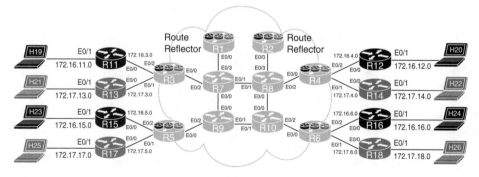

Figure 6-4   *MVPN Troubleshooting Topology*

Taking a bottom-up approach, let's start with the core or transport network and follow these steps:

Step 1.   Receiver check. Make sure a receiver is subscribed via IGMP and that the correct (*, G) is present.

Step 2.   Source check. Make sure you have an active source before trying to troubleshoot.

Step 3. **State verification.** Ensure that the core network is functioning:

✔ Confirm the appropriate L3 information:

○ For Unicast routing, verify that the unicast routing protocol is working correctly and that the PE devices have reachability to the loopback address via a /32.

IOS-XE troubleshooting commands:

■ **show ip route**

```
R6# show ip route
Codes: L - local, C - connected, S - static, R - RIP, M - mobile,
       B - BGP
       D - EIGRP, EX - EIGRP external, O - OSPF, IA - OSPF inter area
       N1 - OSPF NSSA external type 1, N2 - OSPF NSSA external type 2
       E1 - OSPF external type 1, E2 - OSPF external type 2
       i - IS-IS, su - IS-IS summary, L1 - IS-IS level-1, L2 - IS-IS
          level-2
       ia - IS-IS inter area, * - candidate default, U - per-user
          static route
       o - ODR, P - periodic downloaded static route, H - NHRP,
          l - LISP
       a - application route
       + - replicated route, % - next hop override, p - overrides from PfR


Gateway of last resort is not set


      192.168.0.0/32 is subnetted, 10 subnets
O        192.168.0.1 [110/41] via 192.168.106.10, 01:14:40, Ethernet0/0
O        192.168.0.2 [110/31] via 192.168.106.10, 01:14:40, Ethernet0/0
O        192.168.0.3 [110/41] via 192.168.106.10, 01:14:40, Ethernet0/0
O        192.168.0.4 [110/31] via 192.168.106.10, 01:14:40, Ethernet0/0
O        192.168.0.5 [110/31] via 192.168.106.10, 01:14:40, Ethernet0/0
C        192.168.0.6 is directly connected, Loopback0
O        192.168.0.7 [110/31] via 192.168.106.10, 01:14:40, Ethernet0/0
O        192.168.0.8 [110/21] via 192.168.106.10, 01:14:40, Ethernet0/0
O        192.168.0.9 [110/21] via 192.168.106.10, 01:14:40, Ethernet0/0
O        192.168.0.10 [110/11] via 192.168.106.10, 01:14:50, Ethernet0/0
S     192.168.1.0/24 is directly connected, Ethernet1/3
O     192.168.71.0/24 [110/40] via 192.168.106.10, 01:14:40, Ethernet0/0
O     192.168.73.0/24 [110/40] via 192.168.106.10, 01:14:40, Ethernet0/0
O     192.168.82.0/24 [110/30] via 192.168.106.10, 01:14:40, Ethernet0/0
O     192.168.84.0/24 [110/30] via 192.168.106.10, 01:14:40, Ethernet0/0
O     192.168.87.0/24 [110/30] via 192.168.106.10, 01:14:40, Ethernet0/0
O     192.168.95.0/24 [110/30] via 192.168.106.10, 01:14:40, Ethernet0/0
O     192.168.97.0/24 [110/30] via 192.168.106.10, 01:14:40, Ethernet0/0
```

```
        192.168.106.0/24 is variably subnetted, 2 subnets, 2 masks
C          192.168.106.0/24 is directly connected, Ethernet0/0
L          192.168.106.6/32 is directly connected, Ethernet0/0
O       192.168.108.0/24 [110/20] via 192.168.106.10, 01:14:40, Ethernet0/0
O       192.168.109.0/24 [110/20] via 192.168.106.10, 01:14:40, Ethernet0/0
```

This output indicates that all the PE and P devices are present in the routing table.

IOS-XR troubleshooting commands:

- **show route ipv4**

✔ Ensure that the appropriate routes in the unicast routing table have associated labels and that the labels are consistent between LDP neighbors.

IOS-XE troubleshooting commands:

- **show mpls forwarding-table**

```
R6# show mpls forwarding-table
Local   Outgoing   Prefix        Bytes Label Outgoing Next Hop
Label   Label      or Tunnel Id  Switched    interface
16      Pop Label  192.168.0.10/32  0          Et0/0   192.168.106.10
17      16         192.168.0.9/32   0          Et0/0   192.168.106.10
18      17         192.168.0.8/32   0          Et0/0   192.168.106.10
19      18         192.168.0.7/32   0          Et0/0   192.168.106.10
20      20         192.168.0.5/32   0          Et0/0   192.168.106.10
21      21         192.168.0.4/32   0          Et0/0   192.168.106.10
22      22         192.168.0.3/32   0          Et0/0   192.168.106.10
23      23         192.168.0.2/32   0          Et0/0   192.168.106.10
24      24         192.168.0.1/32   0          Et0/0   192.168.106.10
25      25         192.168.73.0/24  0          Et0/0   192.168.106.10
26      26         192.168.71.0/24  0          Et0/0   192.168.106.10
27      31         192.168.84.0/24  0          Et0/0   192.168.106.10
28      29         192.168.97.0/24  0          Et0/0   192.168.106.10
29      28         192.168.95.0/24  0          Et0/0   192.168.106.10
30      30         192.168.87.0/24  0          Et0/0   192.168.106.10
31      27         192.168.82.0/24  0          Et0/0   192.168.106.10
32      Pop Label  192.168.108.0/24 0          Et0/0   192.168.106.10
33      Pop Label  192.168.109.0/24 0          Et0/0   192.168.106.10
34      No Label   172.16.6.0/24[V]  0          aggregate/RED
35      No Label   172.16.16.0/24[V] \
Local   Outgoing   Prefix        Bytes Label Outgoing Next Hop
Label   Label      or Tunnel Id  Switched    interface
                                  0          Et0/2   172.16.6.16
36      No Label   172.17.6.0/24[V]  0          aggregate/BLU
37      No Label   172.17.18.0/24[V] \
                                  0          Et0/1   172.17.6.18
```

This output show that labels have been assigned to IP routes.

IOS-XR troubleshooting commands:

- **show mpls forwarding**

IOS-XE and IOS-XR troubleshooting commands:

- **show mpls interface**

- **show mpls ldp neighbor**

```
R10# show mpls ldp neighbor
    Peer LDP Ident: 192.168.0.6:0; Local LDP Ident 192.168.0.10:0
   TCP connection: 192.168.0.6.646 - 192.168.0.10.28964
   State: Oper; Msgs sent/rcvd: 37/38; Downstream
   Up time: 00:11:14
   LDP discovery sources:
     Ethernet0/2, Src IP addr: 192.168.106.6
        Addresses bound to peer LDP Ident:
           192.168.106.6   100.64.4.13     192.168.0.6
     Peer LDP Ident: 192.168.0.8:0; Local LDP Ident 192.168.0.10:0
   TCP connection: 192.168.0.8.646 - 192.168.0.10.32691
   State: Oper; Msgs sent/rcvd: 37/37; Downstream
   Up time: 00:11:02
   LDP discovery sources:
     Ethernet0/0, Src IP addr: 192.168.108.8
        Addresses bound to peer LDP Ident:
           192.168.108.8   192.168.87.8    192.168.84.8    192.168.82.8
           100.64.4.17     192.168.0.8
     Peer LDP Ident: 192.168.0.9:0; Local LDP Ident 192.168.0.10:0
   TCP connection: 192.168.0.9.646 - 192.168.0.10.55053
   State: Oper; Msgs sent/rcvd: 37/37; Downstream
   Up time: 00:11:01
   LDP discovery sources:
     Ethernet0/1, Src IP addr: 192.168.109.9
        Addresses bound to peer LDP Ident:
           192.168.97.9    192.168.109.9   192.168.95.9    100.64.4.19
           192.168.0.9
```

✔ From the output, you can verify that R10 has LDP neighbor relationships with R6, R8, and R9.

  ○ Depending on the profile used to implement multicast within the VPN, you may not have native multicast traffic in the core or transport network.

For profiles using GRE:

✔ Is multicast established in the core? Are there MDT default and data trees?

IOS-XE troubleshooting commands:

■ show ip mroute

```
R10# show ip mroute
IP Multicast Routing Table
Flags: D - Dense, S - Sparse, B - Bidir Group, s - SSM Group,
         C - Connected,
       L - Local, P - Pruned, R - RP-bit set, F - Register flag,
       T - SPT-bit set, J - Join SPT, M - MSDP created entry,
         E - Extranet,
       X - Proxy Join Timer Running, A - Candidate for MSDP Advertisement,
       U - URD, I - Received Source Specific Host Report,
       Z - Multicast Tunnel, z - MDT-data group sender,
       Y - Joined MDT-data group, y - Sending to MDT-data group,
       G - Received BGP C-Mroute, g - Sent BGP C-Mroute,
       N - Received BGP Shared-Tree Prune, n - BGP C-Mroute suppressed,
       Q - Received BGP S-A Route, q - Sent BGP S-A Route,
       V - RD & Vector, v - Vector, p - PIM Joins on route,
       x - VxLAN group
Outgoing interface flags: H - Hardware switched, A - Assert winner,
p - PIM Join
 Timers: Uptime/Expires
 Interface state: Interface, Next-Hop or VCD, State/Mode

(192.168.0.6, 232.0.0.1), 00:59:45/00:02:45, flags: sT
  Incoming interface: Ethernet0/2, RPF nbr 192.168.106.6
  Outgoing interface list:
    Ethernet0/0, Forward/Sparse, 00:59:45/00:02:45
    Ethernet0/1, Forward/Sparse, 00:59:45/00:02:42

(192.168.0.3, 232.0.0.1), 00:59:45/00:02:44, flags: sT
  Incoming interface: Ethernet0/1, RPF nbr 192.168.109.9
  Outgoing interface list:
    Ethernet0/2, Forward/Sparse, 00:59:45/00:02:44

(192.168.0.5, 232.0.0.1), 00:59:45/00:02:52, flags: sT
  Incoming interface: Ethernet0/1, RPF nbr 192.168.109.9
  Outgoing interface list:
    Ethernet0/2, Forward/Sparse, 00:59:45/00:02:49
    Ethernet0/0, Forward/Sparse, 00:59:45/00:02:52

(192.168.0.4, 232.0.0.1), 00:59:45/00:02:45, flags: sT
  Incoming interface: Ethernet0/0, RPF nbr 192.168.108.8
  Outgoing interface list:
    Ethernet0/2, Forward/Sparse, 00:59:45/00:02:45
    Ethernet0/1, Forward/Sparse, 00:59:45/00:02:42
```

```
(192.168.0.6, 232.0.0.2), 00:59:45/00:02:47, flags: sT
  Incoming interface: Ethernet0/2, RPF nbr 192.168.106.6
  Outgoing interface list:
    Ethernet0/0, Forward/Sparse, 00:59:45/00:02:45
    Ethernet0/1, Forward/Sparse, 00:59:45/00:02:47

(192.168.0.3, 232.0.0.2), 00:59:45/00:02:46, flags: sT
  Incoming interface: Ethernet0/1, RPF nbr 192.168.109.9
  Outgoing interface list:
    Ethernet0/2, Forward/Sparse, 00:59:45/00:02:46

(192.168.0.5, 232.0.0.2), 00:59:45/00:02:53, flags: sT
  Incoming interface: Ethernet0/1, RPF nbr 192.168.109.9
  Outgoing interface list:
    Ethernet0/2, Forward/Sparse, 00:59:45/00:02:53
    Ethernet0/0, Forward/Sparse, 00:59:45/00:02:41

(192.168.0.4, 232.0.0.2), 00:59:45/00:02:55, flags: sT
  Incoming interface: Ethernet0/0, RPF nbr 192.168.108.8
  Outgoing interface list:
    Ethernet0/2, Forward/Sparse, 00:59:45/00:02:55
    Ethernet0/1, Forward/Sparse, 00:59:45/00:02:47

(192.168.0.4, 232.0.1.0), 00:01:08/00:03:19, flags: sT
  Incoming interface: Ethernet0/0, RPF nbr 192.168.108.8
  Outgoing interface list:
    Ethernet0/2, Forward/Sparse, 00:01:08/00:03:19

(*, 224.0.1.40), 01:01:43/00:02:17, RP 0.0.0.0, flags: DCL
  Incoming interface: Null, RPF nbr 0.0.0.0
  Outgoing interface list:
    Loopback0, Forward/Sparse, 01:01:42/00:02:17
```

This output reveals some interesting information. In Chapter 3, you configured the MDT default for VRF RED as 232.0.0.1 and for VRF BLU using 232.0.0.2. There are sessions clearly indicated and sourced from P/PE devices. In addition, the highlighted output shows that a multicast session is sourced from 192.168.0.4 (R4) to a data MDT 232.0.1.0 in VRF RED. Further examination shows that multicast traffic is currently being forwarded out interface Ethernet0/2. This indicates an active multicast session. Continue working through the troubleshooting steps.

✔ Is the MTI active when using IOS-XE, or is the MDT interface active when using IOS-XR?

IOS-XE troubleshooting commands:

■ show [vrf vrf-name]

■ show interfaces tunnel [#]

```
R6# show interfaces tunnel 1
Tunnel1 is up, line protocol is up
  Hardware is Tunnel
  Interface is unnumbered. Using address of Loopback0 (192.168.0.6)
  MTU 17916 bytes, BW 100 Kbit/sec, DLY 50000 usec,
     reliability 255/255, txload 1/255, rxload 30/255
  Encapsulation TUNNEL, loopback not set
  Keepalive not set
  Tunnel linestate evaluation up
  Tunnel source 192.168.0.6 (Loopback0)
   Tunnel Subblocks:
      src-track:
         Tunnel1 source tracking subblock associated with Loopback0
          Set of tunnels with source Loopback0, 2 members (includes
             iterators), on interface <OK>
  Tunnel protocol/transport multi-GRE/IP
    Key disabled, sequencing disabled
    Checksumming of packets disabled
  Tunnel TTL 255, Fast tunneling enabled
  Tunnel transport MTU 1476 bytes
  Tunnel transmit bandwidth 8000 (kbps)
  Tunnel receive bandwidth 8000 (kbps)
  Last input 00:00:01, output 00:00:00, output hang never
  Last clearing of "show interface" counters 01:11:52
  Input queue: 0/75/0/0 (size/max/drops/flushes); Total output drops: 0
  Queueing strategy: fifo
  Output queue: 0/0 (size/max)
  5 minute input rate 12000 bits/sec, 12 packets/sec
  5 minute output rate 0 bits/sec, 0 packets/sec
     102124 packets input, 12627804 bytes, 0 no buffer
     Received 0 broadcasts (101511 IP multicasts)
     0 runts, 0 giants, 0 throttles
     0 input errors, 0 CRC, 0 frame, 0 overrun, 0 ignored, 0 abort
     258 packets output, 20872 bytes, 0 underruns
     0 output errors, 0 collisions, 0 interface resets
     0 unknown protocol drops
     0 output buffer failures, 0 output buffers swapped out
```

The highlighted output indicates that the tunnel is passing traffic. This is a good thing!

IOS-XR troubleshooting commands:

- **show pim [vrf vrf-name] mdt interface**

For profiles using MLDP:

IOS-XE and IOS-XR troubleshooting commands:

- **show mpls mldp neighbors**

✔ Ensure that the VPN is functioning.

- ○ Verify that the unicast routing protocol is working correctly and that you are able to ping from PE to PE within a VRF.

- ○ Verify the communication between PE devices. This could be PIM, BGP, MLDP, and so on. The troubleshooting options are dependent on the specific profile you are using. Please refer to Chapter 3 and specific operating system documentation for additional details.

✔ Ensure interoperability between PE and CE.

- ○ Determine whether PIM is enabled between the PE interface or subinterface and the CE device.

IOS-XE troubleshooting commands:

- **show ip pim interface**

- **show ip pim vrf [vrf vrf-name]**

- **show ip pim neighbor**

- **show ip pim vrf [vrf vrf-name] neighbor**

```
R6# show ip pim vrf RED neighbor
PIM Neighbor Table
Mode: B - Bidir Capable, DR - Designated Router, N - Default DR Priority,
      P - Proxy Capable, S - State Refresh Capable, G - GenID Capable,
      L - DR Load-balancing Capable
Neighbor        Interface          Uptime/Expires    Ver   DR
Address                                                    Prio/Mode
172.16.6.16     Ethernet0/2        00:35:33/00:01:35 v2    1 / DR S P G
192.168.0.5     Tunnel1            00:33:40/00:01:31 v2    1 / S P G
192.168.0.4     Tunnel1            00:33:40/00:01:30 v2    1 / S P G
192.168.0.3     Tunnel1            00:33:40/00:01:33 v2    1 / S P G
```

The output from R6 shows a neighbor adjacency to R15 on the Ethernet0/2 interface; this is in VRF RED. The adjacencies on the Tunnel1 interface connect to other PE devices in the network that are participating in the same MVPN.

IOS-XR troubleshooting commands:

- **show pim [vrf *vrf-name*] [ipv4 | ipv6] interface**

- **show pim [vrf *vrf-name*] [ipv4 | ipv6] neighbor**

Following these steps allows you to successfully troubleshoot path error problems in an MVPN cloud. It is likely, given the configuration complexity of MVPN, that many errors will occur due to misconfiguration of some type. Some of the most common configuration errors to watch out for in an MVPN network include the following:

- Alternative paths/interfaces are not configured for MPLS.

- Multicast routing is not established in the core or transport network when using profile 0. Source-Specific Multicast (SSM) or Any-Source Multicast (ASM) needs to be functional.

- There is a missing BGP address family on the provider edge or route reflector.

- The RP is not configured correctly within the VPN. A provider edge, customer edge, or customer device can be configured as the RP.

- The RP is not reachable within the VPN.

- Multicast routing has not been enabled.

Verifying Multicast in VXLAN

This section provides the commands needed to troubleshoot multicast behavior within a VXLAN environment. If the output for data plane multicast traffic does not have the appropriate baseline as stated in these steps, then the troubleshooting efforts need to start with baseline check as defined by the three steps. However, it can be assumed that the receiver and source are operational because they are components of a specific configuration and can be easily checked. Thus, the real troubleshooting, once again, starts with Step 3, state verification.

Let's review the steps mentioned previously:

Step 1.   Receiver check – verify the receiver as sent the appropriate IGMP join

Step 2.   Source check – has source sent the traffic to FHR, and the FHR is registered with RP (in case of PIM sparse mode)?

Step 3.   State verification – state verification hop by hop, where the VXLAN fabric is single hop (ingress Virtual Tunnel End-Point (VTEP) and egress VTEP has to be reviewed first for state information)

  ✔ Check the Network Virtualization Endpoint (NVE) is up and functional

  ✔ Check the multicast group aligned to the active VXLAN Network Identifiers (VNI)s

  ✔ Check the Multicast group information, and make sure the VTEP peer information is seen and the outgoing information is tied to NVE1 interface

  ✔ Check if the VXLAN is set up on multicast underlay

Let's start with NVE functionality (the first check). As you remember, VTEPs hold a VxLAN forwarding table that maps destination mac address to remote VTEP IP address where the destination is located. The VTEP also maintains a local table that represents VLAN to VXLAN mappings. The data plane is represented by an NVE. For the VXLAN functions, it is important to verify if NVE peers are UP and operative, as seen by using the **show nve peers** command. Generic output from this command is shown in Example 6-23

Example 6-23   *Showing NVE Peers Output*

```
VTEP-1# show nve peers
Interface Peer-IP          State LearnType Uptime   Router-Mac
--------- ---------------  ----- --------- -------- -----------------

nve1      10.50.1.1        Up    DP        00:05:09 n/a
```

Now you need to check the multicast group aligned to the active VNIs (as reviewed in the second check). This is accomplished using the **show nve vni** command. Example 6-24 gives a generic output from this command.

Example 6-24   *Showing Active VNI Groups*

```
VTEP-1# sh nve vni
Codes: CP - Control Plane        DP - Data Plane
       UC - Unconfigured         SA - Suppress ARP


Interface VNI      Multicast-group   State Mode Type [BD/VRF]       Flags
--------- -------- ----------------- ----- ---- ------------------ -----
nve1      2901     239.1.1.1         Up    DP   L2 [2901]

```

In flood and learn mode, the NVE is aligned with the underlay multicast, in this case **nve1** of 2901 is mapped with 239.1.1.1. In this scenario, VTEP-1 is the source for 239.1.1.1, and the other VTEPs in the VxLAN domain are the receivers. The data plane is the Broadcast and Unknown Unicast and Multicast (BUM) traffic that uses the multicast group.

Now check the Multicast group information, and make sure the VTEP peer information is seen and the outgoing information is tied to NVE1 interface (as reviewed in the third check). This is to confirm the multicast group as (*,G) & (S,G) entry in the control plane. Confirm this by using a simple **show ip mroute** command on the VTEP. Example 6-25 shows this output from the generic VTEP.

Example 6-25   *Verifying Mroute with VNI Interface*

```
VTEP-1# sh ip mroute
IP Multicast Routing Table for VRF "default"


(*, 232.0.0.0/8), uptime: 5d10h, pim ip
  Incoming interface: Null, RPF nbr: 0.0.0.0, uptime: 5d10h
  Outgoing interface list: (count: 0)


(*, 239.1.1.1/32), uptime: 00:05:18, nve ip pim
  Incoming interface: Ethernet1/58, RPF nbr: 10.19.9.2, uptime: 00:05:18
  Outgoing interface list: (count: 1)
    nve1, uptime: 00:05:18, nve


(10.11.2.2/32, 239.1.1.1/32), uptime: 00:05:18, nve ip mrib pim
  Incoming interface: loopback0, RPF nbr: 10.11.2.2, uptime: 00:05:18
  Outgoing interface list: (count: 1)
    Ethernet1/58, uptime: 00:02:34, pim
(10.50.1.1/32, 239.1.1.1/32), uptime: 00:02:26, ip mrib pim nve
  Incoming interface: Ethernet1/59, RPF nbr: 10.19.10.2, uptime: 00:02:21
  Outgoing interface list: (count: 1)
    nve1, uptime: 00:02:26, nve
```

Note   The first three checks verify multicast set up in the control plane in flood and learn mode. The working state should be confirmed before you proceed to the final check.

Finally, check if the VXLAN is complete on the multicast underlay for the last check. This is accomplished by checking the multicast flow for 239.100.100.100 via the overlay infrastructure. This is also accomplished by using the same **show ip mroute command**, adding the detail option for group 239.100.100.100. Example 6-26 provides this output, and shows that the flow has VXLAN flags and that the outgoing interface is nve1.

Example 6-26   *Verify Multicast Underlay for VXLAN*

```
VTEP show ip mroute 239.100.100.100 detail
IP Multicast Routing Table for VRF "default"


Total number of routes: 4
Total number of (*,G) routes: 1
Total number of (S,G) routes: 2
Total number of (*,G-prefix) routes: 1
```

```
(*,239.100.100.100/32), uptime: 5d02h, nve(1) ip(0) pim(0)
  Data Created: No
  VXLAN Flags
    VXLAN Decap
  VPC Flags
    RPF-Source Forwarder
  Stats: 1/64 [Packets/Bytes], 0.000   bps
  Stats: Inactive Flow
  Incoming interface: Ethernet1/7, RPF nbr: 192.168.10.6
  Outgoing interface list: (count: 1)
    nve1, uptime: 5d02h, nve

(192.168.2.1/32, 239.100.100.100/32), uptime: 5d02h, nve(0) ip(0) mrib(0) pim(0)
  Data Created: Yes
  VXLAN Flags
    VXLAN Encap
  VPC Flags
    RPF-Source Forwarder
  Stats: 5/521 [Packets/Bytes], 0.000   bps
  Stats: Inactive Flow
  Incoming interface: loopback1, RPF nbr: 192.168.20.1
  Outgoing interface list: (count: 0)
(192.168.20.5/32, 239.100.100.100 /32), uptime: 5d02h, ip(0) mrib(0) pim(0) nve(1)
  Data Created: Yes
  VXLAN Flags
    VXLAN Decap
  VPC Flags
    RPF-Source Forwarder
  Stats: 29218/2409710 [Packets/Bytes], 13.600   bps
  Stats: Active Flow
  Incoming interface: Ethernet1/7, RPF nbr: 192.168.10.5
  Outgoing interface list: (count: 1)
    nve1, uptime: 2d02h, nve
```

Summary

Troubleshooting large multicast environments can be daunting. As with eating an elephant, it involves determining where to start—trunk, tail, or somewhere in the middle. Now that you are familiar with the three fundamental troubleshooting steps, you know where to start:

Step 1.   Receiver check

Step 2.   Source check

Step 3.   State verification

You can use this methodology to troubleshoot any multicast problem, including those explained in this chapter (interdomain, traffic engineering, MVPN, and VXLAN) and those that are not.

The key to quickly and effectively determining the root cause of a multicast problem is to be familiar with the different technologies and follow the methodology outlined in this chapter.

Index

Symbols

(*, G) state entry, 10, 49
  checking, 50, 96, 289–290
  data MDT traffic flow, 148–149
  learning, 32–34
  multicast reachability failure, 34–35
(S, G) state entry, 10, 49
  checking, 96
  completing, 50
  data MDT traffic flow, 148–149

A

access control
  firewalls, 83
  prefix filtering, 84–88
access points (APs), 244
ACI (Application Centric Infrastructure), 258–260
  data center networks, 227–228
  fabrics and overlay elements, 229–230
  Layer 2 IGMP snooping in, 231–235
ACKs (acknowledgements), eliminating, 87
actions (MSDP), 41–42
activate command, 27

AD (Auto Discovery), 182–183
address-family information (AFI)
  BGP (Border Gateway Protocol), 28
  MBGP (Multiprotocol Border Gateway Protocol), 27–28
advertisements
  PIM auto-RP advertisements, 235
  SAs (source actives), 40, 47–50
AFI. *See* address-family information (AFI)
Application Centric Infrastructure. *See* ACI (Application Centric Infrastructure)
APs (access points), 244
ASM (Any-Source Multicast), 6
ASNs (autonomous system numbers), 3
ASs (autonomous systems), 3–6.
  See also interdomain design
  ASNs (autonomous system numbers), 3
  borders of, 22–24
  intra-AS multidomain design, 62–71
Auto Discovery (AD), 182–183

B

badging systems, 253
best-effort forwarding, 1–4
BGP (Border Gateway Protocol), 2, 5
  AD (Auto Discovery), 182–183

D

E

J-K-L

M

N

W-X-Y-Z